OBJECT-
ORIENTED
DESIGN AND
PROGRAMMING
WITH C++

OBJECT-
ORIENTED
DESIGN AND
PROGRAMMING
WITH C++

RONALD LEACH

Howard University
Washington, D.C.

AP PROFESSIONAL

Boston   San Diego   New York
London   Sydney   Tokyo   Toronto

AP PROFESSIONAL
1300 Boylston Street, Chestnut Hill, MA 02167

An imprint of ACADEMIC PRESS, INC.
A Division of HARCOURT BRACE & COMPANY

United Kingdom Edition published by
ACADEMIC PRESS LIMITED
24–28 Oval Road, London NW1 7DX

Library of Congress Cataloging-in-Publication Data
Leach, Ronald (Ronald J.)
    Object-oriented design and programming with C++ / Ronald J. Leach
        p.   cm.
    Includes bibliographical references and index.
    ISBN 0-12-440215-1 (acid-free paper)
    1. Object-oriented programming (Computer science)   2. C++
(Computer program language)   I. Title.
    QA76.64.L43   1995
    005.13'3--dc20   95-13535
                                                        CIP

Printed in the United States of America
95 96 97 98 IP 9 8 7 6 5 4 3 2 1

Contents

Preface

This book is intended for persons who are reasonably familiar with the C programming language and wish to understand the issues in object-oriented programming using C++. The reader should have had enough experience with higher-level languages to understand pointers, arrays, and structured data types. The reader should also have written at least some simple programs in C using these language features.

Although the book provides complete coverage of the C++ language, it covers the elementary syntax features quickly in order to be able to discuss the fundamental issues of software design in C++ (or any object-oriented language)—design, testing and reuse. These issues are repeated throughout the book.

As with the author's book *Using C in Software Design* (AP PROFESSIONAL, 1993), this book is organized into two parts. Part I describes the fundamental features of C++: classes control structure, member functions, templates (parametrized classes), C++ data structures, and I/O. Special emphasis is given to testing of objects. This will provide the reader with a complete understanding of the fundamental issues of programming in C++ using object-oriented techniques.

Part II describes more advanced, software-engineering-specific features of C++. Part II contains information on program structure, object-oriented design, and the proper use of techniques such as exceptions. The draft ANSI standard C++ class library is discussed in detail, as are several existing class libraries, such as those included with the standard distribution of the Borland and AT&T C++ systems. Part II includes two case studies with considerable amounts of C++ code so that the reader can see the application of the object-oriented software engineering principles discussed in the book.

A more detailed description of the book's contents is given below.

First, a list of software engineering principles is provided to guide the software development process.

Chapter 1 provides an overview of C++. It describes object-oriented programming and the history of C++ and briefly introduces classes, inheritance, polymorphism, and overloading.

Chapter 2 contains a more detailed introduction to C++. It describes classes, fundamental data types, output with the **<<** operator and **cout**, input with the **>>** operator and **cin**, and control structures. This chapter contains a section on testing issues for overloaded operators and for user-defined I/O.

Chapter 3 provides a description of functions, including **friend**, **virtual**, and **inline** functions. Base classes and derived classes are introduced here. We also describe the C++ preprocessor and organization of class libraries. The chapter closes with a discussion of testing issues.

In Chapter 4, we describe arrays and pointers in C++. We use multidimensional arrays as the starting point for development of a class called Matrix, which is used with standard matrix operations. The power of the object-oriented approach is illustrated by development of a system of functions to treat sparse matrices. (A sparse matrix is one that has most of its entries 0.)

Chapter 5 contains descriptions of the fundamental data structures and some typical implementations in C++. In this chapter we describe stacks, lists, queues, and trees and some typical implementations for them. Templates, or parameterized classes, are introduced in this chapter. Each section that discusses an implementation of one of these data structures is followed by a section that discusses implementation of the same data structure using templates.

Chapter 6 concludes the discussion of the fundamental principles of small-scale C++ programming in Part I. It provides a detailed discussion of file I/O in C++. It also completes the discussion of stream-based I/O.

Part II of the book begins with Chapter 7, which initiates a discussion of larger software systems and their implementation in C++. It includes a discussion of scope rules, separate compilation, class libraries and their organization, browsers, exceptions, and exception handling. Standard libraries are discussed in detail.

Chapter 8 is devoted to object-oriented design. Several different object-oriented design methodologies are discussed. The major example is the development of a class of string operations. The related design techniques of information modeling and entity–relationships diagrams are also discussed in this chapter.

In Chapter 9, we discuss the design of a system to implement a graphical database. This will provide another example of the use of the design methodology presented in Chapter 8. C++ code for the implementation of this system is provided in the book.

In Chapter 10 we discuss the design of a moderately complex system that provides a file system simulation. The system is developed using both a procedurally based description and an object-oriented one. This will be especially helpful to the programmer wishing to transform a procedurally described (or coded) system to an object-oriented one. C++ code for both implementations of the system is also provided in the book.

There are six appendices: the set of reserved words in C++, a formal description of the syntax of C++, a summary of the C language, the ANSI C standard library, the draft ANSI C++ standard library, and answers to selected exercises. The draft C++ library is likely to be the basis for an ANSI standard that is adopted by the time that this book appears.

I would like to thank the following people for their assistance during the preparation of this book. Many thanks to my colleagues at Howard University (Don M. Coleman, Bernard Woolfolk, and Reza Hashemi) for many helpful discussions of object-oriented design and programming and C++ in particular and for reading portions of this manuscript. Bernard also provided excellent insights into the object-oriented paradigm when he was a Visiting Professor at Howard on leave from AT&T. Anne Santos of After-Math provided helpful technical services. My editor at AP PROFESSIONAL, Charles Glaser, deserves special thanks for the continued encouragement to do this project and many helpful suggestions during the writing process. Many thanks to the AP PROFESSIONAL "book team," Cindy Kogut and David Hannon.

Software Engineering Principles

T he term "software engineering" refers to a generally accepted set of goals for the analysis, design, implementation, testing, and maintenance of software. These software engineering goals include efficiency, reliability, usability, modifiability, portability, testability, reusability, maintainability, interoperability, and correctness. These terms refer both to systems and to their components. Many of the terms are self-explanatory; however, their definitions are included for completeness.

Efficiency: The software is produced in the expected time and within the limits of the available resources. The software produced runs within the time expected.

Reliability: The software performs as expected. In multiuser systems, the system performs its functions even with other loads on the system.

Usability: The software can be used properly without a huge investment in training. This generally refers to the ease of use of the user interface but also concerns the applicability of the software to the computer environment.

Modifiability: The software can be easily changed if the requirements of the system change.

Portability: The software system can be transferred to other computers or systems without major rewriting of the software. Software that needs only to be recompiled in order to have a properly working system on the new machine is considered to be very portable.

Testability: The software can be easily tested. This generally means that the software is written in a modular manner.

Reusability: Some or all of the software can be used again in other projects. This means that the software is modular, that each individual module has a well-defined interface, and that each individual module has a clearly defined outcome from its execution. This often means that there is a substantial level of abstraction and generality in the modules that will be reused most often.

Maintainability: The software can be easily understood and changed over time. This term is used to describe the lifetime of systems such as the air traffic control system that must operate for decades.

Interoperability: The software system can interact properly with other systems. This can apply to software on a single, stand-alone computer or to software that is used on a network.

Correctness: The program produces the correct output.

These goals, while noble, do not help with the design of software that meets such goals. The choice of proper software design methodologies is currently a matter of considerable debate in academia, government, and industry. Some commonly used methods are data-structured systems design, Jackson structured design, data-flow design, rapid prototyping, spiral designs, etc. All these methods are useful in certain software projects. These methods were originally developed for programs written in procedural languages such as Ada, Pascal, or C.

This book will emphasize the use of object-oriented methods in software engineering. We are not going to follow a particular object-oriented method of software engineering and exclude consideration of all others. Instead we will show how systems can be designed in C++ using the software engineering principles described in this chapter.

Software engineering will be a recurring theme in this book. The early chapters will emphasize correctness and reusability along with an introduction to the fundamentals of object-oriented design, object-oriented programming, and their implementation in the C++ programming language. The later chapters will include discussions of larger software systems and will describe some of the trade-offs involved in design decisions and methods used. The effect of a programming language such as C++ that supports object-oriented programming for the software engineering goals described in this chapter will become evident when we study larger systems. (Technically, C++ is considered to be a hybrid language, because it contains support for both object-oriented and traditional procedurally oriented software engineering.)

Fundamental Principles

I

Overview of C++

1

1.1   What Is Object-Oriented Programming?

You have probably heard a lot of discussion about the C++ language and object-oriented programming. Some people claim that using the technique of object-oriented programming with languages such as C++ will automatically solve most of the major problems in software engineering. This was the intention of Bjarne Stroustrup, who is commonly considered to be the creator of the C++ language. Object-oriented languages are actually much older than C++; one of the earliest object-oriented languages was Simula, which was developed in 1967.

Proponents of the object-oriented approach believe that the combination of object-oriented design and object-oriented programming provides a more natural framework for the software development process and for the reuse of previously developed software. Unfortunately, most experienced computer professionals have a healthy skepticism about the ability of any new programming paradigm to provide easier solutions to software engineering problems. It is difficult for the person new to this subject to distinguish between what is clearly true, what is clearly untrue, what is likely to be true but is currently unproven, and what requires special analysis of its utility in a given situation.

We will not indulge in hyperbole. Instead, we will present a relatively complete description of the C++ programming language and develop several relatively large systems in order to demonstrate the utility of the object-oriented paradigm.

You may also have heard the statement that C++ is a superset of C. This is technically correct. C++ is a superset of ANSI C in the sense that a program in ANSI C can generally be compiled without major changes by a C++ compiler, except for differences in access to the standard libraries. However, anyone faced with the problem of using C++ for a software system of any size has found that there are several subtle differences in the semantics of C and C++, at least in the way that the semantics of the languages are implemented by various compiler writers. At the time that this book is being written, there is no official standard for C++ that is as universally accepted as the ANSI standard for C.

The basic principle of object-oriented programming is that a software system can be viewed as a sequence of "transformations" on a set of "objects." The terms "transformations" and "object" are difficult to define in a precise sense for a variety of technical reasons and therefore we will not attempt formal descriptions.

To see the difficulty in making a precise definition, consider the following definition of an object by Yourdon and Coad:

An object is an abstraction of something in the domain of the problem or its implementation, reflecting the capabilities of a system to keep information about it, interact with it, or both.

An alternative definition was made by Booch:

An object has state, behavior, and identity.

Many other authors have different, but similar, definitions.

Don't worry if you have trouble understanding the differences between the various definitions. We will illustrate the concepts by many examples so that you will be able to recognize them when they appear.

Object-oriented programming differs from the more familiar "procedural programming" in which the basic principle is that a software system is a sequence of operations on data. (The term *imperative programming* is often used instead of procedural programming.) The level of abstraction of object-oriented programming is generally higher than that of procedural programming. (Both views of programming are different from logic programming. We will not discuss logic programming in this book.)

Here is a simple example of the different viewpoints of object-oriented and procedurally oriented programming—a stack. In a procedural language such as C or Pascal, we can define a data type called **stack** (or similar) and define variables of this type. The standard operations on a stack might be implemented in functions called **push( )**,

pop( ), or **empty( )**. Depending on the language and the degree to which the details of implementation of the stack are hidden, the user of a stack within a program can be restricted to the previously defined functions. Recall that in C, use of the **typedef** construction can allow the same functions to be used for stacks of floats instead of stacks of integers. The change of the type of contents of the stack can be done by a simple change of a data type in a header file and a recompilation.

Thus a stack of integer elements might look something like the following:

```
/* Typical C definition of a stack of ints. */

#define MAXSTACK 20

struct stack
   {
   int item[MAXSTACK];
   int top;
   };

typedef struct stack stack;
```

while a stack of floating point numbers might look like

```
/* Typical C definition of a stack of floats. */

#define MAXSTACK 20

struct stack
   {
   float item[MAXSTACK];
   int top;
   };

typedef struct stack stack;
```

However, the support for stack operations is not restricted to the functions designed by the programmer. It is easy to write other functions that manipulate the data within a stack while ignoring the fundamental stack feature of having only last-in, first-out access to the elements of the stack. For example, we could theoretically write a function **change2()** that would change the value of the second element from the top of the stack by directly manipulating the variable **top**. Code for this function might be:

```
stack s;

void change2(int value)
{
   s.item[top - 1] = value;
}
```

In an object-oriented system, there would still be a stack; but there would be a specified object. Included in the definition of the object would be a set of allowable transformations, probably including **push()**, **pop()**, and **empty()**, and a function to create a stack object. No other functions would be allowed to manipulate the internal description of the stack unless access permissions were given. Thus, the function **change2()** that was so easy to write (and possibly interfere with the last-in, first-out stack operation) cannot be implemented directly in an object-oriented system, but must be done as a sequence of operations on the stack:

```
temp1 = pop;
temp2 = pop;
temp2 = new2;
push(new2);
push(temp1);
```

We have described the operations in pseudocode to avoid any discussion of C++ syntax at this time.

A major feature of object-oriented programming is that the set of allowable transformations on an object is restricted. This is especially important in software systems that are developed by a team of programmers working with common data interfaces.

Another advantage of having a restricted set of operations allowed for objects is that an object can be placed into any software system for which the interfaces are designed and that the portion of the program representing that object can be used without any difficulty. This is the dream of software engineers: to have a set of "reusable software components" that have precisely defined interfaces and can be inserted into programs as needed just as an electrical engineer builds a circuit by using a set of well-understood hardware components. The goal of object-oriented software engineering is to use existing software components (objects) when available and to develop new software components (objects) when necessary.

1.2   History of the C++ Programming Language

C++ was originally developed by Bjarne Stroustrup at AT&T Bell Laboratories in 1984. His intention was to incorporate a higher level of abstraction than was available in the C programming language. It incorporated much of the thinking of type checking that was included in the ANSI C revision of the original Kernighan and Ritchie version of C. (The Kernighan and Ritchie version of C was also developed at AT&T Bell Laboratories.) The name C++ was chosen to be a spin on the C programming language, since the C language incrementation operator ++ means "add one to the variable," and hence the language C++ is supposed to be one more than C.

The original implementation of C++ was as a preprocessor to a C compiler. Thus, there were both compile-time and run-time performance problems. These problems have largely been eliminated in later implementations that have an integrated compilation system. In general there is little performance penalty for well-designed object-oriented programs in terms of performance.

There are many different C++ compilers for a variety of hardware platforms and operating systems. Some of the most common ones are those by Borland, Microsoft, and Symantec for personal computers and ones by AT&T and CenterLine for UNIX-based workstations. In addition, the Free Software Foundation's GNU project produces high-quality software that is portable to many different environments. Their C++ compiler is readily available.

Each system contains its own interpretation of the language, development environment, and a set of class libraries.

Many of the ideas of object-oriented programming can be traced to the Smalltalk language developed at the Xerox Palo Alto Research Center. The earliest popular object-oriented language was Simula, which was developed in 1967. Both these languages influenced C++.

1.3 What Is C++?

C++ is not yet a standard language, because there are so many different implementations. There are some common features, however.

- C++ is essentially a superset of ANSI C.
- C++ has essentially the same typing features as ANSI C for non-object-oriented features.
- C++ compilers frequently accept code written in the older Kernighan and Ritchie version of C. C++ compilers generally give either warnings or error messages when given C code without function prototypes.
- C++ compilers are bundled with a "class library" of previously written and tested classes of objects.

The major differences between various C++ compilers include the common ones of price, development, environment (editors, debuggers, etc.), speed of compilation, speed of executable code, size of the compilation system on disk, size of executable code, run-time system, quality of error messages, and interoperability of code with other software such as operating systems, window systems, linkers, or applications programs.

Other differences include support for exception handlers and templates. The most complete C++ systems provide support for both features.

Exception handlers are constructions that allow programs to recover from unexpected run-time errors. Exceptions will be discussed in Chapter 7.

Templates allow classes (discussed in the next section) to be distinguished by parameters. We will study templates in detail in Chapter 5.

Of special importance to C++ compilers is the class library and the ease of browsing through the class library to find classes that might be useful for a given software system. In this book, we will describe the C++ language in general and limit our discussion of class libraries to those classes that are generally available. You will probably need a manual describing the class library for the particular system that you are using. This is especially true if you are using any implementation-specific class libraries such as those for graphics or for interfacing directly with the operating system.

1.4   Classes

The "class" is the fundamental building block in C++. A class should be considered as an abstract data type, together with a set of allowable transformations on the abstract data type. The code for the functions that make up the set of allowable transformations for a class is considered to belong to the class.

A class may also define its interface to other classes or functions by describing what portion of its internal data description or set of allowable transformations can be made public. The default is that nothing in a class is public unless explicitly declared as such by the software developer who defined the class.

Although it is not completely a standard terminology in object-oriented programming, the term *object* is often used to denote an instance of a "class." Another view of a class is that it is a run-time description of a class and as such has a state, a behavior, and an identity. This view is consistent with the definition given by Booch described earlier. The distinction is probably not that important unless you are writing a compiler for an object-oriented programming language.

A class in C++ is different from a struct in C in that a class description restricts the set of allowable transformations. A C structure can have any set of operations performed on the fields of the struct such as assignments and tests for equality. Many operations on structs are allowed explicitly by the C language. By comparison, classes in C++ essentially have no operations available unless the designer of the class includes them explicitly.

1.5   Inheritance, Polymorphism, and Overloading

A major feature of classes is that new classes can be built upon old classes. This allows the software designer to reuse code easily, thereby reducing development time.

Here is a simple example. Suppose that we have a class of objects called "rectangles," for which we defined transformations that compute the area and perimeter. If we now wanted to consider a class of objects called "squares," we could always write the code for the new class from scratch.

However, the problem becomes simpler if we note that a square is a special case of a rectangle in which all sides are equal. We can develop a new class called "square" that is derived from the class called "rectangle" by incorporating this information. The class "square" will inherit the properties of having four sides and equal angles from the class "rectangle." Suppose also that we have another function called "area" that we have defined as part of the class "square." Which one do we use if we are asked to compute the area of an object that is a square? A human would resolve this by choosing a formula appropriate to the most specific description, that is, the square. In C, the programmer might have used the union construction and had the C compiler make the selection of the proper formula for computing the area at run time. (See Chapter 9 of the author's *Using C in Software Design* for a description of the data structures to do this.)

The relationship between the two classes "rectangle" and "square" is illustrated in Figure 1.1. The relationship is called *inheritance*. It is presumed that the class "rectangle," which is the *base class*, contains a function to compute the area of a rectangle.

Figure 1.1 The relationship between the square and rectangle classes.

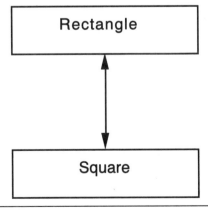

In C++, the compiler's compile-time system makes the correct decision as to which function should be used to compute the area. This selection of the proper function based on the arguments to the function is called *polymorphism*. Polymorphism is a fundamental feature of object-oriented programming. We will meet this concept many times during our study of C++.

The final topic of this section is called *overloading* and is related to polymorphism. You have already met overloading in the C programming language.

Consider the statement

```
c = a + b;
```

and think about the meaning of the symbol +. If the operands are both of type **int**, then the symbol indicates that integer addition is to be performed and the type of the result is **int**. If the operands are both of type **double**, then double-precision addition is to be performed and the type of the result is **double**. There are additional complications if the two operands have different types.

Note also that there may be implicit type conversions if the type of the right-hand side of an assignment expression is different from the type of the left-hand side and hence the = operator is also overloaded. Note that pointer arithmetic also overloads the + and – operators.

In C++, we are able to do additional overloading. For example, we can define classes to represent complex numbers, one-dimensional arrays, multidimensional matrices, or binary integers and in each case we can define a function named + that belongs to the set of allowable transformations on the class. The determination of which of the many + operations to use is made by the C++ run-time system. This makes programs easy to read and avoids problems with having names like **complex_add**, **array_add**, **matrix_add**, or **binary_add**.

Names such as those in the previous paragraph would lead to program statements such as

```
result = complex_add(argument1, argument2);
```

and this is harder to understand than

```
result = argument1 + argument2;
```

which is a legitimate statement in C++ if the operator + has been defined properly for this type of argument.

There is a potential problem with overloading. It is now possible for a program statement such as

```
c = a + b;
```

to be encountered in which the operand **a** is a member of the class **complex_number** and the operand **b** is a member of the class **three-dimensional matrix**. In such a case, the + operation is nonsense and the program will abort. It is unlikely that any programmer would write anything like:

```
c = complex_add(a, b);
```

where **b** was not an element of the class **complex_number**, so that this example was somewhat far-fetched. However, a situation such as

```
c = a + b;
```

where **a** is an element of the class **complex_number** and **b** is a floating point number, is quite common and is consistent with standard mathematical usage, but will result in a run-time error unless a function named + is explicitly written to handle mixed arguments and is included in the set of allowable transformations on the class **complex_number**.

Thus the advantages of improving program readability by overloading must be balanced by the potential disadvantage of having run-time errors.

There is a trade-off here. If we wish to have robust software components that can be reused easily, we must incorporate functions to handle these different cases that can occur within the class itself. This will lead to complicated objects and a considerable amount of difficulty in testing. On the other hand, we can reduce the complexity of objects by placing more of a burden on the user of these objects to ensure that no errors are made in usage. The current trend in object-oriented programming is toward more robust objects. We will return to this point many times in this book, especially when we discuss testing.

Summary

Object-oriented programming is based on the idea of explicitly describing the set of allowable transformations that may be used on an object. Object-oriented programming allows a high degree of abstraction and support for abstract data types.

C++ was developed at AT&T Bell Laboratories by Bjarne Stroustrup. It is essentially a superset of ANSI C, although there are some technical differences.

The fundamental notion of object-oriented programming is the class. New classes can be derived from old with new features or restrictions added.

Operators in C++ can be overloaded, which increases program understandability. However, overloading can cause difficulties in testing objects and can require objects to grow in complexity.

EXERCISES

1. Which of the operators in C can be overloaded?

2. How does a class differ from a struct in C? Ignore syntactical issues in your explanation and concentrate on the struct as a data type.

3. Describe the deficiencies of the **typedef** construction in C when it is used in the development of abstract data types.

4. Determine which, if any, of the applications software you commonly use is written in C++ or another object-oriented programming language.

5. For your C++ system, determine the number of entries in the class library and if there is any effective and systematic way of searching the class library for a particular class.

C H A P T E R

2

Elementary Programming in C++

I n this chapter we will meet our first examples of programs in C++. Programs will be short and will illustrate elementary language features. For simplicity, we will consider only programs with a single class and its associated functions.

2.1 Structure of a Single-Unit C++ Program

C++ includes C as a subset and therefore the shortest possible C++ program is the same as the shortest possible C program (Example 2.1).

Example 2.1 The shortest possible C++ program.

```
main()
  {
  }
```

Interesting C++ programs have I/O and use some of the object-oriented features of the language.

C++ programs that use I/O should have an **#include** statement to enable the use of the I/O functions. The most common include statement is

```
#include <iostream.h>
```

The object-oriented features of C++ are demonstrated in the use of classes, which we have described informally in Chapter 1. A class in C++ consists of its data and the set of allowable transformations, or methods, used on the data. The data is called the *member data* and the methods are called the *member functions*.

The formal syntax for a class in C++ is given below in Backus–Naur form. (See Appendix 3 for more information about Backus–Naur form and a formal description of C++ syntax.)

```
class Name
  {
  protection : optional_data_or_functions;
  protection : optional_data_or_functions;
  };
```

The word **class** is a reserved word in C++. It indicates the fundamental building block of object-oriented programs. The word "protection" is not a reserved word; it refers to the set of rules that determine the set of functions that can use the data and functions associated with the class. Functions associated with a class are called *member functions*.

The possible values for protection are:

- **public**, or accessible by any function inside or outside the class, member function or not.
- **private**, or accessible only by member functions of the class.
- **protected**, or accessible only by member functions of the class or by members of any classes derived from the class.

The default value for the optional word protection is **private**. Many standard C++ style conventions require the name of the class to begin with an uppercase letter, although C++ compilers do not require this. This is the standard that we will follow. If you are working for a company that has a C++ coding standard, use that standard in your code and modify the examples in the book accordingly if necessary.

A useful example of a class in C++ is one that manipulates strings of characters. Lets start our discussion of strings by describing the properties that we wish an abstraction of the notion of "string" to have. It will be very helpful if you try to forget everything you have done when writing programs in C to implement character strings and instead concentrate on the fundamental operations.

An abstract description of a string must have the following features:

- It must have a length.
- It must contain character data that can be accessed in sequential order.
- The amount of character data must be less than or equal to the length of the string.
- It should be possible to search the character data in the string for the appearance of any specified character, or indeed any specified character string.
- It must have facilities for creating a new string and for releasing any storage used for a string that is to be discarded.

A class definition allows variables that are defined later in the program to be given the class as their type.

In Example 2.2, we present a simple C++ program that includes the class **String**. The proper treatment of character strings is very important in C++ and we will return to their study several times in this book. At those times, we will extend the description of the class to incorporate all the abstractions indicated in the previous discussion. For now, we will just provide a small example to demonstrate how strings might be implemented in C++.

Example 2.2 Use of the **String** class.

```cpp
#include <iostream.h>
#include <string.h>
#include <stdlib.h>

class String
{
public:
const char    *contents;

String(const char *data)
  {
  length = strlen(data);
  contents = (char *) malloc (length * sizeof (char) );
  }

private:
  int length;
};

main()
{
  char *data = "Hello\n" ;
  String s(data);

  s.contents = data;
  cout << s.contents ;
}
```

Much of the structure of the program given in Example 2.2 should be familiar to you from your previous experience in C. The use of include files, the declaration of the variables before they are used, and the structure of the main program in the function **main()** are all common techniques in C.

However, there are many new features of this program that require discussion. We will describe the new features of this program in the order in which they appear in the source code.

There are three include files, **iostream.h**, **string.h**, and **stdlib.h**. The three files have their names enclosed in angle brackets, < and >, to indicate that they are to be searched for in special directories by the compiler. The first include file is the essential file for I/O in C++. This file, or a variant of it, is included in most C++ programs in order to provide access to the commonly available functions of C++ I/O.

The second include file, **string.h**, is generally part of the ANSI C library distribution. It is used here to provide access to the standard C function **strlen()**, which is used later in the code. It has no other relationship to the C++ class called **String** that we are using in this example.

The remaining file, **stdlib.h**, is used to give access to the familiar function **malloc()** that is used for storage allocation in C. Until we discuss storage allocation in C++, we will use the **malloc()** function.

The next major portion of the code is the definition of the objects that form the **String** class. The name of the class is **String**, as can be seen from the next token after the C++ reserved word **class**. The class has two parts: a public part that contains a character pointer called **contents** and a function named **String** and a private part containing data for which no access is allowed to other functions. The function **String()** appears at first glance to have a peculiar syntax.

The public portion of the class description is identified by the use of the reserved word **public**. This is the programming interface that other functions or classes see.

Similarly, the private part of the class description is identified by the use of the reserved word **private**. This is available only to the class, not to other functions or classes.

The pointer, **contents**, is declared as a constant pointer to char using the **const** declaration. This avoids the possibility that a function using this class can change the pointer's value. (Changing a pointer's value means changing a memory address.) Using a constant pointer protects the location of the data from being totally lost, although the data pointed to by it can be overwritten easily.

The function called **String** is what is known in C++ as a *constructor function*, or *constructor* for short. The purpose of this function is to create an instance of an object of the class **String**. A constructor is an initialization function that determines how the object is to be created. It is very common to have a constructor function have the same name as the class, although this is not absolutely necessary. This function takes a single argument.

Most class descriptions contain a destructor function whose purpose is to remove the object from memory. A destructor function, or destructor for short, always has the syntax

```
~class_name();
```

where **class_name** is the name of the class for which the destructor is created. In our case, the destructor would be named

```
~String();
```

Note that the function **String()** has two variables that appear as lvalues. That is, the values appear on the left-hand side of an assignment statement. The character pointer **contents** has been seen before the description of the function **String()**. However, the value of **length**, which is in the private portion of the class, has not yet been defined (or at least we haven't read it yet). Clearly C++ has more complex scoping rules than does C. We will return to this topic later in this book.

The private portion of the class description consists of a single declaration of the variable **length**, which is of type **int**.

The main program has two data definitions. The definition of the variable **data** as a character string terminated by the null byte **'\0'** is easy to recognize because it is so common in C.

The other definition is much more difficult to detect. It appears on the second line of **main()**. This definition is of a variable named **s**, which belongs to the class **String** and has its contents initialized to the value of the character string represented by the other variable named **data**.

The next line of **main()** is an assignment statement that is similar in syntax to the C language treatment of assignment to fields of a **struct**. This is not surprising. As we shall see later, a **struct** in either C or C++ is just a very special case of a C++ **class**.

The last line of the program is an output statement. It sends output to the standard output stream, **cout**. The standard output in C++ is similar in some ways to the file descriptor **stdout** in C. The output stream is accessed by the operator <<. The operator << is often called the *insertion operator* when used for output in C++. It should not be confused with the left shift operator, which has the same notation but has an entirely different meaning.

This example illustrates some of the basic features of C++. It shows how a class can be separated into a public and a private part and how some of the functions and data in a class are accessed. It also shows some of the typical syntax of C++.

The example does not illustrate the power of information hiding in C++. To see a portion of the C++ compiler's assistance in information hiding, modify this example by adding any of the lines

```
s.length = 7;
i = s.length; /* declare i as int first */
i = length;   /* declare i as int first */
```

to the function **main()** in Example 2.2. The program will not compile, because the variable **length** was declared to be **private**. Declaring a variable (or function) as **private** limits access by other portions of the program.

We will improve upon this example several times in the book as we learn more about C++, I/O, better representations of the **String** class, constructors, and storage allocation.

2.2   Fundamental Data Types in C++

The term "fundamental data types" in C++ refers to those predefined types available without the definition of any classes, functions, structures, unions, etc. Specifically, the fundamental data types in C++ are character, integer, or floating point type. These may be broken down into

```
char
signed char
unsigned char
int
short int
long int
unsigned int
float
double
long double
void
```

An enumeration type such as

```
enum color { red, green, blue };
```

assigns constant integer values to the expressions inside the curly braces. Each expression inside the curly braces must be an identifier whose value is an integer constant or else be of the form identifier = some integer constant. The constant values start at 0 for the expressions being enumerated. That is, an enumerated type is stored internally as a collection of integers starting with 0.

The expressions within an enumeration type must be delimited by the curly braces and preceded by the C++ reserved word **enum**. (Recall that **enum** is also a reserved word in C.)

Most C++ compilers adhere to the draft ANSI C++ standards for storage of these fundamental data types.

For some compilers, there is no presumption about the size of the integer types other than the obvious ones that a short **int** requires no more storage than an **int**, which requires no more storage than a long **int**. There are similar statements for **float**, **double**, and **long double**.

The three character types are all considered to be distinct and use precisely the same amount of storage. The size of a variable or constant of type **char** is guaranteed to be large enough to hold any character that is in the allowable character set of the implementation.

The types **int** (all sizes), **char** (all sizes), and enumeration types are known collectively as the integral types. The types **float**, **double**, and **long double** are known collectively as the floating types. The integral types and floating types are known collectively as the arithmetic types.

The **void** type is used as the return type for functions that return no value.

No other type of object may be declared as having **void** type, although pointers to **void** are allowed. As was the case in ANSI C, pointers to **void** are frequently used together with cast operations.

2.3 Output with cout

Recall that there is an extremely flexible output function named **printf()** that is available for output in C. This function produces output to what is referred to as standard output or **stdout**. This is generally the terminal screen (or personal computer screen). Different control specifications are needed to format output as a character, an integer, or a floating point number. Other output functions such as **putchar()** are also available.

C++ has a general-purpose output operator called << that works with the standard output stream **cout**. An important feature of C++ I/O is that << is an overloaded operator, since it can be given any type of data and will produce output consistent with that data.

In this section, we will illustrate the use of **cout** with the fundamental data types available in C++. Suppose that we have variables **a**, **b**, and **c** declared as

```
int a = 1;
char b = 'b';
float c = 3.14;
```

A simple statement to print these variables might be

```
cout << "a= "<< a <<"b= "<< b <<" c=" << c << "\n";
```

The output is a result of the stream of expressions preceded by the << symbol. Multiple uses of << indicate repeated output from the current position of the cursor. Thus if this line of C++ code is placed within a program with the given initialization, the output is

```
a= 1 b= b c=3.14
```

Compare this method of generating C++ output to the C output statement

```
printf("a=%d b=%c c=%f\n", a, b, c);
```

which has the output

```
a= 1 b= b c= 3.140000
```

The difference in the number of spaces to the right of the last equals sign and the number of zeros displayed to the right of the decimal point is caused by the default settings of the **printf()** function.

We now return to the study of C++ I/O. In each case we have used a single output function to print character strings and three variables of different types. In the C example we had to use an explicit control specification. In the C++ example, no control specification was necessary because the << operator is provided with enough information to print the character strings and the **int**, **char**, and **float** variables in the proper format. There are built-in methods of providing output for each of the fundamental data types in C++.

How is this possible? The << operator is overloaded and can accept operands of different types. The effect of this situation is one we have already seen in C++—different objects may have the same overloaded operation. In this case, **int**, **char**, and **float** data and character strings enclosed in double quotes are each predefined objects in C++.

Note that the statement

```
cout << "This is a test.\n";
```

has the same output as the pair of statements

```
cout << "This is a test.";
cout << "\n";
```

or the three statements

```
cout << "This is ";
cout << "a test";
cout << "\n";
```

This illustrates that << produces its output at the location to which the cursor was moved previously.

In Example 2.3 we present pseudocode to illustrate the overloading of the << operator and the I/O stream **cout**. We have used the dot (.) to indicate that the operation (in this case output) is attached to a particular object of a class. Pseudocode is given instead of actual C++ code in order to avoid some of the technical issues of classes that we will discuss later in this chapter. We use the six dots to indicate that the description of the class has been omitted.

Example 2.3 Pseudocode for output.

```
#include <iostream.h>
class String ......
class List ......
class Other_stuff .......

main()
{
  String string1;
  List list1;
  Other_stuff other;
  string1.output();
  list1.output();
  other.output();
}
```

Here **string1** is an object that belongs to the appropriately defined class named **String**. Similarly, **list1** and **other** are also objects that belong to their respective classes. Recall that a version of << is provided for use with each of the predefined data types in C++. The function named **output()** uses the << operator and either its predefined output for predefined types or some user-defined output mechanism. The function named **output()** that is associated with the class **String** is different from the function named **output()** that is associated with the class **List**, which in turn is different from the function named **output()** that is associated with the class **Other_stuff**.

The important thing to note about the pseudocode given in Example 2.3 is that the meaning of the code in the function **main()** is clear once we get used to the syntax. There are three functions that produce output, one for each of the classes used in the program. The details of how this works are completely hidden from the function **main()**. This is an illustration of *information hiding*, which is a major feature of C++.

We will defer the discussion of formatted output in C++ until Section 2.4 of this chapter.

Just as C has streams for standard output, input, and error (**stdout**, **stdin**, and **stderr**), C++ has **cout**, **cin**, and **cerr**. Errors should generally be sent to **cerr**. We will meet **cin** in Section 2.5.

The repeated use of multiple << statements is somewhat awkward. An alternative is to use a single << statement with the repeated data to be printed spread out over several lines (Example 2.4).

Example 2.4

```
#include <iostream.h>
main()
{
  cout << "The title of this book is:\n"
  << "Object-Oriented Design and \n"
  << "Programming with C++.\n"
  << "The author is Ronald J. Leach.\n"
  << " The publisher is: "
  << "AP PROFESSIONAL.\n";
  }
```

The output is of course:

```
The title of this book is:
Object-Oriented Design and
Programming with C++.
The author is Ronald J. Leach.
The publisher is: AP PROFESSIONAL.
```

Notice the use of the << operator and the lack of intermediate semicolons. The continuation portions of the << statement have been indented for clarity. As indicated earlier, the output of multiple << statements continues from the previous position of the cursor.

2.4   Formatted Output in C++

Output in C++ can be formatted using the **setw()** operator. This operator sets the width to be used when displaying an output item. The number of spaces used for displaying data is given in the argument to **setw()**. The item is displayed with the data right justified.

Thus the sequence of statements

```
cout   << "\n"
       << setw(15) << "FIRST NAME"
       << setw(15) << "LAST NAME"
       << "\n";
```

will produce the output

```
    FIRST NAME    LAST NAME
```

In this output, there are 5 (= 15–10) blank spaces to the left of the first character '**F**' of the string "**FIRST NAME**." Similarly, there are 6 (= 15–9) blank spaces between the first '**F**' and the '**L.**' Note that the initial **\n** forces the cursor's position to be at the start of a new line.

A complete program that uses formatted output must include the header file **iomanip.h.** This standard header file provides access to a set of operators called manipulators. A manipulator takes a stream reference as an argument and returns a reference to the same I/O stream.

A complete program that manipulates the I/O stream is shown in Example 2.5.

Example 2.5

```
#include <iostream.h>
#include <iomanip.h>

main()
{
  cout <<"\n"
  << setw(15) << "FIRST NAME"
  << setw(15) << "LAST NAME"
  << "\n";
}
```

There are other standard library functions that can be used to format output in C++. They are:

setprecision(int n)   This function is used to set the number of decimal spaces used to display digits to the right of the decimal point of a floating point number. The number of spaces remains constant until reset by another call to **setprecision()**.

setfill(char c)   This sets the "fill character," which uses the argument of **setw()** to fill up any unused space in formatted output. The default value of the argument is a blank space.

dec	This displays the output in decimal format. It is similar to the %d control specification used with the **printf()** function in C.
hex	This is used to display output in hexadecimal (base 16) format.
oct	This is used to display output in octal (base 8) format.
ws()	This is used to extract white space (either spaces, tabs, or new lines).
endl()	This places a new line character, **'\n'**, in the output stream. It then "flushes" the output stream from any buffers.
ends()	This places a null byte, **'\0'**, on the output stream. This is useful when an output stream is redirected to another process. (This redirection is a standard feature of both the DOS and UNIX operating systems.)
flush()	This flushes the output stream from any buffers. It differs from **endl()** in that no **'\n'** is placed in the output stream.

You should note that a complete description of output formatting can be quite complicated. For example, 16 pages are devoted to just the **printf()** function in one C programming manual. The most appropriate way to use formatted output in C++ is to understand the guidelines given here and use them in conjunction with the appropriate manual for your system.

In Example 2.6, we illustrate the use of some of the I/O manipulators that format output. The **flush()** manipulator is primarily used when a program uses both C++ I/O and C I/O with **printf()** or similar functions, or else when there are concurrently running processes writing data to the same output screen.

Example 2.6 Use of I/O manipulators.

```
#include <iostream.h>
#include <iomanip.h>

main()
{
  int i = 12;
```

```
    float f = 3.1415259;
    cout <<"\n"
    << setw(15) << "FIRST NAME"
    << setw(15) << "LAST NAME"
    << "\n"
    << setfill('*')
    << setw(15) << "FIRST NAME"
    << setw(15) << "LAST NAME"
    << "\n"
    << setfill(' ')
    << setw(15) << "FIRST NAME"
    << setw(15) << "LAST NAME"
    << "\n";

    cout << i << endl;
    cout << oct << i << endl;
    cout << hex << i << endl;
    cout << dec << i << endl;

    cout << setprecision(5) << f << endl;
    cout << setprecision(10) << f << endl ;
}
```

The output of the program in Example 2.6 is

```
       FIRST NAME      LAST NAME
*****FIRST NAME******LAST NAME
       FIRST NAME      LAST NAME
12
14
c
12
3.14153
3.1415259838
```

Note that the fill character was set to an asterisk (*) and then reset to a blank space. The value of the int **i** is displayed in decimal integer, octal, and hexadecimal formats, after which the default setting for display of integers is reset to decimal integer.

2.5   Input with cin

The primary input operator in C++ is >>, which is used with the stream **cin**. This operator has a similar syntax to the use of << with **cout**. For example, we can read in a variable named **a** of type **int** by the statements

```
int a;
cout << "Please enter an integer.\n";
cin >> a;
cout << "You entered : " << a << "\n";
```

(We have used two output statements to aid in clarity.) Note the use of the >> symbol for input.

Since variables in C++ must be declared before they are used, the type of fundamental data type of the variable **a** is known. Hence, the >> operator is overloaded, just as the << operator was.

When used for input, the >> operator is occasionally called the extraction operator. Recall that the operator << had a double meaning as either the insertion operator, when used for output, or the left shift operator, when used with bit operations. In a similar way, the >> notation can mean either the extraction operator or the right shift operator. There is usually little confusion between the two meanings.

There is one potentially confusing situation—the use of a shift operator within either an input or output statement. The way to resolve the confusion is to recognize that it is merely a problem in precedence and that as such it can be solved by using parentheses. Thus the statement

```
cout << (x << 2)
```

works correctly to print the result of applying the left shift operator << to **x** before output.

Multiple input can be accomplished by repeated use of the >> symbol. Thus we can read in these variables **a**, **b**, **c** of different types by something like:

```
int a;
char b;
float c;
cout << "Enter an int, a char, and float\n";
cin >> a >> b >> c;
```

The input statement can be split up as

```
cin >> a;
cin >> b;
cin >> c;
```

or as

```
cin >> a >> b;
cin >> c;
```

As with displaying output with **cout** and << we can read formatted input with >>.

For example, suppose that we wish to write a program to compute grades. An interactive program might look like Example 2.7.

Example 2.7 Unformatted input to obtain grade information.

```
#include <iostream.h>

main()
{
    int exam1, exam2, exam3, final_exam ;
    float average;

    cout << "Please enter the first exam grade.\n";
    cin >> exam1;
    cout << "Please enter the second exam grade.\n";
    cin >> exam2;
    cout << "Please enter the third exam grade.\n";
    cin >> exam3;
    cout << "Please enter the final exam grade.\n";
    cin >> final_exam;

    average = (exam1 + exam2 + exam3)* 0.2 + final_exam* 0.4;
    cout << "The average is: " << average << "\n";
}
```

The instructions to enter grades can get somewhat annoying if repeated consistently. A way to avoid this is to combine the **cin** statements (after prompting the user), as in the following:

```
cout    << "Please enter the three exam grades"
        << "and the final exam grade"
        << "separated by spaces.\n";

cin     >> exam1 >> exam2 >> exam3
        >> final_exam;
```

This works very smoothly because all data read in is of the same type. There are many problems that occur if the data is of different types.

For example, suppose that we try to read in two values, one of type **int** and one of type **char**. If we prompt the user to enter two such variables, then we must also tell him or her to enter the data in a particular order.

Suppose we have declared a variable **ch** to be of type **char** and a variable **val** to be of type **int**. The statement

```
cin >> ch >> val;
```

will read the first character (other than white space) and assign it to the variable **ch.** It will then skip any white space and interpret the next input as an **int** as much as possible. This will be assigned to **val.** Thus the input

```
A 99
```

will assign the value 'A' to **ch** and '99' to **val**, while the input

```
A 99.44
```

will still assign 'A' to **ch** and '99' to **val** but will ignore the three characters ' . ', '4,' and '4.'

A more complicated situation arises when the order of input is reversed. The statement

```
cin >> val >> ch;
```

together with an input of

```
99 A
```

will work, properly assigning '99' to **val** and 'A' to **ch,** but the input

```
99.44 A
```

will assign '99' to **val** (since **val** is an **int**) and will assign the ' . ' to **ch**, ignoring the rest of the input.

There are many potential sources of error when a program requests user input. Many cascading errors can occur in such situations if there is additional code to read more data from the input stream.

The need for defensive programming in such situations is obvious. Many commercial interactive systems devote a large portion of their code to defensive programming against errors in user input.

One common defensive technique against cascading errors is flushing the input stream using a function called **ignore()** that will read and discard characters obtained from input. The number of characters read and ignored by this function is the smaller of the number specified as its first argument and the number of characters that are actually read and discarded before a delimiter character (specified in the second argument) is encountered.

Since the function **ignore()** is actually a member function of the class **istream**, it should be properly referred to as

```
cin.ignore();
```

to illustrate its attachment to the object **cin** in the class **istream**.

We illustrate the use of **ignore()** for defensive programming in Example 2.8.

Example 2.8 Defensive programming using `ignore()`.

```cpp
#include <iostream.h>

#define MAXCHAR 80

main()
{
  int val;
  char ch;

  cin >> val >> ch;
  cout << ch << val << endl;
  cin.ignore(MAXCHAR, '\n');

  cin >> val >> ch;
  cout << ch << val << endl;

  cin >> val >> ch;
  cout << ch << val << endl << endl;
}
```

With an input of

```
99.44 A
99 A
99 A
```

the output from the program of Example 2.8 is

```
.99
A 99
A 99
```

The first line of output from the program of Example 2.8 is wrong, since we gave incorrect input. However, the remaining two lines of output are correct. Note that all lines of input have been read.

Here is what happens if we use the code of Example 2.8 without the use of the `ignore()` function. With an input of

```
99.44 A
99 A
```

the output from the program of Example 2.8 would have been

```
.99
A 44
A 99
```

Note that only two lines of input were accepted by the program. Note also that only the third line of the output is what was intended. The errors in the second line of output are caused by attempting to recover from the error in the first line of input.

Clearly the use of **ignore()** reduced the amount of erroneous data that was read into the program.

The ability to reduce the possibility of future errors in a program can be very helpful when writing programs that are to be used by people other than yourself. Such programs are often susceptible to data entry errors. When we study C++ exceptions later in this book, we will learn how to recover from such errors and restart the initialization procedure to make sure that we get correct data into the program.

There are other ways to read streams of input data in C++. We can read in string data one character at a time, checking for `'\n'` to indicate the end of a line and checking for `'\0'` in certain instances. (Recall that the **endl** operator can be used with **cout** and << to insert the `'\n'` character in an output stream.)

There are often better and more efficient ways to read in data. Character strings can be read using a new function, **getline()**. This function is similar to the **getline()** function commonly included in standard C libraries. Technically the **getline()** function in C++ is an operator used on the input stream **cin**, because it is a member function of the class **iostream**, and **cin** is an object in that class. Therefore the proper usage of **getline()** is

```
cin.getline(char *stringname, int length, char delimiter);
```

where the `'.'` indicates that **getline()** is associated with the input object **cin**.

The arguments to **getline()** are used in a very precise way and the details are slightly tricky (at least at this point in our discussion of C++).

The first argument to **getline()**, **stringname**, is the same as that of an array that has been defined earlier. Recall from your knowledge of the C programming language that to define a variable in C is to set aside space for the storage of that variable. If we intend to read in a variable named address which we expect to have a maximum of 30 characters, then we should make sure that the data has at least that much storage. (We will need two additional bytes for reasons to be explained later.) Thus we will need to have a definition of

```
char address [32];
```

for the variable address. This variable is actually an array of characters, just as in C. We will discuss arrays in C++ more completely in Chapter 4.

The next argument, **length**, is used to represent the length of the string read in, plus a `'\n'` character, which flushes the input buffer and sends the data to **getline()**, plus a null byte `'\0'` to terminate the string. Thus the value of this argument should be the length of the expected string plus 2 for the extra bytes. In any event, this number should be less than or equal to the size of the storage area set aside for the array, to avoid overwriting other data.

The third argument, **delimiter**, is a character used to terminate the string. In most applications, the delimiter will be the **'\n'** character. As we will see in Chapter 3, C++ functions can have "default values" for some of their arguments. If no value is presented for the argument that has a default value, that argument can be omitted in that function call.

Thus the two statements

```
cin.getline(address, 32, '\n')
```

and

```
cin.getline(address, 32);
```

are equivalent in that they read in a line of at most 32 characters; the delimiter that indicates the end of a line is **'\n'**.

In any event, the delimiter character is always used as the next-to-last character in the string.

An example of the use of **getline()** is shown in Example 2.9.

Example 2.9 Typical use of **getline()**.

```
#include <iostream.h>

main()
{
  char address[80];

  cout << "Please enter a line of text, terminated "
  cout << "by a return"<< endl;
  cin.getline(address, 80, '\n');
  cout << address;
}
```

Use of the **getline()** function may cause some problems when combined with reading other types of data using the standard >> operator with **cin**.

As an example, consider the problem of keeping a (simplified) database of students ordered according to their grade point average. We might attempt to collect data by the following sequence:

```
cout << "Enter grade.\n";

cin >> GPA;

cout << "Enter name.\n";

cin.getline(name, 32);
```

The difficulty is that the user cannot send the GPA to the program without processing the carriage return key. When the return key is pressed, it is used as the delimiter for the name string. Hence the name will never be read into the appropriate variable and will remain in the input buffer until it is read into some other variable. This is incorrect (and seems especially unfair to the 'A' students).

There are several kluges that can be used when combining **getline()** with other input functions. (A *kluge* is a term that means an awkward, ugly programming trick.) A better solution is to restrict the use of **getline()** to situations in which we are processing a stream of character data. If we must mix reading in a stream of characters with other input, then **getline()** should be replaced by a function such as **get()**, which is a member function of the class **istream**.

For a moment, we digress to discuss two common I/O functions that are available in C: **gets()** and **fgets()**. Each of these two functions reads in an input string and changes the '**\n**' character at the end of the line to a null byte '**\0**'.

The C function **gets()** has a function prototype declared in the header file <**stdio.h**>; this file should be included in the program. Its syntax is

```
gets(name)
```

The related function **fgets()** also requires <**stdio.h**> to be included. Its syntax is

```
fgets(name, length, file stream);
```

The length argument is treated the same as that of **getline()**; it should be two bytes larger than the intended maximum length of the string.

The file stream argument can be any file; to apply to the standard input it should be **stdin**.

Both **gets()** and **fgets()** should be very familiar to C programmers.

We would prefer to use a solution to the problem of the extra carriage return needed for this application of **getline()** that avoids mixing C++ and C output functions. At the same time, we wish to avoid some of the complexity of the **getline()** member function of the **istream** class.

The solution can be found in the set of member functions available in most C++ implementations of the **iostream** class. These member functions include

eatwhite()	This function reads and removes all white space characters (blanks, tabs, and returns) from the input stream until a non–white space character is read.
int gcount()	This function returns the count of the number of characters read in the last operation on the input stream.
int get()	reads and removes the next character from the input stream.

There are several other versions of the **get()** function. That is, the function **get()** is overloaded. The additional versions of **get()** are listed below.

- **istream & get(signed char *, int len, char = '\n');**
- **istream & get(unsigned char *, int len, char = '\n');**

  The two versions of **get()** listed above read and remove characters from the input stream until either **len −1** characters have been read, the delimiter is read, or the end of file is detected. The delimiter is not placed onto the output stream, although a terminating NULL byte character **'\0'** is.

- **istream & get(signed char &);**
- **istream & get(unsigned char &);**

  The two versions of **get()** listed above read and remove a single character from the input stream and place it as a reference (address) on the given stream.

- **istream & get(streambuf &, char = '\n');** This version of **get()** reads and removes characters from the input stream until the delimiter is read.

- **istream & getline(signed char *buffer, int, char = '\n');**
- **istream & getline(unsigned char *buffer, int, char = '\n');**

  These two versions of **getline()** differ from **get()** in that the delimiter is removed from the input stream by **get()**. The delimiter is not placed onto the buffer.

- **istream & ignore(int n = 1, int delimiter = EOF)** Causes up to **n** characters to be ignored. This action stops if the delimiter is encountered.

- **int peek()** This function reads the next character from the input stream, but does not remove it. The character is available for future reading or removal.

- **int putback()** This function places a character back in the initial position of the input stream so that it is the next character read. It is similar to the **ungetc()** familiar to C programmers.

- **istream & read(signed char *, int);**
- **istream & read(unsigned char *, int);**

  This function reads and removes the number of characters given in the second argument and places them into an array. It is different from the UNIX system call **read()**. There are two forms given because the function is overloaded.

- **istream & seekg(long int position);**　Moves to an absolute position in the input stream. Similar in use to the functions **lseek()** and **fseek()** used for random file access in C. (Random file access is often called direct file access in C.)

- **istream & seekg(long int offset, seek_dir);**　The function **seekg()** is a version of **seek()** with relative movement instead of absolute movement, as was the case in the first version of **seek()**. The use of the **offset** depends on the value of the second argument **seek_dir**, which is an enumerated type with the definition

  enum seek_dir {beg, cur, end};

  It is easiest to understand this using the concept of a stream pointer. If the value of **seek_dir** is **beg**, then the movement is to an absolute position **offset** bytes from the beginning of the stream. If the value of **seek_dir** is **cur**, then the movement is to a relative position that is **offset number of** bytes from the value of the current stream pointer. If the value of **seek_dir** is **end**, then the movement is to an absolute position **offset** bytes from the "end" of the stream. (There is a member function named **seekp()** of the class **ostream** that is similar to **seekg()**, but is used to place characters back on the output stream.)

- **streampos tellg();**　Returns the value of the current stream pointer in the input stream. This function is similar to the C function **ftell()**.

We illustrate the use of some of the alternatives to the function **getline()** in Example 2.10. Note the use of the extra **get()** in the second and third sets of I/O. This extra call to **get()** is intended to read a single character and remove it from the input stream. The extra call was not necessary in the first set of I/O statements because **getline()** reads its input delimiter and removes it from the input stream.

Example 2.10 Alternatives to the use of **getline()**.

```
#include <iostream.h>
#define MAXCHAR 80

main()

{
  char address[MAXCHAR];
  char temp;
```

```
    cout << "Please enter a line of text, terminated by a";
    cout << "return\n";
    cin.getline(address, MAXCHAR, '\n');
    cout << "OUTPUT USING GETLINE\n";
    cout << address << endl<< endl;

    cout << "Enter second line of text, terminated by a";
    cout << "return\n";
    cin.get(address, MAXCHAR, '\n');
    cout << "OUTPUT USING GET WITH CHARACTER COUNT\n";
    cout << address<< endl << endl;
    cin.get(temp);

    cout << "Enter third line of text, terminated by a";
    cout << "return\n";
    cin.get(address, '\n');
    cout << "OUTPUT USING GET WITHOUT CHARACTER COUNT\n";
    cout << address << endl << endl;
    cin.get();
}
```

The output from one execution of the program of Example 2.10 is

```
Please enter a line of text, terminated by a return
abc

Please enter second line of text, terminated by a return
OUTPUT USING GET
abc

Please enter third line of text, terminated by a return
OUTPUT USING GET WITH NO CHARACTER COUNT
abc

Please enter fourth line of text, terminated by a return
OUTPUT WITH GET AND LINE WRAP
abc
```

2.6 Documentation and Commenting of C++ Programs

All of the usual guidelines for program documentation apply to C++ programs. In fact, there is probably a greater need for documentation because of the current lack of an ANSI standard and some substantial differences in class libraries between different C++ installations.

How are comments written in C++? Since C++ is essentially a superset of C, the standard form of delimiting comments by /* and */ is available. However, C++ allows a new form of comments using the single delimiter //.

The // is used on a line-by-line basis. Any characters between the // and the end of the line will be treated as a comment and ignored by the C++ compiler. Each line to be commented must contain the // delimiter symbols. The delimiter need not be the first two characters on a line, but can be used for comments after any statement.

Comments delimited by // can be nested, but there is no reason to do so.

The standard style of commenting for C++ programs is to use only the // form of comments and not to mix and match with the older delimiters /* and */ of C.

Note that we have gained the flexibility of not requiring explicit termination of comments by an explicit delimiter, since the // indicates that all succeeding characters to the end of the line will be ignored. On the other hand, the use of the // delimiter means that we cannot easily use the common technique of commenting out a block of code while debugging, as we could do in C.

This would appear to be a loss while we are learning C++ by means of small examples. However, when we examine larger C++ programs in Part II, we will see that a typical C++ program has many classes declared and that programs often appear to be a glue holding together many objects. Such programs have most of their debugging efforts directed toward classes, and the number of lines of code used to implement a class is often relatively small. In any event, the lack of ability to comment out a block of C++ code with // presents no hardship in practice.

Since C++ does not require that all declarations of variables must precede all executable statements within a block of code, the program of Example 2.11 is legal.

Example 2.11 Variable definition.

```
// Program to demonstrate the definition of
// variables after executable program
// statements have been encountered.

#include <iostream.h>

main()
{
  int count;

  cout << "Enter the number of repetitions\n";
  cin >> count;

  int i;
  for (i = 0; i < count ; i++)
    cout << i<< endl;
}
```

In this example the variable **i** is declared after the executable statements for output and input are reached. The declaration of this variable could also have been made in the loop control statement, as in

```
for (int i = 0; i < count ; i++)
    cout << i<< endl;
```

This somewhat rare usage certainly requires the programmer to indicate by a comment what is intended. A properly commented version of the program of Example 2.11 is given in Example 2.12.

Example 2.12 Properly commented version of the code shown in Example 2.11.

```
// Program to demonstrate the definition of variables after
// executable program statements have been encountered.

#include <iostream.h>

main()
{
  int count;

  cout << "Enter the number of repetitions\n";
  cin >> count;

  // Local variable used for this loop only.
  int i;
  for (i = 0; i < count ; i++)
    cout << i<< endl;
}
```

2.7   Control of C++ Programs

The main control structures in C++ are the same as those for C programs. The **if**, **if-else, break, continue**, and **switch** statements are available for branching, and the familiar **for-loop, while-loop**, and **do-while-loop** allow repetition. Their syntax is precisely the same as for C programs and should present no problems if you have used these control structures when programming in C.

For example, the integers from 0 to 10 can be printed using the **while-loop**

```
i = 0;
while (i <= 10)
  {
  cout << i<< endl;
  i++;
  }
```

or the do-while-loop

```
i = 0;
do
  {
  cout << i << endl;
  i++;
  }
while (i <= 10);
```

The **for-loop** in C has the following semantics:

```
for( expression1; expression2; expression3)
   zero_or_more_statements
```

Since C++ is essentially a superset of C, any **for-loop** organization that is valid in C will also work in C++. However, the C++ semantics of a **for-loop** are slightly more general than they are in C. The formal syntax of a **for-loop** in C++ is

```
for( statement1; statement2; statement3)
   zero_or_more_statements
```

C++ allows the use of statements in a **for-loop**, not just expressions. This means that the C++ controlling statements can have data declarations and not just expressions. (The same organization holds for **while-loops** and **do-while-loops**.) Example 2.13 illustrates this point. Notice the syntax of the first part of the **for-loop** definition.

Example 2.13 Use of declarations inside **for-loop** control.

```
#include <iostream.h>
main()
{
  for (int i = 0; i <= 10; i++)
    cout << i << endl;
}
```

The **if-else** statement in C++ has familiar semantics:

```
if (expression1)
   zero_or_more_statements
else
   zero_or_more_statements
```

The switch statement has the same semantics in C++ as it does in C. The Backus–Naur form for the switch statement looks something like the following:

```
switch (expression1)
  {
  case constant_int_1: zero_or_more_statements_1
  case constant_int_2: zero_or_more_statements_2

     .

     .

  case constant_int_n: zero_or_more_statements_n
  default: zero_or_more_statements_default
  }
more_statements;
```

As was the situation with the corresponding statement in C, the use of the **default** statement within a **switch** statement is optional.

Except for the **for-loop** in C++, the syntax for control statements is the same in C and C++.

2.8 Operators in C++

All the operators available in C are also available in C++. They are used with the same syntax and their semantics are similar when applied to C language constructions in C++ programs. There are some differences, however.

The first obvious difference is that C++ has more reserved words than C and therefore a C program using these additional reserved words as operands cannot be correct as a C++ program. See Appendix 1 for a list of reserved words in C++.

The second difference is that C++ allows operators to be overloaded. That is, the operator has different meanings in different contexts, depending only on the types of the operands. C allows this for the standard arithmetic operators +, -, *, and so on. As we will see, operator overloading is much broader in C++ than in C, since we will be able to overload an operator named '+' for user-defined classes with very different meanings, such as complex numbers (normal complex addition), and strings (concatentation).

A third difference involves the scope of an operator. Since C++ permits, and in fact encourages, the use of operator overloading, there are new issues of operator resolution in C++. There are other differences between C++ and C involving the scope of operators .

The overloading of operators in C++ can be shown most easily by an example. Suppose that we have a class called **Complex**, whose elements have been defined to have two parts: a real part and a complex part. We assume that there is a constructor function **Complex** defined as part of the class. The class should be designed to allow us to perform normal operations on complex numbers and to be able to consider a complex number whose imaginary part is 0 as a real number.

We can define a method of addition of complex numbers by the definition of the member function + as follows. The function prototype for the overloaded operator + is:

```
Complex operator + (Complex, Complex);
```

The function prototype indicates that the operator + takes two arguments, each of which is of type **Complex**, and returns a value that is also of type **Complex**. It is also clear from the use of the C++ reserved word **operator** that the type **Complex** refers to a class, rather than merely to a data type declared by a **typedef** construction.

The details of the implementation of this operator are

```
Complex operator + (Complex a, Complex b);
{
  Complex C(0,0); // Call to constructor function.
  C.real = a.real + b.real;
  C.imag = a.imag + b.imag;
  return C;
};
```

The use of this overloaded operator named + is the same as for any other function call:

```
c = a + b;
```

if **a**, **b**, and **c** are complex numbers.

The natural question to ask at this point is whether this use of + causes any difficulty. Ordinarily, we would have to define addition in all the special cases:

```
Complex operator + (Complex, int);
Complex operator + (Complex, float);
Complex operator + (Complex, double);
Complex operator + (int, Complex);
Complex operator + (float, Complex);
Complex operator + (double, Complex);
```

(Technically the last three cases would be declared as being **friend** functions, rather than member functions. We will discuss **friend** functions in detail in Chapter 3.)

A typical definition of a member function might be

```
Complex operator + (Complex a, int b);
{
  Complex C(0,0) ; //constructor
  C.real = a.real + b;
  C.imag = a.imag;
};
```

We can avoid the extra coding in this case by using the default value of 0.0 for the imaginary part of a constructor as in

```
Complex (double x, double y = 0.0)
{
  real = x;
  imag = y;
};
```

Note that the default value of the imaginary part is overwritten by any assignment to this field. (The term *constructor* refers to a function that creates an object belonging to a class. The name of the constructor function is the same as the name of the class. We will study constructors in Section 3.2.)

Recall from Chapter 1 that the term *overloading* means that an operator can be used with multiple sets of argument types. The selection of which operation is used when a symbol such as + is encountered during compilation is determined by the types of the argument.

Suppose that **i** is of type **int**, **f** is of type **float**, and the variables **c1**, **c2**, **c3**, and **c4** are of type **Complex**. The + operation refers to integer arithmetic, floating point arithmetic (with a copy of the argument **a** promoted to the appropriate floating point type), and complex arithmetic in the examples below, respectively.

```
c1 = i + i;// integer addition, ints promoted to Complex

c2 = i + f;// float addition, int and float promoted to
           // Complex

c3 = i + c4;// complex addition, int promoted to Complex
```

Note that the use of default values in the constructor of a complex number means that the results of complex arithmetic are correct when performed with arguments whose imaginary part is 0.

C++ resolves conflicts in operator overloading by the algorithm given in Table 2.1. The symbol **f()** will denote the operator in this example. (Recall that the two terms "operator" and "function" are synonymous in this context.)

Here is an example of how the overloading algorithm works for the case of the operation

```
z = a + c;
```

The operator under consideration is + and there are many possibilities, since there are many combinations of predefined types and the user-defined type **Complex**. We will select an operator + for which we have an exact match of the **Complex** argument **c** and use an appropriate predefined conversion for the first argument.

You may have noted that there is another operator that is overloaded in the previous example, the assignment operator =. The overloading of this operator is familiar when the operands are of any one of the predefined types in either C or C++. There is a default assignment operator in C++. However, it is dangerous to use it since this default assignment operator does not automatically assign storage to an object being assigned

Table 2.1 Algorithm for resolving conflicts in operator overloading.

1. Determine the set of all functions that have the same name as the operator **f()**. Consider only those names that are visible to the current function call. Call this set of functions **S**.
2. For each function **g()** in the set **S**, apply each of the rules 3 through 5.
3. For each argument of the operator **g()**, determine if there is an exact match of the type of the argument of **g()** with the corresponding argument of **f()**.
4. If an argument of **g()** does not exactly match an argument of **f()**, determine if a conversion of its argument will convert its type to that of the corresponding argument of **f()**.
5. Mark each function **g()** in the set **S** for which there is a match of an argument of **g()** to the corresponding argument of **f()**.
6. Among all marked functions in the set **S**, determine if there is a function **g()** that matches **f()** in all arguments.
7. If there is a single such function **g()** in step 6, then this function is returned and the algorithm terminates.
8. Otherwise the set of matching functions is ordered by the preferences that an exact match is better than any conversion and that a standard conversion of one of the predefined types in C++ is better than any user-defined conversion.
9. If there is a single "best" match, as determined by the ordering in step 8, then that is the selection for the operator and this function is returned by the algorithm. If there is more than one such match, then the algorithm terminates with failure.

to. It is probably safe in this example, since the class structure that we have used for the class **Complex** is very simple.

C++ has relatively few restrictions on the overloading of operators. The primary requirement is that the syntax of the operator must remain the same after overloading. Thus a binary operator cannot be overloaded as a unary or ternary operator, a unary operator cannot be overloaded as a binary or a ternary operator, and so on. The five operators

```
. .* :: ?: sizeof
```

cannot be overloaded, nor can the preprocessor symbols # and ##. (There are some differences in the syntactical and semantic treatment of the overloading of the operators **new** and **delete**. We will discuss these operators when we study C++ pointers in Chapter 4.

The scope resolution operator **::** is used to distinguish between operators (and functions) of the same name that are members of different classes. The presence of the two colons **::** indicates that the expression to the right is a function that is a member of the class specified on the left.

Thus the code fragment

```
Binary :: read() { //rest of code omitted}
```

indicates that **read()** is a member function of the class **Binary**.

There is nothing in C that is directly analogous to the scope resolution operator **::** that is available in C++. If a function is called in a C source file but not defined there, then the C compiler looks for it elsewhere. If the function is not defined in any of the source files compiled with this system and is not included in one of the libraries linked to the program, then an error message is produced and no executable file will be produced. If the function is defined in another file (and the prototype agrees with the function definition, at least in the return type) then the compilation process can proceed.

All statements in the previous paragraph are true regardless of the presence or absence of the C reserved word **extern**.

There is no such problem with classes and member functions in C++.

2.9 An Example: Processing an Input Stream

By the term *input stream*, we mean a collection of input data terminated by a special symbol denoting the end of input. There is no format assumed for the input other than these characters. The most common construction in the C language for handling an input stream is shown in Example 2.14.

Example 2.14 C program to process an input stream.

```
#include <stdio.h>

extern void process(int ch); /* defined elsewhere*/

/* Note use of int type to avoid problems with EOF */
main()
{
  int ch;

  while ((ch=getchar()) != EOF)
    process(ch);
}
```

The most important action of this C program takes place in the evaluation of the expression that controls the **while-loop**. The function **getchar()** reads characters from the input stream one at a time. As each character is read, it is assigned to the variable **ch**, which is of type **int**. The value of **ch** is then compared to the symbolic constant **EOF**, which is defined in the standard C header file <**stdio.h**>. If the variable is not **EOF**, then the expression controlling the **while-loop** is nonzero and the body of the **while-loop**, which in this example is the single statement process (**ch**), is executed. The program stops when the value read in to **ch** is equal to **EOF**. (The reader should recall that the variable **ch** was declared to be of type **int** in order to treat the case where **EOF** might have had the value –**1** because of a particular operating system; such a negative value frequently cannot be obtained from a character variable.)

Additional structure of the input can be treated in the function **process()**.

In C++, a program that processes an input stream can have a similar structure. Note the improvement in program simplicity. There is no need to concern ourselves with the potential problems with EOF that are so annoying when reading input streams in C, since the **get()** member function of **cin** does this work for us.

Example 2.15 Reading an input stream in C++.

```
#include <iostream.h>

extern void process(char ch); // defined elsewhere

// Note use of char type. No problems with EOF.

main()
{
  char ch;

  while (cin.get(ch) )
    process(ch);
}

void process(char ch)
{
  cout << ch;
}
```

An alternative method of reading an input stream is from a file. We can read the contents of a file and echo them to the terminal screen (**cout**) by using the **ifstream** object of the **fstream** object described in the standard header file **fstream.h**. We will treat this concept briefly here and return to the study of file **I/O** in Chapter 6.

An example of a program to echo the contents of a file whose name is "**infile**" is given in Example 2.16. We will modify this program to allow the use of command-line arguments or user-defined file names in Chapter 4 when we study pointers. This is just one example of a program to read from a file; we will meet many others.

Example 2.16 Echoing a file to the screen.

```
#include <fstream.h>

extern void process(char ch); // defined elsewhere

// Note use of char type. No problems with EOF.
main()
{
  char ch;
  ifstream f1 ("infile");

  if (!f1)
    cerr << "Error opening input file.\n";

  while (f1.get(ch) )
    process(ch);
}
```

There are several things worth noting in this example. The file name is enclosed within quotes and then inside parentheses. An object of the class **ifstream** is declared, indicating that we are using an input file. We check for an error when opening the file named "**infile**" by using a simple negation construction using the logical not operator with the symbol **!**. Error messages are sent to **cerr**.

Note also the use of the notation **f1.get()**. It refers to the use of the function **get()**, which is a member function belonging to the class **f1**.

2.10   **Differences in I/O between C and C++**

The title of this section is somewhat misleading. Since C++ is essentially a superset of C, all C I/O functions will also work with C++ programs (assuming proper header files are used). However, standard C I/O functions often cause problems when combined with the C++ << and >> operators and the standard streams **cin**, **cout**, and **cerr**.

The difficulty is essentially due to buffering of output. A C++ program using the two statements

```
printf("Please enter an integer.\n");
```

and

```
cout << "Use -1 to exit.\n";
```

in succession would expect the two lines of text

```
Please enter an integer.
Use -1 to exit.
```

to be printed in that order. However, the two output statements use different buffers. The actual output on most systems is

```
Use -1 to exit.
...other output from the << operator
```

with the output

```
Please enter an integer.
```

appearing only after all << operations have been performed and the program execution terminates. (The order of output might be different on your system.) The reason that the **printf()** statement's data gets printed at this time is that flushing of all output buffers is a standard action that is taken by the operating system when a program completes its execution.

The situation can be remedied somewhat on UNIX and some other systems that allow user control of output buffers within a program. The programmer can include the statement:

```
fflush(stdout);
```

to force emptying the contents of standard output buffers. This use of **fflush()** should precede each occurrence of a **printf()** statement to flush the print buffer. (Recall that in C, the contents of this buffer are not printed until flushed by a request to output a new line character **'\n'**, or by successful termination of the program.)

Whether this will work with other standard output functions such as **fprintf()**, **putc()**, **putchar()**, or **puts()** is problematical. The best solution is not to mix any of the I/O functions from C with the I/O operators << and >> of C++. This means extra programming when converting C programs to C++ but is worth the effort. We will not encourage unnecessarily complex, nonportable programming practice by mixing C and C++ I/O in this book.

2.11 Testing Issues

The new C++ features we have seen in this chapter cause some problems for testing. The primary difficulty at this point occurs in operator overloading, although we have seen some I/O problems if the program uses both C and C++ I/O functions.

We present two checklists of items to be considered when testing C++ programs that use the constructions of this chapter. Additional checklists will be given when we learn more of the features of C++ in the later chapters. For simplicity, we will concentrate on those features specific to C++ and ignore general questions of testing non-object-oriented software.

The first checklist describes the steps necessary for testing programs that use an overloaded operator. This checklist is given in Table 2.2.

For example, an operator such as + is already overloaded for **int** and **float**. If we have some new type for which the operator is redefined, then we must test the + operator for the following combinations of arguments:

```
int new_type
new_type int
float new_type
new_type float
new_type new_type
```

We need not test the cases that can be assumed to have been previously tested, such as

```
int int
float float
int float
float int
```

The second checklist describes the steps necessary for testing C++ programs that use the standard I/O functions of the C language instead of those available in C++. This checklist is given in Table 2.3.

These checklists can help avoid some of the more common errors that beginning C++ programmers make. We will study more complex testing issues later in this book. For now, we will be content with a discussion of how to test a somewhat larger object-oriented program such as that shown in Example 2.17.

Example 2.17 uses some C++ constructs that are unfamiliar to us at this stage of our knowledge. The constructs occur in the declaration of the overloaded extraction operator <<. Ignore these constructs and concentrate on the testing issues discussed in this section.

Note that we have three overloaded operators in this program: +, >>, and =. The first two have been explicitly declared as functions that can access all of the data in the class **Complex**. (Nothing in the class **Complex** has been declared as being **private**.) We have used the default overloading of the assignment operator =.

Table 2.2 Checklist for testing overloaded operators.

1. Make a list of all overloaded operators. (The operators that we discuss in this section will already be defined for some of the standard types.)
2. For each overloaded operator, make a list of each type of operand that can be used with that operator. Be sure to include all predefined types to which the operator can be applied.
3. For a unary operator, test the operator on the new object type.
4. For a binary operator, list all possible combinations of types of the operands.
5. Test each possible combination of allowable operands.

Table 2.3 Testing of I/O functions.

1. Replace all **printf()**, **putc()**, **putchar()**, and **puts()**, function calls with the operator << and either **cout** or **cerr**, as appropriate.
2. Replace all **scanf()**, **getc()**, **getchar()**, and **gets()** function calls by the operator >> and **cin**.
3. Include the header file **iostream.h.**
4. Rerun the program and compare the results on some standard inputs with those obtained previously.
5. If there are differences, apply manipulators to the I/O stream in order to obtain correct results. Be sure to use the include file **iomanip.h** if you use any I/O manipulators.

Three functions are presented for testing purposes. The member function **print()** is included to make sure that different functions work correctly. It is much more difficult to find errors if the I/O functions do not work properly. The output function call corresponding to this function's definition would have been

```
z2.print(z2);
```

The functions **realpart()** and **imagpart()** were also used for testing the program.

Example 2.17 A testing example.

```
#include <iostream.h>

class Complex
{
public:
  double real;
  double imag;

  Complex() {double real = 0.0; double imag = 0.0; }

  double realpart (Complex z) { return z.real; }
  double imagpart (Complex z) { return z.imag; }
```

```
    // Code not used, but presented for clarity.
    void print(Complex z) {cout << z.real<< " + "
                        << z.imag <<"i\n";}
};
Complex operator + (Complex a, Complex b)
{
  Complex C;

  C.real = a.real + b.real;
  C.imag = a.imag + b.imag;
  return C;
}
ostream & operator << (ostream & stream, Complex a)
{
  cout << a.real << " + " << a.imag << "i\n";
  return stream;
}
main()
{
  Complex z1, z2;
  float x1, x2,y1,y2;

  cout << "Enter the real and imaginary parts of "
     << "the first complex number" << endl;
  cin >> x1 >> y1;
  cout << "Enter the real and imaginary parts of "
     << "the second complex number" << endl;
  cin >> x2 >> y2;
  z1.real = x1;
  z1.imag = y1;
  z2.real = x2;
  z2.imag = y2;
  z2 = z1 + z2;
  cout << z2;
}
```

Some testing was done using the default conversions of predefined arithmetic arguments in C++.

Summary

The C++ language is essentially a superset of C. The fundamental additional feature of C++ is the class. Control structures in C++ are essentially the same as control structures in C.

Comments in C++ can be marked by the use of two slashes (**//**). A comment delimited by **//** extends to the end of the line on which the **//** appears.

Output in C++ is performed primarily by the << operator. There are two primary output streams, **cout** and **cerr**. It can be performed on the **ostream** class.

Input in C++ is performed primarily by the >> operator. There is one primary input stream in C++, **cin**. It can be performed on the **istream** class.

The **ostream** and **istream** classes are related to a class **iostream**. These classes are used for interactive (not file-based) I/O. Input and output for files should use the **fstream**, **ifstream**, and **ofstream** classes.

The C++ << and >> operators should not be used with the C language I/O functions **printf()**, **scanf()**, **getc()**, **putc()**, **getchar()**, **putchar()**, **gets()**, or **puts()** because of several problems with synchronization of the different I/O buffers.

Testing of an overloaded operator should include testing of all possible combinations of operands.

Exercises

1. Test some of your ANSI C programs to determine if they are compatible with your C++ compiler. Do they compile without any errors or warning messages?

2. Repeat Exercise 1 for some program written in the earlier Kernighan and Ritchie version of C.

3. List all different classes described in this chapter. After you have made this list, examine the source code for the header file **iostream.h** that is provided with your system and see if you had described all the classes provided there.

4. Devise a new class to describe floating point numbers. The precision of the floating point numbers will be part of the class. The three precisions to be considered are **float**, **double**, and **long double**.

5. Assume that you have created the class described in Exercise 4. Assume also that functions have been written to perform all arithmetic operations on this class and that these functions overload the +, -, *, and / operators. What combinations of arguments must be tested for the overloaded + operator for this class?

6. List the special cases that should be tested for correct treatment of overloading of the + operator in Example 2.17. List the special cases needed for testing of the << and assignment operators also.

7. Write a C++ program that assigns grades. The program will have the control structure that will indicate a grade of '**A**' if the value of average is greater than or equal

to 90.0, `'B'` if the value of average is greater than or equal to 80.0 but less than 90.0, and so on down to `'F'` if the value of average is less than 60.0. Test your program logic by running it several times.

8. Rewrite the grading program of the previous exercise using the enumeration data construction for the possible letter grades. Compare the two programs. Which is easier to read?

9. We have seen a fairly large number of simple C++ language statements and a few C++ programs, probably enough to be able to distinguish most of the simple notations that are used in C++ programs. Describe an algorithm that will take as input a file that contains a C++ language program and that produces as output a listing of the separate tokens that make up the program. Assume that tokens are anything other than blanks, tabs, or new lines. Be sure that your algorithm can handle such things as the comment delimiter `//`. Do not attempt to implement this algorithm at this time.

Elementary C++ Program Structure

3

3.1 Derived and Base Classes

In the previous chapter, we described some of the primary building blocks of C++ programs and the relation of C to C++. We described the notion of a class and the overloading of operators. We have already made progress toward our software engineering goals by improving understandability of programs using overloading. With overloading, we were able to replace statements like

```
a = plus(b,c);
```

by much clearer statements such as

```
a = b + c;
```

As we will see, these are only minor improvements compared to the object-oriented features that we will meet later.

We are now ready to make a major advance by learning how to construct new classes from old. The idea is to determine the properties provided in the description of the old class that are appropriate for the desired new class and to use these properties as the start of the new class.

These concepts are formalized in object-oriented language as a *base class* and a *derived class*. The presumption is that the base class is already defined along with the transformations that are appropriate for the abstract object described by the class. The derived class will "inherit" the basic structure and the defined functions. The derived class will be able to keep those portions of the base class that it needs and replace others with appropriate functions.

A major advantage of this approach is that much of the code describing the base class can be used for the derived class. The ability of a derived class to inherit code from a base class is a major step toward software reuse.

Here are some of the issues involved in any possible organization of classes. Suppose that we have a class called **Rectangle** that has already been defined and suppose that we want to develop a new class called **Square**. From our knowledge of geometry, we know that the objects in this class are also rectangles and hence are also members of the class **Rectangle**.

In fact, we can do everything that we want to do with squares by restricting our attention only to rectangles whose length and width are equal, with no additional attempt to represent any geometric knowledge. This allows complete reuse of any code already developed for rectangles and therefore has much to commend it.

This approach has one weakness—we have no way of capturing the fundamental property of two rectangles being equal. It is possible to have a rectangle whose adjacent sides are 2.000000001 and 1.999999999 being considered as a square because of rounding errors when the two numbers are converted to binary representations, at least on some computers. This can happen if the lengths of the two sides are computed by different procedures, which may have different accuracy. We cannot have the essential concept of a square having two sides equal depend on the numerical accuracy of the calculations determining their length.

In fact, it is not necessary for us to compute the lengths of the sides of a rectangle to know that the sides are equal. Think of being in one of two long line of cars waiting to pay a toll on a bridge. If the lines are equally backed up (the last cars are parallel), it doesn't really matter if there are 100 or 101 cars in front of you. Equality of the length of the two lines is relevant to determining which line is better, not the actual length. (Of course the length is relevant to the amount of time that you will spend waiting in line.)

Thus, the approach of considering only those rectangles whose length and width are equal is not adequate. The major problem is that we have not captured the property of being a square.

Another (extreme) approach is to develop totally new code for the implementation of squares and not use any of the code developed for rectangles. This is an inefficient way of developing code. It is inconsistent with nearly everything that we have learned about software engineering and is particularly inconsistent with the goal of software reusability.

What we need is some middle ground that allows us to reuse as much as possible of the existing code for rectangles and that also allows us to capture the abstraction of a square. We will do this using the C++ notions of base and derived classes.

The program shown in Example 3.1 provides one possible implementation of the class **Rectangle**. Note that there is no abstraction of the possibility of the rectangle being a square.

Example 3.1 One possible organization of the class **Rectangle**.

```
#include <iostream.h>

class Rectangle
{
private:
  double length;
  double width ;
public:
  Rectangle(double L = 0.0, double W = 0.0);
  double area() { return (length * width) ; }
  double perimeter() {return (2.0 * (length + width)) ; }
};

// Member function of class Rectangle.
Rectangle :: Rectangle(double L, double W)
{
  length = L;
  width = W;
}

main()
{
  Rectangle R1(3,4);
  Rectangle R2(5,5);

  cout << "Area of first rectangle: " << R1.area() << endl ;
  cout << "Perimeter is " << R1.perimeter() << endl;

  cout << "Area of second rectangle:" << R2.area() << endl ;
  cout << "Perimeter is " << R2.perimeter() << endl;
}
```

The output of this program is what is expected, namely a printing of the area and perimeter of each of the two rectangles.

Now we turn to the development of a class that describes the abstract concept of a square. We will call this new class **Square** to be consistent with the naming of the class **Rectangle**. An inefficient way to develop this new class would be to include the existing lines of the description of the class **Rectangle** in the class **Square** by copying them. This would be wasteful and would make modifying any program using these classes a nightmare, because there would be two copies of essentially the same code to keep track of.

The preferred method in C++ is to treat the existing class, **Rectangle**, as a base class and determine the properties of the new class, **Square**, that are the same as those of the base class. The new class is called a "derived class" and is said to inherit information from the base class. The concept of inheritance is fundamental in C++.

Lets examine the way that this is done in Example 3.2. For completeness, we have grouped the code for both the **Rectangle** and **Square** classes into the same file. In most situations, the code would be grouped into separate files, with the class descriptions placed in header files and the definitions of the member functions, and probably the main program, also in separate files. We will discuss separate files later in Chapter 7.

The key step is the definition of the class **Square.**

Example 3.2 A base and a derived class.

```
#include <iostream.h>

class Rectangle
{
private:
  double length;
  double width ;
public:
  Rectangle(double L = 0.0, double W = 0.0);
  double area() { return (length * width) ; }
  double perimeter() {return (2.0 * (length + width)); }
};

// Member function of class Rectangle.
Rectangle :: Rectangle(double L, double W)
{
  length = L;
  width = W;
}

// Description of the class Square.
class Square : public Rectangle
```

```
{
private:
  double side;
public:
  Square()  {side = 0.0;}};
  Square(double s) : Rectangle(s,s){side = s;} ;
};

main()
{
  Rectangle R1(3,4);
  Rectangle R2(5,5);
  Square S1(4.0);
  Square S2(3.99999999999);

  cout << "Area of first rectangle: " << R1.area() << endl;
  cout << "Perimeter is " << R1.perimeter() << endl;

  cout << "Area of second rectangle:" << R2.area() << endl;
  cout << "Perimeter is " << R2.perimeter() << endl;

  cout << "Area of first square is " << S1.area() << endl;
  cout << "Perimeter is " << S1.perimeter() << endl;

  cout << "Area of second square is " << S2.area() << endl;
  cout << "Perimeter is " << S2.perimeter() << endl;
}
```

The output of the program is

```
Area of first rectangle: 12
Perimeter is 14

Area of second rectangle: 25
Perimeter is 20

Area of first square: 16
Perimeter is 16

Area of first square: 16
Perimeter is 16
```

Note that the two squares have the same area and perimeter. The results displayed depend upon the accuracy of the computer's internal representation of numbers and the default settings for output. Note that the inputs of 4.0 and 3.99999999999 for the sides of the two squares are different values and that the computer handles any discrepancy.

The syntax of the definition of the class **Square** begins with the line

```
class Square : public Rectangle
```

This line indicates that the class **Square** is derived from the class **Rectangle**. The appearance of the reserved word **public** indicates that each **public** member function from the base class is to be treated as public in the derived class, which is what we want.

The derived class **Square** has a single hidden data value: the entity represented by the **side** variable. Note that the base class, **Rectangle**, has two hidden entities: **length** and **width**.

The most interesting part of the class description of **Square** is the constructor **Square()**. The constructor is overloaded. The default value for the value of the side of an element of the class **Square** is 0. Our description of a constructor for the derived class builds upon the previous existence of a constructor for the base class **Rectangle**. This is clear from the code statement

```
Square(double s) : Rectangle(s,s){side = s;} ;
```

The appearance of the colon '**:**' in this statement illustrates that we are to use something from the base class. What we are using is the constructor for the base class, with the length and width being equal, which is exactly what we want for a rectangle.

There are no other public member functions for the class **Square**. However, the functions of this class can use any of the member functions of the base class, because of the use of the reserved word **public** in the definition of the class **Rectangle**. Therefore, we can call the functions **area()** and **perimeter()**, just as if they were members of the class **Square**. They *are* members of that class and they were placed there by the action of inheritance in C++, since they belong to a derived class.

Inheritance is a powerful concept in C++ and we will return to it often.

Clearly we need to have an existing base class before we can consider having derived classes that inherit properties from this base class. You might be a little concerned that we appear to have developed the descriptions of the base class **Rectangle** and the derived class **Square** simultaneously. This seems to be counter to the experience of most programmers in maintaining existing systems. Programmers performing software maintenance rarely have the opportunity to make major changes to older portions of the code in order to make new portions easier to write.

What we have touched upon here is a fundamental change in the software development paradigm—incorporating ease of modifiability into the initial design of software. This is a major advantage of object-oriented programming. We can reduce future coding by proper design of our systems, even if the new systems are used in ways different from the original intention of the software designer.

Incidentally, this issue is a major reason for some of the hyperbole associated with object-oriented programming. Some proponents of object-oriented technology claim tremendous savings in the costs of software maintenance, which are often from 50 to 80 percent of the total software life cycle costs. These savings will not occur in the maintenance of existing procedurally based systems, which must be reengineered into an object-oriented framework before any projected savings in maintenance costs can be achieved because of object-oriented technology. The costs to reengineer software are often much larger than anticipated and there is little hard data on improvements in maintenance costs for large systems that have been reengineered.

What *is* true is that a careful design of a system from scratch can reduce maintenance costs because of the possibility of inheritance reducing the amount of code being written. Object-oriented programming, when coupled with careful object-oriented design, can reduce maintenance costs by encouraging software reuse. If having code written in C++ instead of older languages automatically meant that the code would be easier to maintain, then automatic line-by-line program translation from, say, FORTRAN to C++ would reduce maintenance costs easily. Line-by-line translators are easy to write, but the resulting code appears to be written in what many people call "C++TRAN," which is effectively useless. Most complex language translators that attempt to abstract some of the data and functional organization of the program being translated are available commercially and are often quite expensive. It is not easy to modify systems to become object-oriented.

Let's return to the study of inheritance. There is no apparent reason why a class cannot be derived from more than one base class. Example 3.3 shows how the concept of "squareness" can be inherited from two different base classes. In this example, there are now two base classes, **Rectangle** and **Quadrilateral**, and two derived classes, **Square** and **Square2**. (Because of the difficulty of determining the area of a quadrilateral from a knowledge of its sides, no member function to compute the area of a general quadrilateral is given.)

The C++ reserved word **public** is used as an access qualifier in this context. It indicates how the member functions of the base class are to be treated with respect to the derived class. The use of the word **public** in this case means that the derived class will have access to all member functions of the base class.

The possible values for access qualifiers and their meanings are:

private   Only member functions, member initializers, and friends of the class in which it is declared can use an object declared as being private.

protected   Less restrictive than private because member functions and friends of any classes that are derived from the class can have the same access as do member functions, member initializers, and friends of the class in which it is declared.

public   Any function or initializer can use the object.

(We will define the terms "initializer" and "friend" later in this book.)

The default value for an access qualifier is **public**. It is good programming practice to indicate explicitly each access qualifier for a class to make sure that the correct access is used.

Example 3.3 Two different ways of inheriting "squareness."

```
#include <iostream.h>

class Rectangle
{
private:
  double length;
  double width ;
public:
  Rectangle(double L = 0.0, double W = 0.0);
  double area() { return (length * width) ; }
  double perimeter() {return (2.0 * (length + width)) ; }
};

// Member function of class Rectangle.
Rectangle :: Rectangle(double L, double W)
{
  length = L;
  width = W;
}

// Description of a new class Quadrilateral
class Quadrilateral
{
  double side1, side2, side3, side4;
public:
  Quadrilateral(double s1 = 0.0, double s2 = 0.0,
                double s3 = 0.0, double s4 = 0.0);
  double perimeter()
                { return (side1 + side2 + side3 + side4);}
};

// Constructor for the new class Quadrilateral
Quadrilateral :: Quadrilateral(double s1, double s2,
                double s3, double s4)
{
  side1 = s1;
  side2 = s2;
  side3 = s3;
  side4 = s4;
}
```

```cpp
// Description of the class Square.
class Square : public Rectangle
{
  double side;
public:
  Square()  {side = 0.0;};
  Square(double s) : Rectangle(s,s){side = s;} ;
};

// Description of the new derived class Square2
class Square2 : public Quadrilateral
{
  double side;
public:
  Square2() {side = 0.0;};
  Square2(double s) : Quadrilateral(s, s, s, s)
                   { side = s;};
}

// Main program.
main()
{
  Rectangle R1(3,4);
  Rectangle R2(5,5);
  Square S1(4.0);
  Square S2(3.99999999999);
  Quadrilateral Q(1,2,3,4);
  Square2 sq(4.0);

  cout << "Area of first rectangle is " << R1.area()
            << endl;
  cout << "Perimeter is " << R1.perimeter() << endl;

  cout << "Area of second rectangle is " << R2.area()
            << endl;
  cout << "Perimeter is " << R2.perimeter() << endl;

  cout << "Area of first square is " << S1.area() << endl ;
  cout << "Perimeter is " << S1.perimeter() << endl;

  cout << "Area of second square is " << S2.area() << endl ;
  cout << "Perimeter is " << S2.perimeter() << endl;

  cout << "Perimeter of Quadrilateral is " << Q.perimeter()
            << endl;
  cout << "Perimeter of Square2 is " << sq.perimeter()
        << endl;
}
```

Figure 3.1 illustrates the relationships among the various classes in Example 3.3.

We have drawn the lines between the base and derived classes with arrows at both ends. This is to indicate that the derived class gets its data and functions from the base class and that the derived class sends requests to the base class for information about missing functions and data.

The relationship between a base class and a class derived from it is often called the "is-a" relation. The is-a relation can provide a strong indication that your inheritance hierarchy is correct. If you can say that an object of the derived class "is a" object of the base class, then the hierarchy is probably correct. Since a square *is-a* rectangle, and a square *is a* quadrilateral, we have confidence that our hierarchies are correct. (Ignore the difference between the indefinite articles "a" and "an" when doing this; concentrate on the semantics and not on the English grammar of how you say it.)

There is one major problem with the code of Example 3.3. We had two different derived classes for the same concept. It would be smoother if we could have a single derived class called **Square** that would inherit the appropriate properties of each base class from which it is derived. This would be an example of multiple inheritance. **Note:** multiple inheritance is not available on all C++ compilers.

Figure 3.2 illustrates the way that we would prefer to have a single derived class inherit properties from two different base classes. Note how this figure is in agreement with the is-a relationship between squares and rectangles, and between squares and quadrilaterals.

In Example 3.4, we illustrate the use of multiple inheritance. The interesting syntax is in the statement

```
class Square:public Rectangle, public Quadrilateral
```

Figure 3.1 The inheritance relationships in the program of Example 3.3.

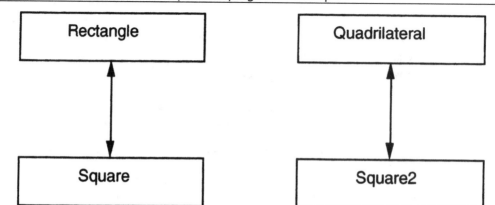

Figure 3.2 The preferred way to inherit from two different base classes.

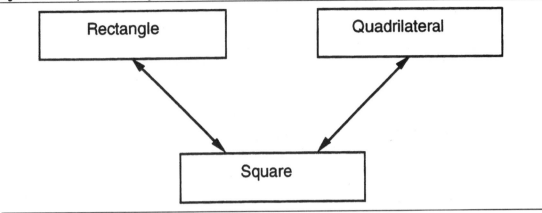

which indicates that there is inheritance from each of two base classes because of the repeated use of the access qualifier **public**.

To vary the syntax of our sequence of examples, we used the access qualifier **protected** for some members of the base classes. This was done to emphasize their visibility to derived classes. Since the default value of the access qualifier is **public**, no information was lost by making this change, since the other (nonsharable) portion of the class description was already declared as private.

The determination of which **perimeter()** function to use in the derived class is interesting. Because the name of this function appears in each of the base classes, the compiler does not know how to resolve the ambiguity in the selection of the proper function with that name.

The surprising values of **0** for the area of the second square and for the perimeter of the square treated as a quadrilateral are due to deliberate errors in the resolution of the ambiguity in multiple inheritance. These errors may be due to a deficiency in the semantic analysis of the C++ compiler used. It might have been better to have used a compiler with more accurate warning messages of ambiguities in multiple inheritance.

Example 3.4 Multiple inheritance.

```
#include <iostream.h>

class Rectangle
{
```

```
protected:
  double length;
  double width ;
public:
  Rectangle(double L = 0.0, double W = 0.0);
  double area() {return (double) (length * width) ; }
  double perimeter()
           {return (double) (2.0 *(length + width)); }
};


// Member function of class Rectangle.
Rectangle :: Rectangle(double L, double W)
{
  length = L;
  width = W;
}


// Description of a new class Quadrilateral
class Quadrilateral
{
protected:
  double side1, side2, side3, side4;
public:
  Quadrilateral(double s1 = 0.0, double s2 = 0.0,
     double s3 = 0.0, double s4 = 0.0);
  double perimeter()
     {return (double) (side1 + side2 + side3 + side4);}
};


// Constructor for the new class Quadrilateral
Quadrilateral :: Quadrilateral(double s1,
         double s2, double s3, double s4)
{
  side1 = s1;
  side2 = s2;
  side3 = s3;
  side4 = s4;
}


// Description of the class Square.
class Square : public Rectangle, public Quadrilateral
{
  double side;
public:
  Square(double s): Rectangle(s,s) {length= s; width = s;};
```

```
    // Ignore all but first argument in constructing Square.
    Square(double s, double t) : Rectangle(s,s)
            {length = s; width = s;};

    // Ignore all but first argument in constructing Square.
    Square (double s, double t, double u, double v):
            Quadrilateral(s, s, s, s) { side = s;};

    double perimeter();
};


double Square:: perimeter()
{
  Rectangle :: perimeter();
  Quadrilateral :: perimeter();
}



// Main program.
main()
{
  Rectangle R1(3,4);
  Rectangle R2(5,5);
  Square S1(4.0, 4.0);
  Square S2(3.99999999999, 3.99999999999, 3.9999999999,
            3.99999999);
  Quadrilateral Q(1,2,3,4);

  cout << "Area of first rectangle is " << R1.area()
          << endl ;
  cout << "Perimeter is " << R1.perimeter() << endl;

  cout << "Area of second rectangle is " << R2.area()
          << endl ;
  cout << "Perimeter is " << R2.perimeter() << endl;

  cout << "\nArea of first square is " << S1.area()
          << endl ;
  cout << "Perimeter is " << S1.Rectangle::perimeter()
          << endl;

  cout << "Area of second square is " << S2.area() << endl ;
  cout << "Perimeter is " << S2.Quadrilateral::perimeter()
          << endl;

  cout << "\nPerimeter of Quadrilateral is "
          << Q.perimeter() << endl;
```

```
cout << "Perimeter of first Square as a Quadrilateral is "
    << S1.Quadrilateral::perimeter() << endl;

}
```

The output of the program of Example 3.4 is

```
Area of first rectangle is 12
Perimeter is 14
Area of second rectangle is 25
Perimeter is 20

Area of first square is 16
Perimeter is 16
Area of second square is 0
Perimeter is 16

Perimeter of Quadrilateral is 10
Perimeter of first Square as a Quadrilateral is 0
```

The important thing to note about Example 3.4 is that multiple inheritance is possible in C++, but care must be taken to be certain that there are no ambiguities when resolving possible conflicts in the selection of member functions from a base class.

3.2 Constructors, Destructors, and Other Functions

Since C++ is essentially a superset of C, one viewpoint of functions is that they can be used in precisely the same way in C++ that they are used in C. This viewpoint is of little interest to the designer wishing to build an object-oriented system and hence we will not pursue it further. Instead, we will consider primarily functions attached to objects.

The simplest way to attach a function to an object is to include the function in the description of the object. The functions can be attached to the class in the public, protected, or private parts. An example of this is shown in Example 3.5. Note that the header file **math.h** must be included in order to use the standard function **sqrt()** from the mathematics library. Successful linking of the math library may require special treatment on different C++ environments. See your system manual for more information on how to link libraries.

Example 3.5 Functions associated with the private, protected, and public parts of a class.

```
#include <iostream.h>
#include <math.h>

class Rectangle
{
private:
  double length;
  double width ;
  double long_side() { return ((length > width) ? length
                      : width) ;}
protected:
  double diagonal() {return sqrt( length * length +
                                  width  * width);}
public:
  Rectangle(double L = 0.0, double W = 0.0);
  double area() { return (length * width) ; }
  double perimeter() {return (2.0 * (length + width)) ; }
};


// Member function of class Rectangle.
Rectangle :: Rectangle(double L, double W)
{
  length = L;
  width = W;
}



main()
{
// details omitted
}
```

Note also that in Example 3.5, we have used the conditional operator **?:** in the function **long_side()**. This was done to illustrate that even some of the more unusual features of C are incorporated in C++.

Functions defined this way are called *member functions*. They can be written as part of the code describing a class.

The most common instance of a member function is known as a constructor function, or constructor for short. The purpose of a constructor is to create and initialize an instance of an object in the class. The initialization can use default values or assign no values whatsoever. Some constructor functions were **String()** for the **String** class of Example 2.2 and **Rectangle()**, **Square()**, and **Quadrilateral()** for the geometric examples given earlier in this chapter.

Most of the semantics of constructors are straightforward. However, there are some unusual features that require special attention:

- A constructor function for a class must have the same name as the name of the class.
- A constructor function cannot have any return value, not even **void**.
- The name of a constructor function (which is also the name of the class) may be overloaded and default values will be assigned. If no arguments are given to a constructor, then the constructor is called a *default constructor*. (Default constructors are especially important when the class is used with a template class. We will study templates in Chapter 5.)
- If no constructor function is present for a class, then the C++ compiler will generate a default constructor for the object. The default constructor created by the compiler will be public. Initialization of any object created by the default constructor cannot be assumed.
- There is a special constructor called a *copy constructor* that can be used to initialize an object to the value of another object of the same type. We will study copy constructors when we study pointers in Chapter 4.
- A derived class cannot inherit a constructor from a base class. However, objects in a derived class can call a constructor from the base class. This is essentially the only limit to inheritance by the base class.
- If a class is derived from more than one base class (multiple inheritance), then the calling of a constructor from different base classes is done in a precise order by the C++ compilation system. The base classes are initialized in the order in which they were declared, after which any member functions are initialized in the order in which they are declared.

Typical constructors are

```
Complex(0,0);
Stack();
List();
Rectangle(4.0, 5.0);
Rectangle();
```

A constructor function can have an *initializer* associated with it. An initializer will set specified data values belonging to the object before control passes to the body of the constructor. This essentially avoids some situations where arguments might lead to an unwanted error.

An initializer generally has the form

```
class_name(argument_list) : (list_of_initial_values)
{
    // body of constructor
}
```

I tend not to use initializers because I learned to program in Pascal and Ada before I learned C (and C++). The colon on the first line suggests a function's return value to me, which can cause confusion because of my training. Initializers are not needed very often.

It is also possible to remove objects gracefully from a system. The simplest and most common mechanism for doing this is to use a member function called a destructor function, or destructor for short. The standard notation for a destructor for a class is the name of the class preceded by a tilde symbol (~).

Destructors are easier to use than constructors. The important points to keep in mind about destructors are listed below:

- A destructor function for a class must have the same name as the name of the class preceded by a ~.
- A destructor function cannot have any return value, not even **void**.
- A destructor takes no arguments.
- If no destructor function is present for a class, then the C++ compiler will generate a default destructor for the object.
- A destructor is called implicitly for each local variable within a function when the function or local block of code is exited. However, when a pointer is a local variable, no destructor is implicitly called when the function or local block of code is exited. (We will study pointers in Chapter 4.)

Some typical destructors are

```
~Complex();
~Stack();
~List();
~Rectangle();
```

We now consider other types of member functions. There is no reason to assume that any member function can be written in a few lines. The more complicated member functions can still be written as part of the description of a class. Clearly, including member functions with many lines of code within the description of a class can make the organizational structure for the class difficult to determine.

The solution is to include a brief declaration of the "signature" of the function within the class description, with the body of the function to be described elsewhere. (The *sig-*

nature of a function is its return type and its argument list, including the number and types of arguments.) The function is then linked to the appropriate class, since the name of the function is known to the class. This use of a signature is essentially the same as the use of a function prototype in C except that we generalize the function prototype in C++ by allowing all arguments and return types to be either classes or data types.

For example, a function named **pop()** might be declared as part of the set of allowable transformations on a object described by a class named **Stack** in either of the following two ways:

```
// One method of providing a class description.

// Class description using member functions
// with the code inside the class explicitly.

class Stack
{
private;
  some_type item;
  int top;
public:
  Stack(); // constructor
  ~Stack(); // destructor
  void push(item_type item)
    {// Code for push() could be here}
  some_type pop();
    {// Code for pop() could be here}
};
```

```
// Another method of providing a class description.

// Class description using member functions
// with the code outside the class proper.

class Stack
{
private;
  some_type item;
  int top;
public:
  Stack(); // constructor
  ~Stack(); // destructor
  void push(item_type item);
  some_type pop();
};
```

```
Stack::void push(item_type item)
{
  // Code for push() would go here.
}


Stack::some_type pop();
{
  // Code for pop() would go here.
}
```

The two colons '**::**' are used in the second method as a way of linking the member function to the object. Here the term **"some_type"** is pseudocode for the type of items that are placed in the stack.

The natural place to put the implementation details of the function **pop()** is somewhere physically near the description of the class **Stack**.

In C, there would be no question about the function **pop()** being used to operate on a stack. There can be one such function in any C program; having more than one function with the name **pop()** in a C program would result in the error

```
pop: multiply defined
```

when the object files are linked.

Suppose that we had two objects in our C++ program: queues and lists. It is likely that each of these two classes would have associated member functions **insert()** and **remove()**. This situation is called *polymorphism.*

Polymorphism occurs when a function can be called with different numbers and types of arguments. In other words, polymorphic functions can be called with multiple signatures. This situation presents a challenge for a compiler. How can we resolve the conflicts that can occur if there are multiple function signatures for the same function?

C++ solves this problem by having a new operator called the *scope resolution operator,* which is denoted by the symbol **::** (two colons together). Then our **Stack** class would have its member function **pop()** declared as

```
Stack :: pop()
{
  // code for pop() goes here
}
```

and the member functions **insert()** and **remove()** associated with the classes **Queue** and **List** would be something like

```
Queue :: insert()
{
  // code for queue insert() goes here
}
```

and

```
Queue :: remove()
{
  // code for queue remove() goes here
}
```

for the queue operations, and

```
List :: insert()
{
  // code for list insert() goes here
}
```

and

```
List :: remove()
{
  // code for list remove() goes here
}
```

for the list operations.

The scope resolution operator **::** provides a partial solution to the problem of proper selection of a function from a set of multiple functions with the same names. (We will see a complete solution when we study virtual functions in Section 3.6).

Note that there are several possible ways of determining which of several different functions can be applied to an object if there is no inheritance:

- Matching the object to the class itself, as in a call such as in the two statements **List.insert()** or **Stack.pop()**, is unambiguous.
- The signature of the function provides information if there is polymorphism. Thus the three different constructor calls **Complex(5)**, **Complex(5,2)**, and **Complex(1.0, 2.0)** refer to creating objects of the class **Complex** with a single argument of type **int**, two arguments of type **int**, or two arguments of type **float**, respectively. The default values are handled correctly. Recall that the signature of a function is the name of the function together with its number, type, and position of arguments, and the function's return type.
- The scope resolution operator indicates clearly which functions are associated with each class when using statements such as

```
void List.insert();
```

  or

```
void Stack::push(Item data);
```

All these methods of resolving name conflicts are performed at compile time, since the information is available then. This early resolution is often called early binding or static binding.

Multiple inheritance can cause problems in determining which inherited function we are considering. We discussed this potential ambiguity previously. The solution is the same as the one presented there—use the scope resolution operator **::** to make clear which inherited member function is being used. This is the proper way to treat multiple inheritance.

3.3 Passing Parameters to Functions in C and C++

There is a subtle difference between the methods of passing parameters to functions in the C and C++ programming languages. (The term *argument* is used interchangeably with *parameter*.)

There is one basic method of passing arguments to functions in C: passing parameters by value. In this method, a copy of the argument is made by the run-time system and this copy is given to the function. After exiting the function, the copy is destroyed and so the value of the argument is unchanged by the function.

Using the address operator **&** and passing a pointer allows the contents of the address to be changed (although the copy of the address is still made and destroyed after exiting the function). This is called passing parameters by reference. However, it is not implemented as efficiently in C as in several other languages.

C++ allows each of the mechanisms of passing parameters by value and by reference that are available in C. However, it also allows a new mechanism for passing parameters by reference that is more efficient than the mechanism provided in the C language.

This method of providing information to functions is called passing parameters by constant reference. It requires using the address operator **&** together with the reserved word **const** as in

```
f(const & x);
```

which allows fast access to the data stored in the argument **x** and ensures that the contents of **x** are not changed.

We will use all these methods in this book.

3.4   The `inline` Qualifier for Functions

There is a way to improve the efficiency of some C++ programs by avoiding the overhead of function calls. If we declare a function with the qualifier **inline** before its definition, then it is expanded at each succeeding point in the code where it is used, thereby removing a function call and return each time. This is similar to the use of macros to speed up program execution time.

We now illustrate the use of the **inline** directive to speed up program performance. We will use an extremely simple function that does nothing other than increment its argument. The illustration consists of four examples. In Example 3.6, we show a main program with a single loop. In Example 3.7, we show the same program using a function call. These two programs are written in C. In Examples 3.8 and 3.9, we show programs with the same functionality, using two artificially written classes, with and without the use of **inline**. The expectation is that the program of Example 3.6 will execute fastest, with the program of Example 3.9 running much faster than the program of Example 3.8.

Example 3.6   Simple C program.

```
/* Simple C program with one main loop. */

main()
{
   int i;

   for (i = 0; i < 10000; i++)
      ;
}
```

Example 3.7   Simple C program with a function call.

```
/* Simple C program with loop and one function call. */

int increment(int i)
{
   return i++;
}
```

```
main()
{
  int i;

  for(i = 0; i < 10000; i++)
     increment(i);
}
```

Example 3.8 Simple C++ program with a function call that is not **inline**.

```
// Simple C++ program with one main loop and
// one function call.  Function is not inline.

class Toy
{
public:
  int i;
  int increment(void) { return i++;}
};

main()
{
  int i;
  Toy T;

  for(i = 0; i < 10000; i++)
     T.increment();
}
```

Example 3.9 Simple C++ program with a call to an **inline** function.

```
// Simple C++ program with one main loop and
// one function call.  Function is declared inline.

class Toy
{
  int i;
  inline int increment(void) { return i++;}
};

main()
{
  int i;

  for(i = 0; i < 10000; i++)
     increment();
}
```

On a very slow computer, the program of Example 3.8 took about 20% longer to execute than did the program of Example 3.9. We did not set any of the compiler options in order to optimize performance. The timing difference indicates some of the potential benefits of using the qualifier **inline** in C++ programs. The improvements in execution time will depend upon the compiler's run-time system, compiler options set, the computer used, and the nature of the function whose code is expanded **inline**.

You should be aware of some potential problems with the **inline** qualifier. The most obvious problem is that the amount of code specified in a function to be placed **inline** may be too large for proper insertion and in fact may hurt performance because the program's executable code overlaps memory segment boundaries.

Less obvious is the fact that any function calls within a function that is declared **inline** may cause problems because of library access. This type of code is often flagged with a warning by compilers on high-performance computers.

The final problem with the **inline** qualifier is the same one that C compilers have with variables whose storage qualifier is **register**. The use of this qualifier is based on an assessment by the programmer that he or she wishes to have a particular variable accessed frequently. It is extremely difficult for a programmer to specify precisely which register is to be used. It also causes some problems for advanced compilers that attempt to perform a global optimization of the code generated by the compiler.

It is probably best to restrict the use of the **inline** qualifier to those situations in which performance is critical and the use of a profiler has determined that a substantial amount of time is being spent in the overhead of calls to and returns from a particular function which itself makes no function calls and has only a few lines of code. We will use the **inline** qualifier sparingly in this book.

3.5   Member and Friend Functions

One potential implementation of multiple inheritance can cause problems in program efficiency, especially in memory usage. To understand the problem, consider what happens if a class inherits some member functions from two different base classes. It is clearly wasteful to have the same code of the same member function belong to two different classes.

These issues of program efficiency also occur if we wish to use code that logically belongs to two different classes, but the two classes are not related by any form of inheritance.

One way that we can reuse code without any problems in ownership and without redundancy is to use *friend functions*. The purpose of a friend function is to allow access to a class by either a different class or a function defined outside the original class. Note that there is no requirement that the two classes be related as a base class and a derived class. (Having access to the contents of a class by a friend function does not mean that the friend function is required to use the access.)

A friend function can have access to the private and protected members of a class. However, a friend function is not considered a member function of a class.

In Example 3.10 we present an example of the use of friend functions. The code of this example is a modification of the code of Example 3.4. In that example, we used multiple inheritance to select an appropriate **perimeter()** function to determine the perimeter of a member of the class **Rectangle**, **Square**, or **Quadrilateral**.

We now wish to share the function **perimeter()** between the classes **Rectangle** and **Square**. This function will be declared as a friend in the class **Rectangle** using the C++ reserved word **friend**. It then will be made available to the other class because it is not a member function of the class **Rectangle**.

Example 3.10

```
#include <iostream.h>

class Rectangle
{
protected:
  double length;
  double width ;
  friend double perimeter(Rectangle R)
          {return (double) (2.0 * (R.length + R.width)); }
public:
  Rectangle(double L = 0.0, double W = 0.0);
  double area() {return (double) (length * width) ; }
};


// Member function of class Rectangle.
Rectangle :: Rectangle(double L, double W)
{
  length = L;
  width = W;
}


// Description of the class Quadrilateral
class Quadrilateral
{
```

```
protected:
  double side1, side2, side3, side4;
public:
  Quadrilateral(double s1 = 0.0, double s2 = 0.0,
                   double s3 = 0.0, double s4 = 0.0);
  double perimeter()
          {return (double) (side1 + side2
          + side3 + side4);}
};


// Constructor for the new class Quadrilateral
Quadrilateral :: Quadrilateral(double s1, double s2,
               double s3, double s4)
{
  side1 = s1;
  side2 = s2;
  side3 = s3;
  side4 = s4;
}



// Description of the class Square.
class Square : public Rectangle, public Quadrilateral
{
  double side;
public:
  Square(double s): Rectangle(s,s) {length= s; width = s;};

  // Ignore all but first argument in constructing Square.
  Square(double s, double t) : Rectangle(s,s)
                {length = s; width = s;};

  // Ignore all but first argument in constructing Square.
  Square (double s, double t, double u, double v):
          Quadrilateral(s, s, s, s) { side = s;};

};



// Main program.
main()
{
  Rectangle R1(3,4);
  Rectangle R2(5,5);
  Square S1(4.0, 4.0);
  Quadrilateral Q(1,2,3,4);
```

```
    cout << "Area of first rectangle: " << R1.area() << endl;
    cout << "Perimeter is " << perimeter(R1) << endl;

    cout << "Area of second rectangle:" << R2.area() << endl ;
    cout << "Perimeter is " << perimeter(R2) << endl;

    cout << "\nArea of square is " << S1.area() << endl ;
    cout << "Perimeter is " << perimeter(S1) << endl;

    cout << "\nPerimeter of Quadrilateral is "
            << Q.perimeter() << endl;
}
```

There were several different uses of a function named **perimeter()** in the program of Example 3.10. For the objects **R1** and **R2** of the class **Rectangle**, the calls were

```
    perimeter(R1);
```

and

```
    perimeter(R2);
```

while for the object S1 belonging to the class **Square**, the call was **perimeter(S1)**;. Note that the notation used in describing these calls did not use any connection to objects, since a function declared as being a **friend** within a class description is not a member function of the class.

The syntax of the last call to **perimeter()** is different. This call was for an object of the class **Quadrilateral**. A member function named **perimeter()** is defined for this class, and we can call this member function in the usual way, using the dot notation

```
    Q.perimeter();
```

A friend function can use the private and protected areas of a class. This is useful if a function needs to have access to the private areas of two or more distinct classes. This situation occurs more often than you might think.

There is one danger with the use of friend functions. Their use can reduce the modularity of programs. A fundamental reason for object-oriented programming languages is to reduce the interfaces between program subunits and increase program modularity. To some extent, the use of friend functions decreases modularity, because it makes private or protected data visible.

A strong recommendation is that you use any private or protected data in friend functions only as an rvalue and not as an lvalue. That is, private or protected data should appear only on the right-hand side of an assignment statement. If you follow this suggestion, your programs will not allow any modification of the values of private or protected data, although this data can be used in computations and copies can be made. This will reduce the danger of using friend functions.

We will use friend functions several times in the remainder of this book. However, you should be aware of a potential problem with their use. Allowing access to the private or protected members of a class is somewhat inconsistent with the information hiding and abstraction that are at the heart of the object-oriented program design paradigm. Their use is slightly controversial in C++. Indeed, the concept of a friend function is not part of many object-oriented programming languages. Clearly, friend functions should be used sparingly. Just be careful when combining friend functions and object-oriented programs.

3.6   The C++ Preprocessor

Since C++ is essentially a superset of C, the C preprocessor can be used for C++ programs. Thus the directives **#include** and **#define** are available in C++ and have the same meaning that they have in C.

In addition, conditional compilation using constructions such as

```
#ifdef POSIX
... code goes here
#endif
```

and

```
#ifndef SUN
... code goes here
#endif
```

are available in both C and C++.

The ANSI version of C made it appropriate to use the constant qualifier, as in

```
const int MAX = 10;
```

instead of the simple preprocessor statement,

```
#define MAX 10
```

This can be helpful in many circumstances.

The same rationale holds for the use of the C++ preprocessor with programs that use the object-oriented features of C++.

The C++ preprocessor also allows macro expansion so that we may define such computations as the absolute value of a number x using something like

```
#define abs(x) ((x) >= 0) ? (x) : (-x)
```

The lack of type checking in the C (or C++) preprocessor makes the use of macros inappropriate in most situations. (Recall from Section 3.3 that declaring functions as the keyword **inline** can reduce the overhead of a function call.)

Warning: macro expansion in the C++ processor does not always behave in a consistent manner. Example 3.11 illustrates some of the problems that can occur with certain compiler implementations. Be aware that the problem indicated here is not intended as a criticism of a particular compiler, but is a warning that a large amount of software has errors and one should not blindly assume that all compilers and other commonly used applications or software are error free.

The code in Example 3.11 was communicated to me by Eric Charles, while he was a graduate student at Howard University. It was based on an exercise given by Professor Bernard Woolfolk. It uses some constructions that we have not discussed yet, especially those in the user-defined file **string.c**. This file in turn contains a header file named **string.h**. The two include files contain the basic definitions for the class **String** and its member functions. We have also included friend functions and free functions for the String class. (The term *free function* refers to functions that are not member functions nor friend functions of any class.)

The code for the two include files is given in Examples 3.12 and 3.13, respectively. They are included in the text proper at this point to aid in completeness of our discussion. Source codes for both of these files are on the disk that is included with this book. Ignore the details of these two files at this time. We will discuss the development of string classes in detail in several places later in this book and thus the code may be skipped over at this time. However, you should note the wide range of operations on strings that are illustrated in Example 3.11.

Example 3.11 An example of the macro substitution feature of the C++ preprocessor.

```
//////////////////////////////////////////////////////////////////
Role: serves as main driver for program.
//////////////////////////////////////////////////////////////////

#include <iostream.h>  // I/O
#include <string.h>    // string manipulation
#include <memory.h>    // for memcpy use.
#include "string.c"    // file containing function definitions

// print macro
#define PRINT(X) cout < "( X ) = \"" < (X) < '"' < endl;
```

```
void main ()
{
  String a = "abc";
  String b = "def";
  String c = a + b;
  String d = "";
  PRINT(a)
  PRINT(b)
  PRINT(c)
  PRINT(d)
  PRINT(a + b)
  PRINT(a == b)
  PRINT(a > b)
  PRINT(a <= b)
  PRINT(a = b)
  PRINT(a += c)
  PRINT(d+d)


  char *foo = "foo";
  char *bar = "bar";
  char *null = "";
  char *big = "Now is the time for all good men...";
  PRINT (foo)
  PRINT (bar)
  PRINT (null)
  PRINT (big)
  PRINT(a == foo)
  PRINT(foo == a)
  PRINT(a = foo)
  PRINT(a == foo)
  PRINT(foo == a)
  PRINT(a += bar)
  PRINT(foo >= a)
  PRINT(foo == a)
  PRINT(foo <= a)
  PRINT(a > foo)
  PRINT(foo + a)
  PRINT(b + bar)
  PRINT(c = null)
  PRINT(c)
  PRINT(c = big)
  PRINT(c)
  PRINT(c = null)
  PRINT(c)
  PRINT(c + null)
  PRINT(c)
  PRINT(c += null)
```

```
    PRINT(c)
    PRINT(c += foo)
    PRINT(c)
    PRINT(c += bar)
    PRINT(c)
    PRINT((const char *) d)
}
```

On a Sun SPARC 2 running AT&T C++ version 3.0, the program of Example 3.11 worked correctly, providing the following output. Note that both occurrences of the expression **X** are expanded correctly.

Output from Example 3.11 under AT&T C++ version 3.0

```
( abc ) = "abc"
( def ) = "def"
( abcdef ) = "abcdef"
(  ) = ""
( abc ) = "abcdef"
( 0 ) = "0"
( 0 ) = "0"
( 1 ) = "1"
( def ) = "def"
( defabcdef ) = "defabcdef"
(  ) = ""
( foo ) = "foo"
( bar ) = "bar"
(  ) = ""
( Now is the time for all good men... ) = "Now is the time
for all good men..."
( 0 ) = "0"
( 0 ) = "0"
( foo ) = "foo"
( 1 ) = "1"
( 1 ) = "1"
( foobar ) = "foobar"
( 0 ) = "0"
( 0 ) = "0"
( 1 ) = "1"
( 1 ) = "1"
( foofoobar ) = "foofoobar"
( defbar ) = "defbar"
(  ) = ""
(  ) = ""
( Now is the time for all good men... ) = "Now is the time
for all good men..."
```

```
( Now is the time for all good men... ) = "Now is the time
for all good men..."
(  ) = ""
(  ) = ""
(  ) = ""
(  ) = ""
(  ) = ""
(  ) = ""
( foo ) = "foo"
( foo ) = "foo"
( foobar ) = "foobar"
( foobar ) = "foobar"
(  ) = ""
```

However, on a personal computer running Borland C++ version 4.0, the following incorrect output was obtained. Notice that the expression **X** at the beginning of each line of output is not expanded properly, although the expansion of the second occurrence of **X** at the end of the line is correct. Similar errors occurred in the gnu C++ compiler on an HP workstation.

Output from Example 3.11 under Borland C++ version 4.0

```
( X ) = "abc"
( X ) = "def"
( X ) = "abcdef"
( X ) = ""
( X ) = "abcdef"
( X ) = "0"
( X ) = "0"
( X ) = "1"
( X ) = "def"
( X ) = "defabcdef"
( X ) = ""
( X ) = "foo"
( X ) = "bar"
( X ) = ""
( X ) = "Now is the time for all good men..."
( X ) = "0"
( X ) = "0"
( X ) = "foo"
( X ) = "1"
( X ) = "1"
( X ) = "foobar"
( X ) = "0"
( X ) = "0"
( X ) = "1"
( X ) = "1"
```

```
( X ) = "foofoobar"
( X ) = "defbar"
( X ) = ""
( X ) = ""
( X ) = "Now is the time for all good men..."
( X ) = "Now is the time for all good men..."
( X ) = ""
( X ) = ""
( X ) = ""
( X ) = ""
( X ) = ""
( X ) = ""
( X ) = "foo"
( X ) = "foo"
( X ) = "foobar"
( X ) = "foobar"
( X ) = ""
```

Unfortunately, the occurrence of errors in C++ compilers is not unusual. Every C++ compiler that I have used has at least one error. This is probably due to the newness of the language and the current lack of standardization. The best strategy for a C++ programmer at this point is to use only the most standard features of the language.

Example 3.12 The user-defined file **String.c.**

```
///////////////////////////////////////////////////////////////////
File Name: string.c
Contains member and nonmember function definitions.
///////////////////////////////////////////////////////////////////

#include "string.h"

static char *init (const char *str)
{
  int size;
  char *string = new char[size = strlen(str) + 1];

  memcpy(string, str, size);
  return string;
}


// constructor
String::String()
{
  d_string_p = init("");
}
```

```cpp
// constructor
String::String(const String& string)
{
  d_string_p = init(string.d_string_p);
}


// constructor
String::String(const char* str)
{
  d_string_p = init(str);
}

// constructor
String::~String()
{
  delete d_string_p;
}


String & String::operator = (const String& string)
{
  return *this = string.d_string_p;
}


String & String::operator = (const char* str)
{
  int len = strlen(str);          // get length of str
  char *s = new char[len + 1];    // alloc mem for s

  strcpy(s, str);                 // copy str to s
  delete [] d_string_p;           // dealloc mem of old string
  d_string_p = s;                 // reinitialize pointer
  return *this;                   // return
}


String &String::operator += (const String& string)
{
  return *this += string.d_string_p;
}


String &String::operator += (const char* str)
{
  int len = length();    // get length of str1
```

```
    len += strlen(str);              // add length of str2
    char *s = new char[len + 1];     // alloc memory

    strcpy(s, d_string_p);           // copy str1 to new str
    strcat(s, str);                  // concatenate strings
    delete [] d_string_p;            // dealloc mem of str1
    d_string_p = s;                  // reinitialize pointer
    return *this;                    // return
}


// returns length of string
int String::length() const
{
  return strlen(d_string_p);
}


String String::operator + (const String& string) const
{
  String str = *this;       // create new object

   str += string;           // concatenate strings
   return str;              // return new object
}


String String::operator + (const char* str) const
{
  String Str = *this;    // create new object
  Str += str;            // concatenate strings
  return Str;            // return new object
}



// The following functions use the standard string.h
// library function, strcmp(), to overload operators.
// strcmp() returns 0 if the strings are equal, < 0 if
// str1 is lexicographically less than str2, and > 0 if
// str1 is greater than str2.  The actual return values
// are being tested in these functions.

int String::operator == (const String& string) const
{
  return ( strcmp(d_string_p, string.d_string_p) == 0 );
}
```

```
int String::operator == (const char* str) const
{
  return ( strcmp(d_string_p, str) == 0 );
}


int String::operator!=(const String& string) const
{
  return ( strcmp(d_string_p, string.d_string_p) != 0 );
}


int String::operator != (const char* str) const
{
  return ( strcmp(d_string_p, str) != 0 );
}


int String::operator < (const String& string) const
{
  return ( strcmp(d_string_p, string.d_string_p) < 0 );
}


int String::operator < (const char* str) const
{
  return ( strcmp(d_string_p, str) < 0 );
}


int String::operator <= (const String& string) const
{
  return ( strcmp(d_string_p, string.d_string_p) <= 0 );
}


int String::operator <= (const char* str) const
{
  return ( strcmp(d_string_p, str) <= 0 );
}


int String::operator > (const String& string) const
{
  return ( strcmp (d_string_p, string.d_string_p) >  0 );
}


int String::operator > (const char* str) const
{
```

```
    return ( strcmp (d_string_p, str) >  0 );
}


int String::operator >= (const String& string) const
{
  return ( strcmp(d_string_p, string.d_string_p) >= 0 );
}


int String::operator >= (const char* str) const
{
  return ( strcmp(d_string_p, str) >= 0 );
}


// Next functions also use the overloaded operators that
// were defined above to operate on operands of different
// types.
String operator + (const char* str, const String& string)
{
  String newstr = str;        // create new object
  newstr += string;           // concatenate strings
  return newstr;              // return object
}


// pass str as parameter to overloaded operator function
int operator == (const char* str, const String& string)
{
  return ( string.operator == (str) );
}


// pass str as parameter to overloaded operator function
int operator != (const char* str, const String& string)
{
  return ( string.operator != (str) );
}


// pass str as parameter to overloaded operator function
int operator < (const char* str, const String& string)
{
```

```
    return ( string.operator > (str) );
}


// pass str as parameter to overloaded operator function
int operator <= (const char* str, const String& string)
{
    return ( string.operator >= (str) );
}



// pass str as parameter to overloaded operator function
int operator > (const char* str, const String& string)
{
    return ( string.operator < (str) );
}


// pass str as parameter to overloaded operator function
int operator >= (const char* str, const String& string)
{
    return ( string.operator <= (str) );
}


// overloaded I/O operator
ostream &operator < (ostream& s, String &str)
{
    // << is friend of String class
    s << str.d_string_p;    // get output string from str
    return s;               // return output
}
```

The header file **String.h** includes the basic definitions needed for the class used in Examples 3.11 and 3.12.

Example 3.13 The user-defined include file **String.h**.

```
//////////////////////////////////////////////////////////////////////
File Name: string.h:
Contains the class definition of String, as well as
non-member overloaded operator functions.
//////////////////////////////////////////////////////////////////////

class String
{
public:
    // Constructors
```

```
    String();
    String(const String& string);
    String(const char *str);

    // Destructor
    ~String();

    // Assignment
    String &operator = (const String& string);
    String &operator = (const char* str);

    // Manipulators
    String &operator += (const String& string);
    String &operator += (const char* str);
    // Concatenation (to this string)

    // Accessors
    int length() const;
    String operator + (const String& str) const;
    String operator + (const char* string) const;
    // Concatenation (to a new string)

    // Comparison Operators (lexical)
    int operator == (const String& string) const;
    int operator == (const char* str) const;
    int operator != (const String& string) const;
    int operator != (const char* str) const;
    int operator < (const String& string) const;
    int operator < (const char* str) const;
    int operator <= (const String& string) const;
    int operator <= (const char* str) const;
    int operator > (const String& string) const;
    int operator > (const char* str) const;
    int operator >= (const String& string) const;
    int operator >= (const char* str) const;


  // overloaded conversion operator converts String to char*
  operator char*()  // converts to standard type
  {
    return d_string_p;
  }

  // friend — for overloaded I/O operator of ostream class
  friend ostream& operator < (ostream& s, String &str);
private:
  char *d_string_p;  // pointer to string of characters
};
```

```
// Non-Member (Free) Operators
String operator + (const char* str, const String& string);
int operator == (const char* str, const String& string);
int operator != (const char* str, const String& string);
int operator > (const char* str, const String& string);
int operator >= (const char* str, const String& string);
int operator < (const char* str, const String& string);
int operator <= (const char* str, const String& string);
```

The C++ preprocessor; has a new operator denoted by the symbol **##**. It is most commonly used with the **#** operator in a "**#define**" statement. The **##** operator is used within an **#define** statement of the following form:

> `#define function(arg) <tokens> ## <tokens>`

The meaning of the **##** operator is that if either of the tokens adjacent to the **##** is replaced with a call to the function in the **#define** statement, then the two sets of tokens are concatenated, with the **##** and its surrounding white space removed.

Thus the **#define** statement

> `#define concatenate(a) public baseclass ## a;`

when used with the call

> `concatenate name`

provides the following output:

> `public baseclass name`

The **##** operator is not used frequently, although it is discussed briefly in the *C++ Annotated Reference Manual.* A check of six C++ books and some publicly available C++ source code showed no usage of this operator. Use the **##** operator at your own risk. (This admonition is especially valid in view of the C++ preprocessor macro expansion error described earlier in this section.)

3.7 Library Functions and Class Libraries

Much of the power of object-oriented programming in C++ lies in the class libraries available with the system. By the term *class library* we mean the collection of classes and methods previously encoded. (Recall that the terms *method* and *member function* are synonymous in C++.)

Most C++ development systems provide both source code and object code for the associated classes and members. The object code is often organized to match the source code and object code for the associated classes and members. The object code often matches the source code directly, so that objects and methods in a file named **class1.c** (or **class 1.cpp**) will have the associated object code in a file named **class1.o** (or **class1.obj**). On computers running either a variant of MS-DOS systems or Microsoft Windows, object files end with the **.obj** extension and executable files end with the **.exe** extension. On UNIX systems, the **.o** extension generally indicates an object file and the default name for an executable file is **a.out**. (There are other ways to determine the type of a file on UNIX systems. See the author's *Advanced Topics in UNIX* or any other reference that describes formats of object and executable files and the meaning of the term *magic number* in UNIX.)

You should be careful about moving C++ programs from UNIX to PCs or vice versa. The most common PC C++ compilers use the extension **.cpp** to indicate a C++ source code file. In UNIX, a **.cpp** extension indicates a file created by the preprocessor, which is also known as **cpp**.

Another common organization, especially for UNIX systems, is to use a "random archive library," which includes object code for each predefined class and method in a compressed format. The appropriate code is automatically included by the linker when an appropriate linking command is used. The updating of a class means recompilation of the object code and reorganization of the random archive library. The linking involves only the most recent form of a function in a random archive library and is called *dynamic linking*.

In any event, some sort of class library will be included with any C++ development system. It is very likely that you will want to create your own libraries. This brings up some organizational and testing issues. We will consider organizational issues in this section and the testing issues will be discussed in Section 3.7. For a discussion of the organizational issues for C programs, see the author's *Using C in Software Design*.

The most common organization of user-defined class libraries is by the organization of the data. The organization should also take into account the likelihood that code in your class library can be reused in more than one software project. We will discuss organization of larger C++ systems in Chapter 7.

3.8 Testing Issues

The availability of inheritance causes new testing problems for C++ programs. One issue is what needs to be tested in a derived class (assuming that the base class was sufficiently tested). Clearly, testing a derived class requires complete knowledge of the base class from which it was derived.

We will assume that the logic of the member functions has been tested (at least by hand) and that the major concerns are the interfaces between objects.

In order to test a derived class, we should first test all possible member functions not derived from the base class to make sure that there is no interface problem. This is the easiest situation to test, since there is no possible ambiguity between member functions of the same name.

After we have tested the new member functions of the derived class, it is time to test the member functions that have been inherited. These should be tested by making sure that the correct information (base class or derived class) is being used.

Additional problems arise when testing multiple inheritance. Certainly, every test that was applied with single inheritance should also be applied here. In addition, each case of possible ambiguity should be tested carefully.

Recall that friend functions are not members of a class, although they have access to the private and protected member of the class in which they are declared. The use of friend functions can cause a breakdown in the modularity of an object-oriented program. Any testing of friend functions should include code reading to make sure that no private or protected data is used as an lvalue (on the left-hand side of an assignment statement). Other testing should make sure that the program using the object and the friend function avoids hiding one function by another.

Note that there is a potential "combinatorial explosion" in the number of possible test cases for classes with many member functions or many levels of inheritance. If the testing seems excessive, begin with reading the code and determining if good coding practices were used. Follow this by careful testing of those objects that you believe are the most complex (because of their internal structure, or their most likely use within C++ programs).

Summary

One of the major features of C++ is that new classes and methods can be defined using existing classes and methods. The existing class is called the base class and the new class is called the derived class. The derived class may have additional features using the existing data organization and methods of the base class and adding to them. Alternatively, the derived class can have some of the methods or organization of data changed in the derived class.

The methods applied to a class are called the member functions of that class. Member functions can have their source code included within the definition of the class. If the source code for the member function consists of many lines or the class is complicated, then the function can be given within the class with a function prototype and have its code given elsewhere using the scope resolution operator **::** as in

```
class name :: function()
{
   // Code goes here.
}
```

The signature of the function prototype and the function definition must agree.

A derived class can inherit from more than one base class. This is called multiple inheritance.

A function may be shared between two or more classes by declaring it as a friend function, using the **friend** keyword. A friend function is not a member function of a class, although it does have access to the protected and private members of the class.

Functions may be declared **inline** to reduce the overhead of a function call.

The C++ preprocessor performs all the functions of the preprocessor for C. It encourages use of constant values instead of using the **#define** statement.

EXERCISES

1. Design an experiment to determine the speedup, if any, produced by using the function given below:

   ```
   inline int f(int i) {return i++;}
   ```

2. Repeat Exercise 1 using the functions

   ```
   void f(int i) { cout < i;}
   ```

   and

   ```
   int g(int i) {int j; for(j=0; j<i; j*=i); return j; }
   ```

   Explain any warning messages from the compiler.

3. We did not use destructors in many of the examples in this chapter. Write destructors for each of the three classes **Rectangle**, **Square**, and **Quadrilateral**. Do this without using any inheritance.

4. Repeat Exercise 3, but use the inheritance described in Example 3.2.

5. Repeat Exercise 3, but use the multiple inheritance described in Example 3.3.

6. List all test cases that you believe are necessary to test the objects defined in Example 3.1.

7. List all test cases that you believe are necessary to test the objects defined in Example 3.2. Compare your answer to the set of test cases that you determined for Example 3.1. Which new test cases are due to the presence of inheritance?

8. List all test cases that you believe are necessary to test the objects defined in Example 3.4. Compare your answer to the set of test cases that you determined for Examples 3.1 and 3.2. What changes are caused by the presence of multiple inheritance?

9. Describe the differences between member functions, friend functions, and free functions. Which of these can be polymorphic?

10. List the member functions, friend functions, and free functions for the **String** class indicated in Examples 3.12 and 3.13.

Arrays and Pointers

I n this chapter, we describe some of the fundamental changes from C to C++ in the three areas of pointers, arrays, and pointer arithmetic. The changes are all designed to provide more type checking and to enable better run-time and compile-time control of array indices and memory allocation. For completeness, we briefly discuss some of these three areas in C and describe some well-known deficiencies of the C language implementations of these features. The effective use of pointers in C++ classes is emphasized.

4.1   Pointers, Arrays, and Pointer Arithmetic

C++, being essentially a superset of C, treats pointers and arrays as related objects. Thus the C statement

```
float *p;
```

declares p to be a pointer to an address that contains a floating point number. The C statement

```
float a[];
```

declares that **a** is an array of floating point numbers, with the address to be used as the starting address for the storage of elements, if any, of the array **a**. Nothing is stated about the amount of storage necessary for the array named **a**.

There is no conceptual difference between the two declarations given above. They each indicate a single address and a C compiler has no way of distinguishing between a pointer and an array declaration. Indeed, the meanings of the two notations

```
a[0];
```

and

```
*a;
```

are identical, as are the two declarations

```
a[n];
```

and

```
*(a+n);
```

for any integer **n**. This is the basis for the use of pointer arithmetic in C (and C++).

Thus it is impossible for either a human reader of source code, or a compiler attempting to translate the source code, to determine if the statement

```
char *a;
```

refers to the address of storage for a single character or if it refers to the address where the initial element of an array of characters (with the array possibly being terminated by a null byte ‘ **\0** ’) is stored.

The C function **malloc()** does not provide an easy way to check for memory errors. Consider the two C statements

```
char *str;
str = (char*) malloc (5*size of (char));
```

that allocate space for storage of five characters and return a pointer to this space.

A later C statement of:

```
str = "Hello"
```

causes great difficulties in programs because the string "Hello" requires *six* characters for storage, since there is a final ‘ **\0** ’ that terminates the string.

The difficulty here is a fundamental one. The C language treats pointers and arrays as identical concepts and cannot distinguish between the two notations

```
char *p;      /* a pointer to a single char*/
```

and

```
char *s;      /* a pointer to a string of char*/
```

Some very good C software development environments include the ability to find errors such as the one indicated here. However, most C compilers will provide little assistance in this situation.

The actual allocation of space in C is performed by a function called **malloc()** or by one of a related set of functions. We will describe the use of **malloc()** in detail and touch upon the others only briefly.

In C, **malloc()** returns a pointer to a set of bytes whose size is an integer specified in its argument. The type of the pointer in the ANSI version of C is *pointer to void,* although the convention in the earlier versions of C was *pointer to char.* The ANSI C return type was chosen to enable hiding of information about the nature of regions allocated by **malloc()**.

The typical use of **malloc()** in C involves the built-in **sizeof()** operator and a *cast* operation. This typical use is of the form

```
ptr = (p_type *) malloc(sizeof(p_type));
```

where **p_type** is the type of the memory object pointed to by **ptr**. In most C applications, **p_type** is a structured data type. Alternatively, the argument to the **sizeof()** operator can be a variable that has been declared previously so that the compiler can determine the number of bytes that must be allocated for storage of the variable.

Allocation of memory for an array of, say, 10 floats can be done by either

```
ptr = (float *) malloc(10 * sizeof(float));
```

or

```
ptr = (float *) malloc(10 * sizeof(f));
```

where **f** is a variable whose type is **float**.

This use of **malloc()** is somewhat complex and is a major source of errors for beginning C programmers. These errors are often caused by initialization of space or improper use of the cast operator.

Here is a set of typical errors in pointer allocation:

- Failure to initialize the space allocated by a call to **malloc()**.
- Improper matching of allocated space to desired space.
- Overwriting an allocated space.

An example of the first situation is shown by the code fragment

```
struct stack *ptr ;
int current_top;

ptr = (struct stack *)malloc(sizeof(struct stack));
current_top = ptr->top;
```

Here an attempt is made to access a field of the struct pointed to by **ptr**, even though the fields of the struct have not been initialized at this time.

An example of the second error situation occurs in code fragments something like the following:

```
char string[8];
*string  = "I like C";
```

The problem in this code fragment is that no space was allocated for the null byte **'\0'**. The visible part or the character string contains eight characters.

The third error situation occurs when an array index exceeds the allocated space. An example of this common situation can be found in Example 8.8 of the author's book *Using C in Software Design*. The source code used in this example and the resulting discussion are repeated here.

Example 4.1 A subtle error in pointer access.

```
/* code has a subtle error */
#include <stdio.h>
#define NUM_ELEMENTS 100

main(void)
{
  int i,  key;
  int arr[NUM_ELEMENTS];

  puts("Please enter the key to be searched for");
  scanf("%d",&key);


  /* The error is here. */
  for(i=0;i <= NUM_ELEMENTS;i++)
     arr[i] = 300 + i;
  i=0;
  while (i < NUM_ELEMENTS )
    {
    if (arr[i] == key)
          {
          printf("The key is in position %d.\n",i);
```

```
            break;
            }
          else
            i++;
      }
    if (i == NUM_ELEMENTS)
      printf("Key %d is not in the array.\n",key);
  }
```

The error is extremely difficult to spot, at least without the comment showing where it occurs. To make matters worse, the program worked correctly on one computer but on the other computer always gave the output

```
Key 400 is not in the array.
```

even if the value entered for **key** was 324, which is obviously present in the array.

What happened in this example is that the compiler generated very tightly written code to minimize the use of storage. The array **arr** was intended to be placed in **NUM_ELEMENTS** contiguous memory locations, each of which stored an integer variable. The integer variables **i** and **key** were to be stored immediately after the memory area where the array **arr** was stored. Notice that the **for-loop** will execute **NUM_ELEMENTS + 1** times since array indices begin at 0 in C. The body of the assignment portion of the loop will thus be executed **NUM_ELEMENTS + 1** times. The statement

```
    a[i] = 300 + i;
```

is equivalent to

```
    *(a + i) = 300 + i;
```

and this statement will be executed **NUM_ELEMENTS + 1** times. This will place the number **400 (= 300 + NUM_ELEMENTS)** in the next location after the area that was set aside for the array **arr**. Since the compiler used the next memory location for the storage of the variable **key**, the value of **key** read in was overwritten by the value of the extra array element. This explains the constant output of the statement that 400 was not in the array, at least on one computer.

The error in this situation is caused by the unexpected array element

```
    arr[100]
```

overwriting the value of the memory area assigned to the variable named **key**. (There are 100 array entries preceding it.) This error can be extremely difficult to find, because it does not always appear on all C compilers.

The success of a memory allocation in C++ is often checked in programs using statements such as

```
p = (struct *p_type) malloc(sizeof(struct p_type));
if (p == NULL)
   error();
```

Here the symbolic constant NULL represents the value 0 and indicates an error condition.

There are some commercial software tools that attempt to find potential errors in pointer usage in C and C++ programs. At the time that this book was written, the most prominent are MemCheck from StratosWare Corporation, Purify from Pure Software, Centerline from Centerline Systems, ObjectCenter, and TestCenter. A comparative review of the capabilities of some of these tools in detecting errors in pointer usage was given in the December 1993 issue of *Sun Expert* magazine. Because each tool has evolved since the writing of that article, we will not discuss their evaluation in this book.

The use of **malloc()** is marginally acceptable in C++ because C++ is essentially a superset of C. However, there is a better way to allocate space in C++.

C++ has an operator that simplifies the allocation of memory for complex objects. The operator is called **new** and it has the syntax

```
ptr = new p_type;
```

The new operator allocates necessary memory and returns a pointer to this memory, with the pointer accessing the correct type of object. This is much cleaner and more elegant than the two steps

1. Allocating the memory
2. Performing a type cast

that were necessary with **malloc()**. The simplified system for memory allocation is similar to that of languages like Pascal and Ada, although the parentheses used in Pascal are not used in C++. Note that we can let the compiler handle all the details of the size and organization of the object that is pointed to by **ptr**.

The formal syntax of the **new** operator is described in the formal grammar of C++ as an "allocation_expression." The syntax of C++ is described in the formal grammar given in Appendix 2 using yacc format. Two common forms of an allocation_expression are

```
allocation_expression  :  new new_type_name
```

and

```
allocation_expression  :  new  new_type_name  new_initializer
```

(Italics are used to indicate expressions that need further parsing and semantic analysis before they are recognized. The C++ keyword **new** is not italicized because it is a token that can be recognized by the compiler.)

Thus an allocation expression (which is the replacement for statements that use **malloc()** in C++) has the reserved word **new** followed by some type name that is to be used with the allocator **new**. An initializer is optional. If no initializer is present, then a default initializer is used.

An allocation expression must do three things:

1. Find storage space for the object being created by **new**.
2. Initialize the object created.
3. Return a pointer to the object.

Let us examine each of these actions in turn.

The use of **new** can also avoid some of the problems of using different storage allocator functions such as **calloc()** and **realloc()**, which can have slightly different semantics from **malloc()**. Recall that the function **calloc()** is used to initialize multiple spaces such as for arrays of data, all of which are of the same type.

Unfortunately, the memory allocated by a call to **new** is not guaranteed to be initialized. A call to **new** can include an initializer, in which case the object created has its memory initialized. Without an initializer, no assumption can be made about the memory allocated.

Examples of the use of an initializer with **new** are

```
char *ch_ptr = new char;
char *ch_ptr = new char('a');
Rectangle *rect_ptr = new Rectangle(0, 0);
Rectangle *rect_ptr = new Rectangle(3, 4);
```

Note the syntax that is used in these four statements. In the first statement, a pointer to a **char** is created. In the second statement, a pointer to a **char** is created and an initializer is used. In the last two statements, a pointer to an object of type **Rectangle** is created, and the contents of the object (that is, the contents of the memory allocated by the call to **new**) are initialized.

The formal syntax of an allocation expression that uses an initializer was given previously. More information on formal C++ syntax can be found in Appendix 2.

The type of the data that occupies the memory allocated to the object by the **new** operator can be an elementary data type or structured data type as allowed in C, or can be an object in a class in C++. Thus the new operator in C++ is more powerful than the **malloc()** function in C.

One important difference between the new operator in C++ and the **malloc()** function in C occurs in the treatment of arrays. The C++ statement

```
int *int_ptr = new int[10];
```

returns a pointer to an **int** (the first element of an array of 10 items of this type).

Compare this to the C language statement

```
int *int_ptr = (int *) malloc( 10 * sizeof(int));
```

This statement allocates space for an array containing 10 items of type int and returns a pointer to **void** (or a pointer to **char** in pre-ANSI C). A cast operation is needed to coerce the return type to be the type of the left-hand side of the assignment operator.

In each case, the pointer is to the first item of the array (the one with index 0).

There are several features of the **new** operator that should be emphasized:

- The **new** operator can be used with or without an initializer.
- If no initializer is given, then the data stored in the memory allocated by **new** may have arbitrary values.
- The **new** operator may be overloaded. A call to **new** without the scope resolution operator **::** uses the globally available standard **new**. (The overloaded **new** operator must have the same syntax as the standard **new** operator that it overloads, as is the case for every overloaded operator.)
- In C++, the convention is to use the value 0 to indicate that a pointer allocation failed, rather than the constant **NULL**, which is usually defined to be 0.

The complete formal syntax for an allocation expression is given below. Note the use of the familiar scope resolution operator **::**.

You should also note the use of the term placement in an allocation expression. It is used for positioning an object at a specific location, such as an absolute memory address (for use in programs that interact with an operating system) or a relative memory address (as in the middle of an array). It can even be used for an embedded system that interacts with the hardware directly, without any intervening operating system.

```
allocation_expression :
        new placement  new_type_name new_initializer
      | new placement ( type_name ) new_initializer
      | new placement new_type_name
      | new placement ( type_name )
      | new new_type_name new_initializer
      | new ( type_name ) new_initializer
      | new new_type_name
      | new ( type_name )
      | :: new placement  new_type_name new_initializer
      | :: new placement  ( type_name ) new_initializer
```

```
|   :: new placement   new_type_name
|   :: new placement   ( type_name )
|   :: new   new_type_name   new_initializer
|   :: new   ( type_name )   new_initializer
|   :: new   new_type_name
|   :: new   ( type_name )
;

placement   :
        ( expression_list )
        ;
```

There is another operator in C++ for handling dynamic memory allocation: **delete**. The most commonly used syntax of this operator is even simpler than that of the **new** operator:

```
delete ptr;
```

This operator is much more reliable than the **free()** function available in C. It does actually release memory in such a way as to allow it to be reused as necessary. Many C language implementations of **free()** remove the address of the memory from a process's symbol table but do not place this memory on a heap (a structure containing addresses of available locations) for use by subsequent calls to **malloc()**.

The formal syntax for the **delete** operator is described using a deallocation expression, which is related to the allocation expression used to describe the formal syntax of **new**.

```
deallocation_expression   :
        delete cast_expression
        |delete[] cast_expression
        |:: delete cast_expression
        |:: delete [] cast_expression
        ;
```

The simplest way to use the **delete** operator is to keep in mind several rules.

- The **delete** operator should be used only to remove a pointer that was obtained from a call to the operator **new**.
- Use of **delete** to remove a pointer that was declared directly using a construction such as

```
char *p;
delete p ;
```

leaves the memory state undefined and is to be avoided.

- Use of **delete** to remove a pointer that was declared directly using a construction such as

```
char *p = (char *) malloc(sizeof(char));
delete p ;
```

leaves the memory state undefined and is to be avoided.
- Use of **delete** to remove a pointer that has been obtained from a correct call to **new** followed by use of pointer arithmetic leaves the memory state undefined and is to be avoided. Thus the code

```
int *p = new char;
p++;
delete p;
```

is to be avoided.
- Deleting a pointer with the value 0 is guaranteed to be harmless, regardless of how the pointer was obtained.
- The return type of the **delete** operator is **void**.

The operator **delete** differs from the C function **free()** in several ways. Many implementations do not ensure that a call to **free()** will make the memory accessed by the removed pointer available for later use in a program. This is partially due to the difficulty that the **delete** operator has with deleting a pointer that was subjected to pointer arithmetic. The code fragment

```
char *char_ptr = (char *) malloc(sizeof (char));
char_ptr ++;
delete char_ptr;
```

will not work properly in C++.

4.2   Array Indexing and Pointer Arithmetic in C++

Since C++ is essentially a superset of C, we should expect that array indexing is the same in both languages, since it is such a standard feature. The syntax and semantics are identical, as are those of pointer arithmetic.

This means that statements such as

```
int arr[10];
arr[7] = 46;
```

and

```
k = arr[i++];
```

are equally valid in both C++ and C and have the same meaning in each language.

Unfortunately, this means that both languages suffer from the same well-known deficiency. There is no direct way to make sure that indices of arrays stay within allocated bounds. Thus a statement such as

```
arr[46] = 46;
```

is legal in both C and C++, although it is likely to lead to disaster.

We discussed this point earlier in this chapter in Example 4.1. Additional evidence of the severity of the problem is the existence of the bounds-checking tools mentioned previously.

Note that the view that "C++ is a better C" doesn't seem to apply here because the syntax and semantics are the same in this situation. Fortunately, we can use additional features of C++.

We can use the object-oriented features of C++ to define an array object with run-time checking for indices being out of range. The basic idea is to have a member function of a class designed to detect if an array index is within the allowable array bounds. In Example 4.2, we show one possible class description using a member function named **within_limits()**. The function is declared as private, since we do not wish users of the class to be able to access this information. The class is named **Array** in this example.

Example 4.2 A portion of the **Array** class.

```
class Array
{
public:
  int lower, upper;      // For array limits.
  int index ;            // For the array index.
  int valid;             // For users of this class.
  Array(int low, int high);        // Constructor
private:
  int within_limits();
  int arr[];
};
```

```
int Array:: within_limits()
{
  if ((index >= lower) && (index <= upper))
    return 1;
  else
    return 0;
}


Array::Array(int low, int high)
{
// code goes here
}
```

Some comments on the code of Example 4.2 are in order. The first thing to note is that it is the first example that we have presented that is not a complete program. There is no function **main()** provided in the example, and thus the code cannot be linked successfully into an executable file.

The next observation is that any use of this **Array** class will have additional run-time overhead because of the checking of indices to determine if they are valid (within the specified range of indices).

The third observation is that there does not seem to be any way of representing the type of the elements of the **Array** class. Thus it would seem that we would need to have different class descriptions for arrays of **char**, **int**, **float**, **double**, and any user-defined types. Fortunately, this is not the case. We will see a way of avoiding this in Chapter 5 when we study the C++ construction known as a template, or a parameterized class.

Note that we have not included the details of writing a constructor for the class **Array** in this example. Several different constructors could be written for this class. One possible constructor could use a "super array" whose size is large enough to include most sizes of arrays specified in the range of valid indices. This would look something like the code in Example 4.3.

Example 4.3 Use of a "super array" constructor for the **Array** class.

```
Array::Array(int low, int high)
{
  const int MAX = 10000;
  int *arr = new int[MAX];
  int *array = int_ptr + low;
}
```

There would be similar constructors for arrays of **char**, **float**, etc.

A second constructor could allocate space properly on an "as-needed" basis using the **new** operator. A constructor based on this idea might look something like the code of Example 4.4, with similar constructors for arrays of **char**, **float**, etc. There is likely to be some problem with this type of declaration because the specification for C++ requires that the array size in a declaration be a constant.

Example 4.4 A different constructor for the **Array** class.

```
// Won't compile - need constant size.
Array::Array(int low, int high)
{
    int *int_ptr = new int[high - low]; // watch for constants
    int *array = int_ptr;
}
```

Perhaps the most flexible constructor would be one in which a linked list is used for the internal storage of the array elements. We will illustrate the implementation of this design in an efficient way in Section 5.3 when we study linked lists.

4.3 Multidimensional Arrays in C++

The title of this section is somewhat misleading in that C does not actually allow two-dimensional arrays. (C++ does allow two-dimensional arrays, but they are not predefined language features and must be encoded by the programmer as classes.) For completeness, we review the C definitions before continuing to their interpretation in C++.

A two-dimensional array is an object composed of elements of the same type that is organized so that any element can be accessed by using the starting position of the array (which is known to the compiler) and the two indices that describe the position of the desired element. Every two-dimensional array must have the same number of elements in each row; the number of elements in each column must also be the same although it does not have to be the same as the number of elements in each row. The term *row* means the index for the first dimension, and *column* means the index for the second dimension. For example, a two-dimensional array with 4 elements in the first dimension and 5 elements in the second dimension has a total of 20 elements and is said to be a 4 by 5 array; that is, it has 4 rows and 5 columns. One such two-dimensional array is shown in Figure 4.1, in which we use the common representation in which rows extend horizontally and columns extend vertically.

Figure 4.1 A two-dimensional array.

```
 2  4  6  8 10
12 14 16 18 20
22 24 26 28 30
32 34 36 38 40
```

The elements of this two-dimensional array are all of the same type.

The 20 numbers in Figure 4.1 can be represented by the data definition

```
int arr[4][5] ;
```

which says that **arr** is an array of 4 elements, each of which is an array of 5 elements, with the last-mentioned elements all being of type **int**. The element 22 is found by using the indices appropriately so that the value of **arr[2][0]** is equal to 22.

Consider what happens in C after a two-dimensional array is defined and has storage space allocated to it. The elements in an array called **arr** must be accessed using the form **arr[i][j]** instead of the form **arr[i,j]**, which is common in many other languages. The expression **arr[i,j]** has an entirely different meaning in C using a concept called the *comma operator*; the value of the expression **arr[i,j]** is **arr[j]**, which is certainly not what we intend. You should follow this warning: **Use the form arr[i][j] instead of arr[i,j] to access elements of two-dimensional arrays.**

The array of Figure 4.1 is stored in row-major form; that is, the index that changes first is the second or column index. Figure 4.2 shows the way that this particular array would be stored on a computer that places the beginning of the array at the bottom of the picture.

For ordinary, rectangular arrays with both dimensions fixed, there is no essential difference between the two methods of having two-dimensional arrays being represented either as a single entity or as a one-dimensional array of one-dimensional arrays as in C. There is a distinct advantage to the C method if the array size is not known at compile time. An examination of the storage indicated in Figure 4.1 suggests that the critical need is for the C compiler to know the number of elements in a row. The actual picture of memory is represented more accurately in Figure 4.2.

The storage for the first five **ints** would be exactly the same if we used the statement

```
int arr[][5];
```

since the only thing that we must know is the size of an arbitrary element of the array. The elements of the array **arr** are one-dimensional arrays of five **ints** each, and thus the storage allotted for any element of **arr** must be precisely the space needed for five expressions of type **int**.

Figure 4.2 Storage of a two-dimensional array of fixed size.

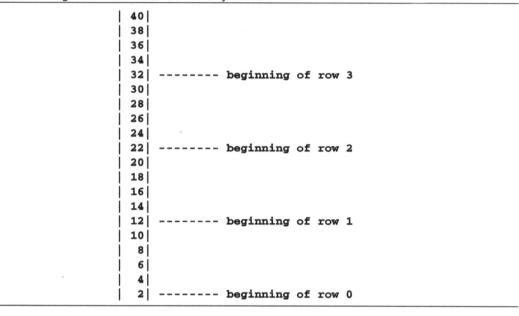

```
                    | 40|
                    | 38|
                    | 36|
                    | 34|
                    | 32|  -------- beginning of row 3
                    | 30|
                    | 28|
                    | 26|
                    | 24|
                    | 22|  -------- beginning of row 2
                    | 20|
                    | 18|
                    | 16|
                    | 14|
                    | 12|  -------- beginning of row 1
                    | 10|
                    |  8|
                    |  6|
                    |  4|
                    |  2|  -------- beginning of row 0
```

The two notations

```
    int arr[][5];
```

and

```
    int arr[4][5];
```

are not the same. Strictly speaking, the first notation does not declare a two-dimensional array. It declares a pointer to an array whose elements are themselves arrays of five **ints**. The second notation says that we are to set aside enough storage for a total of 20 **ints**.

A two-dimensional array can be initialized using the same construction used for one-dimensional arrays. It is probably easier to group the rows together in order to make the assignment of elements to their proper positions easy to understand. Examples 4.5 and 4.6 show alternative methods of declaring and initializing two-dimensional arrays; that represent the values of coordinates of a pentagon. The pentagon is described as a polygon with six vertices. Six vertices are used, since the data must interface with a graphics function that will draw the pentagon as a sequence of line segments. Having six vertices with the first and last identical ensures that the pentagon is a closed figure. The vertices are given as a two-dimensional array of dimensions 6 by 2. The first

Figure 4.3 Storage of a two-dimensional array of variable size.

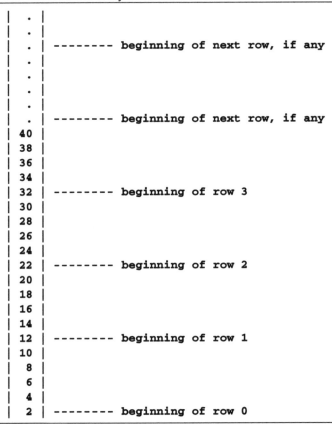

dimension indicates that there are six vertices and the second indicates two coordinates per vertex; we expect the first coordinate to correspond to the x coordinate and the second to correspond to the y coordinate.

Example 4.5 Initialization of two-dimensional arrays—readable form.

```
float pentagon1[6][2] =
     {
     {0.0, 0.0},
     {1.0, 1.0},
     {2.0, 2.0},
     {10.0, 10.0},
     {0.0, 10.0},
     {0.0, 0.0}
     };
```

Example 4.6 Initialization of two-dimensional arrays—unreadable form.

```
float pentagon2[6][2] = { 0.0, 0.0, 1.0, 1.0, 2.0, 2.0, 10.0,
10.0, 0.0, 10.0, 0.0, 0.0};
```

To summarize, there are four major things to remember about the treatment of two-dimensional arrays in C:

1. Elements of the array must be accessed by the **arr[row][column]** notation rather than by using the **arr[row,column]** notation.
2. The number of elements in each row of the array must be the same, but the number of rows need not be specified. However, no space is allocated if the number of rows is not specified, and unpredictable results can occur. Thus this omission of the leading dimension of an array is useful only within the context of a formal argument to a function.
3. The elements in the array must have the same type.
4. The array may be initialized using the construction

```
arr[row][column] =
   { { first row separated by commas },
     {second row separated by commas},
           .
           .
     {last row separated by commas} } ;
```

It is important to understand the way that two-dimensional arrays are stored in C programs. The address of the element **arr[i][j]** is obtained by using the expression

```
START + (i*NUMBER_OF_COLUMNS + j)*sizeof(arr[0][0])
```

where **START** is the address of the first element **arr[0][0]**.

Higher-dimensional arrays can also be simulated in C. The method is the same as for two-dimensional arrays: write the array as an array of elements, each of which is itself an array of lower dimension. For example, a declaration for a three-dimensional array of floating point numbers, with the array name of **arr** and with **N** values in the first dimension, **M** values in the second dimension, and **P** values in the third dimension is

```
float arr[N][M][P];
```

The same array with a variable number of elements in the first dimension can be declared by something like

```
float arr[][M][P];
```

As was the case for two-dimensional arrays, every range of values for each of the indices, except for the first dimension's indices, must be specified so that the compiler can store the proper size elements. Omission of the first dimension is appropriate only if the array is a formal argument to a function.

We now turn to the discussion of two-dimensional arrays in C++. Of course, nearly all of the preceding discusion will hold for C++, since C++ is essentially a superset of C. We might expect some problems with initialization of arrays because of the existence of default constructors in C++.

The first issue that we discuss is the proper creation of two-dimensional arrays in C++ using the **new** operator. The syntax is the same as for the creation of a one-dimensional array, since multidimensional arrays in C++ (and also in C) are simply one-dimensional arrays of elements that are also one-dimensional arrays.

Recall that for a one-dimensional array, a declaration such as

```
int *int_ptr = new int[10];
```

indicates that there is a one-dimensional array of 10 elements of type **int** and that this array is accessed by the pointer **int_ptr**.

The first attempt at declaring a two-dimensional array of **int** might be something like

```
int *int_ptr[5] = new int[5][10]; // semantic error
```

This is an error because of the problems with pointer conversion that are detected by nearly all C++ compilers. This incorrect statement attempts to convert a variable of type "pointer to an array of 10 elements of type **int**" to an array of 10 "pointers to **int**."

Note that C is much more forgiving of type mismatches. See the author's book *Using C in Software Design* for some examples of the freedom granted by most C compilers.

The correct way to do this is to use parentheses to be consistent with the C++ (and C) language treatment of multidimensional arrays as one-dimensional arrays of one-dimensional arrays. As such, the rightmost dimension in a two-dimensional array determines the size and type of the array. One possible declaration might look something like

```
int (*int_ptr)[10] = new int[5][10];
```

There are other alternatives, depending upon the structure desired for your program.

4.4   Matrices in C++

We now turn to the study of matrices in C++. For convenience, we will use the term *matrix* for a two-dimensional array. In this section we will present a set of object-oriented C++ programs to perform some important matrix operations.

Let us list the operations that we wish to perform on matrices:

- add
- subtract
- transpose
- multiply

For square matrices, there are additional operations:

- find the determinant
- determine if singular (determinant = 0)
- find the inverse of a nonsingular matrix

In order to add two matrices, they must have the same dimensions. The result of the addition of two matrices of the same dimension is a matrix whose dimensions are the same as the dimensions of the two original matrices. The entries of the sum are the sum of the corresponding entries in the two original matrices.

Let's develop a class for operations on two-dimensional matrices. The public portion of the class would be its size and its entries. How the entries are actually stored will remain private, for reasons to be discussed later.

The class description is given in Example 4.7. For simplicity of storage, we have allocated a relatively large array of dimensions 50 by 50 to hold the entries of a matrix. This size was chosen because of resource limitations on one computer on which the program was run.

Example 4.7 The class **Matrix**.

```
// Modified class Matrix for ordinary matrices.

typedef int boolean;

class Matrix
{
private:
  #define max_rows 50
  #define max_columns 50
  int num_rows, num_columns;
  double entry[max_rows][max_columns];
public:
  Matrix(int rows, int columns); //Constructor
  ~Matrix (); // Destructor
  Matrix operator + (Matrix );
  Matrix operator - (Matrix);
  Matrix transpose();
```

```
  Matrix operator * (Matrix);
  boolean conformable (Matrix);
  boolean same_dimension (Matrix);
};


/////////////////////////////////////////
// Constructor that initializes a matrix.
Matrix :: Matrix(int rows, int columns)
{
  int i, j;

  num_rows = rows;
  num_columns = columns;
  for (i = 0; i < num_rows; i++)
    for (j = 0 ; j < num_columns; j++)
      entry[i][j] = 0.0;
}



/////////////////////////////////////////
// Trivial destructor - does not release space.
Matrix:: ~ Matrix()
{
  int i, j;

  for (i = 0; i < num_rows; i++)
    for (j = 0; j < num_columns; j++)
      entry[i][j] = 0.0;
  num_rows = 0;
  num_columns = 0;
}



/////////////////////////////////////////
// Tests if argument has same dimensions as the object.

boolean Matrix :: same_dimension (Matrix a)
{
  if ((a.num_rows == num_rows)
          && (a.num_columns == num_columns))
    return 1;
  else
    return 0;
}
```

```
/////////////////////////////////////
// Tests if argument can be multiplied by the object.

boolean Matrix :: conformable (Matrix a)
{
  if (a.num_columns == num_rows)
    return 1;
  else
    return 0;
}




/////////////////////////////////////
// Adds argument to object.
// Assume matrices are of same dimension.
Matrix Matrix :: operator + (Matrix a)
{
  Matrix C(a.num_rows, a.num_columns);
  int i,j;

  C.num_rows = a.num_rows;
  C.num_columns = a.num_columns;
  for (i = 0; i < a.num_rows; i++);
    for (j = 0; j < a.num_columns; j++);
      C.entry[i][j] = a.entry[i][j] + entry[i][j];
  return C;
};




/////////////////////////////////////
// Multiplies matrix argument by object.
// Assume matrices are "conformable."
Matrix Matrix :: operator * (Matrix a)
{
  Matrix C(a.num_rows, num_columns);
  int i, j, k;

  C.num_rows = a.num_rows;
  C.num_columns = num_columns;
  for (i = 0; i < C.num_rows; i++);
    for (j = 0; j < C.num_columns; j++);
      {
      C.entry[i][j] = 0.0;
      for (k = 0; k < a.num_columns; k++)
        C.entry[i][j] += a.entry[i][k] * entry[k][j];
```

```
        }
    return C;
};


/////////////////////////////////////////
// Computes the transpose of a matrix.
Matrix Matrix ::transpose ()
{
    Matrix C(num_columns, num_rows);
    int i,j;

    C.num_rows = num_columns;
    C.num_columns = num_rows;
    for (i = 0; i < num_columns; i++);
      for (j = 0; j < num_rows; j++);
          C.entry[i][j] = entry[j][i];
    return C;
};
```

The best way to describe the class of square matrices is to use the technique of a base class and a derived class that we met in Chapter 3. One possible organization is given below:

```
class Square_Matrix: public Matrix
{
private:
    #define maxsize 50

public:
    Square_Matrix();   // Constructor
    double det();
    boolean singular();
    Square Matrix inverse();
}
```

Function definitions for these member functions are given in Example 4.8. We have used well-known, straightforward algorithms for these functions and have not attempted to use the most efficient algorithms. We have also presented straightforward implementations of these algorithms. For example, we have used the method of "expansion by minors" for the computation of a determinant and the method of Gauss elimination for the computation of the inverse of a matrix.

Example 4.8 Some member functions for the class **Square_Matrix**.

```
// Include the class description for the base class Matrix.

#include "ex4_7.cpp"

typedef int boolean;

class Square_Matrix: public Matrix
{
private:
  #define maxsize 50
  double entry[maxsize][maxsize];
public:
  int size;
  Square_Matrix(int m_size) : Matrix(m_size, m_size){size =
m_size;}};
  double det();
  boolean singular();
  Square_Matrix inverse();
};



//////////////////////////////////////////
//Square_Matrix :: Square_Matrix(int matrix_size)
//{
//  size = matrix_size;
//  Matrix::Matrix(size, size);
//}


//////////////////////////////////////////
// Details of this function are omitted.
// See the exercises.
double Square_Matrix :: det ()
{
  double temp;
  // code goes here

  return temp;
}


//////////////////////////////////////////
// Returns 1 if the determinant of the matrix is 0,
// returns 0 otherwise.
```

```
boolean Square_Matrix :: singular()
{
  if (det() == 0.0)
    return 1;
  else
    return 0;
}



///////////////////////////////////////////
// Compute inverse of a nonsingular matrix
// using the method of Gausss elimination.
///////////////////////////////////////////
#include <math.h>
Square_Matrix Square_Matrix :: inverse()
{
  Square_Matrix inv(size);
  int i, j, k, pivot;
  double temp;

  for (i = 0; i < size; i++)
    for(j = 0 ; j < size; j++)
      inv.entry[i][j] = (i == j);

  for(i = 0; i < size; i++)
    {
    pivot = i;
    for (j = i + 1; j < size; j++)
      if (fabs(entry[i][j]) > fabs(entry[pivot][j]))
          pivot = j;
    for (k = i; k < size; k++)
      {
      temp = inv.entry[i][k];
      inv.entry[i][k] = inv.entry[pivot][k];
      inv.entry[pivot][k] = temp;
      }
    for(j = i + 1; j < size; j++)
      for (k = size; k >= i; k--)
      inv.entry[j][k] -= (inv.entry[i][k]* inv.entry[j][i])
                                /inv.entry[i][i];

    }
  return inv;
}
```

Note that using object-oriented designs for the class **Matrix** or **Square_Matrix**
allows us to pass the objects to functions easily. This is a great improvement over the

passing of two-dimensional arrays as arguments in C. In C, we would often have to pass a two-dimensional array using **double** indirection such as

```
double ** array_elements;
```

or by passing arguments as pointers to **void** and then casting it as a pointer to **double**, using pointer arithmetic and our knowledge of how two-dimensional arrays are stored in C and C++. We will treat this issue in the exercises. (Many thanks to my colleague Will Craven at Howard University for suggesting the use of pointers to **void** in this context.)

4.5   Interfacing with the Command Line: Parameters to main()

The function **main()** can interact with its own environment—the operating system of the computer. The communication between the program and the operating system can go in two directions. If the program has an error such as division by 0, then the program communicates with the operating system and the program is halted. Communication in the other direction is done by means of command-line arguments.

In Example 4.9, we present an example of a program that has command-line arguments. Notice the form of the arguments to **main()**. These arguments are character strings that are put into the program by an interface between the command shell, which is part of the operating system, and the running program.

Example 4.9 Echoing command-line arguments.

```
#include <iostream.h>

main(int argc, char *argv[])
{
int i;

cout << "The arguments to this function are:\n";
for (i = 0; i < argc; i++)
    cout << argv[i] << endl;
}
```

Type in this program and run it. If your executable program was named **a.out** (which is the default name for executable files under the UNIX operating system), then your output would be the character string

```
The arguments to this function are:
a.out
```

with the name of the executable file on a line by itself. (The corresponding output in computers running under MS/DOS would be the character string

```
The arguments to this function are:
progname.exe
```

assuming that the executable file was named **progname.cpp**.) If you typed in the line

```
a.out Fred Marie Harry Computer Science types
```

the output would be

```
The arguments to this function are:
    a.out
    Fred
    Marie
    Harry
    Computer
    Science
    types
```

with each string of characters printed on a line by itself. The command-line arguments in the first run of the program were

```
a.out
```

In the second run of the program, there were the seven command-line arguments listed previously. The value of **argc** was 1 in the first run and 7 in the second run. The value of **argc** is always at least 1 since the name of the executable file (**a.out** in this example) is always counted as a command-line argument. The other command-line arguments are stored in **argv[]**. (On systems running under MS/DOS, the output would be identical except for the name of the executable file.)

This example shows that the command line, which included the name of the executable file and other character strings, was processed by the operating system and the information was given to the program.

Example 4.10 shows how we can read in a command-line argument as a string of characters (the only way to get commands from the operating system) and change it into an integer.

Example 4.10 A counting program.

```
#include <iostream.h>

main(int argc,char *argv[])
{
  int i,lim;

  lim = atoi(argv[1]);
  for(i = 1; i <= lim; i++)
    cout << i << endl;
}
```

Type in this program and test it with several different arguments. It gives the correct answer if you type in a command line such as

```
a.out 2
a.out 23
```

or something similar. It also gives a correct output (nothing) if the command line is

```
a.out c
```

where **c** can be any character. However, there is a serious error if you simply type the command line

```
a.out
```

The program terminates ungracefully with a core dump. One of the exercises at the end of this chapter suggests a way of fixing this problem. The program is not well written from the standpoint of defensive programming, since it can fail unpleasantly when presented with only minor errors in input. The exercise illustrates an extremely important principle of programming: be sure that possible errors in interfaces do not cause the program to crash. This warning applies both to interfaces to a human user entering data and to regular processing in the program. We will discuss this point in more detail in Chapter 7 when we study exceptions in C++.

The best way to write this program defensively is to insert some defensive code immediately after the type declarations. We will use the fact that the variable **argc** keeps track of the number of command-line arguments. We can use the argument count to exit if there are not enough arguments. This allows the program to terminate gracefully rather than dump the in-core memory into a file.

The defensive code is

```
if (argc == 1)
  {
  printf("Error - not enough arguments\n");
  exit(1);
  }
```

This code allows the termination of the program by using the **exit()** function, which is called with an argument of 0 to indicate that no abnormal action should be taken by the operating system. A call to **exit()** always terminates the program.

4.6   Pointers to Functions

This section might be a little difficult to understand at first reading. It is reasonable to ask why anyone would want to use such a strange construction, even if it were available in a programming language. Certainly, languages such as Pascal, FORTRAN, and BASIC have no such facility.

Consider the function whose rule of operation is "add 1 to the value of the input parameter and then square the result." We can write the action of this function as the composition

```
result = f(g(x)),
```

where **f()** might be the squaring function (whose rule is "square the value of the input parameter") and **g()** might be the function whose rule is "add 1 to the input parameter." In this case the composition of the two functions would be "add 1 to the input value and then square the result." For most languages, this is easy to do for a single value of the input such as in the loop

```
for (x = 0; x <= 1.0; x += .01)
    cout << (x+1)*(x+1);
```

Note that in this example, we have only computed individual values using the rules of the function and have combined the results in a single statement.

Perhaps a better example might be

```
for (x = 0; x <= 1.0; x += .01)
  cout << f(g(x));
```

where **f()** and **g()** are defined by

```
float f(float x)
{
  return x*x;
}
```

```
float g(float x)
{
   return x + 1;
}
```

Even in this example, what we have is the passing of values of a function **g()** at specific values of the input **x** to another function **f()** by computing the value of **u = g(x)** and then passing the value of **u** to **g()** as an input.

A language that has pointers has the ability to change the values of parameters to functions simply by changing the contents of the location accessed by the pointer. If the language allowed pointers to functions, then it might be possible to pass functions as parameters to other functions such as is done in mathematical functions that have rules or that describe their action such as "find all real roots of the function," "find the maximum value of a function," or "compute the definite integral of a function over a given interval," where the function on which we perform these actions is not fixed. This is not passing a function to another function in the sense of communicating a rule. We need the notion of pointers to functions to be able to do this.

A nonmathematical example of the use of this idea occurs in the UNIX system call function **signal()** that is used for communicating the existence of certain events such as the termination of a process or an interrupt from a keyboard. The syntax for the **signal()** system call is

```
int (*signal(int sig, int (*fcn) () ) )   ()
```

On the next few lines we have separated the declaration of the **signal()** system call into several lines for clarity.

```
int (*signal (
        int sig,
        int (*fcn) ()
        )
     )
     ()
```

The first line indicates that the value returned by **signal()** is of type "pointer to a function whose return type is **int**," with the rest of the declaration to follow. The second line is simple. The third line indicates that the second argument is also a pointer to a function whose return value is **int**.

The system call using the signal function in UNIX is quite complex and will be discussed here only at a very high level in this and the next two paragraphs. The only thing that you need to know at this time is that such a construction using pointers to functions is used in certain nonmathematical programs.

When an event such as overflow of a register or division by 0 occurs, a signal is sent by the operating system. The signal has been been given a predetermined integer value in the operating system header file **signal.h**. A typical signal for these arithmetic faults is **SIGFPE**, which is a mnemonic for "signal floating point exception." The user's program should have a statement in it such as

```
... signal( SIGFPE, signal_catcher) ...
```

that indicates that a detection of this particular signal has been made by the operating system and that the program should take appropriate action. The appropriate action is to do what the programmer wishes to do, assuming that he or she has anticipated this error state and has previously included the signal catcher function in the program. If there is no signal handler in place, then the operating system generates a signal **SIGKILL**, which always terminates the program, and a message such as

```
Floating Point Violation

Bus Error - Core dumped

EMT Violation - Core dumped
```

or similar is given to the user.

As another example, consider the UNIX **rpcgen** utility used to aid in low-level network programming. This utility uses pointers to functions. This utility takes as input a very simple data file including the name of a function to be executed on a remote computer and the name used for its arguments. The output of the **rpcgen** utility is a set of C source code files with a mechanism for taking the general source code output and linking it to the user-defined function.

A common statement in the middle of the **rpcgen** output might look something like

```
(char *) (*local)();
```

which represents a pointer to a function named **local()**. This local function pointer is used as a link to a user-defined function. The cast operation is used for consistency with the wide variety of possible functions.

Here is another example. You are probably familiar with the concept of a window system in which one or more processes run in different windows. The choice of an active window is often made by a mouse or other pointing device. The movement of the mouse causes an interrupt of the CPU in order to have the mouse's movement translated into movement of a "mouse cursor" on the screen. The positioning of the mouse cursor on a window and the pressing of a button on the mouse are events that must be interpreted by the display system. The event might mean that a window is to be closed, hidden from view by another window, placed in front of other windows that partially cover it, changed in size, or changed into some other form such as an icon. Each of these possible actions can be chosen according to the state of the mouse cursor and button. The pressing of the mouse button sends a signal, usually **SIGINT**, that is "caught" by a "signal catcher" function that is accessed by a pointer. How does the display system decide what to do? It looks at the function pointed to by the signal-catching function. The design of a signal-catching function can be quite complex and is best left to an advanced monograph on the UNIX operating system. However, we will meet some of these features when we discuss the notion of an exception and an exception handler in Chapter 7.

We now turn to the discussion of another use of pointers to functions. Mathematical examples of pointers to functions are somewhat simpler to understand than the use of the signal system call in UNIX. As an example, we consider the problem of writing a function to obtain the maximum and minimum values of an arbitrary function defined on an interval. We will do this with a function called **max()** that gets its information by using pointers to other functions.

What information do we need? We must know the rule describing the function and the endpoints of the interval that we are interested in. The program is given in Example 4.11. It includes a subtle error in the function **max()** that we will discuss later.

Example 4.11

```
// Illustrates the use of function pointers.

#include <iostream.h>
#include <math.h>

// function prototypes
double max(double a, double b, double tol,
                      double (*gptr)(double) );
double f(double x);

main(void)
{
double a, b, tolerance;
double maxval;    // Value returned from max().
char choice;

cout << "Enter the endpoints of the interval\n";
cin >> a >> b;
cout << "Enter the accuracy of the calculation\n";
cin >> tolerance;
cout << "Enter the choice of function\n\n";
cout << "sin(x)   ..... 1\n\n";
cout << "exp(x)   ..... 2\n\n";
cout << "2 x -3   ..... 3\n\n";
cout << "------------->";
```

```
cin >> choice;
cout << "The choice was " << choice << "\n\n";
switch (choice)
  {
  case '1':
    maxval = max(a,b,tolerance,sin);
    break;
  case '2':
    maxval = max(a,b,tolerance,exp);
    break;
  case '3':
    maxval = max(a,b,tolerance,f);
    break;
  }
cout << "The maximum value of the function is"
    << maxval << endl;
}


///////////////////////////////////////////////////
//   FUNCTION TO FIND THE MAXIMUM OF A FUNCTION
//   INPUTS: POINTER TO ANOTHER FUNCTION AND
//   THREE FLOATING POINT VARIABLES
//   ARGUMENTS:
//   double a,b --- endpoints of the interval
//   double tol --- accuracy of interval divisions
//   double (*gptr) () --- pointer to a function
///////////////////////////////////////////////////

double max(double a, double b, double tol, double
(*gptr)(double))

{
double x, ymax;

cout << "Address of function " << (*gptr)(a) << "\n";
ymax = (*gptr)(a);
cout << ymax ;

// be careful of round-off errors
for (x= a; x <= b; x += tol)
  {
  cout << (*gptr)(x)  << endl;
    if  ((*gptr)(x) > ymax)
      ymax = (*gptr)(x);
  }
return ymax;
}
```

```
// user-defined function
double f(double x)
{
  return 2.0 * x - 3.0;
}
```

A portion of the output from two runs of the program of Example 4.11 is given in Examples 4.12 and 4.13.

Example 4.12 First run of the program of Example 4.11.

```
Enter the endpoints of the interval
        0.0
        3.0
        Enter the accuracy of the calculation
        0.1

        Enter the choice of function

        sin(x)   ..... 1

        exp(x)   ..... 2

        2 x -3   ..... 3

- - - - - - - - - - - - - ->1

The choice was 1

The address of the function is 14
0.000000
0.000000
0.099833
0.198669
0.295520
0.389418
0.479426
0.564642
0.644218
0.717356
0.783327
The maximum value of the function is 0.783327
```

Example 4.13 Second run of the program of Example 4.11.

```
Enter the endpoints of the interval
0.0
1.0
Enter the accuracy of the calculation
0.1
Enter the choice of function

sin(x)   ..... 1

exp(x)   ..... 2

2 x -3   ..... 3

---------->3
The choice was 3

The address of the function is -1073217536

-3.000000
-3.000000
-2.800000
-2.600000
-2.400000
-2.200000
-2.000000
-1.800000
-1.600000
-1.400000
-1.200000
The maximum value of the function is -1.200000
```

There are many features of this program and its output that need discussion.

The first observation is that we have used the mathematics library and therefore need to include the standard header file **math.h** in our program.

The first part of the code prior to the **switch** statement is relatively clear and straightforward. Note the declaration of the functions **max()** and **f()** as having returned values of type **float** so that the compiler can link properly. The interesting features occur in the **switch** statements that contain the calls to the function **max()**.

The function **max()** is called three times corresponding to the three choices of the **switch** statement. There were four parameters in the first call to **max()**; **a, b, tolerance**, and **sin**. The parameters **a, b**, and **tolerance** were defined in the first line of the function **main()**. Where was **sin** declared or defined? Since the program worked, the compiler must have understood the meaning of **sin** (at least in this context). The three characters **"sin"** are the name of a C function that is not defined in the program proper but in the standard math library that was included using the header file. In a similar manner, the call to **max()** with the parameter **exp** is also known to the compiler in the same way.

The third call to **max()** that could have been selected as an option in the **switch** statement is slightly different in that the symbol "**f**" is not in the standard math library but instead is in the set of functions already declared in the program.

Each of the three possible calls to **max()** includes the name of a function. In order to communicate the rule describing the function to **max()** and not simply give values returned by the function, **max()** had to include in its heading a statement such as

```
double (*gptr) (double);
```

and a similar syntax was used in the evaluations of values of the function that was passed to **max()**. The reasoning is that the name of the function is known to the compiler when the calling statement is encountered. However, inside the function **max()** itself no such knowledge is available. Both C++ and C expect that every argument to a function will be either an expression or a pointer; the only operations allowed on functions are calling them or using their address. Since the address of the function is used in this example, each function call will make use of the contents of the function that is stored at the desired address. Thus we used statements such as

```
ymax = (*gptr)(a);
```

in this example instead of something like

```
ymax = gptr(a);
```

The second notation is more like standard mathematical notation. The idea behind using the second notation is that we are replacing the contents of the function pointer **gptr()** by the function that is pointed to. It actually made no difference which of the two notations was used; use whichever one seems easier for you.

The use of pointers to functions as parameters is likely to cause some problems in portability. Some of the difficulty is caused by differences between C++, ANSI C, and Kernighan & Ritchie C. The general rule is that type checking is stronger in the newer languages.

Example 4.11 is a good indication of some portability issues. The example is taken from the author's book *Using C in Software Design* (AP PROFESSIONAL, 1993). After making minor changes to the include files and I/O statements, the program was expected to compile and execute correctly. However, the new program did not even compile, generating 10 errors on one compiler. The problem was in the declaration

```
double (*gptr) ();
```

which worked perfectly in C, but had to be changed to

```
double (*gptr) (double);
```

in order to work in C++ because the type of arguments to the function had to be specified. The calls to the function pointed to by **gptr** also had to have an argument of type **double** in order for the program to run correctly.

Unfortunately, not all C or C++ compilers implement pointers to functions correctly.

Using pointers to functions can provide your C++ programs with considerable power to do things that would be impossible in other languages. However, issues such as portability, strangeness of syntax, and possible type-matching problems such as those shown by lint indicate that this language feature should be used sparingly in C++ programs, especially for the beginning programmer.

Another example of a pointer to a function is the standard C++ (and C) library function **qsort()**. There are four parameters to this library function: a pointer to the array to be sorted, the number of elements in the array, the size of each of the array elements, and a user-defined function for performing comparisons between the individual array elements. The syntax of this function is

```
void qsort( void *arr_ptr, size_t num_elements,
    size_t element_size,
    int (*compare)( const void *, const void *)
    );
```

The first argument is the address of the array to be sorted (with an explicit **void** so that the function works independently of data types). The second and third arguments are the sizes, which are unsigned **ints**. The last argument is a function of return type **int** that takes two arguments, each of which is a pointer to the array elements being compared.

This last function argument must be a function that is written by the programmer. The name of this function can be anything but must agree with the character string used for the argument to the library function **qsort()**. It can be as simple as comparing two **ints** with:

```
int compare(const void * xptr, const void * yptr)
{
  if (*xptr < *yptr)
    return 1;
  else
    return 2;
}
```

comparing two character strings with

Table 4.1 Conversions from pointers to **char**.

Language	Conversions Allowed from Pointers to Functions
C++	Pointers to **void**
ANSI C	None
K & R C	Pointers to **char**

```
int compare(const void *first, const void *second)
{
    return (strcmp(first, second));
}
```

or allowing a comparison of some user-defined data types, depending on the wishes of the programmer.

The C++ language has facilities for pointers to functions, since it is essentially a superset of C. Therefore most C programs that use pointers to functions will also work as C++ programs. However, there is one difference between the two languages' treatment of pointers to functions: conversions to and from a pointer to a function from a pointer to **void**.

Pointers to functions are also treated differently in the original Kernighan and Ritchie C and the later ANSI C dialects. ANSI C prohibits any conversions, while the older version of C allows casting to the type "pointer to **char**."

The situation is summarized in Table 4.1.

4.7 Functions with a Variable Number of Arguments

The C language has always had the facility for having some functions, such as **printf()** and **scanf()**, with a variable number of arguments. ANSI C went one step further and allows user-defined functions to have a variable number of arguments using the **varargs** construction.

This is probably as good a time as any to mention the ability of C to have functions with variable numbers of arguments. The topic is relevant to C++ because C++ is essentially a superset of C.

There is a header file named **varargs.h** that provides access to the standard C and C++ library functions that allow variable arguments. This header file is part of the

ANSI C specification.   A moment's reflection reminds us that the functions **printf()**, **scanf()**, and **main()** can all take a variable number of arguments. The use of command-line arguments also requires that **main()** be allowed to have a variable number of arguments.

A function that uses the variable number of arguments feature will have to have some way of determining the beginning and the end of the list of variable arguments as well as moving to the next argument on the list. Such a function will have a format similar to that of the following pseudocode:

```
#include <varargs.h>
/* prototype */
return_type var_arg_function(arg_type arg1, ...);

/* other stuff here */

return_type var_arg_function(arg_type arg1, ...)
{
/* start list for variable argument */
va_list   start;

/* other variables */

va_start(ap, arg1);

/* other part of function using   */
/* va_arg(start, arg_type)              */
/* va_arg() helps move to the next      */
/* argument in the list                 */

va_end(ap); /* End list of variable arguments. */

/* Rest of code goes here,        */
/* including return value, if any       */
}
```

We illustrate the use of this construction in a simple example of a function that returns the maximum of its arguments (Example 4.14). (This is similar to the function **MAX0** and related functions available in FORTRAN.)

Example 4.14 Illustration of the use of variable number of arguments.

```
// File ex4_14.cpp
// Illustrates use of variable number of arguments.
```

```
//#include <varargs.h>
#include <stdarg.h>
#include <iostream.h>
#include <limits.h>

// prototype — first arg holds number of other args.
int max(int arg1, ...);

void main(void)
{
  int i = 1, j = 3, k = 2;

  cout << "MAX of first two = " << max(2,i,j) << endl;
  cout << "MAX of first three = " << max(3,i,j,k) << endl;
}


int max(int arg, ...)
{
  // start list for variable arguments.
  va_list  ap;

  // other variables
  int temp1, temp2, i = 1;

  va_start(ap, arg);
  temp1 = INT_MIN;
  while (i <= arg)
    {
    temp2 = va_arg(ap,int);
    i++;
    if (temp1 <= temp2)
      temp1 = temp2;
    }
  va_end(ap); // End list of variable arguments.
  return temp1;
}
```

There are some issues here that need additional discussion. The need for appropriate header files and having a function prototype should be very familiar by now. There is one part of the syntax here that might be overlooked. We have previously used three dots (...) in some examples as a notation in order to indicate to you that there is more source code than what we have written explicitly. The three dots in the function prototype in this example and the function definition are used to indicate to the compiler the need for a variable number of arguments.

The use of the functions **va_start()** and **va_end()** delimits the portion of the code that requires a variable number of arguments. (Technically these are macros, not functions.) The macro **va_list()** is used to keep track of the linked list that is used to hold the variable set of arguments.

Since we used integers instead of pointers to integers in this example, we could not use any standard list operations such as ending the list iteration when a pointer becomes 0.

There is one final note about this example. The Borland C++ compiler would not compile this program when the header file **varargs.h** was included. We used the file **stdargs.h** and the program worked perfectly. You might find similar deviations from the standard when using this language feature.

The variable number of arguments feature of C is described in the ANSI C standard, but is not available in most earlier dialects of the C language, or even in all current versions. You should probably expect some portability problems if you use this feature. There is a large amount of testing necessary when using the variable number of arguments feature of either C or C++.

You might find it convenient at times to have a smooth way of parsing command-line arguments if you write software that has many options. The function **getopt()** is available on many C compilers and is especially common on some AT&T-based UNIX systems. However, it is not generally available on C compilers for personal computers.

Here is an example of the use of **getopt()** in a software system that was used to analyze a set of C source code files. The command line of the software system included the name of the executable file (**"measure"**), a set of options (including **'a'**, **'A'**, **'c'**, **'C'**, **'d'**, **'g'**, **'h'**, **'m'**, and no option specified at all, which meant that all options were selected by default), and a list of input files to be analyzed by the software. The user of the system was allowed to enter command lines such as

```
measure -d file1.c
```

and

```
measure -c file2.c file3.c
```

with single options,

```
measure -d -h file1.c

measure -c -m file2.c file3.c

measure -d -C -m file1.c

measure  file2.c file3.c
```

with multiple options that were flagged with minus signs, and

```
measure -cdm file2.c file3.c
```

where multiple options were allowed to be flagged by a single minus sign. The syntax for our use of a call to **getopt()** in this software system was

```
while ((option = getopt(argc, argv, "hcmdCAag"))
                        != EOF )
  {
  switch (option)
    {
    case 'a :
    case 'A' :
      ANSIoption = TRUE;
      break;

      .
      .
      .
    }
  }
```

Note that this code fragment uses a **while-loop** to check for each one of the arguments being present. Note also the use of **EOF** to check for the end of the argument list.

C++ has a similar facility for functions with variable numbers of arguments. Recall that overloading of functions allows multiple versions of functions to be associated with the same object. The values of any missing function arguments are then replaced by predetermined default values.

The best way to think of the idea of variable numbers and types of arguments to functions in C++ is to regard them as examples of unchecked substitution of arguments. They should probably be avoided unless there is no other alternative. If we know that a function will have a maximum number of arguments, and the types of the potential arguments are known in advance, then it is probably better to use overloaded functions instead of variable lists of arguments.

4.8   Virtual Functions

Many situations arise in which it is inconvenient to resolve all possible conflicts in overloading of function definitions at compile time. This can occur if a function is defined in a base class and is also defined in a derived class. A C++ compiler must have some mechanism for determining which function to apply to an object that belongs to either the base class or the derived class. The mechanism that applies at run time is called virtual functions.

If the member functions are hard-coded as part of the description of both the base and derived classes, then this determination should be made at compile time, not run time.

However, it may be more efficient from the viewpoint of both programming and run-time execution time for the C++ run-time system to make the determination at run time. Virtual functions were developed in order to allow this selection process to happen smoothly, with a minimum of run-time overhead.

In Section 3.2, we listed possible ways of determining which of several different functions can be applied to an object:

- by the signature of the function
- by the scope resolution operator, which is denoted by the two characters **: :**.
- by matching the object to the class itself.

Virtual functions allow additional information about which function should be applied to an object if the object is in either base classes or classes derived from base classes. Virtual functions provide a mechanism for resolution of names at run time. This delayed resolution of conflicts in names is known as *late binding* or *dynamic binding*.

Virtual functions can be used in base classes to provide an efficient way of organizing information in derived classes.

The syntax for virtual functions is simple: use the keyword **virtual** as a type specifier before a function declaration.

The semantics of virtual functions are more complex and depend to some extent upon the organization of any classes derived from a base class. For example, suppose that a base class has a virtual function named **V()** and that a derived class has a function, which is also called **V()**, that has the same argument signature and the same return type. Then any call to the function **V()** in the derived class could be either the function **V()** in the base class (using inheritance) or the function of the same name in the derived class. The distinction is made by the C++ run-time system, depending on the use of the reserved word **virtual** in the derived class.

In Example 4.15 we illustrate the use of virtual functions. This example is a modification of the code previously presented in Example 3.2. The code of Example 3.2 used inheritance to describe a class named **Square**, which was derived from a class called **Rectangle**. Both classes used functions called **area()** and **perimeter()** that were declared in the base class **Rectangle** as member functions of that class. These two functions were made available to the derived class **Square** by means of inheritance.

The code of Example 4.15 is somewhat different. We have declared the two member functions **area()** and **perimeter()** of the base class as being virtual. This makes selection of the proper function in the derived class happen at run time. The derived class has only one of these two functions, **area()**, which is also declared to be a virtual function by use of the reserved word **virtual**. (The two other member functions for the derived class are constructor functions.)

Example 4.15 Use of virtual functions.

```
// Code to illustrate the use of virtual functions.

#include <iostream.h>

class Rectangle
{
private:
  double length;
  double width ;
public:
  Rectangle(double L = 0.0, double W = 0.0);
  virtual double area() { return (length * width) ; }
  virtual double perimeter()
          {return (2.0 * (length + width)) ; }
};


// Member function of class Rectangle.
Rectangle :: Rectangle(double L, double W)
{
  length = L;
  width = W;
}


// Description of the class Square.
class Square : public Rectangle
{
  double side;
public:
  Square()  {side = 0.0;};
  Square(double s) : Rectangle(s,s){side = s;} ;
  virtual double area() {return (double) side * side; };
};
```

```
// Main program.
main()
{
  Rectangle R1(3,4);
  Rectangle R2(5,5);
  Square S1(4.0);
  Square S2(5);

  cout << "Area of first rectangle is " << R1.area() <<endl;
  cout << "Perimeter is " << R1.perimeter() << endl;

  cout << "Area of second rectangle is " << R2.area()<<endl;
  cout << "Perimeter is " << R2.perimeter() << endl;

  cout << "Area of first square is " << S1.area() << endl ;
  cout << "Perimeter is " << S1.perimeter() << endl;

  cout << "Area of second square is " << S2.area() << endl ;
  cout << "Perimeter is " << S2.perimeter() << endl;
}
```

The output of this example is identical to the equivalent statements in Example 3.2. The essential thing to understand is that the determination of the proper **perimeter()** function was made at run time. Note that the determination of the proper **area()** function was made at compile time using inheritance rules, since there was no member function of that name in the derived class.

There are some potential problems with the use of virtual functions. The classes must be designed carefully to resolve conflicts if there is multiple inheritance. Other issues involve the overloading that occurs whenever virtual functions are used. The scope resolution operator can be very helpful in this regard.

4.9 **Pointers to** void

Pointers to **void** are an effective method of passing arguments to functions. (We described this technique earlier, in Section 4.4.) However, there are problems with the indiscriminate use of such pointers. The problems generally occur when we attempt to combine existing C source code and new C++ programs.

The C and C++ languages differ in their treatment of pointers to **void**. The primary reason for this is the emphasis on "type safety" in C++.

Consider the two declarations below. They are valid in both C and C++.

```
char * char_ptr;
void *fcn_ptr = f();
```

In C, the statement

```
char_ptr = fcn_ptr;
```

is legitimate and the conversion causes no problems. In C++, this statement is not valid because the pointers are of different types.

In C++, we would have to use an explicit cast operation such as

```
char_ptr = (char *) fcn_ptr;
```

in order to allow assignment of the pointers.

The technical difficulty is caused by the distinction between the constant value 0, which is frequently used in a symbolic constant **NULL**, and the expression (**void ***) **0**, which is frequently used. The ANSI C standard defines the term *null pointer* to be either the constant expression 0, or else such an expression that is cast to type **void ***.

This difficulty is especially likely to occur when using older C language header files with C++ code. The problem will occur with both ANSI C and the older Kernighan and Ritchie C. You should expect to make appropriate cast operations if necessary.

Some of the material in this section is based on the published deliberations of the ANSI C++ committee X3J16. These are available by anonymous **ftp** from the source **research.att.com.**

4.10   A Special Pointer: this

A common C construction used with pointers within a function involves declaring a temporary pointer that points to an object of a particular type such as a C struct, union, or function. After proper initialization of the object, the pointer is then returned by the function.

An illustration of this type of construction is given in Example 4.16.

Example 4.16 A use of temporary pointers in C.

```
#include <stdlib.h>

struct tel
  {
```

```
char name[20];
int telno;
char  *address[50];
};


struct tel *make_entry()
{
 struct tel * temp;

 temp = (struct tel *) malloc(sizeof (struct tel)) ;
 temp->name = "John Smith";
 temp->telno = 5551212;
 temp->address = "123 Fourth Street Anywhere USA 56789" ;
   return temp;
}
```

Of course, the same construction will also work in C++. However, we can provide a more elegant solution in C++. Recall that the **new** operator allows us to avoid the type cast used to coerce the return type of the pointer in Example 4.16.

Use of the new operator simplifies things somewhat, but still requires the explicit declaration and use of a temporary pointer. The scope of the pointer **temp** in Example 4.16 is only within the function. Of course, confusion can arise if there is another global declaration of **temp**. The local declaration hides the global declaration. Unfortunately, because of the scoping rules of C, if no local declaration of **temp** is available within a function, a global one (if any) is used. Omission of a declaration of a local temporary pointer causes a modification of a global pointer, which was probably not the intention of the programmer.

C++ uses a new reserved word, **this**, to avoid the slight possibility of the misuse of global temporary variables. The idea is simple: use the reserved word **this** to indicate a pointer to the type of object being created by the functions. Since the intention of the pointer **this** is to reduce the possibility of confusion with global pointers, its scope is only the function in which it is declared.

There are two additional essential restrictions on the use of the reserved word **this**.

- There can be only one type of object returned by the function. (Otherwise there would be confusion about which pointer to be returned from the function.)
- The function must be a member function of some class, so that the return type of this is a pointer to the class to which the member function belongs. The pointer should not be modified after it is declared so that the return type is essentially **Object * const**, where **"Object"** is the type of the object to which the member function containing the reference to the pointer **this** belongs.

The most common use of the pointer **this** is illustrated in the code of Example 4.17. Note the improvement in readability of the code and the reduction in the number of possible errors. This is a considerable improvement in the treatment of pointers in C++.

Example 4.17 Use of the **this** pointer in C++.

```
class Toy
{
public:
  char *name;
  int telno;
  char  *address;

  Toy *make_entry();  // A member function
};



Toy * Toy :: make_entry()
{
  this->name = "John Smith";
  this->telno = 5551212;
  this->address = "123 Fourth Street Anywhere USA 56789" ;
  return this;
}
```

We will use the special pointer **this** throughout the remainder of this book. It clearly simplifies the development of C++ code that uses pointers to objects inside member functions.

Summary

There is no concept of a multidimensional array in C. Instead, C considers one-dimensional arrays, all of whose elements are of some fixed data type, one-dimensional arrays each of whose elements is a one-dimensional array, etc. As a result of this organization, the statements

```
        float a[10][10];
```

and

```
        float a[][10];
```

are legal, but

```
        float a[10][];
```

and

```
        float a[][];
```

are not, since the C compiler cannot properly allocate space for the underlying one-dimensional array.

There is no obvious way to get around this fundamental problem in C++ if we use the pure C data organization. Instead, the object-oriented features of C++ can be used to build some classes to make up for the unavailability of the concept of a multidimensional array in C. The classes will allow some simple matrix operations on multidimensional matrices.

C++ has an operator called **new** that combines the allocation of space with the type-cast conversions that were both necessary when using the **malloc()** function within C programs.

Along with the operator **new**, C++ has the **delete** operator, which frees up memory and returns the space to the heap for later allocation. These two operations allow a safer mechanism for programs that use dynamic memory allocation.

Pointers to functions are powerful constructions in both C and C++. Unlike pointers to functions in ANSI C, a pointer to a function in C++ can be cast to a pointer to **void**.

Classes can be developed in C++ to allow safer use of array access. In particular, more checking of index bounds is available in C++, using special array classes.

A special pointer, **this**, can be used to provide access to an object. The **this** pointer can only be defined for a member function of a class.

EXERCISES

1. Write a C program that will find roots of the equation

   ```
   sin(x) - x = 0
   ```

   The program should have an opening message to the user requesting entering the input of three floating point numbers, **a**, **b**, and **tolerance**. The first two numbers are to be parameters to two functions, **maximum()** and **minimum()**, that produce the larger and smaller of these two numbers, respectively. The values returned by **maximum()** and **minimum()** as well as the value of **tolerance** are to be used as parameters to a function named **locate** that will implement the following algorithm on the function **f(x) = sin(x) – x**. Note that the use of the function **sin(x)** in this problem will require the use of the mathematics library.

```
high = maximum(a,b);
low = minimum(a,b);
if f(low) and f(high) have the same sign then exit;
while (low < high) do
  {
  mid = (high + low)/2;
  if f(mid) and f(low) have the same sign)
    low = mid;
  else
    high =  mid;
  }
if absolute value of f(mid) is less than tolerance
  then print "root is near x = " mid;
else
  print("No root within given limits")
```

The method that is applied in this algorithm is often called the method of bisection by numerical analysts; it is a variant of the binary search technique.

2. Repeat Exercise 1 for the function **f(x) = exp(x) – x**, where **exp(x)** denotes the exponential function.

3. A common technique in the storage management of data that must be accessed rapidly is called *hashing*. The idea here is that the data is to be accessed by a key. Rather than store all the data in some type of sorted order, the data is to be stored and accessed on the basis of a hashkey that is computed by a function called a hash function. The value returned by the hash function is typically an integer that represents the actual storage location either directly or indirectly. We will return to this idea in the next chapter and in Chapter 9. For now, we just want to compute a hash function.

The hash function that you will compute in this problem takes as its input an array of at most 10 characters. The output will be the sum of the integer equivalents of the character values, with each value being multiplied by 10 raised to the power of the index (as read from left to right) –1. Only the first eight characters will be used. If the array has fewer than eight characters, then only those characters will be used. The end of array symbol **'\0'** is not to be included in the count. To keep the range of values returned by the hash function within appropriate limits, the value accumulated will be decreased by replacing it by its remainder mod 127; the remainder after the mod function is used will be the value returned by the hash function.

4. Write a C++ program that prints C and C++ programs in an attractive fashion. Output from the program should consist of the lines of the input file preceded by the line numbers. That is, if the input looks like

```
main()
{int i,j;
i=1;
j=2;
i = i + (j-1);
if (i > j)
        cout << "Hello";
}
```

then the output should be

```
1     main()
2     {
3       int i,j;
4       i=1;
5       j=2;
6       i = i + (j-1);
7       if (i > j)
8           cout << "Hello";
9     }
```

Your program should make sure that no more than 60 lines of the input will be printed on a page (standard page length = 66 lines). In addition, you should be careful about long lines. Thus a long line such as

```
alphabet = if (found == -1) cout << "The key " << key << "is
not in the array.\n";
```

should be printed like

```
100   alphabet = if (found == -1)
        cout << "The key "<< key << is not in the array.\n";
```

instead of

```
100   alphabet = if (found == -1) cout << "The key " << key
<< " is not in the array.\n";
```

In the second print, the line runs off the page and the tail end will probably not be printed on most printers that print 80 characters wide. The choice of break points in the line is up to you; however, you should be careful not to separate any tokens.

5. Write two C++ functions called **bin_to_dec()** and **dec_to_bin()** that will convert binary (base 2) integers to decimal (base 10) and vice versa. The input to the function **bin_to_dec()** is to be an array of characters, each of which is either 0 or 1. The array of characters might be something like

   ```
   0101011
   ```

   and this is to be interpreted as a binary number. The value returned by the function **bin_to_dec()** should be of type **int**. For the function **dec_to_bin()**, the input and output types should be reversed. Test these functions by creating an appropriate main program.

6. Write a C++ program that will read in pairs of integers and add them. The input will be integers that are entered in the binary format. This should be done somewhat differently from the previous problem. In this problem, the input will be in the form

   ```
   char first[], second[];
   ```

   and **first** and **second** will be arrays of characters with each entry in the array being either 0 or 1. Assume that the input can fit on one line and hence the maximum size of the input arrays is 80. The addition will be done in binary format and you will have to write the actual routines to add 0 + 0, 0 + 1, 1 + 0, and 1 + 1, placing the results of each addition in the appropriate position and carrying any excess to the next position.

   The output of this addition should be a variable named sum that is also a representation of a number in binary form. That is, the result will be in the form

   ```
   char sum[];
   ```

   The output array can hold up to 81 entries because of the carry; be sure to allocate enough room.

   Describe the alternatives that can be used for the objects in this program.

7. Perform the same task as in Exercise 6, except that your program should multiply the two inputs.

8. This exercise involves writing a C++ program that emulates the behavior of a classic program in the artificial intelligence community, the Eliza program that was

designed by Jerome Weitzenbaum at MIT. The program was intended to act like a "nondirectional analyst" who never answered a question but responded instead with a new question related to the patient's last response. A sample session might go something like this:

> *Analyst*: How are you feeling?
> *Patient*: I am tired today.
> *Analyst*: Has anything happened recently to make you tired?
> *Patient*: No. Do you think I look tired?
> *Analyst*: Why do you think you look tired?
> *Patient*: I have looked tired since childhood.
> *Analyst*: Tell me about your childhood.
> *Patient*: I had a happy childhood.
> *Analyst*: Really? Why are you so unhappy now?

The original program simply used string-matching techniques to look for patterns in the input. Write a simple program to do something similar. Your program should parse the input into separate words and look for the appearance of one or more key words in the patient's description. To limit the size of the program, limit the patient to 100 responses and match from a list of 20 key words that you choose. Use a binary search on the key words.

9. Write two C++ functions **ftoa()** and **atof()**. The first function, **ftoa()**, has as input a floating point number and will produce an ASCII string that is identical in appearance to the original input number. The function **atof()** changes an ASCII string to an equivalent floating point number.

10. Write an algorithm that efficiently computes the sine of an angle. The input to this function is an angle that is to be given in degrees. The computation is to be done as follows:

   - The angle is to be converted to an angle in the range 0..359 that has the same sine as the given angle. Be sure to allow for the possibility that an input angle might be negative.
   - The converted angle is to be converted again to an equivalent angle in the range 0..90 where the sine of the new and old angles may differ but the absolute values are identical.
   - The new angle has its sine determined by looking at the values of the sines of the angles from 0 degrees to 90 degrees.
   - These angles between 0 and 90 degrees have had their sines computed and entered into a table. You are to create this table at the beginning of the program.

Perform an experiment to test the speed of your function as compared to the standard function **sin()** in the standard C++ math library.

11. Repeat the previous problem for a function called **cosine()**.

12. The functions might be sped up somewhat by reducing the size of the arrays of sines and cosines of angles from the range 0..90 to the range 0..45 by using the trigonometric identity

        sin(A) = cos(90 - A)

    Before coding, indicate if this is likely to be of any use.

13. Write a program that will solve a system of linear equations of the form

        A X = B

    where **A** is an n by n array of floating point numbers that has all entries other than those on the main diagonal equal to 0, **X** is an n by 1 array of floating point numbers that represents the array of unknowns to be solved for, and **B** is an n by 1 array of floating point numbers.

14. (For those with a knowledge of linear algebra.) Repeat Exercise 13 but this time simply assume that the array **A** is an n by n array that has all of its elements above the main diagonal equal to 0. This problem will require access to arbitrary elements of the array and not just the diagonal ones.

15. This program compares methods of accessing two-dimensional square arrays. Consider the 10 by 10 array **arr** of floating point numbers that looks like this:

```
 0.0  1.0  2.0  3.0  4.0  5.0  6.0  7.0  8.0  9.0
10.0 11.0 12.0 13.0 14.0 15.0 16.0 17.0 18.0 19.0
20.0 21.0 22.0 23.0 24.0 25.0 26.0 27.0 28.0 29.0
30.0 31.0 32.0 33.0 34.0 35.0 36.0 37.0 38.0 39.0
40.0 41.0 42.0 43.0 44.0 45.0 46.0 47.0 48.0 49.0
50.0 51.0 52.0 53.0 54.0 55.0 56.0 57.0 58.0 59.0
60.0 61.0 62.0 63.0 64.0 65.0 66.0 67.0 68.0 69.0
70.0 71.0 72.0 73.0 74.0 75.0 76.0 77.0 78.0 79.0
80.0 81.0 82.0 83.0 84.0 85.0 86.0 87.0 88.0 89.0
90.0 91.0 92.0 93.0 94.0 95.0 96.0 97.0 98.0 99.0
```

(a) Write a program to create this array.

In the remainder of this problem, you will write different functions to repeat the following operation 100 times: assign the value 123.456 to each of the elements of the array.

(b) Measure the time for the loop below to execute.

```
for (i= 0;i <10; i++)
  for (j= 0; j < 10; j++)
    arr[i][j] = 123.456 ;
```

(c) Use pointer arithmetic and the "good quality code" that is generated for the location of element **arr[i][j]** by the formula

$$\texttt{START + (i * TEMP) + j * sizeof(arr[0][0])}$$

to count the number of additions and multiplications that are needed for all the assignment statements in this nested loop to be performed.

(d) and (e) Repeat parts (b) and (c) of this problem using the loop

```
for (j=0;j <10; j++)
   for (i= 0; i < 10; i++)
      arr[i][j] = 123.456 ;
```

(f) Compare the ratio of the running times for the two versions with the following three ratios: the ratio of the number of either additions or subtractions, the ratio of the number of multiplications, and finally the ratio of the total number of arithmetic operations.

(g) Repeat parts (b)–(f) using pointer arithmetic instead of direct access of the element **arr[i][j]**. Be careful in how you declare the array arr using pointer notation.

16. Write an ANSI C program that creates a two-dimensional array of size 10 by 10 and initializes the first three rows and columns. The entries of the array are to be of type **int**. The main program is to perform the initialization and call a function named **print_matrix()**. This function will take a pointer to **void** and the maximum number of rows to be printed as its arguments and produces as output the initialized contents of the 10 by 10 array.

17. It is often a good idea to check the performance and accuracy of system-supplied functions. This exercise will suggest how to do this for the standard library function **qsort()**.

(a) Write a program to initialize an array of 1,000 entries of size **int**. The entries are to be randomly selected using the standard library function **rand()**.

(b) Find the time needed for the initialization. You might wish to use the functions in the standard library that can be accessed by the header file **time.h** however, a watch will probably suffice.

(c) Sort this array using the standard library function **qsort()**.

(d) Compute the times for steps (a) and (c).

(e) Write a quicksort function and use it to sort the array in part (a).

(f) Compare the time for steps (a) and (e) with the times for steps (a) and (c).

(g) Repeat the experiment for array sizes of 10,000, 100,000, and 1,000000. Which is faster, your routine or the library one?

18. Use the variable number of arguments feature of C++ (and C) to obtain the output of the program in Exercise 4.9.

19. Write a C++ function that takes a two-dimensional array of data of type **int** as an argument and produces the sum of the entries as its return value. Use the technique of pointers to **void** to pass the information.

20. Rewrite the function of Exercise 19 using an object-oriented function. What are the objects that your program uses as arguments?

Structured Data Types in C++

5.1 Classes, Structs, and Templates

The C++ concept of a class has some aspects in common with structs in C. This is clear from the historical origin of C++. We now examine the relationship between classes and structs in more detail.

Suppose that we wish to have an object that is purely data, in the sense that the only member functions for the class are constructor, destructors, or functions that change the value of some data "field" of the object. It is easy to implement this in C as a struct something like:

```
struct Data
{
    type_1  data1;
    type_2  data2;
    type_3  data3;
};
struct Data data;
```

This allows us to assign values to portions of a struct by statements such as

```
data.data1 = val1;
data.data2 = val2;
```

or to use the values already present in portions of an object by statements such as

```
temp = data.data3;
```

or similar. (We assume that the three types **type_1, type_2,** and **type_3** either were predefined types or else were previously declared in a **typedef** statement.)

The simplest corresponding C++ class definition for this type would be:

```
class Data
{
  type_1  data1;
  type_2  data2;
  type_3  data3;
};
```

and we could declare **data** to be of this type by the statement:

```
Data data;
```

The distinction between the two definitions appears to be one of syntax and not worth further discussion. However, we can use the hiding power of C++ to create a higher level of abstraction.

We can perform one operation in C++ that is not allowed in C—assigning entire data structures. Suppose that we have defined an object named **data1** of type **Data** by the statement

```
Data d1;
```

Defining a member function `=` by something like

```
void operator = (Data d2)
{
  d1.val1 = d2.val1;
  d1.val2 = d2.val2;
  d1.val3 = d2.val3;
};
```

allows us to overload the assignment operator and change all of the data fields at once. We can pass arguments effectively by using this type of organization.

Suppose that we wished to hide one of the values in a particular field of a struct from some functions using it. This is not possible in C, at least not directly. (There is some possibility that this can be done if all structs are accessed as pointers and they are cast as pointers to **void** whenever they are used as arguments by other functions. This is a relatively rare construction in C programs.)

We can hide the contents of the component fields of a class in C++ from functions using the class by declaring the values in these components to be private, thereby hiding them from functions other than member functions. This is a major advantage of C++ over C.

Another major difference between classes and structs is that an object can limit the functions that can act on it. (This is an extension of the ideas described in the previous few paragraphs.)

We illustrate this point in Example 5.1. The two statements that are commented out illustrate the information hiding possible with objects in C++. These transformations are illegal in C++ (they won't even be accepted by most C++ compilers), but their equivalents would be carried out in C.

Example 5.1 Classes and structs.

```
// Program illustrates the difference between a
// class and a struct in information hiding.


class Object
{
private:
  int test1;
  int test2;
public:
  int test3;
  int test4;
};



struct structure
{
  int test1;
  int test2;
};


main()
{
  Object object;
  struct structure structure;

  structure.test1 = structure.test2 = 7;
  object.test3 = structure.test1;

  // object.test1 = structure.test1; -- Not legal
  // object.test2 = structure.test2; -- Not legal
}
```

Objects such as those of Example 5.1 are known as *static* objects. An object is called static if it does not use dynamic storage allocation and does not include any member functions. Static objects have several important features. An object that is not static is called a *dynamic* object.

A static object uses the default constructor provided by the compiler. This constructor is invoked before any executable statements (statements other than data definitions or declarations) are executed.

A default destructor is used with static objects. These destructors are created by the compiler. The default destructor is invoked for a static object when the function **main()** is exited.

There is one other C language feature that is somewhat helpful when writing programs that emphasize data abstraction—**typedef**. This construction allows a name change for variables as in the code of Example 5.2 that might belong to a C header file for stack operations. (We will discuss object-oriented implementations of stacks in C++ later in this chapter.)

To make the code relatively portable and to avoid conflicts with files of the same name in a class library, we will include the name of the file within the source code so as to make it easier to combine source code files with the appropriate header files.

Example 5.2 Header file for stack operations using **typedef** in a C program.

```
/**********************************************************/
/*      FILENAME : ex5_2.h                      */
/*      CONTAINS CONSTANTS FOR STACK OPERATIONS   */
/*      STACK USES AN ARRAY OF FIXED SIZE         */
/*       ELEMENTS OF ARRAY ARE OF TYPE GIVEN BY   */
/*      typedef STATEMENT  TYPE STACK_ITEM        */
/*      STACK_ITEM IS int IN THIS FILE            */
/*      stack is a structured data type           */
/**********************************************************/

#define MAXSTACK 20              /* max. stack size*/
typedef int STACK_ITEM;
struct stack
   {
   STACK_ITEM stack[MAXSTACK];   /* array of int */
   int top;
   };

typedef struct stack STACK;
```

The only change that is necessary to be able to use precisely this same code for other projects with stack operations is to change the header file.

Of course, the consistent use of the type **STACK_ITEM** must be enforced by the programming team. I knew a programmer who was fired from a project for not following the company's required pattern for the names of data types. Each of the individual program modules written by this programmer was correct, but together they were useless since they had to be rewritten in order to interface with the rest of the system.

Clearly, the use of the **typedef** statement supports the idea of using code in different contexts, which is one of the benefits of software reuse. However, it is not sufficient, because it is not enforced by the C or C++ programming languages.

C++ provides additional strong support for abstraction in a language construction known as *templates*. A template is a method of declaring a class whose underlying data is not specified in the class description but instead is determined by the type of the class that will use it. Since the class that is using the template is not specified, the term *parameterized class* is often used instead of template. The template construction in C++ programs allows the abstraction to be used in different contexts. We will use templates many times in this chapter.

A template allows us to develop a general set of operations and data that apply to any type of abstraction of data organization. The abstract operations are the same; only the underlying structure of the data changes. Thus we can have stacks, queues, lists, and trees of integers, stacks, queues, lists, and trees of floating point numbers, stacks, queues, lists, and trees of rectangles, and so on, provided that we develop stacks, queues, lists, and trees as templates.

5.2   Stacks in C++

The major problem with using the **typedef** declaration for pure object-oriented programming is that many C compilers do not normally check for type agreement even without **typedef** and therefore are not likely to check if the program uses **typedef**. In addition, only one renaming of any **typedef** definition is active in a program at any one time. The unfortunate conclusion is that C does not really support the use of object-oriented programming.

Even with this limitation, we can provide some of the facilities for an abstract data type in C. By the term *abstract data type* we mean that the essential features of the concept can be hidden completely from the person using this type.

We want the abstraction of a stack to be consistent with the stack organization indicated in Figure 5.1.

Figure 5.1 Stack operations.

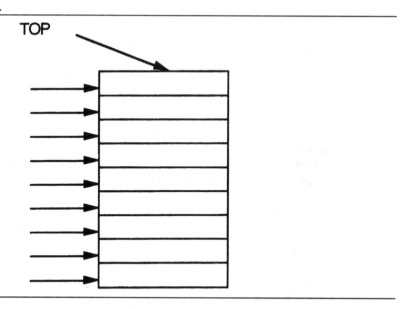

One problem with the previous code for stack operations is the direct visibility of the top of the stack to the rest of the program. We can remedy this lack of hiding by redefining the data type stack as a structured type. One way to do this in the C language is shown in Example 5.3.

Example 5.3 C code for operations on **STACK_ITEM** abstract data type.

```
/**********************************************************/
/*      FILENAME : ex5_3.c                              */
/*      FILE CONTAINS FUNCTIONS FOR OPERATIONS ON A STACK  */
/*      STACK IS IMPLEMENTED USING AN ARRAY OF FIXED SIZE  */
/*      ELEMENTS OF THE ARRAY ARE OF THE TYPE GIVEN BY A   */
/*      typedef STATEMENT AS BEING OF TYPE STACK_ITEM */
/*      STACK_ITEM is a synonym for int                 */
/*      A STACK is an abstract data type                */
/*      elements on STACK are of type STACK_ITEM        */
/*      CONSTANTS ARE IN THE FILE stack.h               */
/*      FUNCTIONS IN FILE:                              */
/*          initialize()                                */
/*          push()                                      */
/*          pop()                                       */
/**********************************************************/
```

```
#include "ex5_2.h"


/* New function needed because of new declaration       */
/* initializes the stack top to -1              */
void initialize(STACK s)
{
  s.top = -1;
};


/* pushes an argument onto the stack if not full.  If */
/* stack was already full, then print error message      */
void push (STACK s, STACK_ITEM n)
{
  if (s.top < MAXSTACK - 1)
    {
    s.top++;
    s.stack[s.top] = n;
    }
  else
    printf("error -- stack full.\n");
}


/* pops the top value off stack. Prints an error message  */
/* if one tries to "pop" from an empty stack.         */
/* A negative value for top means that the stack is empty */
STACK_ITEM pop(STACK s)
{
  int temp = s.top;

  if (s.top >= 0)
    {
    s.top--;
    return (s.stack[temp]);
    }
  else
    {
    printf("error -- stack empty.\n");
    return (0); /* stack empty: return 0 to clear stack */
    }
}
```

Any C programmer wishing to use the stack operations on the abstract data type may simply include the two files of Examples 5.2 and 5.3 and change the **typedef** statement to agree with the appropriate type. The size of the arrays could be changed as needed. In fact, a change to the **STACK** data structure that allows a linked list representation of a stack using pointers instead of a representation that uses arrays should affect only the two stack operations files and not the rest of the code. This is a fairly high level of abstraction—the highest that is available in C.

Note that a high level of abstraction such as the use of abstract data types allows any function using an instance of the abstract data type to be completely independent of the details of this type. In the exercises you will be asked to confirm this statement by writing a program that operates on a stack using the code for array implementation of stacks given in this section and to modify the stack operations without changing the rest of your system. An appropriate data structure for a linked-list implementation of a stack would be

```
typedef int STACK_ITEM;

struct stack
{
  STACK_ITEM info;  /* array of int  */
  struct STACK *top;
};


typedef struct stack STACK;
```

With the three functions **push()**, **pop()**, and **initialize()** recoded to meet this interface, any other portions of the program can be used without modification to use this implementation. Of course, the program will have to be recompiled since the include file has been changed.

Clearly, C++ classes are far more powerful than C structs in their level of support for good software engineering practice. There is an additional feature of C++ that can make program errors easier to detect. Early detection of errors is far better than detecting them after a software system is delivered.

The C++ feature that we are describing is the assert mechanism. The basic idea is to test for a boolean expression having the value 0 at some point of a program. If this happens, then the C++ run-time system calls a function named **abort()** in the standard C++ library. This function does what you would expect—it prints an error message and halts program execution.

This can be used as follows. First we include the standard header file **assert.h** in our program. We then use statements of the form

```
assert(boolean_condition);
```

at each place where an error might occur.

Consider the function **pop()** given in Example 5.3. We used an **if-else** structure to treat the usual condition properly, with the alternative code to be executed if the value of **s.top** is less than 0. We can use **assert()** to write the code something like the following:

```
STACK_ITEM pop(STACK s)
{
  assert(s.top >= 0);
  s.top--;
  return (s.stack[s.top]);
}
```

This code is much shorter and simpler to read and yet is essentially equivalent to the previous one when the stack is in a correct state.

There is another advantage to using **assert()**. It eliminates any possibility of the occurrence of a particular run-time error, or exception, that is known in the Ada programming language as the program being "not well-formed." The error of a program being "ill-formed" will occur if a function has a return type declared, but some program execution path leads to an exit from the function without a value being returned. An **else** statement of the **pop()** function that was written as

```
else
  {
  printf("error -- stack empty.\n");
  }
```

would not have a return value and the remainder of program execution would be very difficult to verify because of the garbage value in the location where a returned result was expected.

The advantage of using **assert()** is that an error can be pinpointed more easily than if we allow the program to crash at a later point in its execution. Many companies have software engineering standards that encourage the use of **assert()** during program development, especially if the company encourages the rapid prototyping methodology. In these software engineering environments, the **assert()** mechanism can be turned off by placing the statement

```
#define NDEBUG
```

at the beginning of each file in which assertions are used. The software then works correctly in the main case, without much error checking. The code is then elaborated to handle the unusual error cases in order to make the software more robust. The elaboration consists of blocks of code and functions that are used to treat error conditions. Exception handling, which we will meet in Chapter 7, is often included at this time.

C++ supports a far greater amount of information hiding than does C. We would like to be able to use stacks in programs without any chance of a user accidentally changing the internal representation of the stack.

A class description of an object called **Stack** that represents a stack is provided in Example 5.4.

Example 5.4 One description of a **Stack** class in C++.

```
// FILENAME: ex5_4.h
// Class Stack


typedef int STACK_ITEM;   // for completeness.


class Stack
{
private:
#define MAXSTACK 20
  int top;
  STACK_ITEM item[MAXSTACK];
public:
  Stack();         // Constructor
  int empty();
  void initialize();
  void push(STACK_ITEM s);
  STACK_ITEM pop();
};
```

In Example 5.5, we show a typical implementation of stacks in C++ using an array implementation. This example uses the class description of stacks that was given in Example 5.4.

Example 5.5 C++ code for operations on **STACK_ITEM** data type.

```
//
//      FILENAME : ex5_5.cpp
//      FILE CONTAINS FUNCTIONS FOR OPERATIONS ON A STACK
//      FILENAME : ex5_5.cpp
//      FILE CONTAINS FUNCTIONS FOR OPERATIONS ON A STACK
//      STACK IS IMPLEMENTED USING AN ARRAY OF FIXED SIZE
//      ELEMENTS OF THE ARRAY ARE OF THE TYPE GIVEN BY A
//      typedef STATEMENT AS BEING OF TYPE STACK_ITEM
//      STACK_ITEM is a synonym for int
//      A STACK is an abstract data type
//      elements on STACK are of type STACK_ITEM
//      CONSTANTS ARE IN THE FILE stack.h
//
//      FUNCTIONS IN FILE:
//                  Stack();           // Constructor
//                  int empty();
//                  initialize()
```

```
//                      void push(STACK_ITEM)
//                      STACK_ITEM pop()

#include <iostream.h>
#include "ex5_4.h"                    // "stack.h"

// New function needed because of new declaration
// initializes the stack top to -1
void Stack :: initialize(void)
{
  top = -1;
};


// Pushes an argument onto the stack if not full.  If
// stack was already full, then print error message.
void Stack :: push (STACK_ITEM n)
{
  if (top < MAXSTACK - 1)
     {
     top++;
     item[top] = n;
     }
  else
     cout << "error -- stack full.\n";
}


// Pops the top value off stack. Prints an error message
// if one tries to "pop" from an empty stack.
// A negative value for top means that the stack is empty.
STACK_ITEM Stack :: pop()
{
  int temp = top;

  if (top >= 0)
     {
     top--;
     return (item[temp]);
     }
  else
     {
     cerr << "error -- stack empty.\n";
     return (0); // stack empty: return 0 to clear stack.
     }
}
```

5.3   Implementing Stacks in C++ Using Templates

Our intention in this section is to introduce the complex syntax of templates, not provide the most elegant design of stacks possible in C++. An abstract, more general design will be presented after we have studied object-oriented representations of linked lists in C++ later in this chapter.

The typical syntax of templates in declarations is shown in Example 5.6, which is a class description of a stack. The class type, **T**, is used in several different places in this example within the template description. Note the use of the C++ reserved word **template**. Note also the use of two angle brackets as delimiters that indicate that we have a description of the parameterization of the template class.

Example 5.6 Templates and stacks.

```
// File ex5_6.h
// Illustrates the use of templates with stacks.

template <class T> class Stack
{
private :
  #define MAXSTACK 20
  int top;
  class T item[MAXSTACK];
public:
  Stack();
  ~Stack();
  virtual int empty();
  virtual T pop();
  virtual void push(T item);
};
```

This sort of description allows the use of the stack abstract data type in many different situations. It is easy to have stacks whose entires are integers, floating point numbers, pointers to characters, or indeed any possible data type that is valid in C++. (Even though it is required in template declarations, the use of the reserved word class is misleading within the angle brackets.) Thus we can have stacks of stacks, stacks of queues, stacks of arrays, and so on.

The member functions of this class might have definitions something like the code presented in Example 5.7. Note the different usage of the angle brackets in this example in statements such as

```
template <class T> Stack<T>:: Stack()
{
// Code goes here.
}
```

Example 5.7 Member functions for a template-based implementation of stacks.

```
//
// FILE ex5_7.cpp
//

#include "ex5_6.h"
#include <iostream.h>


// Constructor function.
template <class T> Stack<T> :: Stack()
{
  top = -1;
}


// Destructor function.
template <class T> Stack<T>:: ~Stack()
{
  top = -1;
}



// Returns 1 if the stack is empty, (top is -1)
// otherwise returns 0.
template <class T> int Stack<T>:: empty()
{
  if (top == -1)
    return 1;
  else
    return 0;
}


template <class T> T  Stack<T>:: pop()
{
  int temp = top;
```

```
   if (top >= 0)
      {
      top --;
      return(item[temp]);
      }
   else
      {
      cerr << "Error -- stack empty." << endl;
      return (item[top]);
      }
}


template <class T>  void Stack<T>:: push(T data)
{
  if (top < MAXSTACK -1)
     {
     top ++;
     item[top] = data;
     }
  else
     cerr << "error -- stack full." << endl;
}



/////////////////////////////////////////////////
// Simple function main() to illustrate the use of
// templates in a stack organization.
/////////////////////////////////////////////////

main(int argc, char * argv[])
{
  int i;
  float f=  3.14;
  char c = 'A';  // Not used, for illustration only.

  Stack<int>  Stack1;
  Stack<float>  Stack2;
  Stack<char>  Stack3; // Not used, for illustration only.

  cout << endl;
  for( i = 0; i < 30; i++)
     {
     Stack1.push(i);
     cout << Stack1.pop()<< endl;
     Stack2.push(f = f + i);
```

```
    cout << Stack2.pop() << endl;
    }
}
```

Note the use of the C++ keyword **virtual** in the code of Example 5.6. Recall from Section 4.7 that declaring a function as being **virtual** means that it can be overridden by methods with the same names if there is a child class that is a derived class of the base class. This applies to the three methods **empty(), pop()**, and **push()**.

It is now simple to define and manipulate stacks, as Example 5.7 shows. For example, to declare a stack of integers, we would simply use the statement

```
    Stack<int>  Stack1;
```

in a program. For a stack of floating point numbers, we would use the statement

```
    Stack<float>  Stack2;
```

Similarly, we would use the statement

```
    Stack<struct tel>  Stack3;
```

to declare a stack whose entries are the structured data type used to represent telephone numbers in the program of Example 4.16. Finally, we would use the statement

```
    Stack <class Rectangle>  Stack4;
```

for a stack whose entries are objects of the class **Rectangle** we met in Chapter 2.

In each case, the push operations are done using object-oriented C++ syntax such as

```
    Stack1.push(7);
    Stack2.push(7.0);
    Stack3.push(tel_7);
```

or

```
    Stack4.push(Rectangle7);
```

Note that there is no need for the fragile information hiding of the **typedef** construction. Clearly C++ templates provide a higher level of abstract data types.

It is important to understand the importance of default constructors for the base class used to parameterize a template. Recall that a default constructor is a constructor function for which no arguments are required. Each of the predefined types; (**int, float, double, char,** etc.) in C++ has a default constructor.

A default constructor must be available for the class parameterizing a template. If no constructor is present in the class, then the compiler will attempt to generate a default constructor for a class. A default constructor will be generated, provided that there are no other constructors (default or otherwise) or references (pointers) that are members of the class. Since pointers must point to specific locations in order to be useful, the semantics of C++ do not allow automatic generation of default constructors in classes with pointers as members. Keep this in mind when we study template-based implementations of lists in C++.

Unfortunately, not all implementations of C++ incorporate templates, even though they are described in *The Annotated C++ Reference Manual* by Margaret Ellis and Bjarne Stroustrup. In fact, one commonly applied measure of the completeness of an implementation of the C++ language is the implementation's support of templates and exceptions. (Exceptions are discussed in Chapter 7.)

In order to present only the most portable C++ code examples, we will discuss the fundamental data structures of lists, trees, and queues in separate sections. Each of these sections will discuss the C++ implementation of the data structure without the use of templates and will be followed by a section that discusses the implementation of the data structure using templates.

One last point needs to be made about the use of templates with stacks. Our implementation makes use of C++ constructs to implement this data structure as an abstract data type. We showed how to write one class that can be used easily with stack items of arbitrary types.

However, the code we have presented in this section does not make full use of the power of object-oriented programming. The operations of insertion and deletion from a stack and the testing of a stack for being empty are much more general than merely applying to stacks. Our future implementations of data structures will attempt to encapsulate the highest-level view of the abstract data type that we are implementing. We will use a hierarchy of objects to motivate our organization of data structures. In the Exercises, you will be asked to rewrite the stack code using more generality and abstraction than we used in this section.

5.4   Lists in C++

In this section we will describe a simple data structure in C++. We assume that you are familiar with the basic uses of these data structures and so we will concentrate on the abstract data types and their C++ implementations rather than on common applications of the data structures. You should recall that we used a stack as one of our primary examples of a C++ data structure.

The first C++ data structure that we consider is a **linked list**. The first order of business is to examine the set of operations we can perform on a list. These operations are

- create the list
- remove the list
- determine if the list is empty
- insert an element into the list
- remove an element from the list
- search the list in order to locate a specific item
- merge two lists into a single list
- split a list into two different lists

The insert operation can be broken down further into the following operations:

- insert item after a particular element
- insert item before a particular element

Note that all of these operations are abstract and that none of them say anything about the organization of the **list** (singly linked, doubly linked circular, etc.) or about the organization of the links (implicit links using pointers, or explicit links using array indices in an array implementation). Figure 5.2 illustrates the abstract view of a linked list.

Let us assume for simplicity that the type of data to be stored in the list has already been determined as either a **class** or a **typedef**. We will use the notation **Item** for the data type to be stored in the list.

Note that several list operations require examining list entries in sequence. Typical examples are searching the list for the presence of a particular piece of data and examining the list to determine a place to insert a new node containing some data. These operations all use some form of list iteration. A function that performs list iterations is commonly called an *iterator*.

Figure 5.2 Representation of a linked list.

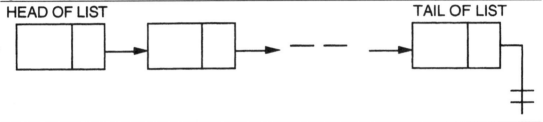

For reasons of efficiency, an iterator function is sometimes coded as a **friend** of the list class. A friend function can have access to all data in the class, including private and protected portions. We choose not to do this in our example in order to encourage information hiding, since friend functions can increase access to restricted data of objects.

A class description for the **List** object might look something like the code given in Example 5.8.

Example 5.8 A non-template version of the class **List**.

```
// FILE ex5_8.h
//
// Non-template description of the class List.
// Each element of the List is of type Data.
// The data type must be declared using a typedef statement.
//


typedef int Item;


class List
{
private:
  struct Node
      {
      Item info;
      struct Node *next;
      };
  struct Node *head; // head of list;

public:
  List(Item data);
  List();
  ~List();
  int empty();

  Item iterator();
  insert(Item data);
  remove(Item data);
  int search(Item data);
  List merge(List list1);
  List split(List list1);
};
```

The implementation of these methods for the **List** class is given in Example 5.9.

Example 5.9 Member functions for the non-template version of the class **List**.

```cpp
// FILE: ex5_9.cpp
//
// Non-template-based linked list class.
//

#include "ex5_8.h"
#include <iostream.h>
#include <iomanip.h>

// Constructor function.
List:: List(Item D)
{
  Node * temp;

  temp = new Node;
  temp->info = D;
  temp->next = 0;
  head = temp;
}




// Constructor function.
// Leaves the contents of the node defined as -1.
List:: List()
{
  struct Node * temp;

  temp = new Node;
  temp->next = 0;
  temp->info = -1;
  head = temp;
}




// Destructor
List :: ~List()
{
  struct Node *runner, *trailer;
```

```cpp
    for(trailer = head; trailer != 0; trailer = runner)
        {
        runner = trailer->next;
        trailer->next = 0;
        delete trailer;
        }
}


// Insertion function.
List:: insert(Item data)
{
    struct Node * temp, *temp_head = head;

    temp = new Node;
    temp->info = data;
    temp->next = head;
    head = temp;
    head->next = temp_head;
}



// Remove data from the list.
List:: remove(Item data)
{
}



// List search function.   Returns 1 if found, 0 otherwise.
int List:: search(Item data)
{
}



// Function to merge two lists.
List List:: merge(List List1)
{
}



// Function to split the list into two lists.
List List:: split(List List1)
{
    List temp;
}
```

```
// List iterator.
Item List:: iterator()
{
  struct Node * runner;
  int i = 0;

  runner = head;
  while(runner != 0)
     {
     // Process the contents of the node.
     cout << "Iterating\n";
     cout << setw(4) << runner->info;
     runner = runner ->next;
     cout << endl;
     }
  cout << endl;
}



/////////////////////////////////////////////////
// Function main() to illustrate the List class.
/////////////////////////////////////////////////
main()
{
  List List1(6);

  List1.insert(7);
  List1.iterator();
  List1.insert(8);
  List1.iterator();
  List1.insert(9);
  List1.iterator();
}
```

This is a first attempt at a description of a list class. Other organizations are possible. For example, we might wish to specify the relative location of the node in which an item of data is placed. In this situation, the **insert()** function might be replaced by the two functions

```
    insert_after (Item data, node N);
    insert_before (Item data, node N);
```

Alternatively, these two functions might be incorporated into a single **insert()** function which now would have the prototype

```
    int insert(Item data, Node n, int where);
```

In this case, the variable "**where**" should either be an enumeration type (**before**, **after**) or else an **int**.

For simplicity, we will consider only the simplest situation in our discussion and use the declaration in Example 5.8 as our guide.

5.5   Implementation of Lists Using Templates

Lists are easy to implement using templates. Example 5.10 provides a description of the class structure. It includes descriptions of two classes: a class called **List_Node** that provides a description of the contents of an arbirtrary node in the linked list, and a more complex class called **List** that includes the set of standard list operations. Example 5.11 provides the code for the member functions of objects of the class **List**.

Two classes are used in Example 5.10 because we wish to hide all details of the organization of a node from a function accessing an instance of the **List** object. Templates are used in both classes to aid in information hiding and to provide flexible code.

The object description presented in Example 5.10 is quite general. For instance, we have included two different functions that insert data into a list. These two member functions are called **insert_before()** and **insert_after()**. They reflect the way that insertions are used for stacks and queues, respectively. A similar organization is available for the functions that delete nodes from a list.

Example 5.10 Description of the class of singly linked lists using templates.

```
// File ex5_10.h
//
// This file contains three class descriptions.
// The first is for the class List_Node, which serves
// as the nodes of the linked list.
// The next class described here is the list itself.
// The final class described here is an iterator class.
// All three classes use templates.
//

// Define the class of nodes for the linked list class.

template <class T>  class List_Node
{
```

```
public:
  // Constructor
  List_Node (T, List_Node *);
  List_Node * insert(T);
  ~List_Node();
  T get_data();
private:
  T info;
  List_Node * next;
  List_Node * copy();
protected:
  friend class List<T>;
  friend class List_Iterator<T>;
};
```

```
// Constructor function for class List_Node.
template<class T>  List_Node<T>  ::List_Node(T val,
List_Node<T>  *p)

{
  info = val;
  next = p;
}
```

```
// Destructor.
template <class T>  List_Node<T>  :: ~List_Node()
{
  delete this;
}
```

```
// Examine the contents of a node.
template <class T>  T List_Node<T>  :: get_data()
{
  return info;
}
```

```
////////////////////////////////////////////
// Define the class List that uses the nodes
// defined in the class List_Node.
////////////////////////////////////////////
```

```
template <class T>  class List
{
public:
  // Constructor
  List()  {head = 0;} ;
  // Copy constructor
  List(const List & );
  //Destructor
  ~List();

  void remove_first();
  void insert(T value);
  void clear();
  int empty() const;
  T get_data();
  List_Node<T>  * head;
protected:
  friend class List<T>;
  friend List_Iterator<T>;
};



// Destructor.
template <class T>  List<T>  :: ~List()
{
  List_Node<T>  * temp = head;
  while (temp != 0)
     {
     head = temp;
     delete temp;
     temp = head->next;
     }
  head = 0;
}



// Makes a copy of each List_Node by following pointers.
template <class T>  List_Node<T>  * List_Node<T>:: copy()
{
  List_Node<T>  * temp;

  if (next != 0)
     temp = new List_Node<T>(info, next->copy());
  else
     temp = new List_Node<T>(info, 0);
```

```
    return temp;
}




/////////////////////////////////////////
// Define the iterator class.
/////////////////////////////////////////
template <class T>  class List_Iterator
{
public:
  List_Iterator( List<T>  &);
  void init();

  virtual int operator ++();
  void remove();
  void insert_before(T val);
  void insert_after(T val);
  List_Node <T>  *forward;
  List_Node<T>   *backward;
protected:
  List<T>  & List_Head;
};




// Constructor for List_Iterator class. It uses an
// initializer and then calls a function init.
template <class T>  List_Iterator<T>:: List_Iterator(
                List<T>  &list1): List_Head(list1)
{
}




template <class T>  void List_Iterator<T>:: init()
{
  backward = 0;
  forward = List_Head.head;
}




// Operator ++ to indicate moving through the nodes of
// a list one element at at time.
#include <iostream.h>
```

```
template <class T>  int List_Iterator<T>:: operator ++ ()
{
  if (forward == 0)
     {
     if (backward == 0)
        forward = List_Head.head;
     else
        forward = backward->next;
     }
  else
     {
     cout << forward->info << ' ' ;
     backward = forward;
     forward = forward->next;
     }
  return (forward !=0);
}



//Remove current node from list.
template <class T>  void List_Iterator<T>:: remove()
{
  if (backward == 0)
     List_Head.head = forward->next;
  else
     backward->next = forward->next;

  delete forward;
}



// Function to insert a node before the current node.
template <class T>  void List_Iterator<T>::
                                  insert_before(T value)
{
  // Insertion before the start of list.
  if (!backward)
     {
     List_Head.List<T>::insert(value);
     backward = List_Head.head;
     forward = backward->next;
     }
  else
     backward = backward->next;
}
```

```
// Function to insert after a node.
template <class T>  void List_Iterator<T>::
                                   insert_after(T value)
{
  // Insertion in normal situation.
  if (forward)
     forward->insert(value);

  // Insertion at end of list.
  else if (backward)
     forward = backward->insert(value);

  else // Insert at start list.
     List_Head.List<T>:: insert(value);
}
```

We now describe the member functions for the class **List**. Note the syntax of the function declarations, which illustrate the use of the template class, the return type, and the scope resolution operator. (Recall that the scope resolution operator is denoted by the symbol **::**.)

Example 5.11 Member functions for the class of singly linked lists (using templates).

```
// File ex5_11.cpp
//
// Template-based description of List class.
//


#include "ex5_10.h"
#include <iostream.h>


// Constructor for List_Node class.
template <class T>  List_Node<T>:: List_Node(T val,
                            List_Node<T>  *p)
{
  info = val;
  next = p;
}



// Insert function.
template <class T>  List_Node<T>  *List_Node<T>  ::
                            insert(T value)
```

```
{
  next = new List_Node<T>(value,next);
  return next;
}


// Constructor for List class.
template <class T>  List<T>:: List()
{
  head = 0;
}


// Copy constructor for List class.  It calls the
// recursive routine copy() for the class List_Node.
template <class T>  List<T>  :: List(const List<T>  & from)
{
  if (from.empty())
     head = 0;
  else
     {
     List_Node<T>  *temp  = from.head;
     head = temp-> copy();
     }
}



// Insert new List_Node at front of list.
template <class T>  void List<T>::insert(T val)
{
  head = new List_Node<T>(val, head);
}



// Function to determine if List is empty.
// Returns 1 if empty, 0 otherwise.
template <class T>  int List<T>  :: empty() const
{
  if (head == 0)
     return 1;
  else
     return 0;
}



// Function to return contents of first node in list.
template <class T>  T List<T>:: get_data()
```

```
{
  return (head->info) ;
}



// Remove first List_Node from head of list.
template <class T>  void List<T>:: remove_first()
{
  List_Node<T>  *temp = head;
  head = temp->next;
  delete temp;
}



//////////////////////////////////////////
// main() function to test the list class.
//////////////////////////////////////////

main()
{
  int i;
  List<int>  list1;
  List<float>  list2;
  List<char>  list3;
  List_Iterator<int>  list_it1(list1);

  for(i = 10; i > 0; i--)
     list1.insert(i);
  list1.insert(77);
  for (list_it1.init(); list_it1.forward != 0; ++list_it1)
     ; // All work is done in iterator.
  cout << endl << endl;
}
```

5.6 Using Lists with Sparse Matrices

Recall from Chapter 4 that we can develop an object-oriented description of a matrix class. In Section 4.4, we gave the following class description, which we repeat here for clarity.

```
     // The class Matrix.

     typedef int boolean;
```

```
class Matrix
{
public:
  int num_rows, num_columns;
  Matrix(); //Constructor
  ~Matrix (); // Destructor
  Matrix operator + (Matrix);
  Matrix operator - (Matrix);
  Matrix transpose ();
  Matrix operator * (Matrix);
  boolean conformable (Matrix);
  boolean same_dimension (Matrix);
};
```

The definitions of the member functions of this class were given in Section 4.4 in Examples 4.7 and 4.8 and will not be repeated here.

Developing matrices as objects provides a relatively easy way to have our classes efficiently treat one of the fundamental problems in applied linear algebra—operations on sparse matrices.

A *sparse matrix* is one in which most of the entries are 0. Two examples of sparse matrices are shown in Figures 5.3 and 5.4.

Figure 5.3 A sparse matrix.

```
1 0 0 0 0 0 0 0 0 0 0 0 0 0 0 0 0 0 0 0 0 1
0 1 0 0 0 0 0 0 0 0 0 0 0 0 0 0 0 0 0 0 1 0
0 0 1 0 0 0 0 0 0 0 0 0 0 0 0 0 0 0 0 0 0 0
0 0 0 1 0 0 0 0 0 0 0 0 0 0 0 0 0 0 0 0 0 0
0 0 0 0 1 0 0 0 0 0 0 0 0 0 0 0 0 0 0 0 0 0
0 0 0 0 0 1 0 0 0 0 0 0 0 0 0 0 0 0 0 0 0 0
0 0 0 0 0 0 1 0 0 0 0 0 0 0 0 0 0 0 0 0 0 0
0 0 0 0 0 0 0 1 0 0 0 0 0 0 0 0 0 0 0 0 0 0
0 0 0 0 0 0 0 0 1 0 0 0 0 0 0 0 0 0 0 0 0 0
0 0 0 0 0 0 0 0 0 1 0 0 0 0 0 0 0 0 0 0 0 0
0 0 0 0 0 0 0 0 0 0 1 0 0 0 0 0 0 0 0 0 0 0
0 0 0 0 0 0 0 0 0 0 0 1 0 0 0 0 0 0 0 0 0 0
0 0 0 0 0 0 0 0 0 0 0 0 1 0 0 0 0 0 0 0 0 0
0 0 0 0 0 0 0 0 0 0 0 0 0 1 0 0 0 0 0 0 0 0
0 0 0 0 0 0 0 0 0 0 0 0 0 0 1 0 0 0 0 0 0 0
0 0 0 0 0 0 0 0 0 0 0 0 0 0 0 1 0 0 0 0 0 0
0 0 0 0 0 0 0 0 0 0 0 0 0 0 0 0 1 0 0 0 0 0
0 0 0 0 0 0 0 0 0 0 0 0 0 0 0 0 0 1 0 0 0 0
0 0 0 0 0 0 0 0 0 0 0 0 0 0 0 0 0 0 1 0 0 0
0 0 0 0 0 0 0 0 0 0 0 0 0 0 0 0 0 0 0 1 0 0
0 0 0 0 0 0 0 0 0 0 0 0 0 0 0 0 0 0 0 0 1 0
0 0 0 0 0 0 0 0 0 0 0 0 0 0 0 0 0 0 0 0 0 1
```

Figure 5.4 Another sparse matrix.

1	4	0	0	0	0	0	0	0	0	0	0	0	0	0	0	0	0	0	0
4	1	4	0	0	0	0	0	0	0	0	0	0	0	0	0	0	0	0	0
0	4	1	4	0	0	0	0	0	0	0	0	0	0	0	0	0	0	0	0
0	0	4	1	4	0	0	0	0	0	0	0	0	0	0	0	0	0	0	0
0	0	0	4	1	4	0	0	0	0	0	0	0	0	0	0	0	0	0	0
0	0	0	0	4	1	4	0	0	0	0	0	0	0	0	0	0	0	0	0
0	0	0	0	0	4	1	4	0	0	0	0	0	0	0	0	0	0	0	0
0	0	0	0	0	0	4	1	4	0	0	0	0	0	0	0	0	0	0	0
0	0	0	0	0	0	0	4	1	4	0	0	0	0	0	0	0	0	0	0
0	0	0	0	0	0	0	0	4	1	4	0	0	0	0	0	0	0	0	0
0	0	0	0	0	0	0	0	0	4	1	4	0	0	0	0	0	0	0	0
0	0	0	0	0	0	0	0	0	0	4	1	4	0	0	0	0	0	0	0
0	0	0	0	0	0	0	0	0	0	0	4	1	4	0	0	0	0	0	0
0	0	0	0	0	0	0	0	0	0	0	0	4	1	4	0	0	0	0	0
0	0	0	0	0	0	0	0	0	0	0	0	0	4	1	4	0	0	0	0
0	0	0	0	0	0	0	0	0	0	0	0	0	0	4	1	4	0	0	0
0	0	0	0	0	0	0	0	0	0	0	0	0	0	0	4	1	4	0	0
0	0	0	0	0	0	0	0	0	0	0	0	0	0	0	0	4	1	4	0
0	0	0	0	0	0	0	0	0	0	0	0	0	0	0	0	0	4	1	4
0	0	0	0	0	0	0	0	0	0	0	0	0	0	0	0	0	0	4	1

Suppose that we wanted to add two sparse matrices of the same dimensions, say 20 by 20. Using the notations **a[i][j]** and **b[i][j]** for the entries in the ith row and jth column of matrices **a** and **b**, we would probably have a loop something like

```
for (i = 0; i < num_rows; i++);
    for (j = 0; j < num_columns; j++);
        c[i][j] = a[i][j] + b[i][j];
```

using the notation **c[i][j]** for the elements of matrix **c**. (The notation suggests an array implementation, but we do not wish to commit to this yet.)

Since **num_rows** and **num_columns** are both 20, the addition and the assignment statements in the inner loop are each executed 400 times. However, an examination of the sparse matrix shown in Figure 5.4 shows that there are only 20 entries on the longest diagonal and 19 entries on each of the two diagonals immediately above or below the longest diagonal. Thus we need to perform only 58 computations, since all other entries in the sum matrix are 0. The presentation and this loop cause a great increase in program execution time. This is also a waste of space—there is no need to store all these 0 entries.

In a sparse representation, a linked list or similar structure is often used to connect the non-zero entries. A typical organization of a node in such a linked list might be

```
struct node
{
  int row, column;
  double entry;
  struct node * next_row_element;
  struct node * next_column_element;
};
```

The space overhead of a node structure is the storage of an additional two **ints** and two pointers. This is negligible compared to the savings in space for matrices such as the ones shown in Figure 5.3 or 5.4.

The reduction in execution time is somewhat harder to estimate. For a first approximation, we assume that the time for any memory access is a constant, say M, which is the same for pointer access, assignment or any address calculation. Then the sparse representation of the array requires two pointer accesses for each entry together with the address used for the left-hand side of an assignment statement:

```
(2 + 2 + 2 + 1)M
```

for the sparse representation, compared to M+M+M, or 3M, for the non-sparse representation.

Thus for our example, the execution time is roughly

```
298 [7M + A]
```

where **A** represents the item for an addition. This compares favorably to the approximation:

```
1000 [3M + A]
```

for the running time of the loop for a non-sparse matrix. This is clearly much larger than the time needed for the sparse representation.

Note that the internal details of the representation of the array are hidden from the user. Thus a program that computed a determinant, say, of a sparse matrix; would have an identical interface with a program that computed a determinant of an array that uses the standard representation. This hiding of detail is a feature of C++ that we have seen several times before.

From a numerical analysis perspective, the approach here is more than adequate for both types of matrices, as long as we do not take computation times into account. You should note, however, that there are some types of problems in numerical linear algebra for which the abstraction here is not sufficient because different algorithmic techniques are needed for certain problems, not just better methods of performing arithmetic on different types of matrices. For more information on this point, see any book on analysis of algorithms such as those given in the references.

We now describe two possible methods of describing the class of sparse matrices. Note that the interface is the same as for ordinary (non-sparse) matrices, so that either one can be used in programs.

The first method involves including the location of the entries in the sparse matrix within the matrix entry data structure itself. This would probably be implemented as something like

```
struct Matrix_Entry
{
  int row, column;
  double contents;
  Matrix_Entry *next;
};
```

In this case, the sparse matrix would have a description such as

```
class Sparse_Matrix
{
private:
  int num_rows, num_columns;
  Matrix_Entry *matrix;
};
```

In this first method of organization, we are considering the matrix to be a linked list of elements that are accessed in linear order. Anything other than linear access order is likely to be inefficient.

The second method of organization makes use of the fact that many sparse matrices have the property that at least one element of each row is non-zero. In this case it is more logical to implement the sparse matrix as an array of pointers to rows, each of which is a linked list containing pointers to the non-zero entries in that row.

In this situation, a data structure might look like

```
struct Matrix_Entry
{
  int column;
  double contents;
  Matrix_Entry *next;
};
```

In this case the sparse matrix would have a description such as

```
class Sparse_Matrix
{
private:
  int num_rows, num_columns;
  Matrix_Entry **row_array;
};
```

Often sparse matrices that do not have this non-zero row property in each row have all the rows with all entries 0 appear in blocks, so that other techniques can be applied. Consult a modern book on linear algebra such as those suggested in the References for more information.

Our code examples are based on the first method of sparse matrices.

You should be aware of a trade-off in our development. The reduction in storage requirements and in loop iterations is balanced by the overhead of pointer management when using sparse matrices. In addition, we have very inefficient traversals of the matrix, because of the lack of ordering in the matrix. The implementation of the over-loaded + operator for sparse matrices illustrates this potential for inefficiency.

Example 5.12 Class description and member functions for the class **Sparse_Matrix**.

```
// File: ex5_12.h
//
// This file contains the class description and member
// functions for the Sparse_Matrix class.
//

#include <iostream.h>

typedef int boolean;


// Class Sparse_Matrix
class Sparse_Matrix
{
private:
  int num_rows, num_columns;
  struct Entry
    {
    int row, column;
    float value;
    Entry * next;
    } *entry;
  Entry * entry_start;
public:
  // Constructor function.
  Sparse_Matrix(int rows, int columns);
  // Destructor function.
  ~Sparse_Matrix();

  void init(int row, int column, float value);
  Sparse_Matrix operator + (Sparse_Matrix);
```

```
    boolean conformable (Sparse_Matrix);
    boolean same_dimension (Sparse_Matrix);
};



// Constructor function for the class Sparse_Matrix.
Sparse_Matrix :: Sparse_Matrix(int rows, int columns)
{
  num_rows = rows;
  num_columns = columns;
  entry_start = new Entry;
  entry_start->row = 0;
  entry_start->column = 0;
  entry_start->value = 0;
  entry_start->next = 0;
}



/////////////////////////////////////////
// Trivial destructor—does not release space.
Sparse_Matrix:: ~ Sparse_Matrix()
{
  num_rows = 0;
  num_columns = 0;
  delete entry_start;
}



/////////////////////////////////////////////////
// Initializes the contents of the given row and
// column to the third argument.
/////////////////////////////////////////////////
void Sparse_Matrix::init(int row, int column, float val)
{
  struct Entry *temp;

  temp = entry_start;
  while (temp != 0)
    if ((temp->row != row) && (temp->column != column))
      temp = temp->next;
  // If found, assign value to this row and column.
  if (temp != 0)
    temp->value = val;
```

```
    else // insert after start for lack of better place.
     {
     temp = new Entry;
     temp->row = row;
     temp->column = column;
     temp->value = val;
     temp->next = entry_start->next;
     entry_start->next = temp;
     }
cout << temp->row << ' '<< temp->column<< ' ' << val;
}




/////////////////////////////////////////////////////
// Tests if argument has same dimensions as the object.

boolean Sparse_Matrix :: same_dimension (Sparse_Matrix a)
{
  if ((a.num_rows == num_rows)
                    && (a.num_columns == num_columns))
    return 1;
  else
    return 0;
}




/////////////////////////////////////////////////////
// Tests if argument can be multiplied by the object.
// NOTE: no multiplication is done member functions.
/////////////////////////////////////////////////////
boolean Sparse_Matrix :: conformable (Sparse_Matrix a)
{
  if (a.num_columns == num_rows)
    return 1;
  else
    return 0;
}




//////////////////////////////////////////////
// Adds argument to object.
// Assume matrices are of same dimension.
Sparse_Matrix Sparse_Matrix :: operator + (Sparse_Matrix a)
{
  Sparse_Matrix C(a.num_rows, a.num_columns);
```

```
          int i,j;
          struct Entry *temp_a, *temp_b, *temp_c, *temp;

          C.num_rows = a.num_rows;
          C.num_columns = a.num_columns;
          temp_a = a.entry_start; // first arg's entry_start
          temp_b = entry_start ; // object's entry_start
          temp_c = C.entry_start;  // return's entry_start

       while (temp_b != 0)
         {
         // Assign object's nonzero entries to C.
         temp_c->value = temp_b->value;
         temp_c->row = temp_b->row;
         temp_c->column = temp_b->column;
         temp_c->next = temp_b->next;
         temp_b = temp_b->next;
         temp_c = temp_c->next;
         }

       // Reinitialize pointer to C's data.
       temp_c = C.entry_start;
       // Now add elements of argument's matrix to C.
       while (temp_a != 0)
         {
         // Use linear search on C.
         temp_c = C.entry_start;
         while ((temp_c->row != temp_a->row) &&
                 (temp_c->column != temp_a->column) &&
                 (temp_c != 0))
          temp_c = temp_c->next;

         if (temp_c != 0) // Found a match of row, column
          temp_c->value += temp_b->value;
         else // Make a new entry in C.
           {
           temp = new Entry;
           temp->row = temp_a->row;
           temp->column = temp_a->column;
           temp->value = temp_a->value;
           temp->next = C.entry_start->next;
           C.entry_start->next = temp;
           }
         temp_a = temp_a->next;
         }
       return C;
      }
```

Example 5.13 Driver function for the class of sparse matrices.

```
// FILE ex5_13.cpp
//
// Contains a main driver
// function for the class Sparse_Matrix.
//

#include "ex5_12.h"


// Function main() to illustrate the use of the
// class Sparse_Matrix.
main()
{
  float x;
  int i, j;
  Sparse_Matrix m1(20,10),m2(20,10);

  m1.init(2, 5, 3.14);
  m1.init(5, 2, 6.28);
  m2.init(5, 2, 6.28);
  m2 = m1 + m2;
}
```

There is another problem with our development of sparse matrices. The user of such a matrix must identify the matrix as being of the proper type (sparse or standard) and we have not described any way of combining the two organizations. Overloading the + operator requires us to consider statements such as

```
C = A + B;
```

where **A** might be a standard matrix and **B** might be sparse. There are many more combinations that must be tested.

Perhaps the easiest way is to define a new matrix class that inherits from both the standard matrix and sparse matrix class. We will consider this in the Exercises.

5.7   Queues in C++

It is easy to implement queues as abstract data types in C++. The approach is the same one that we have used for the other data types that have been discussed previously in this book—list the set of allowable operations.

The most common operations that can be performed on a queue are:

- create the queue
- delete a queue
- determine if the queue is empty
- insert an element into the queue
- delete an element from the queue
- merge two queues
- split a queue into two queues

Note that a queue is like a stack in that the method of access is fixed. Data in a queue must be inserted and removed in a first-in, first-out manner. Thus we do not have to consider the different possibilities for the insert and delete operations as we did with linked lists. An illustration of the action of a queue is given in Figure 5.5. Compare this with the illustration of the action of a stack that was given in Figure 5.1.

Figure 5.5 A queue.

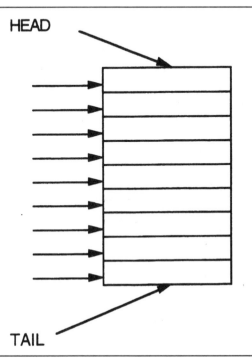

The initial description of the class **Queue** is given in Example 5.14. As was the case in our treatment of linked lists, the merge and split operations will be discussed in the Exercises.

Example 5.14 Description of the class **Queue**.

```
// FILE: ex5_14.h
//
// This is the class description of the class Queue
// for queue manipulation - non-template version.
// The code in this file is a slight modification
// of the code for the non-template implementation
// for the List class given in the file List.h (ex5_8.h).
//

#include <iostream.h>
#include <iomanip.h>

typedef int Item;


class Queue
{
public:
  Queue(Item data);
  ~Queue();
  int empty();
  void insert(Item data);
  Item remove();
  Item iterator();
private:
  struct Node
    {
    Item info;
    struct Node * previous;
    struct Node *next;
    };
  struct Node *front; // head of queue
  struct Node *rear; // rear of queue
};




// Constructor function.
Queue:: Queue(Item data)
```

```
{
  Node * temp;
  temp = new Node;
  temp->info = data;
  temp->next = 0;
  temp->previous = 0;
  front = rear = temp;
}




// Destructor function.
Queue:: ~Queue()
{
  struct Node *runner, *trailer;

  for(trailer = front; trailer != 0; trailer = runner)
    {
    runner = trailer->next;
    trailer->next = 0;
    delete trailer;
    }
}




// Function tests if queue is empty.
// Returns 1 if queue is empty, 0 otherwise.
int Queue :: empty()
{
  if (front == rear == 0)
    return 1;
  else
    return 0;
}




// Insert function—inserts at rear of queue.
void Queue:: insert(Item data)
{
  struct Node * temp;

  temp = new Node;
  temp->info = data;
```

```
    temp->previous = rear;
    temp->next = 0;
    rear->next = temp;
    rear =temp;
    cout << "Done insert of "<< data << endl;
}




// Remove an item from the front of the queue.
Item Queue:: remove()
{
    Item data;
    struct Node *temp;

    data = front->info;
    temp = front->next;
    temp->previous = 0;
    delete front;
    front = temp;
    return data;
}




// Queue iterator — prints contents of queue
// from front to rear and returns contents of rear.
Item Queue:: iterator()
{
    struct Node * runner;
    Item temp_data;

    runner = front;
    temp_data = -999;   // Indicates queue is empty.
    while(runner != 0)
      {
      // Process the contents of the nodes.
      cout << "Iterating the queue." << endl;
      cout << setw(4) << runner->info;
      temp_data = runner->info;
      runner = runner ->next;
      }
    cout << endl;
    return temp_data;
}
```

The implementation of the methods for the class **Queue** is given in Example 5.15.

Example 5.15 Driver function for a non-template version class of the class **Queue**.

```
// FILE: ex5_15.cpp
//
// This file contains the implementation of
// the driver function for the non-template-based
// queue class.
//

#include "ex5_14.h"
#include <iostream.h>


main()
{
  Queue q(-1);
  int i;

  for (i = 0; i < 5; i++)
    {
    q.insert(i);
    cout<< "Iteration " << i<< ", the queue is :"<< endl;
    q.iterator();
    cout << endl <<endl;
    }

  for (i = 0; i < 3; i++)
    {
    cout << "Now remove elements and iterate." << endl;
    cout << "Removed:" << q.remove() << endl;
    q.iterator();
    }
}
```

5.8   Implementation of Queues Using Templates

Not surprisingly, queues are also easy to implement using templates. One possible class description is given in Example 5.16. This organization is based on the code presented in the previous section, without using an iterator function.

Example 5.16 Description of the class **Queue** using templates.

```cpp
// FILE: ex5_16.cpp
//
// Template-based Queue class.
//

#include "ex5_10.h"

template <class T>  class Queue
{
public:
  Queue(T data);
  ~Queue();
  int empty();
  void insert(T data);
  T remove();
private:
  struct Node
    {
    T info;
    struct Node * previous;
    struct Node *next;
    };
  struct Node *front; // head of queue
  struct Node *rear; // rear of queue
};




// Constructor function.
template<class T>  Queue<T> :: Queue(T data)
{
  Node * temp;

  temp = new Node;
  temp->info = data;
  temp->next = 0;
  temp->previous = 0;
  front = rear = temp;
}




// Destructor function.
template <class T>  Queue<T> :: ~Queue()
{
  struct Node *runner, *trailer;
```

```
      for(trailer = front; trailer != 0; trailer = runner)
        {
        runner = trailer->next;
        trailer->next = 0;
        delete trailer;
        }
    }




    // Function tests if queue is empty.
    // Returns 1 if queue is empty, 0 otherwise.
    template <class T>  int Queue<T>  :: empty()
    {
      if (front == rear == 0)
        return 1;
      else
        return 0;
    }




    // Insert function— inserts at rear of queue.
    template <class T>  void Queue<T> :: insert(T data)
    {
      struct Node * temp;

      temp = new Node;
      temp->info = data;
      temp->previous = rear;
      temp->next = 0;
      rear->next = temp;
      rear = temp;
      cout << "Done insert of "<< data << endl;
    }




    // Remove an item from the front of the queue.
    template <class T>  T Queue<T> :: remove()
    {
      T data;
      struct Node *temp;

      data = front->info;
      temp = front->next;
      temp->previous = 0;
```

```
    delete front;
    front = temp;
    return data;
}
```

Since the development of queues was so easy, we should consider the possibility of other organizations that might even be simpler. Let's try to reuse some of the code we have already developed for linked lists.

We have one important feature to include in order to describe—access to the end of the list. There are two obvious ways to do this. We can use a list iterator to get to the last entry in a list and then set the rear of the list to point to this element. Alternatively, we can include a new pointer as part of our data structure.

In either event, a new class description might look something like one of the two following outlines:

```
// One possible outline of template-based Queue class
// making as much use as possible of the previously
// developed List class.

#include "list.h"    // list.h —template version

template <class T>  class Queue
{
private:
  List<T> ;
public:
  void insert(const T &data) {insert_at_rear(data);}
  int remove(T &data) {remove_from_front(data);}
};

// Another possible outline of template-based Queue class
// making as much use as possible of the previously
// developed List class.

#include "list.h"    // list.h —template version

template <class T>  class Queue
{
private:
  List<T> ;
  List_node<T>  * rear;
public:
  void insert(const T &data) {insert_after(rear, data);}
  int remove(T &data) {remove_from_front(data);}
};
```

The simplicity of these class descriptions illustrates the power of object-oriented programming in C++.

5.9 The Tree Data Type in C++

We begin this section by reviewing the definition of an abstract binary tree. A tree is either empty or is composed of a node and two subtrees, each of which is also a tree. A node which is not part of any nontrivial subtree is called the *root*.

Figure 5.6 illustrates the general organization of a tree.

The definition of a tree suggests some operations that can be performed on a tree:

- create the tree
- delete the tree
- determine if the tree is empty
- add an element to the tree
- delete an element from the tree
- merge two trees into a single tree
- split a tree into two different trees

Figure 5.6 A typical tree.

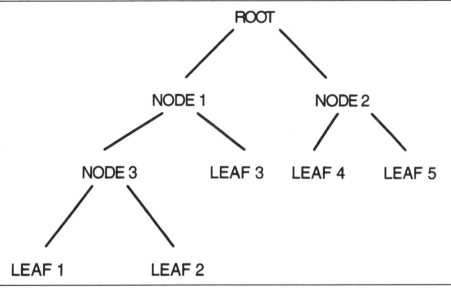

We assume that the data stored in the tree is of type **Item**, which we assume has been previously declared. As before, the merge and split operations will be discussed in the Exercises.

The description of a **Tree** class might look something like the following:

Example 5.17 A description of a **Tree** class.

```
// FILE ex5_17.h
//
// Description of non-template-based Tree class.
//

#include <iostream.h>
#include <iomanip.h>

typedef int Item;


class Tree_Node
{
friend class Tree;

public:
  Tree_Node(const Item &);
  Item process();
private:
  Tree_Node *left;
  Item info;
  Tree_Node *right;
};


// Constructor function for Tree_Node, which will
// hold nodes of Tree.
Tree_Node:: Tree_Node(const Item &data)
{
  info = data;
  left = 0;
  right = 0;
}



// Get information stored in Tree_Node. This simple
// function just prints the contents of the node.
Item Tree_Node:: process()
```

```
{
  cout << setw(4) << info;
  return info;
}



//////////////////////////////////////////
// Definition of class Tree.
//////////////////////////////////////////

class Tree
{
public:
  Tree();
  void insert(const Item &);

  // Traversal functions available to outside world.
  void preorder();
  void postorder();
  void inorder();

private:
  Tree_Node * root;
  void insert_Node(Tree_Node ** , const Item &);

  // Traversal functions available only to member functions.
  void preorder_Node(Tree_Node *);
  void postorder_Node(Tree_Node *);
  void inorder_Node(Tree_Node *);
};



// Constructor function for class Tree without templates.
Tree ::Tree()
{
  root = 0;
}



// Insertion function for trees using insert_Node
// function for trees.
void Tree :: insert(const Item & val)
{
  insert_Node(&root, val);
}
```

```
// Lower-level node insertion function to insert
// data into the tree in "sorted order," assuming
// that the relational operators < and >  are properly
// overloaded for the Item data type.

void Tree:: insert_Node(Tree_Node **p, const Item & val)
{
  if (*p == 0)  // Node set is empty.
    {
    *p = new Tree_Node(val);
    (*p)->left = (*p)->right = 0;
    }
  else
    {
    if (val < (*p)->info)
     insert_Node(& ((*p)->left), val);
    else // value is greater than or equal to contents
     insert_Node(& ((*p)->right), val);
    }
}




////////////////////////////////////////////////////////
// Tree traversal functions.  For each type of traversal
// (inorder, preorder, postorder), the higher-level
// function is followed by a lower-level function for
// doing the actual work of the traversal.
////////////////////////////////////////////////////////

void Tree :: preorder()
{
  preorder_Node(root);
}


void Tree :: preorder_Node(Tree_Node *p)
{
  if (p)
    {
    (*p).process();
    preorder_Node(p->left);
    preorder_Node(p->right);
    }
}

/////////////////////////////
```

```
void Tree :: postorder()
{
  postorder_Node(root);
}


void Tree :: postorder_Node(Tree_Node *p)
{
  if (p)
    {
    postorder_Node(p->left);
    postorder_Node(p->right);
    (*p).process();
    }
}

/////////////////////////////

void Tree :: inorder()
{
  inorder_Node(root);
}


void Tree :: inorder_Node(Tree_Node *p)
{
  if (p)
    {
    inorder_Node(p->left);
    (*p).process();
    inorder_Node(p->right);
    }
}
```

As was the case with linked lists, we have made no assumptions about data storage.

A main program to use this direct implementation of the methods without using inheritance might look something like Example 5.18.

Example 5.18 Member functions for the **Tree** class—non-template version.

```
// FILE ex5_18.cpp
//
// Non-template tree member functions.
//
```

```
#include "ex5_17.h"
#include <iostream.h>
#include <iomanip.h>

typedef int Item;


//
// Main function to illustrate the use of the Tree class.
//

main()
{
  Tree tree1;
  int value1, i;

  cout << "Enter 10 integer values." << endl;

  for (i = 0; i < 10 ; i++)
    {
    cin >> value1;
    tree1.insert(value1);
    }
  cout << "Preorder traversal:" << setw(3) << endl;
  tree1.preorder();
  cout << endl <<"Inorder traversal:" << endl;
  tree1.inorder();
  cout << endl << "Postorder traversal:" << endl;
  tree1.postorder() ;
}
```

5.10 Implementation of Trees Using Templates

Trees are easy to implement using templates. Unfortunately, binary trees require two links from a node of the tree (one to each of two possible children). Thus we will not be able to use our abstract linked list class as a basis for the organization of a tree.

However, we can write a template-based class description of trees using the recursive definition of trees. The basic idea might look something like Example 5.19.

Example 5.19 Description of the class **Tree** using templates.

```cpp
// FILE ex5_19.h
//
// Contains class definitions for nodes and trees
// using templates.
//

#include <iostream.h>
#include <iomanip.h>


///////////////////////////////////
// Definition of class Tree_Node.
///////////////////////////////////

template<class T>  class Tree_Node
{
friend class Tree<T> ;

public:
  Tree_Node(const T &);
  T process();
private:
  Tree_Node *left;
  T info;
  Tree_Node *right;
};


// Constructor function for Tree_Node, which will
// hold parameterized nodes of Tree.
template<class T>  Tree_Node<T> :: Tree_Node(const T &data)
{
  info = data;
  left = 0;
  right = 0;
}


// Get information stored in Tree_Node. This simple
// function just prints the contents of the node.
template<class T>  T Tree_Node<T> :: process()
{
  cout << setw(4) << info;
  return info;
}
```

```
/////////////////////////////////////
// Definition of class Tree.
/////////////////////////////////////

template <class T>  class Tree
{
public:
  Tree();
  void insert(const T &);

  // Traversal functions available to outside world.
  void preorder();
  void postorder();
  void inorder();

private:
  Tree_Node <T>  * root;
  void insert_Node(Tree_Node<T> **, const T &);

  // Traversal functions available only to member functions.
  void preorder_Node(Tree_Node<T>  *);
  void postorder_Node(Tree_Node<T>  *);
  void inorder_Node(Tree_Node<T>  *);
};



// Constructor function for class Tree using templates.
template<class T>  Tree<T>  ::Tree()
{
  root = 0;
}



// Insertion function for trees using insert_Node
// function for trees.
template<class T>  void Tree<T>  :: insert(const T & val)
{
  insert_Node(&root, val);
}



// Lower-level node insertion function to insert
// data into the tree in "sorted order," assuming
// that the relational operators < and >  are properly
// overloaded for this template class.
```

```
template<class T>  void Tree<T>  :: insert_Node(
                        Tree_Node <T>  **p,
                        const T & val)
{
  if (*p == 0)  // Node set is empty.
    {
    *p = new Tree_Node<T>(val);
    (*p)->left = (*p)->right = 0;
    }
  else
    {
    if (val < (*p)->info)
      insert_Node(& ((*p)->left), val);
    else // value is greater than or equal to contents
      insert_Node(& ((*p)->right), val);
    }
}


/////////////////////////////////////////////////////
// Tree traversal functions.  For each type of traversal
// (inorder, preorder, postorder), the higher-level
// function is followed by a lower-level function for
// doing the actual work of the traversal.
/////////////////////////////////////////////////////

template<class T>  void Tree<T>  :: preorder()
{
  preorder_Node(root);
}


template<class T>  void Tree<T>  :: preorder_Node(Tree_Node<T> *p)
{
  if (p)
    {
    (*p).process();
    preorder_Node(p->left);
    preorder_Node(p->right);
    }
}

/////////////////////////////

template<class T> void Tree<T> :: postorder()
{
  postorder_Node(root);
}
```

```
template<class T> void Tree<T> :: postorder_Node(Tree_Node<T> *p)
{
  if (p)
    {
    postorder_Node(p->left);
    postorder_Node(p->right);
    (*p).process();
    }
}

///////////////////////////////

template<class T> void Tree<T> :: inorder()
{
  inorder_Node(root);
}


template<class T> void Tree<T> :: inorder_Node(Tree_Node<T> *p)
{
  if (p)
    {
    inorder_Node(p->left);
    (*p).process();
    inorder_Node(p->right);
    }
}
```

A main driver program for a typical implementation of this class is shown in Example 5.20.

Example 5.20 A template-based implementation of trees.

```
//
// FILE ex5_20.cpp
//
// This file illustrates the use of the template-based
// tree class given in the file ex5_19.h.
//

#include <iostream.h>
#include <iomanip.h>
#include "ex5_19.h"      //tree.h
```

```
//
// Main function to illustrate the use of the Tree class.
//

main()
{
  Tree<int> tree1;
  Tree<float> tree2; // Not used - for illustration only.
  int value1, i;
  float value2; // Not used.

  cout << "Enter 10 integer values." << endl;

  for (i = 0; i < 10 ; i++)
    {
    cin >> value1;
    tree1.insert(value1);
    }
  cout << "Preorder traversal:" << setw(3) << endl;
  tree1.preorder();
  cout << endl <<"Inorder traversal:" << endl;
  tree1.inorder();
  cout << endl << "Postorder traversal:" << endl;
  tree1.postorder() ;
}
```

5.11   The Standard
C and C++ Libraries

One way to make the process of writing programs more efficient is to reuse existing software components when they are appropriate for your application. One obvious place to look for a reusable software component is the standard library included with your C++ compiler.

Since C++ is essentially a superset of C, we will begin our discussion of standard libraries with the standard C library. This is the set of functions and macros whose interfaces and functionality are specified as comprising the ANSI C standard library. The contents of this library can be determined by looking at the standard header files. The header files are listed in Table 5.1. A detailed listing of the contents of this library is given in Appendix 4.

Table 5.1 Header files for the standard C library.

Header File	Function Prototypes
`assert.h`	No
`ctype.h`	Yes
`errno.h`	No
`float.h`	No
`limits.h`	No
`locale.h`	Yes
`math.h`	Yes
`setjmp.h`	Yes
`signal.h`	Yes
`stdarg.h`	No
`stddef.h`	No
`stdio.h`	Yes
`stdlib.h`	Yes
`string.h`	Yes
`time.h`	Yes

The ANSI C standard has greatly aided the development of portable C programs. Unfortunately, there is no such thing as a standard C++ library at the time that this book is being written. The standardization process is relatively far along, and there is some consensus of the likely organization of any standard library for C++.

In the case of C++, the relevant committee is the C++ working group of the X3J16 standards committee. The first working paper available for public consumption was provided in late January 1994 and is subject to considerable review.

There are several references that you should consult for more information about the standards for a C++ class library. Each of them provides far more information than can be given in a brief appendix.

The recent book by Plauger provides a readily available, complete discussion of the standard library. It also presents excellent insights into the issues involved for library implementers.

The relevant electronic correspondence of the C++ working group can be found in several files available from **research.att.com** via anonymous **ftp**. Unfortunately, there is no intention of providing an on-line version of the proposed standard (or rationale for decisions made when creating the standard) at this point.

The Internet news group **comp.std.c++** also contains helpful information on standards for C++. It is much more focused on standards than is **comp.lang.c++**, which is a general-purpose news group.

One of the major difficulties encountered by the standards committee is the need for backward compatibility with C. This has influenced the development of standard libraries.

The principles used to relate the draft ANSI C++ and existing ANSI C standard libraries are as follows:

- Allow the use of C library functions in C++ programs without change, unless their use conflicts with standards for type checking and protection in C++.
- Many of the changes in the semantics of standard library functions between C and C++ involve the distinction between constant and non-constant pointers. Thus an argument of type

```
char * p;
```

in ANSI C should be replaced by the argument type

```
const char * p;
```

in several C++ implementations of C library functions.
- C library functions cannot be used in programs without the appropriate C include files.
- When a C construct conflicts with a C++ construct, the C++ construct takes precedence. For example, the construct **wchar_t** that is used for wide characters in the C header files **stddef.h** and **stdlib.h,** is a reserved word in C++ and thus may not be defined in any header file.
- There are sequencing problems when C and C++ I/O functions are used in the same program. (We discussed these problems earlier.)
- Other constructions in C, such as **malloc()** and **free()** may not work well when used with the C++ operators **new** and **delete**. (We also discussed these problems earlier.)
- Conditional compilation, such as

```
#ifdef __cplusplus
// C++ code here
#else
/* C code here */
#endif
```

may help in spots. However, it can make programs very hard to read because this technique obscures program control.

There are new header files in the draft ANSI C++ library. Note that the new header files that access portions of the standard C++ library do not end in the **.h** extension. The new header files are:

bits	for bit operations such as masking
bitstring	for compact storage of bit strings
complex	for complex numbers
defines	for common definitions (also called **stddef**)
dynarray	for common template-based storage of arrays
exception	for exceptions
fstream	for I/O streams using files
iomanip	for manipulation of I/O streams
ios	the base class for I/O streams
iostream	for I/O streams
istream	for input streams
new	for the operator new with scope resolution
ostream	for output streams
ptrdynarray	for pointers to template-based storage of arrays
stddef	for common definitions (also called defines)
sstream	for I/O streams in memory using strings effectively
streambuf	for I/O streams operations
string	for common definitions and operations on strings
strstream	for I/O streams in memory
typeinfo	for common definitions (also called **defines**)
wstring	for strings of wide characters

There are some proposed changes to C header files in order to make C (and C++) programs that use them consistent with C++ programming standards. For more information, see Appendix 5 or the reference by Plauger.

Unfortunately, there is no mention of implementations of the data structures studied in this chapter in the proposed standard C++ class libraries. This will create some problems for code portability in the future. We will briefly discuss one vendor's class libraries in the next section.

5.12   Other C++ Class Libraries

You should be aware that most C++ implementations have substantial class libraries associated with them. Certainly the class library is too large to have a simple file structure and is almost certain to be organized hierarchically. The description of an object is likely to be split into at least two files: a header file containing the description of the objects, and files that contain the implementation code for the member functions of the objects. (The implementation code is often included in both source code and object code formats.)

The class library will often be organized to reflect the object hierarchy to make it easy to find related objects. Thus we will be likely to have at least two parallel hierarchical organizations (header files for class descriptions and files containing the code for the member functions).

A class library is often quite complex in its organization. This is a result of three primary factors: the richness of its objects, the need for compatibility with previous versions, and the desire to have the objects in the class library make efficient use of existing objects so that they can inherit essential functions from previously developed classes.

For example, the Borland C++ system for computers running MS-DOS or Microsoft Windows includes the following data structures as part of the large set of objects in its class library:

- B-trees
- bags
- deques
- hash tables
- lists (singly linked)
- lists (doubly linked)
- queues (priority)
- queues (regular)
- sets
- stacks
- trees

Some of the data structures listed above may be unfamiliar to you. Don't worry about the unfamiliar ones; we will concentrate on the data structures that we discussed earlier in this chapter. For more information about the data structures listed above, consult the references or any good book on data structures.

Let's examine these data structures from the perspective of software reuse. Note that many of the functions that can be applied to lists can also be applied to other data structures. The creation and destruction of a list are simply the common constructor and destructor functions that we have seen many times before. The insertion and deletion operations are also included as part of nearly all other data structures. For these reasons, an object such as a stack or a queue is often defined in terms of an abstract list object.

For example, this is precisely the organization of the Borland C++ class library. The fundamental building block for the data structures in this library is the container class.

A C++ container class starts out empty. When objects are placed in the container, by default they are owned by the container. The objects are destroyed when the container is destroyed.

The classes stack, deque, queue, and priority queue have the following properties:

- The order of insertions and deletions is significant.
- Insertions and extractions can occur only at specific points, as defined by the individual class.

In Turbo C++ terminology, these container classes are known collectively as *sequence classes*. Note that a hash table does not fit the description of a sequence class. Neither does the set data structure.

Another class that can be derived from the abstract container class is a collection class. Examples of collection classes are the unordered collections:

- bag
- hash table
- list (singly or doubly linked)
- abstract array

The collection class has a new feature that the container class did not—it is possible to determine if an object belongs to an object of a collection class by using a member function that tests data for inclusion.

This level of abstraction can be extended considerably. Additional features, such as ordering of the container class, can be used to describe sorted arrays, B-trees, or other structures.

Abstract data types serve as the basis for the organization of the portion of the class library devoted to basic data structures.

The abstract data types stacks, queues, deques, bags, sets, and arrays can be implemented in several different ways using the fundamental data structures vector, list, and DoubleList. Thus, all ADTs are implemented as vectors. In addition, stacks are implemented as a list; queues and deques are implemented as doubly linked lists.

For a variety of reasons, the data structures are implemented in two ways: with direct access to the structure and with indirect access using pointers. Additional functions are given so that the near and far pointers of different 80×86 architectures can be accommodated. (Recall that the terms *near pointer* and *far pointer* refer to the referenced object being within 64K memory segments in this architecture.)

For example, there are two implementations of the stack data structure. The functions

```
BI_OStackAsVector()
```

and

```
BI_TCStackAsVector()
```

refer, respectively, to a stack of pointers to a base class named **Object** and a polymorphic stack of pointers to the base class **Object**. In each case, the implementation is done as a vector. The prefix BI indicates that these functions use what is called the "Borland International;" the O indicates that the code is object-based (nonpolymorphic); and the TC indicates that the code is object-based and compatible with earlier versions of the Turbo C++ class library.

The instantiation using **typedef** statements such as

```
typedef BI_StackAsVector<int> intStack;
```

and

```
typedef BI_StackAsList<int> intStack;
```

are typical of the fine-tuning allowed for data types in this class library.

Each of the data structures is implemented using templates. Each template must be instantiated with a particular data type, which is the type of the element that the data structure will hold. A linked list of objects of type T will include code that looks something like the following:

```
template <class T> class BI_ListImp
{
public:
  void add( T t ) { new BI_ListElement<T>( t, &head );}
  // Add objects at head of list
  T peekHead() const { return head.next->data; }
};
```

What else should you expect to find in a class library? The proper treatment of strings is slightly delicate and requires careful design of objects. Thus you are likely to find a **string** object included in a basic class library. There will usually be a class to describe complex numbers.

Implementations that make heavy use of a target computer's operating system are likely to have objects to represent several operating system functions. These might include access to the system clock, facilities to monitor the performance of running programs, or an interface to the graphical user interface. On an 80×86-based personal computer running Microsoft Windows or an Apple Macintosh, the class library is likely to include access to pop-up and pull-down menus, as well as the ability to locate and configure windows. The same interface to the graphical user interface is expected on class libraries intended for use in a UNIX environment running X-Windows.

There is another way to get access to class libraries electronically. At least one version is available on the Internet using the the Mosaic browser from the National Center for Supercomputing Applications (NCSA). At the time that this book was written, a description of a class library was available from the home page

```
http://info.desy.de/usr/projects/c++.html/
```

Much more information is likely to be available by the time this book appears in print.

Note that there are many objects declared in typical class libraries and that it is very likely that a large portion of the lower-level programming has already been done for you.

The ready availability of class libraries suggests a natural question—how do we replace portions of an existing class library by some of our own code? Using a name such as **list.h** for a header file in your program means that you are including the local header file rather than a system-supplied file of the same name. We can reduce confusion in systems by using include statements such as

```
#include <list.h>
```

instead of

```
#include "list.h"
```

to specify use of a special directory for header files rather than a user-defined directory.

We can also use the C++ preprocessor statements **#ifdef**, **#ifndef**, **#define**, and **#endif** as in the code fragment

```
#ifndef LIST_NULL
#define LIST_NULL 0

#ifndef LIST_H
#define LIST_H
   // body of the definition goes here.

#endif
```

to make clear precisely which files and constants we wish to use in our program.

This technique is called *conditional compilation* and is especially useful when you are developing programs in a changing software environment. For illustrations of the use of conditional compilation in the rapidly changing area of different implementations of the UNIX operating system, see the UNIX books by myself or Stevens listed in the references.

Summary

C++ has many facilities for data abstraction that are not available in C. Even for simple structured data types, the C++ class construction is much more powerful than the C **typedef** construction because it allows the user to indicate explicitly which operations are allowed on the data type.

C++ also allows the use of a template, or parameterized class. A template allows the use of the member functions of a class by several different classes. Thus templates allow us to have a single stack class type instead of a stack of **ints**, stack of character pointers, etc.

The fundamental data structures of stacks, lists, queues, and trees are relatively easy to implement in C++. They become even more powerful when implemented using templates. Templates allow the use of the same code for multiple types of data. Templates require the availability of default constructors (constructors with no arguments).

The class descriptions presented in this chapter illustrate some of the basic issues of object-oriented data abstraction and programming in C++. The code is correct and works reasonably well.

However, most programmers are probably more likely to use the existing objects in a class library than to develop their own from scratch. This approach supports the goal of software reuse, which is a key to increasing programmer productivity. Reusability of code is a major goal of experienced C++ programmers.

EXERCISES

1. Examine the class library for your C++ system to determine if templates are available. If they are available, which of the fundamental data structures are implemented using templates?

2. Write C++ code for the **Stack** data structure in the text using templates and the more abstract features of linked lists presented in Section 5.4.

3. Rewrite the stack code using the abstract array class that we developed in Chapter 4.

4. Rewrite the queue code using the abstract array class that we developed in Chapter 4.

5. Many class libraries allow multiple representation of objects in a similar manner to the Borland C++ class library. Examine the class library on your system and determine if there are multiple representations. If there are, write a small C++ program to initialize a data structure and print the contents of the structure. Initialize the structure, access the contents, and print them using the two different representations.

6. Choose one of the data structures in your system's class library. Rewrite one of the member functions and be sure to include an output statement so that you can tell if your function is being called. Test your new function within a C++ program to see which one is used.

7. Choose one of the data structures in this chapter and determine all possible places for the use of the **assert()** function. Tell if the use of this function makes your code easier to develop.

8. Other operations are possible for the data structures discussed in this chapter. For example, we can merge two lists into one or we can split a single list into two separate ones. Which of the other data structures discussed in this chapter can have the merge and split operations applied to them?

9. Implement methods (member functions) for the merge and split operations for the data structures that you indicated in the previous exercise. After writing the member functions, examine your system's class library to determine if the merge and split operations were already included in the class description. (If your class library contains source code, indicate how the implementations differ.)

10. Implement member functions for each of the two suggested implementations of sparse matrices suggested in this chapter. Perform what is often known as a DAXPY operation (double precision matrix add and multiply) of the form

    A * X + Y

    Use a very large value for the number of rows and columns of the sparse array **A**. The matrices **X** and **Y** should have one column each. Determine which of the two implementations of sparse matrices is faster.

11. Determine a set of appropriate test cases if we combine the standard matrix operations with those of sparse matrices. Consider all possible cases of overloading the + and * operators. Indicate how you would provide test drivers for your testing.

12. We developed sparse matrices using matrix contents that were of type **double**. However, matrices whose entries are of type **int** are also important in many applications. Extend the sparse matrix implementation to include entries of type **int** by rewriting the code to use templates.

13. Extend the previous exercise to use matrices whose entries belong to the user-defined type class **Complex**.

14. Describe a class **General_Matrix** that can inherit from both the **Matrix** and **Sparse_Matrix** classes. To keep things simple, just consider constructors, destructors, and the two member functions **conformable()** and **same_dimension()**.

C H A P T E R

Advanced Input and Output

6.1   Input and Output in C and C++

Input and output are not part of the C++ programming language, just as they were not "officially" part of the C language. However, general-purpose programming languages are not of much use if there is no facility for I/O. Every implementation of C++ has a rich set of I/O facilities, and many of the I/O facilities are included in the draft ANSI standard library that is described in Appendix 5. We will learn the power of C++ I/O facilities in this chapter.

We first review the I/O facilities of the C programming language. The primary general-purpose I/O functions are **printf()** and **scanf()**. These functions are very flexible because they allow variable numbers and types of arguments within programs. However, their flexibility creates many opportunities for errors, since there is no compile-time checking of arguments and their formats.

As an illustration of the problems that can occur when using I/O in C, consider what happens when the two statements

```
x = 'A';
printf("%s", x);
```

are executed. Everything in memory from the location where the variable **x** is stored to the first null byte **\0** is printed. If no null byte is found within the executable program's memory space, then a run-time error will be generated.

A more serious deficiency from the perspective of object-oriented programming is that there is no facility for the input or output of user-defined data structures. The only way to print a structured data type in C is to print each of the fields separately using a function such as **printf()**.

Suppose that a structured data type has been declared previously using something similar to the construction

```
struct data_type
{
  char name[20];
  int number;
};
```

An example of using the function **printf()** for this type of I/O programming in C is

```
printf("%s %d", data.name, data.number);
```

This function prints two fields of a structured data type. Unfortunately, this is not a very satisfactory way of printing user-defined data types. We would have to repeat this type of statement whenever we wish to print the fields of a data structure. The statement must be changed if we change the name of a variable of this particular data type.

Thus we are forced to consider a more flexible method of enclosing the **printf()** statement within a function. We could write a function named **print_data()** that looks something like this:

```
void print_data(struct data_type *data)
{
  printf("%s %d", data.name, data.number);
}
```

This technique solves the problem of printing variables of the type **data_type**. However, the method of solution creates new problems. Our programs now have a new function that is used for I/O. Since overloading of function names is not allowed in C, we must have a new name for each new I/O function that we create. This is inconvenient and can lead to many run-time errors because of the large number of functions with similar names that perform similar, but different, I/O actions. Since C++ allows overloading, the I/O provided in the C++ language is a clear improvement over the I/O available in C.

Because of design decisions based on the UNIX and C heritage of C++, terminal-based I/O and file-based I/O are treated in a similar manner in C++ . The only exception to this idea is that in-core-based I/O is treated in a more elegant manner in C++ than in C (which uses the **sprintf()** function).

Before we begin our study of file I/O in C++, we will briefly describe the nature of the object known as a *file stream*. The term "file stream" is used in essentially the same sense as it is in the UNIX operating system: a file is a collection of data in which no organization of data can be made unless provided by the program. The input stream—commonly referred to as *standard input* (generally from the keyboard), which is also known as **stdin**—is considered to be a file. Similarly, standard output (generally the terminal screen and known as **stdout**) and standard error (**stderr**) are also considered to be files. This consistent view of I/O operations as being operations on files makes a unified treatment of input and output possible. These three file streams are part of the ANSI C specification.

The file stream abstraction of C has been replaced by the **iostream** object in many recent implementations of C++. This is intended to bring the I/O library in line with the object-oriented viewpoint of the rest of the typical C++ class library.

The basic idea is that the file I/O operations in C++ are essentially the same as the I/O operations we have already used, with only minor differences in the syntax. This type of software reuse is the essence of object-oriented programming.

A simple C++ function to print the fields of the structured data type **data_type** given earlier would overload the << operator and might look something like

```
ostream & operator << (ostream &out, data_type d)
{
    return out << d.name << endl << d.number << endl;
}
```

In the rest of a C++ program, the output of a variable that is named **var** and is of this data type would simply be

```
cout << var;
```

Here we have used overloading of the << operator, addresses of streams, and the object-oriented features of C++ to produce a more elegant method of I/O for structured data types. Programs using this structure are very easy to read. We will discuss overloading of the << and >> operators in Section 6.3.

6.2   File Input and Output in C++

We now turn to the study of object-oriented file operations in C++. Before reading the remainder of this chapter, you might find it convenient to review the material in Chapter 2 concerning C++ I/O, with particular attention to the discussion and examples in Sections 2.3, 2.4, and 2.5.

The fundamental stream object is known as an **iostream**. The term *streambuf* was used in earlier versions of C++ library, especially in AT&T C++ release 2.0. The iostream library is much more commonly used than the earlier streambuf library and it is the one that we will discuss in this book.

The first thing to understand about iostreams is the hierarchical nature of the various file stream objects. The base class is known as **ios**. There are two classes that are directly derived from this base class: **istream** (for input) and **ostream** (for output). The class **iostream** is derived directly from each of the classes **istream** and **ostream**. This is an example of multiple inheritance.

Three classes, **ifstream**, **fstream**, and **ofstream**, are directly derived from the classes **istream**, **iostream**, and **ostream**, respectively. The organization is shown in Figure 6.1

The inclusion of the standard header file **iostream.h** in a program guarantees that the class **iostream** is available to the program. The **cin**, **cout**, and **cerr** file streams are then made available automatically, as we have seen many times previously. Recall that these file streams are part of typical implementations of C++, but that they are not part of the standard C++ language.

Figure 6.1   Hierarchical organization of I/O classes.

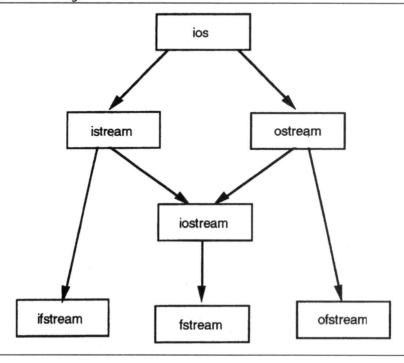

Any other files or file streams are user-defined. Thus we need to have some mechanism for incorporating these user-defined file streams. The idea is to have an abstract class known as a **streambuf** class that represents the essential features of all input and output.

The stream mechanism is obtained from the three classes that are lowest in the hierarchy shown in Figure 6.1: **ifstream**, **ofstream**, and **fstream**. These three classes are used as follows:

- Programs that read data from, or write data to, files must use the header file **fstream.h**.
- Programs that read from files, but do not write data to files, can use the **istream** class and the header file **fstream.h**.
- Programs that write data to files, but do not read data from files, can use the **ostream** class and the header file **fstream.h**.
- Programs that read data from files and also write data to files, can use the **fstream** class and the header file **fstream.h**.

There are several steps that must be used when working with files:

- The proper class must be chosen for the file stream, depending on our requirements for writing data to the file, reading data from the file, or both.
- The file must be opened using the **open()** function provided in the definition of the class.
- The proper file operations must be performed.
- The file must be closed.

The first step is easy. For example, we could declare **"infile"** as an input stream object by the statement

```
ifstream &infile;
```

Similarly, we could declare **"outfile"** as an output stream object by the statement

```
ofstream &outfile;
```

or we could declare **"inoutfile"** as an object stream for both input and output by the statement

```
fstream &inoutfile;
```

(Pointers and the address operator & are generally used with iostreams in this context.)

The next step in the process is to open the file using the **open()** function appropriate for the class of the file stream object. The **open()** function is based on the UNIX system call of the same name. This is not surprising, given that C++ was originally invented at AT&T Bell Laboratories. The design of the UNIX system call **open()** is intended to allow the user to have control over the lower-level details such as the mode of usage of the file and the access permissions. For more details on the UNIX **open()**, see the author's book *Advanced Topics in UNIX* or any other reference on UNIX system calls.

The system of the **open()** function for a file stream object class is

```
stream.open(name, mode, permissions)
```

The **stream** argument is the one previously declared and the name refers to a character string that represents the name of the file.

Note that most implementations of C++ use precisely the same restrictions on file name length and format as does the underlying operating system. Since most DOS implementations of C++ restrict file names to a maximum of eight characters with an optional extension that consists of a dot and a maximum of three characters, these restrictions apply to C++ programs on DOS systems.

The mode is based on a set of predefined constants. These constants are obtained from the fundamental I/O class **ios** and are defined as follows:

ios::in	Open the file for reading.
ios::out	Open the file for writing.
ios::app	Move the file pointer to the end of the file after opening. The file is opened for writing at this portion.
ios::ate	Move the file pointer to the end of the file after opening, but do not require writing at this place. Reading and writing can be done anywhere. (Note the differences between this and the previous mode.)
ios::nocreate	The **open()** function call will fail (and return the value 0) if the file does not already exist.
ios::noreplace	The **open()** function call will fail (and return the value of 0) if the file exists already. Compare to the previous mode.
ios::trunc	The file will be opened with the file pointer set to the location where the first byte should ordinarily be stored. The existing contents of the file are ignored.
ios::binary	The file is in binary, and not in ASCII, format.

These modes are mnemonics that are generally represented as octal or hexadecimal constants. Thus the bitwise OR operation of the C language can be applied to these constants. The expression

```
ios::in | ios::out
```

is therefore legal in C++ and fortunately it represents a mode for a stream that allows both reading and writing.

While the bitwise OR operation can be performed on any constant, not all combinations of modes are allowable as modes. For example, the bitwise OR

```
ios::nocreate | ios::noreplace
```

is clearly meaningless.

The third argument to **open()** is the permissions. Allowable options for the permissions are

S_IREAD	Read only.
S_IWRITE	Write only.
S_IREAD | **S_IWRITE**	Read and write.

Many combinations of mode and permissions can cause the **open()** call to fail. For example, setting the mode as **ios::in** with permission of **S_IREAD** will lead to an error. The permissions set by the operating system override any permissions set within a user's program.

In many C++ environments, especially on personal computers, the concept of permissions is relatively meaningless and hence the permissions argument is often omitted so that the **open()** function call takes the default value of

```
S_IREAD | S_IWRITE
```

for its permissions argument. This is possible because the definition of the function **open()** used default values. These default values are used as arguments when certain arguments are missing, as we have seen several times before.

A C++ programmer in a UNIX environment should be aware that these options for permissions are different from the mnemonic constants used with the UNIX **open()** system call. A call to the object-oriented C++ function **open()** will have a form something like

```
stream.open("name", ios::in, S_IWRITE)
```

and this is clearly different from a call such as

```
open("name", 0660 | O_WRONLY)
```

which refers to the UNIX **open()** system call. This is a convenient way of distinguishing between a function that has a similar name to a UNIX system call and the system call.

We will illustrate the use of C++ file I/O by a sequence of examples. Each of the examples will use the member function **get()** from the appropriate object inside a simple **while-loop**. The **while-loop** is of the form

```
while (infile.get(ch))
  cout << ch;
```

or something similar in the later examples. Note that there is no need to check directly for an end-of-file character **EOF**. Note also that we can declare the contents of the file as being type **char**, since we don't have to worry about the value of **EOF** being –1 on some systems.

Our first example simply echoes the contents of a file to the terminal screen. It uses the **ifstream** object. Notice the syntax of the initial declaration of the **ifstream** named **source** and the linking of this to the name of the file. The word **source** appears several times in the program of Example 6.1. The name of the file is hard-coded within the program in the string **"infile."**

Example 6.1 Copy a file to standard output using a hard-coded name for the input file.

```
//  This program copies a file to standard output.
//  The name of the file is hard-coded into the program.

#include <fstream.h>

main (int argc, char *argv[])
{
  char ch;
  ifstream source ("infile");

  if (!source)
    cerr << "Error opening input file" << endl;
  else
    {
    while (source.get(ch))
      cout << ch;
    source.close();
    }
}
```

The next example also copies the contents of a file to standard output. The name of the file is to be read in as a command-line argument. Hence we wish to avoid the syntax of the previous example, since we cannot determine the name of the input file at compilation time. Of course, the loop that does the copying is the same as in Example 6.1.

Example 6.2 Copying a file to standard output using a command-line argument.

```
//   This program copies a file to standard output.
//   The name of the file is given as a command-line
//   argument.

#include <fstream.h>

main (int argc, char *argv[])
{
  char ch;
  ifstream infile;

  if (argc != 2)
    cout << "Error in arguments \n";
  else
    {
    infile.open (argv [1], ios :: in);
    while (infile.get(ch))
      cout << ch;
    infile.close();
    }
}
```

This program has the expected design—a check for arguments, opening the file stream, reading the file stream in a loop, and closing the file stream.

There are several ways to write a "copy program" that copies the contents of an input file into an output file. Examples 6.3 and 6.4 illustrate two different ways of writing copy programs. The programs will not check to see if the output file already exists before the initial write; you will be asked to do this in the exercises. Note the appearance of the words **source** and **target** in Example 6.3.

Example 6.3 Copy program using hard-coded name for the input and output files.

```
//   This program copies one file to another.
//   The names of the files are hard-coded into the program.

#include <fstream.h>

main (int argc, char *argv[])
{
  char ch;
  ifstream source ("infile");
  ofstream target ("outfile");
```

```
    if (!source)
      cerr << "Error opening input file" << endl;
    else if (!target)
      cerr << "Error opening output file" << endl;
    else
      {
      while (source.get(ch))
        target.put(ch);
      source.close();
      target.close();
      }
  }
```

Example 6.4 Copying one file to another using command-line arguments.

```
// This program copies the contents of one file,
// which is specified by the second command-line argument,
// to another file, whose name is given in the third
// command-line argument.

#include <fstream.h>

main (int argc, char *argv[])
{
  char ch;
  ifstream infile;
  ofstream outfile;

  if (argc != 3)
    cout << "Error in arguments \n";
  else
    {
    infile.open (argv [1], ios :: in);
    outfile.open (argv [2], ios :: out);
    while (infile.get(ch))
      outfile.put(ch);

    infile.close();
    outfile.close();
    }
}
```

6.3   Overloading the << and >> Operators

A major advantage of I/O in the C++ language over I/O in C is that we can overload the << and >> operators. This should not be surprising to you, since we have seen operator overloading many times previously in this book. We have even discussed overloading of << in this chapter when we discussed the deficiencies of the **printf()** function in C.

However, overloading of the << and >> operators is so important that we will devote this section to the discussion of it.

The syntax of overloading << and >> is the same as for overloading any other operator in C++. Function prototypes for some relevant member functions in the **iostream** class are

```
istream & operator >> (int);
istream & operator >> (char);
istream & operator >> (float);
istream & operator >> (double);
```

for input using the **istream** class, and

```
ostream & operator << (int);
ostream & operator << (char);
ostream & operator << (float);
ostream & operator << (double);
```

for output using the **ostream** class. Many other member functions of this class overload the << and >> operators, because there are many possible standard data types for which output must be defined.

Overloading the << and >> operators to allow the same syntax for all I/O operations is easy. We simply define appropriate member functions for the class using the previously developed I/O operations for all component parts of any complicated data objects.

For example, we can produce output of any object of the class **Complex** that was discussed in Section 2.5 by including an appropriate member function. We would have

```
Complex ostream & operator << (Complex C)
{
  cout << C.real << " + i" << C.imag ;
};
```

if we just want to produce results on the output stream **cout**, or

```
Complex ostream & operator << (ostream &out, Complex C)
{
  out << C.real << " + i" << C.imag ;
  return out;
};
```

if we wanted to be able to send output to an arbitrary output stream (object of the class **ostream**).

The overloaded << operator is used in programs in exactly the same way as the ordinary << operator, as the following program fragment illustrates:

```
ostream &out Complex Z (1.0, 2.0);  // Use a constructor.
cout << Z;              // Standard output stream
out << Z;              // Arbitrary output stream.
```

Input of objects using an overloaded >> operator follows the same pattern, assuming that we wish to read the input of a complex number in the form of two successive floats:

```
Complex istream & operator >> (Complex a)
{
  cin >> C.real >> C.imag ;
};
```

if we just want to get input from the standard output stream **cin**, or

```
Complex istream & operator << (istream &in, Complex C)
{
  in >> C.real >> C.imag ;
  return in;
};
```

if we wanted to be able get input from an arbitrary input stream (object of the class **istream**).

The overloaded >> operator is used in programs in exactly the same way as the ordinary >> operator, as the following program fragment illustrates:

```
istream &in
Complex Z (1.0, 2.0); // Use a constructor.
cin >> Z;              // Standard input stream
in >> Z;     // Arbitrary input stream.
```

We need to check for completeness of our overloading of << and >> before we are finished with I/O of objects of the class **Complex**. We need to allow all inputs and outputs that can legitimately be obtained using available constructors. For example, we would need to be certain that numbers of the form **7 + 3i** can be written to output streams, since there is a constructor of the form

```
    Complex(real, real);
```

Fortunately, there is no problem because << and >> are already overloaded for pre-defined types in C++.

This overloading for the predefined types is sufficient because of the overloading rules in C++. Thus we actually have a complete set of I/O operators for this class. You should always check that you have handled all possible cases of conflict with construc-tors and overloaded I/O operators before you are finished with testing the object's member functions. We discussed this aspect of testing in Chapter 2.

Every object can have access to its own version of overloaded << and >> operators using the same techniques. In order to use an overloaded version of the operators << and >>, we might declare the standard **iostream** class operators as friends. As another illustration, consider the class **Matrix** that was presented in Example 4.7. We have eliminated most of the member functions in order to save space.

Example 6.5 A portion of the class **Matrix** with the overloaded << operator.

```
// FILE: ex6_5.cpp
//
// Modified class Matrix for ordinary matrices.
// This class includes a new, overloaded output
// operator.
//
#include <iostream.h>
#include <iomanip.h>

typedef int boolean;

class Matrix
{
private:
  #define max_rows 50
  #define max_columns 50
  int num_rows, num_columns;
  double entry[max_rows][max_columns];
public:
  Matrix(int rows, int columns);
  friend  ostream & operator << (ostream &out, const Matrix &M);
};


// Constructor
Matrix:: Matrix(int rows, int columns)
{
```

```
    int i, j;
    num_rows = rows;
    num_columns = columns;
    for (i = 0; i < rows; i++)
      for (j = 0; j < columns; j++)
        entry[i][j] = 7;
}


// Print output, maximum of 10 numbers per line.
ostream & operator << (ostream & out, const Matrix &M)
{
    int i, j;

    for (i = 0; i < M.num_rows; i++)
      {
      for (j = 0; j < M.num_columns; j++)
        {
        out << setw(5) << M.entry[i][j] ;
        if ( (( j % 10) == 9) )
        out << endl;
        }
      out << endl;
    return out;
}


main(int argc, char * argv[])
{
  Matrix M(5,20);

  cout << "start\n";
  cout << M;
  cout << "done\n";
}
```

There are several things to note about this example. We have declared the overloaded operator << as a **friend** in order to be able to use it for ordinary I/O for simple character strings and the individual matrix entries. We set the precision using the **setw()** manipulator; this required the standard include file **iomanip.h**. Finally, note that we used the ampersand, &, to indicate that the argument **M** was being passed by reference.

6.4 Using C++ File Streams for Random Access

The C programming language has a rich collection of functions such as **rewind()**, **ftell()**, and **fseek()** that directly manipulate the location of a file pointer. They allow what is commonly called random or direct access. The term *random access* does not imply that we are accessing data according to some probabilistic formula. Instead, it refers to the ability to move a "file pointer" to a prescribed location, without having to read all data that is between the location of our current file pointer and the new one. Random access is very useful when reading database files, for example. On UNIX systems, the C functions **rewind()**, **ftell()**, and **fseek()** are often implemented in terms of the UNIX system calls **seek()** and **lseek()**.

Since C++ is essentially a superset of C, these functions are generally available to C++ programs. However, it is more elegant to use the C++ I/O facilities for files in C++ programs, rather than relying on the C facilities. Recall from Section 2.9 that there are potential problems with the timing of I/O statements if both C and C++ I/O functions are used in the same program.

The member functions that change the position of an I/O stream pointer are similar to the corresponding C functions. The relevant C++ functions are **seekg()**, **tellg()**, **seekp()**, and **tellp()**. There are four such functions because different pairs can be used with objects of the classes **istream** and **ostream**.

Perhaps the easiest way to remember which functions are used with objects of the different classes is to use the final ‘**g**’ or ‘**p**’ as a guide. The two functions whose names end in the ‘**g**’ are to be used when we *get* input, that is, with getting input from objects of the class **istream**. The two functions whose names end in the ‘**p**’ are to be used when we *put* output, that is, with putting output to objects of the class **ostream**.

The syntax and use of the two tell functions are similar and we discuss them first. Each of these functions, **tellg()** and **tellp()**, returns the value of the current stream pointer. The value returned is generally used by a subsequent call to either **seekg()** or **seekp()**.

We now discuss these two seek functions.

The **seekg()** function takes two arguments: a **long int** representing the stream position and an **int** determining the mode. The second argument is actually an argument of the type **ios::seek_dir**, since it represents one of three actions depending on the value of the first argument. Since the function is overloaded, the second argument can be omitted and in this case we would use the default argument **ios::beg**.

If the value of the first argument is *N*, then the values of the second argument affect the action of the **seekg()** function as follows. Here we have used **Infile** as the name of an object of the class istream.

ios::beg	Move the file stream pointer *N* bytes from the beginning of the file. The call is either **Infile.seekg(N, ios::beg)** or, if we use the default argument, **Infile.seekg(N)**.
ios::cur	Move the file stream pointer *N* bytes from the current position of the file pointer. The call is **Infile.seekg(N, ios::cur)**
ios::end	Move the file stream pointer *N* bytes from the end of the file. The call is **Infile.seekg(N, ios::end)**

Note that the value of *N* can be positive, negative, or 0, just as in the C function **seek()**. For example, the call **Infile.seekg(10, ios::end)** can be used to move the current position of the stream pointer 10 bytes after the current end of the stream. The call **Infile.seekg(-10,ios::end)** can be used to move the current position of the stream pointer 10 bytes *before* the current end of the stream **Infile**. Finally, the call **seekg(0,ios::end)** can be used to move the current position of the stream pointer to the end of the stream.

We now illustrate the use of the functions **seekg()** and **seekp()** for random access. In Example 6.6, we will read from an input file and copy its contents to an output file. We will do this in a simple loop such as those we have seen several times before in this chapter.

The output file will then be duplicated in place, so that the output file will consist of the same characters as the input file, followed by the same set of characters, in the same order. This second loop is the interesting part of the program.

Be sure that you understand the continual movement of the file position **ios::end** as more data is sent to the output file. In this loop, we always insert the duplicated character after the current value of the end of file, which then moves after the insertion.

Example 6.6 Use of **seekg()** for random access.

```
// This program uses an input file,
// which is specified by the second command-line argument,
// and writes its contents to another file,
// whose name is given in the third command-line argument.
// The output file contains the characters in the same
// order as the characters in the input file, repeated.
```

```cpp
// FILE: ex6_6.cpp

#include <fstream.h>

main (int argc, char *argv[])
{
  ifstream infile; // Read only input file.
  fstream outfile; // Read and write output file.
  int i, file_size = 0;
  char ch, temp[1];

  if (argc != 3)
    cout << "Error in arguments \n";
  else
    {
    infile.open (argv [1], ios :: in);
    outfile.open (argv [2], ios::in |ios :: out);

    // Copy input file to output file in order.
    while (infile.get(ch))
      {
      outfile.put(ch);
      file_size ++;
      }

    infile.close();

    cout << file_size << endl;
    outfile.seekg(0, ios::beg);  // Set "get pointer" to start.
    outfile.seekp(0, ios::end);  // Set "put pointer" to end.

    // Now duplicate file contents.
    for (i = 0; i < file_size; i++)
      {
      // Move i places from start and get a character.
      // Store character in temp.
      outfile.seekg(i, ios::beg);
      outfile.read(temp, sizeof(char));

      // Put temp to end of file.  End of file changes
      // as more data is written to the file.
      outfile.seekp(0, ios::end);
      outfile.write(temp, sizeof(char));
      }
    outfile.close();
    }
}
```

The code of Example 6.6 can be changed to use files with any other type of data object, not just characters. The **read()** and **write()** statements for an object named **outfile** of class **fstream** would be changed to

```
outfile.read((*char) & temp, sizeof(temp) );
```

and

```
outfile.read((*char) & temp, sizeof(temp) );
```

respectively. (Note that we used a temporary array of characters for our reads and writes.)

Be careful when you use files with object-oriented programs. Most operating systems store data in a general form and do not allow the incorporation of higher-level organization, such as objects, to be included in the file structure. This places all responsibility upon the programmer to ensure that the object structure is maintained.

Summary

There are three essential file stream classes in C++ for standard input and output: **istream**, **ostream**, and **iostream**. All three classes may be accessed by including the file <**iostream.h**> in your program. Alternatively, we could include only the input or output stream functions by including the files <**istream.h**> or <**ostream.h**>, respectively.

The related classes for file streams are **ifstream**, **ofstream**, and **fstream**. All three classes may be accessed by including the file <**fstream.h**> in your program. Alternatively, we could include only the input or output stream functions by including the files <**ifstream.h**> or <**ofstream.h**>, respectively.

Files can be opened using the **open()** member function. A file stream named **"filestream"** can be opened using:

```
filestream.open (name, mode, permissions);
```

The mode can be one of

- **ios :: in**
- **ios :: out**
- **ios :: ate**
- **ios :: app**
- **ios :: nocreate**

- **ios :: noreplace**
- **ios :: trunc**
- **ios :: binary**

The permissions argument can be omitted if we wish to use the default values. Other functions that can be used with file streams are **close(), seekg()**, and **tellp()**.

The << and >> operators can be overloaded by a programmer when describing the member functions associated with an object. This is the basic technique used for I/O of objects.

Most operating systems do not allow the incorporation of higher-level organization, such as objects, to be included in the structure of data files. It is the programmer's responsibility to ensure that the object structure is maintained.

EXERCISES

1. List all pairs of modes for the **open()** function whose interactions would leave a file in an inconsistent state.

2. List all of the errors that could occur when opening or closing a file. Be sure to include potential errors in access permissions. Read the description of the header file **fstream.h** (and **iostream.h** if necessary) to determine which values, flags, or functions can be used if one of the errors occurs during an **open()** or **close()** operation.

3. Examine the header file **fstream.h** to determine which functions are available for reading data with different formats.

4. What results do you expect when you attempt to read an executable file using the mode **ios::in**? What do you expect when you attempt to read the same file using the mode **ios::binary**? Test your conjecture with an experiment. (Be sure to close the file after the first set of reads is complete.)

5. A common use of streams is with filters. A *filter* changes the format of a stream slightly. One simple filter would replace a sequence of eight successive blanks by a single tab character '\t.' Which do you think would be fastest?

   (a) Using a function to make this change.

   (b) Using the function in part (a) as **inline**.

   (c) Incorporating the change within the definition of the class.

   Test your conjecture by an experiment. Be sure to modify a *copy* of the file **fstream.h**, not the file **fstream.h** provided with your system.

6. Add a graceful exit to the copy program of Examples 6.2 or 6.4 if the output file exists before the initial attempt to open the file.

7. Write two C functions named **getint()** and **getfloat()** that will read in data of type **int** and **float**, respectively. The data input will be in character form as if the data were stored in a text file. Each piece of data will end with "white space," that is, a blank, tab, or new-line character; no data will be larger than 80 characters long. The two functions will read the data in and will issue an error message if the data is not of the correct form (digits only) or is too large for an **int**. The value that is returned by **getint()** should be of type **int**, and the type returned by **getfloat()** should be **float**. Be sure that the **getfloat()** function handles exponential as well as standard decimal form and that both functions handle positive, negative, and 0 values. Begin this exercise with testing the << operator's treatment of **int** and **float**.

8. There is a small problem with the input routines given for the class **Complex** in Section 6.2. If a user enters a number such as **2 + 5i**, there will be an error, since the input operator >> expects to have the input in the form **2 5**. Provide new member functions overloading the >> operator and thus allowing this type of input. Describe how you would test these new member functions.

9. Use the mode **ios::binary** to read an executable file and determine the number of characters in the file. Measure the time needed for this program. Compare this with the time needed for a program to read the same executable file but without setting the mode as **binary**.

10. Design and implement an experiment to determine the efficiency of the **seekg()** function and its relation to the distance moved in a "random access." Use a loop to repeat the steps

    move the file pointer forward a fixed distance
    move the file pointer backward the same distance

some fixed number of times. Determine the relationship between the time for execution of the program and the distance moved. Be sure to consider at least the numbers 1, the block size of the disk drive (consult your hardware manual for this information), one larger than the block size of disk drive, and 10 times the block size, for the fixed distance moved. (The larger numbers are important when you are using UNIX systems because of the organization of the UNIX file system.)

Software Engineering

Advanced C++ Program Structure

7.1 Separate Compilation

A fundamental motivation in the design of C++ was the ability to reuse classes that were developed previously in C++ programs. Unfortunately, the concept of reuse is of little importance if we have no means of grouping objects as required. Thus the C++ language must, a priori, have some method for physically separating programs into multiple files. Such a method must be based on C's implementation of separate compilation. In particular, the C++ scope rules for visibility of variables and functions in different files must be compatible with the scope rules for C.

Recall that there are three possibilities for the scope of variables in a C program if the program is contained in a single C source file. The rules are

1. If the variable is defined inside a function, then its scope is that function. Static variables retain their values on successive function calls while automatic variables do not. Neither is available outside the defining function.
2. If the variable is defined outside every function, then it will be available to any function defined from that point to the end of the file.
3. If the variable is defined outside every function, then it can be made available to any function in the file by declaring the variable to be **extern** in the function that wishes to use it.

4. The C language does not permit a function to be defined inside another function. That is, a function cannot contain another function body within its own body of code. Thus the concept of a nested scope is meaningless for variables in C.

Since the rules consider only the relationships between variables and functions contained in a single source code file, all these rules are valid even if the program is contained in several source code files. In order to extend the rules to programs with several source code files, it is necessary to distinguish between a declaration and a definition of a variable.

There is no problem with variables that are first declared inside functions. The two functions in Example 7.1 have declarations of variables named **count**. These two variables are completely separate and have no relation to any other variable named **count** regardless of where that name appears in the program. The variable **flag** is external to each of the functions in the file. In addition, **flag** is visible to every function in the file from the point where it is first defined until the end of the file. In order to make **flag** visible to the function **f()**, which appears earlier in the file, we added a statement to the body of the function **f()** which declared **flag** to be external to the function.

Example 7.1 Visibility of variables within a file.

```
// Shows visibility of variables in a file.

void f(void)
{
  int count;
  extern char flag;

  C_statements;
}

char flag;

void g(void)
{
  int count = 0;

  C_statements;
}
```

You should consult Appendix 3 for more information about the scope rules for C.

There are some changes to the C scope rules in the C++ language. We will review the C rules first before indicating the minor changes needed for C++.

For relatively simple classes, it makes sense to have member functions defined in the same file as the classes of which the functions are a member. This is not appropriate for classes whose member functions require a large amount of source code. In such a situation, it makes sense to include the class descriptions and the prototypes for member functions in one file and the source code definitions of the member functions in another file. This requires extra documentation indicating where files are placed and what their contents are.

Separate compilation means that the program may consist of several source code files. The idea is to group those functions and declarations that either use the same data type or perform similar operations together into a single file or set of files. These functions and declarations can then be used in other programs.

This requires the programmer to know precisely which functions are in which files. This can be determined only by a reading of the code, at least at the level of reading the documentation of the program. A better method is to design the code in advance to be sufficiently modular so that it can easily be incorporated into programs as needed. This is the way that libraries for input/output, mathematical computations, and graphics are organized. As an example of how a file can be broken up, consider the following simple situation.

The program in Example 7.2 is written as if it were contained in a single file. In Example 7.3, the program in Example 7.2 is reformed into two separate files. The two programs are identical in function only their physical format has been changed by separating the program into two files. Notice the way that we have included the function prototypes for all the functions in **file1.c**, since all of the functions are either defined or called by other functions in this file.

Example 7.2 A sample program in a single file.

```
void do_input_stuff(void);
void do_analysis_1(int i);
void do_analysis_2(void);
void do_output_stuff(void);

main(void)
{
int i = 1;

do_input_stuff();
do_analysis_1(i);
do_analysis_2();
do_output_stuff();
}

void do_input_stuff(void)
```

```
{-- lots of code --}

void do_analysis_1(int i)
{-- lots of code --}

void do_analysis_2(void)
{-- lots of code --}

void do_output_stuff(void)
{-- lots of code --}
```

We will not follow our coding conventions for indentation of blocks of code and bodies of functions in the examples that show files side by side in order to indicate program decomposition into separate files.

Example 7.3 The program of Example 7.2 broken into two files.

```
FILE1.c                              FILE2.c

void do_input_stuff(void);
void do_analysis_1(int i);           void do_analysis_1(int);
void do_analysis_2(void);            void do_analysis_2(void);
void do_output_stuff(void);

main(void)
{
int i = 1;                           void do_analysis_1(int i)
do_input_stuff();                    {-- lots of code --}
do_analysis_1(i);
do_analysis_2();
do_output_stuff();                   void do_analysis_2()
}                                    {-- lots of code --}

void do_input_stuff(void)
{-- lots of code --}

void do_output_stuff(void)
{-- lots of code -- }
```

Notice that in Example 7.3, the only function prototypes that we have placed in the file **file2.c** are those of the functions that are actually used in that file. This seems to make the program slightly easier to understand than having a long list of function prototypes at the beginning of a source code file when many of the functions are not actually used in the particular file. No harm would have been done if we had included all the function prototypes in the beginning of both files.

You may have noticed that there is another way to treat the function prototypes when the program of Example 7.2 is separated into multiple files. We can group all the appropriate function prototypes into a file that consists only of function prototypes and then include this in each source code file using the C preprocessor. This has the advantage of reducing the amount of typing necessary and also often reduces the potential confusion about precisely which functions are included in a file, since this information is somewhat hidden. The program now contains three files: **file1.c**, **file2.c**, and a header file that we have named **prototype.h**. This is an easy solution that works quite well in simple examples like this one. We will consider more complex organization of function prototypes later in this chapter.

The new code is shown in Example 7.4. Note the use of the double quotation marks around the name of the include file **prototype.h** to indicate that it is a user-defined file and should be searched for in the same directory as the rest of the source code.

Example 7.4 The program of Example 7.1 with an include file for function prototypes.

```
INCLUDE FILE prototype.h

void do_input_stuff(void);
void do_analysis_1(int i);
void do_analysis_2(void);
void do_output_stuff(void);
```

```
FILE1.c                            FILE2.c

#include "prototype.h"             #include "prototype.h"
main(void)
{
int i = 1;                         void do_analysis_1(int i)
do_input_stuff();                  {-- lots of code -}
do_analysis_1(i);
do_analysis_2();
do_output_stuff();                 void do_analysis_2()
}                                  {-- lots of code -}

void do_input_stuff(void)
{-- lots of code -}

void do_output_stuff(void)
{-- lots of code -}
```

Suppose that we wish to use a variable in several files. We must have at least a declaration of the variable indicating the type and size in each file in order to be able to use the variable properly. We must have precisely one place where the variable has had space allocated, that is, where the variable is defined.

Example 7.5 shows how to use the qualifier **extern** to have access to variables that are outside all functions in a file. In this example, the variable **flag** is declared in the source code of **file1.c** in two places: inside the function **f()** and in the statement between the functions **f()** and **g()**. The definition of **flag** occurs at the beginning of **file2.c** before any function is defined so that **flag** is visible throughout **file2.c**. (In Example 7.6 we will show a different way to access the variable **flag** if the program is composed of two source files.)

Example 7.5 A use of the qualifier **extern**.

```
prototype.h:

void f(void);
void g(void);



file1.c:                     file2.c:

#include "prototype.h"        #include "prototype.h"

f()                          char flag ;
{                            void toy(char a,char b)
int count;                   {
extern char flag;            char a,b ;
C_statements;                f();
g();                         }
}
                             main(void)
                             {
extern char flag;            char a = 'a', b = 'b';
                             flag ='Q';
                             toy(a,b);
g()                          }
{
int count = 0;
C_statements;
}
```

In Example 7.6, there is only a single declaration of the variable **flag** in **file1.c** and a single definition of **flag** in **file2.c.** The two source code files use the same header file as before.

Example 7.6 A different use of the qualifier **extern**.

```
prototype.h:

void f(void);
void g(void);

file1.c:                        file2.c:

#include "prototype.h"          #include "prototype.h"

extern char flag;
f()                             char flag ;
{                               void toy(char a, char b)
int count;                      {
C_statements;                   char a,b ;
g();                            f();
}                               }


                                main(void)
                                {
                                char a = 'a', b = 'b';
g()                             flag ='Q';
{int count = 0;                 toy(a,b);
C_statements;                   }
}
```

There are many other ways to arrange the definition and declaration of a variable such as **flag**. Experience has shown that it is better to have all definitions and declarations of external variables at the beginning of the file and not to have the visibility of variables depend on the scoping rule that an external variable defined in a file is visible from the point of definition to the end of the file. If a file is to be used with several other files when being used as a component file in more than one program, then it should be as easy to read as possible. Its purpose should be relatively clear without reading all the code in the file. Thus any use of external variables in another file should be indicated at the beginning of the file.

The situation is identical for functions. For example, the header file **math.h** declares the type of the function **exp()** as

```
extern double exp(double);
```

Recall that any program that uses these functions needs to have the statement

```
#include <math.h>
```

and must be linked to the appropriate library.

You need to be careful about the use of user-defined header files. If they contain only constants and descriptions of variable types, then they should be included in all files that need them.

One additional comment on the use of external variables and functions is in order. We can use both the words **extern** and **static** to describe a variable or function such as

```
extern static int alpha;
extern static float func(float);
```

These external and static variables and functions are known only within the source file in which they are defined and cannot be referenced in any other source file. This deliberate prevention of communication means that we can develop programs using different files and not worry about having two functions or variables causing errors because they have the same name.

We now discuss the relatively minor changes to the C language scope rules that are required for C++. They involve structure names that reside in an "inner scope" and the use of the **extern** qualifier in C++.

If a variable that is of type **struct** *something* resides in the inner scope of a function in C++, then any use of the name of that variable within the function hides any other variable of the same name. Thus if we have a variable named **arr** that is an array of elements of type **int** and is external to a function **f()**, then any variable named **arr** inside the function will be used instead of the external variable of the same name. Thus the output of the code fragment below will be the size needed for 2 **ints**, not 100:

```
int arr[100];
int f(void)
{
  struct x
    {
    int a, b;
    } arr;

  cout << sizeof(arr) << endl;
}
```

The next minor difference in the scope rules between C++ and C is that in C++, a global variable must be defined precisely once, with declarations (references to it) using the reserved word **extern**. C allows multiple definitions of the same variable, each without the use of the word **extern**.

7.2 The make Utility and Separate Compilation

In the previous section, we discussed how to break up a source code file into several files. We now consider the issue of efficient compilation of programs that extend over several source code files. An easy way to compile two files together into a single executable file is either to type something like

```
CC file1.C file2.C
```

which compiles the two source code files into two object files and then links them together into a single executable file, or to compile **file1.C** first, creating its object file, and forming the executable file by compiling **file2.C** and then linking to the object file **file1.o** as in

```
CC -c file1.c
CC file2.C file1.o
```

This works for the standard C++ compiler on many computer systems. (We have assumed that the name of this compiler is **CC**. It might be **gcc**, or something entirely different. Check your system manual.)

You should try this for the simple Example 7.3 and notice the messages that appear on the screen as the compiler compiles each source code file. The executable code works in precisely the same way as when the functions were included in the same file. This works perfectly and easily for any program that follows the format of the decomposition of Example 7.3 in which either all the communication between functions is by means of parameters or else no communication between functions is present at all.

What happens when there are a number of files in your program and you keep making changes to one of the files? As you saw when trying Example 7.2, each of the source code files was recompiled and then the two files were linked together. This seems like a waste of time. What we want is some intelligence in the compiler to be able to recognize that the only files that need to be recompiled are those that changed after the last linking of the compiled files was done. The **make** utility program is exactly what we need to do this. The **make** utility is a standard utility available under the UNIX operating system it is also included with Turbo C++ and many C++ compilers for personal computers.

The **make** utility uses a file created by the programmer, which is generally called a **makefile** or **Makefile**, to interpret a set of instructions for the compiler. The instructions in the **makefile** tell the **make** utility that the program is to be created from a set of source code files by compiling them and linking the object files together, perhaps with certain libraries also linked together. The **makefile** thus tells the make utility about the dependencies of the program and the various source and object files. A call to **make** results in the creation of the executable file, assuming that all goes well in the compilation and linking process.

The power of **make** becomes apparent if there is a change in any of the source code files making up the program (or if the source code is ported to another system). In order to create a new executable file after changing one of the source files, we simply type

```
make executable_name
```

The **make** utility then checks the time stamps on the source code files and the executable file whose name is specified in the **makefile**. If any source code file has a time stamp later than that of the executable file, or if the executable file does not exist, then the only source code files compiled and linked again are those that are necessary for the system. Unchanged source code files (those with a time stamp earlier than the executable file) are not recompiled only their object files are relinked. This can be a great timesaver and can also save a lot of typing.

The syntax of the **make** utility is slightly unusual and is different on different systems. We will give some examples of **makefiles** from two different UNIX systems. The ideas presented here will be helpful even if your system uses a different syntax.

The first **makefile** is taken from a system running AT&T System V UNIX, version 4.1. It uses the instructions in the **makefile** as follows. The executable file is named **complex** and is obtained from the object files (the files whose names have the extension **.o**). The object files are created by using the corresponding C or C++ source code files (the files whose names have the extension **.c** or **.C**).

Warning: make is very sensitive to one particular syntax: the **CC** command on line 2 of the **makefile** *must* be preceded by a tab rather than any collection of blanks.

Example 7.7 shows how the executable file **complex** is obtained from the two source code files called **file1.C** and **file2.C**.

Example 7.7 A simple **makefile**.

```
complex: file1.o y.file2.o
        CC file1.C file2.C -o complex
```

The make utility interprets the **makefile** as follows:

1. The two C++ source code files on line 2 (after the tab) are compiled using the **-o** option of this compiler. This creates two object files. Check your manual for the meaning of this or other options in your system.
2. The object files are then linked together to form the executable file named **"complex."**

This **makefile** is created using any standard editor. After the **makefile** is created, it is used by the UNIX **make** utility by simply typing the command

```
make complex
```

A slightly different syntax for a **makefile** used on a different system (but to solve the same problem) is shown in Example 7.8.

Example 7.8 A **makefile** with slightly different syntax.

```
complex : file1.o file2.o
          CC -o complex file1.o file2.o

file1.o : file1.C
file2.o : file2.C
```

Dependence on libraries can be added to **makefiles**. For example, to have the two files compiled with the math library, we could add the characters **-lm** at the end of the second line (the one with the tab used for indentation). The symbols **-l** indicate that a library is to be linked and the final **m** in the **-lm** indicates the use of the math library.

Many implementations of **make** for C compilers running on personal computers have slightly different syntax. Check the manual for your version of **make** if none of the formats shown in the examples in this section seems to work.

A separate compilation facility is also available in both Turbo C++ and Borland C++. In keeping with our goal of avoiding machine- and compiler-specific features, we have not generally discussed special features of any implementation of C++. The Turbo C++ separate compilation facility will be discussed here because it is somewhat different from the standard UNIX **make** utility, and these differences make it impossible to get started using separate compilation in Turbo C++ without learning a special integrated development environment known as an IDE.

Turbo C has a menu-driven, window-based user interface. This is true for both the MS/DOS and Microsoft Windows–based versions of this compiler family. The easiest way to get separate compilation to work in Turbo C++ is to create what Turbo C++ calls a *project*. A project file has the three-character extension **.prj** and consists of the names of the C++ and other files that make up the system that you are creating. The files could be header files with the **.h** extension, C++ source code files with the **.CPP** extension, or C source code files with the **.C** extension.

For example, the system developed in Example 7.2 would be encoded in a project file whose contents are

```
FILE1.CPP
FILE2.CPP
```

(Recall that DOS uses uppercase for file names and does not distinguish between uppercase and lowercase. We are using uppercase names for clarity.) The two files would be created using the Turbo C++ editor or another text editor.

Once the two source code files are created, the system can be created by using the call to **project**, followed by a call to the compilation facility available in the menu. The program can be executed by using the **"run"** option in the menu. Of course, this can be made faster by selecting the **"make"** menu option.

The separate compilation system in Turbo C++ was efficient and was sophisticated enough to recompile only those source code files that were changed if any of the source code files in the system were edited.

The menu-driven system for separate compilation was easy to learn and could be used easily without reading the manual. There was no syntax to learn, which is a big advantage. However, you should know the principles of the **make** utility even if you do all your work in Turbo C++ or similar software development systems.

You should note that separate compilation places a heavier requirement on a programmer to document his or her work than if the code was incorporated into a single source code file.

A programmer working as part of a programming team must be especially careful to make sure that the functions, variables, and data that he or she uses in one file do not have any unexpected effects on functions, variables, or data that are in files written by other programmers. Thus each source file in a program requires extra documentation. In addition, the documentation of the logical structure of the program must be accompanied by a complete description of the physical structure of the program, that is, of the placement of functions into files.

Software systems that consist of multiple source code files should be placed in a directory by themselves. Many actual systems are so complex that they extend over several directories. A simple file in ASCII format that briefly describes the organization and contents of the directories is very helpful. Such a file is often called a README file. README files are absolutely essential in larger systems.

7.3 Organization of Class Libraries

The key question discussed in this section is how to make classes visible to files other than the one in which the class is defined. Of course, we must include header files.

Many software systems written in C++ consist of a relatively small number of functions written especially for the problem at hand together with a large collection of library functions. (We are using the term "software system" instead of the term "program" since we wish to be able to think about larger amounts of code than before.) The library functions used in a program can be provided with the compiler, such as the standard libraries, as part of an applications system such as graphics libraries, user-defined libraries, or some combination of these. We have already seen examples of how to use a compiler's standard class libraries and how to incorporate the use of libraries into **makefiles** in some of the earlier examples in this chapter. We now briefly describe some of the issues used when developing a user-defined library.

What makes a class a good candidate for inclusion in a user's library? Generally, a class must be modular in design, be needed more than once in a variety of situations, have a simple, well-defined interface, and be extremely well documented and tested.

The need for modular design, multiple uses for the class and its member functions, and a well-defined interface is fairly clear. The other requirements are somewhat less obvious and so we discuss them in more detail.

The whole point of library software is that it is usually considered to be reliable. That is, the library functions are presumed to be carefully tested and to cause no problems in programs that use them. It is as if library functions are considered to be off-the-shelf software components that can simply be fitted into the programs that need them. These functions are subjected to far more severe testing than is typical for other functions or even programs that are used once and then thrown away.

Once one or more functions are subjected to the extensive testing necessary for library functions, they must be documented. The documentation here must be more extensive than the internal documentation of source code files. There should be some external documentation, at least at the level of one or two pages describing the specifications of the interface and action of each library file. This documentation can be stored electronically if you will be the only user of the library functions that you create. There must be additional documentation if the library functions are to be used by others. Creating a manual page can also be helpful for on-line documentation systems.

If there are only a few user-defined library functions, then they can be placed in one file or at worst a small number of files. In more complex software systems, it may be more sensible to organize the user-defined library functions into several directories, grouped by functionality.

We generally wish to separate the source code from the compiled object code and from other related artifacts of these library functions by placing them in separate directories. The following is a reasonably effective method of organizing the various features of any user-defined library.

- Determine logical groupings of the library functions into directories. Use this logical organization consistently for storage of all aspects of library organization.
- Create appropriate header files for all class descriptions, including function prototypes, and place them into directories using the hierarchical organization as appropriate.
- Compile each of the library member functions from the appropriate source code and place the resulting object files into directories using the hierarchical organization as appropriate.
- Create appropriate on-line documentation for each of the new library functions and place them into directories using the hierarchical organization as appropriate. This may be superseded by an existing standard for documentation such as that provided by the UNIX **man** utility.
- Place the source code for each of the library member functions into an appropriate directory. Use only read-only permissions if possible to protect the integrity of the source code. This may not always be provided to purchasers of commercial products.

One approach is to place all definitions of classes in header files. The header files should be organized according to the primary function of the object. Thus a set of classes to describe the most common abstract data types in C++ might include the following classes: stack, queue, tree, linked list, and hash table. Each of these classes would probably be placed in a file by itself.

Thus one organization might lead to five files named

```
stack.h
queue.h
tree.h
linked_list.h
hash_table.h
```

We could place each of these header files in a directory named, say, **data_structure_classes** and use directories and paths in our include statements. Note that the DOS limitation of file names causes some difficulty here when we want to have a name represent functionality.

An alternative organization is to place all related classes (in this case all classes defining the abstract data type (ADT) for the most common data structures) into a single file with an appropriate name. This method simplifies the hierarchical organization of the classes, at the expense of having long searches through files to find the classes that are appropriate for your needs. As a note, at least one system includes the definition of the classes **istream** and **ostream** in the same file as the class **iostream**.

Note that some classes can require a large amount of source code to describe both the class and the set of all allowable methods for the object defined by the class. This brings up some interesting questions.

- How do we organize the code for a class?
- Is there some rule of thumb that can be used to suggest a size limitation for a file describing a class? We would expect something similar to the rule of thumb that the size of a procedure or function should be no more than approximately 80 lines long.

A commonly given suggestion is that if the methods for a class are very short functions, then they should be included in the same header file as the class definition. (It is likely that inline functions will be in the header file.) Otherwise the member functions should be placed into a file with a name related to the name of the header files.

This organization might mean that the header file might be named something like **my_file.h**, with the member functions placed in a file named **my_file.cpp**, or something similar.

A good way to determine at least one set of standards for organization of classes and their functions is to examine the C++ source code provided in the header files for your system. This is easy even on multiuser systems, since the header files must be accessible to everyone for reading (but not writing).

On one system, the header file **iostream.h** was approximately 600 lines long, with approximately 70 functions defined in the file and approximately 85 defined elsewhere. Examine your system to determine its pattern of organization.

We now have some methods of organizing classes and their members. There are other issues that must be addressed before we can claim that we have a true class library.

The proper treatment of friend functions is to allow classes that need to use these functions to have access. This means that the description of the methods used with a class must be complete. It also means that the code for friend functions must be made available to potential users of the friend function. Of course, there is no problem if the code for the friend function is in the header file for the class. In this case, inclusion of the header file is sufficient, assuming that there are no cases of multiple use of the name of a class.

The situation is more complicated if the source code for the friend function is not in the header file in which the class is defined. We will describe two solutions, one for a particular DOS system and one for general UNIX systems. The technical manual for your system will provide additional information.

On DOS (or Windows) systems using either Turbo C++ or Borland C++, we can use the "project" to create systems.

On UNIX systems, the physical directory of a file is not important. For example, we can make a file of friend functions named **friend.cpp** available to files in two different directories named **class1** and **class2** by using *links*. In UNIX, a link is an attachment of a file to a directory.

If we wish to physically locate the file **friend.h** in the directory **class1**, then running the UNIX shell command

```
ln friend.cpp path/class1/friend.cpp
```

from within the directory **class2** will do the job. Here the character string **path** represents either an absolute or relative path leading us from our current directory (**class1**) to the parent directory of **class2**.

The use of the **ln** shell command does not make a copy of the file **friend.cpp** in the **class2** directory. Instead, a link is set up between the **class1** and **class2** directories. Any change to the file is immediately available to both directories.

A link should be set from every directory where a friend function is accessed. To make system maintenance easier, each directory should have a README file explaining the purpose of the links and the directory and file linked to their directory. Even though the UNIX shell command

```
ls - al
```

will indicate the links present among the files in the directory and the files in other directories that they are linked to, a README file can provide insight into the rationale of the class designer and why the choices of friend functions were made.

You should note that there is no problem in using friend functions by means of symbolic links. The scope resolution operator **::** resolves any possible conflicts.

These organizations of friend functions into files that can be incorporated as part of projects (on PCs using Turbo C++ or Borland C++, among others) or as part of system using links (as in UNIX) have ramifications for file organization. We should organize the friend functions (and probably subgroups of classes) into files with relatively few distinct items.

Let's suppose that we have followed the suggestions made previously in this section and organized our classes so as to provide easy access to necessary software. Let's also suppose that we have provided good documentation on the contents of each file. We still have a fundamental problem to address.

Imagine that you took the computer on which this set of classes was created and locked it in a trunk for a year. When you open the trunk, you won't remember much about the organization of the classes and functions. You would be grateful for any software tools that can help you find the files whose contents you need.

The term for a software tool that allows you to search automatically through a set of files, changing directories if necessary, is a *browser*. The most elementary browser will be able to select files that contain certain strings. Thus any browser will be able to find strings such as

```
class iostream
```

or

```
friend getbuf(),
```

whether the strings belong to the file in the current directory or in subdirectories. (You can do this on UNIX systems using the **grep** pattern-matching utility.)

A sophisticated browser can do more. It can search files to determine classes that have specific interfaces. This can be useful if you remember the interface but have forgotten the name of the class.

The existence of a browser enables the collection of classes to be considered to be a well-organized, easily accessible class library.

7.4 Examples of Class Libraries

In this section we describe the class libraries available on several different systems: Borland C++ version 4.0 for the 80×86 architecture, AT&T C++ version 3.0 for a Sun SPARCStation running Solaris (Sun's version of UNIX), and the gnu C++ compiler from the Free Software Foundation.

We will not present source code for any of these class libraries. Because of copyright issues, this would violate proprietary rights for the Borland and AT&T systems.

The Free Software Foundation's gnu C, C++, and other compilers are readily available from the Internet. However, programs that use as is or modify any of their code must include a statement of its origin and must in turn be made available to the public in source code version. This is termed *copyleft* by the Free Software Foundation.

In any event, we choose not to deal with any of these copyright (or copyleft) issues and will content ourselves with a description of the organization and the contents of the class libraries of these systems.

The Borland C++ system version 4.0 organizes its many classes into directories and files. It includes an integrated development environment and a simple browser. It works well under both MS-DOS and Microsoft Windows.

The AT&T system on a Sun SPARCStation contains a set of classes arranged into directories and files. The standard development environment does not integrate a language-sensitive editor and compiler. (Such integrated systems are available from vendors such as CenterLine.)

The gnu C++ compiler for UNIX consists of a very large number of classes organized into directories and files. Many software tools are included in the C++ distribution or other publicly available distribution sources. Their code is probably the most portable, since a goal of the Free Software Foundation (the organizers of the gnu project) is to have open access to source code to aid in portability.

It is not appropriate for a general-purpose book such as this to discuss which class library is the most complete, since the systems were developed for different purposes. We do note that there is considerable overlap in the basic facilities for I/O, standard abstract data types, and mathematical objects such as complex number and matrices.

The Borland class library contains classes that allow easy access to the graphical user interface provided by Microsoft Windows. This would not be expected on a UNIX system. Note, however, that there is a version of the gnu C++ compiler that runs on the 80×86 family of microprocessors.

The availability of source code for a compiler's class libraries can be very useful if you wish to port your source code to other environments. Source code is always available to users of the gnu system. In general, vendors' product information guides contain information on availability of source code.

Source code for other class libraries is also available on the Internet. The Mosaic interface to the World-Wide Web (WWW) listed several repository sites that were available at the time that this book was being written.

7.5   Testing Issues

The goal of software testing is to discover bugs. "Testing cannot show the absence of defects, it can only show that software defects are present" (Pressman). That is, software testing cannot prove that software is correct (meets its specifications) for any realistic system. This is due to the large number of possible execution paths, possible combinations of function arguments, and the general complexity of various program statements.

The statements in the previous paragraph suggest that the best we can hope for is some disciplined procedure that can detect the most likely sources of errors in software. It is becoming clear that the best defense against residual software errors (those that remain after completion of a phase of the software life cycle or release of a system) is proper design and coding practice (Humphrey).

Software testing occurs at several stages in the life of a system these stages are frequently called module level, unit level, and system level.

Testing of traditional, non-object-oriented programs can be done using either "white box" or "black box" methods.

In the *white box* testing method, emphasis is given to tracing execution paths, proper iteration of loops, and checking all branches when a conditional statement is executed.

In the *black box* testing method, the output of each module is compared to the specified results when the same inputs are used. Emphasis here is on the selection of appropriate test cases from the essentially unlimited set of potential arguments to the modules.

The corresponding stages for testing object-oriented programs are method level testing (which considers individual transformation on a class), class level testing, module level testing, and system level testing. (The term *module* is loosely defined as a collection of related classes and a few related functions.)

The class is the most important unit in object-oriented programming. Unfortunately, methods used for a class can be combined in arbitrary ways. One view of the test process for a class is that it is a search process for the order of methods with various collections of arguments that give errors (Lorenz). A common strategy for testing of objects includes (Smith and Robson):

- encapsulation
- minimalization
- exhaustion of a depth
- inheritance
- interactive

The *encapsulation strategy* for testing objects makes use of the abstraction used in defining an object. Any set of abstract methods that can be legitimately applied to the abstract object corresponds to a set of legal combinations of transformations on the class.

The *minimalization strategy* is to develop the smallest number of test cases for the class being tested where the errors that occur can be overridden by any child class of the tested class.

The *exhaustion of a depth strategy* is to consider all legal combinations of methods allowed for an object, with the number of methods in any chain of methods being less than or equal to the previously determined value of the depth.

The *inheritance strategy* is used for subclasses that are inherited from a parent class. A list of methods to be tested is kept and tests are performed on the class depending on the test results for the parent class.

The *interactive strategy* requires the tester to determine which methods to test based on an assessment of the relative complexity of the internal data structures in the class. The method can be summed up as "use your intelligence guided by your experience."

Note that the exhaustion of a depth strategy can be implemented mechanically with relatively little difficulty. Note that the inheritance test strategy also has potential for automation but that the other test strategies do not. In general, automatic testing tools for object-oriented programs are either nonexistent or very primitive (at least compared to the automated testing and analysis tools available for procedural programs in good software development environments).

Several features of object-oriented programming that encourage efficient program development cause some difficulties in testing. We describe some of these in the next few paragraphs.

Multiple inheritance implies that a portion of a class may be inherited along different inheritance paths. Many compilation system handle this potential ambiguity by using a precedence scheme to select proper values. The testing difficulty is due to the potential for a slight change in one of the inheritance paths to lead to an entirely new derived class.

Polymorphism also causes problems. We must determine that when an object receives a message, the object is in the correct form to receive the message, and it will react in the intended manner.

There are also potential problems in concurrent systems, since the creation or destruction of a particular form of an object may not occur instantaneously and hence there may be timing problems. These types of timing problems are notoriously hard to detect by testing.

Note that these issues are not caused by the classes themselves but by the way that they might be combined.

The lack of an implied order in which the methods used for a class are applied appears to make it difficult to use "test data." It is also difficult to use the control flow or data flow techniques commonly used in procedural programming.

For systems of reasonable complexity, there is a trade-off between using many previously tested classes either directly or by inheritance and using more complex objects that require extensive testing. Because testing complex objects is difficult, it appears that the better approach is to use more, but simpler, objects, including those in a class library of data structures. There is little hard data available as yet to support this view, but it is the growing consensus of a large group of project managers and software engineering researchers.

7.6   Exceptions in C++

The term *exception* refers to an unusual event that occurs at run time. Division by 0, attempting to read from a file before it is has been opened, and attempting to write to a memory address that is part of the computer's read-only memory are typical examples of exceptions.

Software systems should be robust. This means that unusual events should not cause them to crash but to remain active, performing the desired computation. If the unexpected event is too severe or unusual, then the software system should halt gracefully, updating an error log so that corrective actions can be taken to restore service.

A system that receives a lot of interactive input must be robust data entry errors should not cause the system to crash. One common problem is the interactive request for a user to select either of the characters **Y** or **N** as an option. The choice of input character is sent to the system after the user presses the return or enter key. It is well known that many novice computer users enter an extra space after their choice of **Y** or **N**. Many users press an extra return in order to "make sure the data is really entered."

A program that checks for correct input options can be complicated to write, test, and maintain. Such a program has many possible execution paths that are traversed in order to get back to a correct state awaiting user input. Since the number of test cases required increases with the number of potential execution paths, such complications in programs can often lead to nightmares when testing.

A major concern is that an unexpected program crash could leave a file (or other persistent system resource) in an inconsistent state, thereby making it impossible to restart the prorgam correctly. We wish to avoid this potential cascading of the effects of runtime errors.

When the user enters input of an incorrect type, an exception has occurred. This is detected by the run-time support system for the program. The C++ run-time support system will send control of the program to an "exception handler."

Exceptions can be powerful aids in programming. Unfortunately, some C++ implementations do not include exceptions.

As an example of exceptions, suppose that we have a program that reads in a stream of two inputs that represent floating point numbers and produces an output that is the quotient of each pair of inputs. The obvious problem is division by 0.

It would be easy to protect against division by 0 by checking that each divisor is nonzero and taking some alternative action in the event that a 0 divisor is encountered. However, this may not be adequate in all situations. The time needed for execution of this simple condition may be unacceptable in systems with real-time requirements.

Presumably the case of a divisor being 0 is relatively rare. Thus an efficient solution might be to allow the program to perform the division for each pair of numbers in the input normally, with an alternative action being taken as a result of the program switching control to an "exception-handling routine" or "exception handler."

There are three steps that must be performed in order to treat exceptions properly:

- Detect that an exception has occurred (and that the function has no means of recovering from the exception). In C++ programs, exceptions are usually considered to be in what is known as a **try** *block*.
- Notify an exception handler that an exception has occurred. This situation is called either *throwing an exception* or *raising an exception*. To throw an exception means that the local try block in which the exception occurred has requested that an exception handler take over responsibility for continuing program execution. There is no guarantee that an exception handler will ever be found, in which case the program terminates ungracefully.
- Treat the exception properly in an exception handler. The exception handler is said to *catch an exception* and processing continues in the exception handler.

At the time that this book is being written, there are no predefined exceptions in C++. This means that the programmer is responsible for defining the types of exceptions that he or she wishes the program to **try**, **catch**, or **throw**. Types of exceptions are usually implemented as classes in C++.

Many steps are necessary to treat exceptions in C++. The exception handler is the easiest to understand and hence we describe it first. We will use a series of examples to illustrate building exceptions into programs and what to do about exceptions in the absence of language standards. (Recall our observation that exceptions and templates are the most likely omissions from many implementations of the C++ language.)

The code of Example 7.9 has no exception-handling features.

Example 7.9 Division by 0 without an exception handler.

```
// Program to demonstrate the division by 0 exception.

#include <iostream.h>

main()
{
  float numerator, denominator;

  cout << "Please enter two numbers"  << endl;
  cin >> numerator >> denominator;
  cout << numerator/ denominator;
}
```

When presented with the input of

```
2.5
0
```

the program in Example 7.9 crashed with the output messages (on one system)

Floating point error: Divide by 0.
Abnormal program termination.

On a UNIX system, this is likely to result in a core dump, using up a considerable amount of disk space. We would like to get a more graceful termination, without a program crash.

Turbo C++ allows access to the assembly language of the 80×87 mathematics co-processor. We illustrate the disabling of these messages in Example 7.10. Note the inclusion of the header file **float.h** to control floating point arithmetic.

Example 7.10 Division by 0 with the default exception handler in Turbo C++.

```
// Program to demonstrate the division by 0 exception.
// It disables error messages by using a macro _control87.

#include <iostream.h>
#include <float.h>

main()
{
  float numerator, denominator, quotient;

  _control87(MCW_EM, MCW_EM);

  cout << "Please enter two numbers"  << endl;
  cin >> numerator >> denominator;

  quotient = numerator / denominator;
  cout << "The quotient is "<< quotient << endl;
}
```

The output from Example 7.10 is in error, but at lease we have avoided the error message:

The quotient is 0e+4933

Other types of exceptions can occur. For example, many mathematical functions have restricted domains. Thus the square root function **sqrt()** in the standard mathematical library requires a nonnegative argument. The Turbo C++ program of Example 7.11 illustrates what can happen if no exception handler is used.

Example 7.11 A domain error in Turbo C++ without a default exception handler.

```
// Program to demonstrate the function domain exception.

#include <iostream.h>
#include <float.h>
#include <math.h>

main()
{
  double x;

  cout << "Please enter a number."  << endl;
  cin >> x;

  cout << "The square root of " << x << " is "<< sqrt(x) <<
          endl;
}
```

The input value of **-1** causes the output

```
The square root of -1 is Floating point error: Domain
Abnormal program termination.
```

The Turbo C++ program given in Example 7.12 illustrates how Turbo C++ allows us to exit gracefully from this error. The program uses the special Turbo C++ function **cdecl()** that is defined in a header file.

Example 7.12 A domain error in Turbo C++ with a simple exception handler.

```
// Program to demonstrate the function domain exception
// and Turbo C++ exception messages.

#include <iostream.h>
#include <float.h>
#include <math.h>

int cdecl matherr(struct exception *e)
{
  cout << " You should be more careful." << endl;
  return 1;
}
```

```
main()
{
  double x;

  cout << "Please enter a number." << endl;
  cin >> x;

  cout << "The square root of " << x << " is "<< sqrt(x) << endl;
}
```

We now consider more standard exception-handling techniques in C++ programs. The examples in the rest of this chapter should work with any C++ compiler that follows the proposed ANSI standard.

An exception is detected in a **try** block. The formal syntax of a **try** block begins with the reserved word **try** and looks like this:

```
try_block  :
       try compound_statement    handler_list
       ;
```

The recursive specification of a *handler_list* indicates that many different types of exceptions can be generated within a single **try** block:

```
handler_list  : handler  handler_list
       ;
```

Exception handlers are specified in a **catch** block. The formal syntax for a **catch** block begins with the reserved word **catch** and starts out something like this:

```
handler: :
       catch { exception_declaration  } compound_statement
       ;
```

For more information about details of the syntax of an *exception_declaration*, see the formal syntax summary of C++ that is given in Appendix 2. We note however, that the type of an exception handler must be included within the **catch** block.

An illustration of an exception handler using both **try** and **catch** blocks is given in Example 7.13. We have illustrated two different types of exceptions in this program in order to illustrate the major features of exceptions.

Example 7.13 Use of **try** and **catch** blocks in an exception handler.

```
// Program to demonstrate the division by 0 exception.

#include <iostream.h>
```

```
main()
{
float numerator, denominator;

  cout << "Please enter two numbers"  << endl;
  cin >> numerator >> denominator;

  try
    {
    float quotient  = divide(numerator, denominator;
    cout << "The quotient is " << quotient << endl;
    }


  catch
    {
    cout << "error" << endl;
    }
}
```

Other exceptions can be handled in C++ using similar techniques. Use the function **cdecl()** in Example 7.12 as a guide if you are using classes of exceptions.

It is important to understand the limitations of C++ exceptions. You may have noticed that each exception handler in this section caused the program to terminate when the handler was invoked. This was intentional. The C++ implementation of exceptions causes program termination and does not allow program execution to resume at some other point of the program's execution.

Compare the treatment of exceptions in C++ to the semantics of exception handling in Ada. Ada is the most widely used language that has exception-handling features. The Ada run-time system first looks for an exception handler in the program unit in which the instruction causing the exception occurs. If an exception handler is found, then it is used. If no exception handler is found, then the search for an exception handler continues the next smallest enclosing program unit.

Thus an exception detected ("raised" in Ada terminology) in a function **f()** requires the search to concentrate first on the function **f()**. If no exception is found, then the smallest program unit (package or task, in this case) containing **f()** is searched.

If no exception handler is found, then the search is directed to the next smallest enclosing program unit (package or task). This process continues until one of two things occurs. Either an exception handler is found, in which case it is invoked and program execution continues, or else no exception handler is found, in which case control is returned to the operating system from which the program was originally executed.

We should have expected that the semantics of exception handling would be different for the two languages, because C++ follows the semantics of the C language, which does not allow nesting of functions, and Ada does.

The advantage of C++ exceptions is that there is a controlled, graceful termination of programs with unexpected run-time conditions. The idea is that the program should be able to restart execution and still have access to all required resources, such as files that were operned by the aborted program execution.

Graceful program termination is especially important in programs with multiple threads of execution that may be interleaved on the same processor or distributed among multiple processors. In such cases, an exception occurring on one processor may not be detected by software running on a different processor. Many client–server systems are distributed among several processors. (Interleaved processes on the same CPU may have the same difficulty detecting errors at run time as do distributed processes.)

We now turn our attention to a discussion of the relationships between **try** blocks, **catch** blocks, and the operating system. The most important relationships are shown in Table 7.1.

You should be aware that there are other options beside exceptions for reacting to unexpected run-time errors. We can use assertions in our code as we did in Section 5.2 when we discussed stacks. This involves the use of the include file **assert.h** and the **assert()** macro.

We could also use the two functions **setjmp()** and **longjmp()** to control the system stack if a run-time error occurs. This is a more powerful technique than C++ exceptions, since it allows for recovery of program execution from some place other than the start of the program in some cases. Unfortunately, these two functions are often available only as UNIX system calls. See Chapter 11 of the author's book

---

Table 7.1 Controlling exception handlers.

- Exception handlers can be thrown only by expressions in a **try** block, or in functions called within the **try** block.
- The handlers indicated in a **try** block are tried in order of appearance for a match of the type of the object specified in the handler. Matching is done by types.
- Destructors are automatically used for all automatic objects created within a **try** block before the point where an exception occurs and an exception handler is invoked.
- The function **unexpected()** is called when a run-time error occurs within a **try** block and no appropriate exception handler is specified within the block using a **throw** statement. This function calls a cleanup function specified in the most recent call to a lower-level function **set_unexpected()**. If no action is called, then the function **terminate()** is called as a default.
- The function **terminate()** is called as a last resort by the run-time system. This function calls a cleanup function specified in the most recent call to a lower-level function **set_terminate()**. If no action is called, then the function **abort()** is called as a default.

Advanced Topics in UNIX for more information on the use of these two functions in a UNIX environment.

Finally, we can use defensive programming if time constraints are not critical. This is often the best approach in many situations.

Summary

C++ allows programs to be separated into multiple files. The scope rules are similar to those for C programs. However, a **struct** defined within a C++ function can hide other variables of the same name. Also, an external variable cannot be multiply defined in different files in C++, although this is allowed in C.

A function that is a member of one class can be made available to another class by declaring it to be a friend function.

Classes can grouped into files and directories. These can be made available to other classes on PCs (in Turbo C++ or Borland C++) by using the project facility of the development system. They can be made available to other classes in other directories on UNIX systems using links by means of the ln UNIX utility.

Class libraries are included with all C++ compilers. A browser is essential for the efficient use of large class libraries.

Testing strategies for classes are different from those for testing ordinary procedurally developed programs. Some common techniques for testing object-oriented programs and classes are encapsulation, minimalization, exhaustion of a depth, inheritance, and interactive methods.

C++ has a facility for detecting, raising, and handling exceptions. A portion of a function that has a potential for a run-time error can be enclosed within a **try** block, using the C++ reserved word **try**. This allows an exception that is detected to be handled by an exception handler, if one is available. This is called "throwing an exception."

The exception handler is said to "catch the exception." The exception handler uses the reserved word **catch** to indicate that it is an exceptional action.

Some of the C++ exception-handling features are based on exception-handling features of Ada. However, C++ programs always terminate when an exception is thrown. In particular, a C++ program cannot resume execution from the point at which an exception occurred.

EXERCISES

1. Examine the class libraries available on your C++ compilation system. Determine the number of classes, directories, and source code files. Use this information to

determine the average number of classes per file and average number of classes per directory.

2. For each file in the class library, list the number of member, **virtual**, **friend**, and **inline** functions used.

3. Explain the potential for an exception in a function such as

```
double f (int x)
{
  if (x >= 0)
    return sqrt(x);
  else
    cerr << "Error—negative argument\\n";
}
```

4. Describe the differences between underflow, overflow, and imprecision.

5. Which run-time error is most likely to generate an exception? Why?

   (a) An error in pointer arithmetic.

   (b) Attempting to access a null pointer.

   (c) Exceeding available memory for the running process.

6. (For those familiar with remote procedure calls [RPC].) Suppose that a client calls a remote procedure **f()** on a server running on another computer. If an exception occurs in the remote procedure **f()**, what happens to the client? Assume both the server and client are written in C++.

7. (For those familiar with UNIX system calls.) Exceptions in C++ cause UNIX signals to be sent. If a process gets two exceptions, is there any way that handling the exceptions can be done in any predetermined order of priority? Explain.

8. Organize the classes that you have developed for the exercises in this book into a class library. Alternatively, use the disk included with this book to organize your personal class library.

Modeling Object-Oriented Systems

8

I n the preceding chapters, we discussed the major features of the C++ programming language. You are now familiar with the terminology of object-oriented programming. You are able to write small programs in C++ and should have some confidence in your ability to read and understand larger programs in this language.

The importance of data abstraction and information hiding in objects should be clear to you. In addition, you should have some appreciation for the power of the concepts of operator overloading and inheritance.

However, you are probably not very confident about your ability to design larger object-oriented systems and implement them in the C++ programming language. All the programs we discussed so far were relatively short and were intended to illustrate one or more language features. We have discussed only small programs and you haven't seen the full power of object orientation.

We now consider the development of larger object-oriented programs in the C++ programming language. In this chapter we will discuss some issues in object-oriented design and indicate how the object-oriented paradigm for software design differs from the procedurally oriented one.

We will also indicate a methodology for the development of object-oriented systems that determines the fundamental objects (and appropriate methods) in these systems. This will be done in the context of the development of a class that describes strings.

The design and implementation of larger object-oriented systems will be discussed in the remaining chapters of this book. In Chapter 9 we will describe the development of a graphical database using object-oriented techniques. In Chapter 10, we will discuss some issues that arise when converting from older, procedurally oriented programs (in our case, programs that are written in C) to object-oriented programs (that are written in C++).

8.1 Design Representations

It is essential to develop a model of a system before writing any software to control a system or to interact with it. This is probably the hardest part of software design. Any notations, techniques, or tools that can help understand systems or describe them should receive serious consideration from the person modeling the system. We will focus our attention in this section on techniques for modeling and will briefly discuss design notations.

The discussion of tools to help with any sort of software modeling, especially object-oriented software modeling, is best left to descriptions of specialized software development environments and CASE (computer-aided software engineering) tools. In any event, it is too specialized a topic for this book.

Design representation techniques for traditional, procedurally organized systems are far more common than techniques for object-oriented systems. This is not surprising given the relative newness of object-oriented techniques.

Design representations for traditional systems often fall into one of two categories: control flow oriented and data flow oriented. We will discuss each category briefly. The discussion will be in the context of a single example of a software system. The same example will be used to illustrate the different techniques.

The models we present are intended for illustration only. Any realistic model of the system would be much more detailed than what we will present in the next six subsections. The models given here describe the system only at its highest level. After reading the next six subsections, you should appreciate the expressive power of several different design representations.

8.1.1 *TERMINAL CONCENTRATORS*

Consider a familiar situation—software that controls a terminal concentrator. A terminal concentrator is a hardware device that allow many different terminal lines to access the same cpu. Input from any of the terminal lines is associated with the terminal to which the line is attached at one end. Corresponding output for a program running on one of the terminals is sent from the cpu to the appropriate terminal screen.

In order to keep the data being sent to and from different terminals from going to the wrong place, the signals are "multiplexed" by the terminal concentrator. Multiplexing hardware and software allow the attachment of many terminals on the same port of the computer, thereby providing more simultaneous users (at a potential cost of reduced processing speed). All terminals on the same terminal concentrator share the same connection to the computer, as shown in Figure 8.1.

Multiplexing means that a single set of wires is used for the connection from the terminal concentrator to the cpu. The decision about which terminal to communicate with along these wires can be made by using different frequencies for the signals or by attaching routing information to each packet of information sent.

The essential data structure in a multiplexed system is a queue. A user's data is sent from his or her terminal to the cpu in a stream in a first-in, first-out manner. The data passes through the multiplexing operation of the terminal concentrator and is sent to the cpu when the process is scheduled for execution. All other processes (and the I/O from their terminals) wait for the process to relinquish control of the cpu. Output is then sent from the cpu to the appropriate terminal, also by means of the multiplexing operation of the terminal concentrator.

Thus there are queues for input, queues for output, and mechanisms for determining which data is attached to which terminal.

Figure 8.1 Organization of a terminal concentrator.

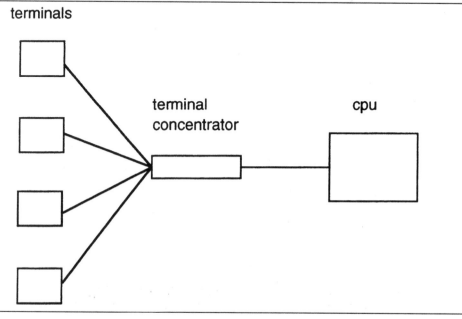

8.1.2 A FLOWCHART REPRESENTATION FOR A TERMINAL CONCENTRATOR

The earliest popular graphical designs were called *flowcharts* and were control flow oriented. The term *control flow* refers to a method of describing a system by means of the major blocks of code that control its operation.

A flowchart was generally drawn by hand using a graphical notation in which control of the program was represented as edges in a directed graph that described the program.

The nodes of a control flow graph are boxes whose shape and orientation provided additional information about the program. For example, a rectangular box with sides either horizontal or vertical means that a computational process occurs at this step in the program. A diamond-shaped box, with its sides at a 45 degree angle with respect to the horizontal direction, is known as a *decision box*. A decision box represents a branch in the control flow of a program. Other symbols are used to represent commonly occurring situations in program behavior.

A flowchart for the software that controls a terminal concentrator is shown in Figure 8.2.

8.1.3 A DATA FLOW REPRESENTATION FOR A TERMINAL CONCENTRATOR

Data flow representations of systems were developed somewhat later than control flow descriptions. The books by Yourdon and deMarco are probably the most accessible basic sources for information on data flow design. Most software engineering books contain examples of the use of data flow diagrams in the design of software systems.

Since different data can move along different paths in the program, it is traditional for data flow design descriptions to include the name of the data along the arrows indicating the direction of data movement.

Data flow designs also depend on particular notations to represent different aspects of a system. Here the arrows indicate a data movement. There are different notations used for different types of data treatment. For example, a node of the graph representing a transformation of input data into output data according to some rule might be represented by a rectangular box. A source of an input data stream such as interactive terminal input would be represented by another notation, indicating that it is a "data source." On the other hand, a repository from which data can never be recalled, such

Figure 8.2 A flowchart for terminal concentrator software.

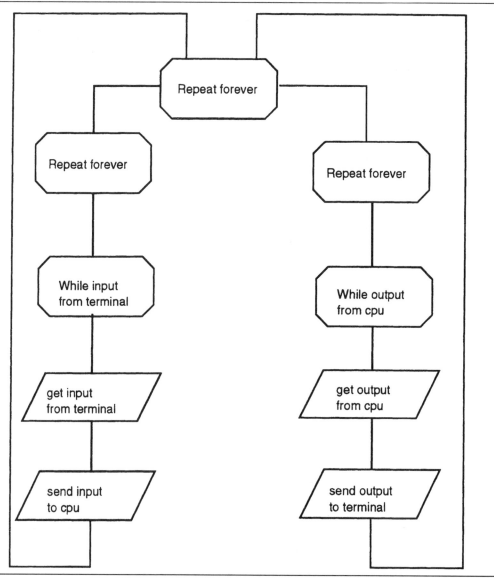

as a terminal screen, is described by another symbol, indicating that this is a "data sink."

Typical data flow descriptions of systems use several diagrams at different "levels." Each level of a data flow diagram represents a more detailed view of a portion of the system at a previously described, higher level.

An example of the data flow description of a program in one graphical notation is given in Figure 8.3. The data flow diagram shown in this figure describes one direction of flow for the terminal concentrator example described previously. The terminal concentrator system can be described completely by a more elaborate diagram. You will be asked to do this in the Exercises.

8.1.4 A PSEUDOCODE REPRESENTATION FOR A TERMINAL CONCENTRATOR

There is one other commonly used method for describing a system. This involves pseudocode, which provides an English-like (at least in English-speaking software development environments) description of the system. The pseudocode is then succes-

Figure 8.3 A data flow representation for a terminal concentrator.

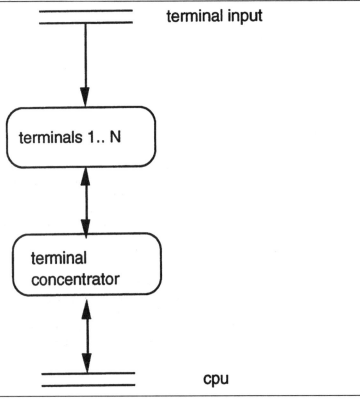

sively refined until the implementation of the source code is straightforward, at least in theory. Note that pseudocode is a nongraphical notation. An example of pseudocode for the terminal concentrator system is shown in Figure 8.4.

Pseudocode representations have one major advantage over the graphical ones: they can be presented as textual information in ASCII files.

8.1.5 OTHER NON-OBJECT-ORIENTED REPRESENTATIONS FOR A TERMINAL CONCENTRATOR

All the previously discussed methods of design representation precede the current interest in object-oriented methods. As a result, they are generally not completely effective in the description of object-oriented designs or systems, although modifications of data flow representations have been used successfully in some instances.

Figure 8.4 A pseudocode representation for a terminal concentrator.

```
For each terminal
  {
  Repeat forever
     {
     When time for input to cpu
        {
        get input data from terminal's input queue
        place on concentrator's input queue to cpu
        include information to identify terminal
        send input data from concentrator to cpu
        remove data from concentrator's input queue
        }
     When time for output from cpu
        {
        receive output data from cpu
        place on concentrator's output queue
        include information to identify terminal
        send output data to terminal's output queue
        remove data from concentrator's queue
        }
     }
  }
```

The design representations described here by no means exhaust the number of representations available. Other commonly used design representations include Buhr diagrams, Booch diagrams, HIPO (hierarchical input process output) charts, and Nassi–Schneiderman charts. Booch diagrams can be used easily with object-oriented systems, while most of the other representations cannot. Descriptions of each of these can be found in most software engineering books and in some of the original writings of the inventors of the notations. Consult the References for more information.

Two related modeling techniques and some commonly associated design representations, information modeling and entity–relationship diagrams, will be described later in this chapter.

8.1.6 *AN OBJECT-ORIENTED REPRESENTATION FOR A TERMINAL CONCENTRATOR*

In this subsection we present a simple object model for the terminal concentrator software system (see Figure 8.5). We will make no attempt to refine the model and will keep it at the same high level that we used for the previous models using different design representations.

The representation is simple (at least at this point). We will use a rectangular box to describe an object, with diamond-shaped boxes and line segments used to indicate relationships between objects. The name of the class is given above a horizontal line inside the box. We will follow the convention of having class names begin with an uppercase letter.

The relationship between the objects is given a name in this representation. The relationship is called "is connected to" and behaves in a similar manner to the "uses" relationship that we will discuss later in this chapter.

Some of the attributes of an arbitrary object in the class are included in the box. We would include all attributes if there were not too many of them.

At the bottom of the diagram, we again list the classes that are in the upper part of the diagram, again using a graphical representation. The classes in this list have typical values for each of the attributes of an object in each class.

Note that this model makes no mention of the queue data structure that will probably be used to keep information going to and from the terminal concentrator in buffers.

Figure 8.5 Representation of an object in the object model notation.

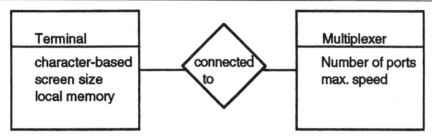

Note that the model presented in this section is object-oriented in the sense that it indicates the action ("is connected to") that is taking place on the two fundamental objects of the system: terminals and terminal concentrator. Attributes of an object are also indicated in this design representation.

Object-oriented models that are both more detailed and provide information about the actual manner in which the terminal concentrator system operates will be discussed later in this chapter.

8.2 Object-Oriented Systems

We now return to the topic of object-oriented modeling of systems. The first fundamental question that we must address is: What are the objects in the system? Once we have determined the objects, we must answer the second fundamental question: What is the set of transformations that can be applied to these objects?

A few definitions may be helpful. An abstract object is said to have *attributes*, which describe some property or aspect of the abstract object. For any instance of an abstract object, each attribute may have values.

The listing of attributes is helpful in assessing our candidate for an object. The attributes must be independent in the sense that a change in the value of one attribute should not affect the value of another attribute.

There is one other judgment that should be made from the attribute list. If there is a single attribute, then it is likely that the object is at a low level of abstraction. This should generally be avoided, and hence we want to have at least two attributes per object.

We will illustrate these concepts by several examples in this and some of the following sections.

Consider the development of a class to describe the abstract concept of a string. Some typical attributes of a string might include its length, its contents, its creation or destruction, and its display. These lead us to some potential values for these attributes—its length might be 22, its contents might be **"I like this C++ book"** (not counting the delimiting quotes), it might be in a state called "created," and it might be displayed on the standard output stream **cout**. Alternate values of some attributes for a string object might be 80 for the length, **"I like this C++ book and wish to buy many copies"** and a file named **"outfile"** for the "display" of the string.

The determination of the attributes of an object and the set of possible values for each attribute then suggests the functions and data types necessary to implement methods to be used with the class. For example, we must have a member function for the **String** class that is able to compute the length of the string. This length must be an **int** (since this is the appropriate elementary predefined data type in C). We must have a constructor function to initialize the contents of the string and we must have a function to display the contents on the appropriate output stream.

Note what we haven't determined yet. There has been no mention of the null byte **\0** to be used as a termination byte to indicate the end of the string; then another question arises as to whether or not their termination byte is to be counted as part of the string, thereby increasing its length by one.

Indeed, there is no requirement that the string should be implemented as a set of contiguous bytes. We could choose to follow the lead of many word processing programs (including the one in which this book is written) and use linked lists to chain together contiguous arrays of characters (and other objects, such as graphs, in the case of the word processor). Other data organizations are possible.

The important point is to note that none of the decisions about the implementation organization or details are relevant to the string object. What we need now is a determination of the attributes of the object and a set of possible values for each attribute.

With such a determination, we can write the first attempt of a description of the class. Thus the first attempt at the definition of a string object will probably have a definition something like the class string defined below. We won't worry about syntax at this point.

```
class String

Member functions:
   int length;
   int strlen( String s);
   void display( String s);
```

with the prototype of the other member functions as necessary.

Some problems arise here because we haven't determined the interface precisely. The constructor member function needs to have a size specified for the length of the string. Other member functions will have to have their interface determined also. Thus we will have to make a second iteration of the design of the class representing strings.

```
class String

Member functions:
   int length;
   String (char *arr);  //array terminated by \0
   int strlen();
   operator <<
```

There are more iterations to be performed in order to have a complete definition of the interfaces of this class. Of course, we still have to develop an implementation of the methods. We omit the details of the iteration for the class description at this point since we will describe them in detail in Section 8.5 after we have discussed some methodologies for developing classes. Implementation of the code for the member functions is left as an exercise.

8.3 Class Design Issues

It is necessary to discuss some difficulty with the development of programs that use the class definition methods described in the previous section. The methodology described in the previous section assumes that the software system has been developed in a vacuum. That is, we have described some of the attributes that we believe are associated with a type of object and have described some potentially useful interfaces between this object and others (such as character arrays and I/O streams). We have not paid any attention to any of the previously developed classes that might be related to our class and that would encourage the use of similar interfaces.

If there is a set of related classes with similar standards for their interfaces, then we must at least consider these interfaces before we set in stone the interfaces that are part of the current description of the object.

This point cannot be emphasized enough. Development of an object must take place along the lines of defining its attributes and typical values for these attributes. This can be done by the usual method of stepwise refinement so familiar to software engineers. Development of a *useful* object (one that can be used in a variety of important situations) requires that one consider the interfaces to existing objects in the development stage. Otherwise the objects that we develop will have very limited utility.

We illustrate the point by an analogy. Consider the current state of development of computer hardware. Unless a hardware designer is designing a special-purpose high-performance supercomputer or a custom microprocessor for control of an embedded system, he or she will use previously developed components with well-defined and well-documented interfaces. These existing well-designed hardware components have predictable levels of performance in terms of clock speed, data transfer rate, reaction to specified interrupts, power usage, etc. A new piece of hardware that does not adhere to these standard interfaces is unlikely to be very useful outside a narrow range of applications. Only a revolutionary design with tremendous applicability or performance is likely to be useful an unusual interface with only mundane applications or average performance is not likely to be very successful.

Exactly the same situation applies to developing classes that can be used as reusable software components. The development of a class cannot be done in a vacuum. It must take into account the other classes in the class library in order to make efficient use of previously developed classes. The library catalog and any software tools for examining the different libraries are extremely important when developing classes to interact with real systems.

Note that we must do one other thing to ensure that the classes we develop make efficient use of resources, especially programmer time. If there is a relationship between our class and one or more preexisting classes, it is possible that then we can make use of previously developed functions that were members of a preexisting class. This is easy to do if we can use inheritance.

We can also use functions associated with an object if the functions were declared originally as being friend functions. Even if the functions were not declared originally as friend functions, we might be able to change the definition of the preexisting class to make the required functions member functions and recompile the system.

In any event, an efficient software design process requires a check of available software resources.

Grady Booch is one of the most highly regarded experts in the object-oriented programming community. He observes that in most high-quality object-oriented programs, many essential objects are clustered into several related classes, rather than being grouped solely by inheritance. He states that the only programs that have all objects related are relatively trivial ones.

Clearly, the determination of available classes in class libraries is only a starting point when designing object-oriented programs. However, it is essential step in designing an object-oriented system.

8.4   What Is an Object?

In this section we give some guidelines for determining the objects that are present in a system that we wish to design. Recall the viewpoint of Section 8.2, in which we stated that an object has attributes and that in any instance of an object, these attributes will have values.

Suppose that you have chosen a candidate to be an object in your system and that you have determined a set of attributes and their possible sets of values. What informal tests can you apply to be sure that your objects are the most appropriate abstractions for your system?

The first test is the *multiple examples test*. Simply stated, if there is only one example of an instance of an object, then the concept is not sufficiently general to have object-oriented techniques used to implement it.

The multiple examples test is consistent with the procedural programming dictum: "If you use it once, just write the code. If you use it twice, write a procedure or function." It is also consistent with the advice commonly given to young mathematicians: "If a concept or theory does not have at least three different hard examples, it is not worth studying."

Once our candiate for an object passes the multiple examples test, it is placed in a set of potential objects. The attributes of the objects are now tested using the "has-a" relationship, which can help to formalize the set of attributes of the objects. We should write an initial set of member functions for this potential object, based on reasonable transformations of the values of some of the attributes of the proposed object.

The next informal rule used for checking the appropriateness of objects concerns the class hierarchy in which new classes are designed from old ones. This relationship between the base class and the derived class is best described as the "is-a" relationship. If the sentence

```
object 1 is a object 2
```

does not seem to make sense, then the relationship is not of the form

```
(base class, derived class).
```

and hence we do not have an inheritance relationship.

On the other hand, if the sentence does seem to make sense, then we have a candidate for such a relationship. This is called the *is-a relation test.* In this case, we should draw a diagram of the object and any relationship between the object and other objects.

We should list the potential member functions and be alert for any examples of polymorphism. The appearance of polymorphism suggests that we have chosen our inheritance relationships properly. If there is no polymorphism, then we should be suspicious that we have not described the member functions correctly, or at least not in sufficient detail.

The set of potential objects and the descriptions of their member functions should be refined at each step.

There is one final relationship that should be performed in order to incorporate the objects into a preliminary object-oriented design of a software system. The concern here is that the objects listed should form a complete set of the objects needed for the software system being designed. The relationship we are looking for is the "uses-a relation."

We use this relationship by asking if the sentence

```
object 1 uses object 2
```

makes sense for the pairs of objects considered. Every meaningful sentence suggests either a client–server or agent-based relationship and is to be considered as part of the program's design. If we cannot find any instances of this sentence making sense, then there are two possibilities: Either the objects are insufficiently specified for us to be able to describe the entire system, or else the natural description of the system is as a procedural program controlling objects.

Note that objects can be related to many other objects. Multiple inheritance is possible, and so are multiple objects. Thus the previous steps should be repeated for groups of three objects, four objects, and so on, until the designer feels that the system's essential object-oriented features have been described.

We summarize the recommended steps for determining objects in Table 8.1.

Make sure you understand the steps in this process of determining objects.

8.5   An Example of Class Development: The String Class

In this section we return to the discussion of the class **String** that we began briefly in Section 8.2. We will apply the rules listed in Table 8.1 to this class and obtain what we hope is a satisfactory abstraction of the properties we want in an abstract **String** class. The **String** class presented in this chapter was originally developed by Eric Charles for a project under the direction of Bernard Woolfolk at Howard University.

Initially, we noted that this class had two member functions: a constructor function **String()** and a function **strlen()** to compute the length of an object of the

Table 8.1 Determination of objects.

1. Choose a candidate to be an object.
2. Determine a set of attributes and their possible sets of values. Use the **has-a** relation. List all relevant transformations on the object.
3. Develop an initial set of transformations on the object to serve as member functions. The list of attributes and their values provide an initial set of transformations by determing the value of, and assigning a value to, each attribute of an object. Constructor, destructor, and I/O functions should also be included.
4. Determine if there is more than one example of the object. If so, then place the proposed object in a set of potential objects. If not, discard it because it fails the multiple examples test.
5. Apply the **is-a** relation by considering all sentences of the form

       object 1 is a object 2

   Objects considered for this relation should include the object under development and any other objects believed to be related. (The class library may be consulted during this step of the process.) Each valid sentence should lead to an inheritance relationship. Each inheritance relationship should be illustrated graphically.
6. Use polymorphism and overloading of operators (and functions) to check if we have described the objects in sufficient detail. Check the object description if no polymorphism or overloading is found.
7. Use the **uses-a** relation

       object 1 uses object 2

   to determine all instances of client–server or agent-based relationships. Use these relationships to determine issues of program design.
8. Review the object, its attributes, member functions, inheritance properties, polymorphism, overloading, and relationships to other objects to determine if the object is complete in the sense that no other functions, attributes, or relationships are necessary.
9. Repeat steps 2 through 8 for all combinations of relevant objects (triples, quadruples, and so on) until the object's role in any proposed system has been described adequately.

class. We are at step 1 of the process described in Table 8.1—we have selected a candidate for an object.

Step 2 in the process requires us to list the attributes of this object. The list of attributes indicated previously was

    length

There was no explicit mention of the data to be stored in **String** in our previous discussion! We clearly expected to use the data in **String** in the function **strlen()**. Let's fix the oversight now by including the data. The next list of attributes for the **String** object is

    length
    data in the **String**

These attributes make sense as potential attributes for **String** objects, because the sentences

A String has a length.

and

A String has data.

both make sense. The second sentence could probably be phrased better as

A String has contents.

and hence we will use the term *contents* instead of *data* in our initial list of attributes.

To make sure that these are reasonable atrributes, we list some typical values in a table:

Attribute	Typical value
length	19
contents	Please buy this book.

In step 3, we consider possible transformations of the object. Relevant member functions include:

* constructor
* destructor
* initialization of a string
* assignment of contents to another string (copy constructor)
* input of a string
* output of a string

It is essential that we begin to consider what the interfaces of these member functions should look like. The C++ default constructor and destructor functions take no arguments and return no values. If we wish to initialze a **String** object, then we should specify this here. It is likely that we will wish to have a constructor of the form

```
String(char * init);
```

or perhaps

```
String(const char * init);
```

Here **init** represents a null-terminated array of characters.

The I/O member functions will almost certainly overload the << and >> operators. It will probably be useful to allow writing of strings to streams other than **cin**, **cout**, and **cerr**, so that our I/O functions will be overloaded again.

Note that we have not addressed issues, such as whether or not the null byte is included as part of the length of the object. These are details that are relevant to either the interface to other objects or the specifics of an implementation.

There are many examples of strings and so our proposed **String** object clearly passes the "many examples test" of step 4.

We now apply step 5 of the process to determine if there are any inheritance relationships. In order to do this, we must determine a set of objects that we believe have an inheritance relationship with our proposed new object. With the possible exceptions of lists and arrays, there are no objects that seem likely at this time and so we proceed to step 6 of the process. If we felt that there was a strong **is-a** relationship between the **String** class and an (abstract) arrray class, then we would have inheritance relationships between these classes. A similar statement holds for the **String** class and an (abstract) linked list class.

We illustrate the state of our **String** class after using steps 1 through 5 of the process in Example 8.1. The header file **String.h** includes the basic definitions needed for the **String** class described so far.

Example 8.1 A user-defined **String** class—first iteration using steps 1 through 5.

```
// File: ex8_1.h
//
// Contains the initial attempt at a class definition
// of the String class using steps 1 through 5 of the
// object development process.
//

class String
{
private:
  char *d_string_p;   // pointer to string of characters
public:
  // Constructors
  String();
  String(const char *str);

  // Destructor
  ~String();

  // Assignment
```

```
String &operator = (const char* str);

int length() const;

// overloaded conversion operator converts String to char*
operator char*()   // converts to standard type
{
  return d_string_p;
}
};
```

As we will see, the code of Example 8.1 is not very complete as a description of the **String** class. We now continue the process of class development.

In step 6, we ask if any polymorphism or overloading is found. If not, we have probably not described all transformations (member functions) for the object. In this case, we have overloading of (at least) the constructor and I/O functions, so that it is likely that we have made at least some use of object-oriented features of the class.

In step 7, we ask if there is any instance of the **uses-a** relationship between our object and other objects. Here we are looking for client–server or agent-based relations. Because of the simplicity of our **String** object, such a relationship is unlikely and so we proceed to step 8.

Step 8 of the process involves reviewing the current state of development of the class and checking for any missing relationships or transformations. This is an ideal time for having a structured walkthrough of the object, preferably with the walkthrough and review being done by someone other than the designer. The purpose of the review is to check for inconsistencies in the design, for missing or misapplied relationships, and for any unnecessary complications.

In our example, we have provided few of the functions available in the standard collection of C functions for string manipulation. Some typical functions accessed in the standard C language header file **string.h** are **strcmp()**, **strcat()**, and **strcpy()**. It would be appropriate to add many of these to our **String** class at this time.

Step 9 allows us to extend the **is-a** relationship to several classes at once, thereby adding the possibility of multiple inheritance to our class description. More complex instances of the **uses-a** relationship will also appear at this time.

It is probably sensible to repeat steps 2 through 8 only up to triples of classes in most beginning designs, unless we expect a more complex relationship to surface.

After completing this process, we will have obtained a description of the internal data and interfaces of the **String** object. The only things we have to do to actually create such a class are to present the definition of the data and member functions in syntactically correct form and encode the details of the member functions.

We present a more complete description of the **String** class in Example 8.2. Note that there are many more member functions than before. Some of the new member functions are included because we wish to have interfaces to other objects of class **String** and not just have interfaces to data of the type **char ***.

We have included the possibility of modifying values of arguments by using the & operator in several places within our member function declarations. The declarations were declared **const**, as in the argument signature

```
const String& string
```

because we wish to avoid the overhead of copying the entire contents of the **String** object, but leave the value of the argument unchanged. Recall that this is called passing parameters by constant reference.

You should also note the wide range of operators in Example 8.2 for such actions as lexical comparison. Many of these operators are overloaded.

We have also included a **friend** operator for interaction with the ostream class in the declaration

```
friend ostream& operator << (ostream& s, String &str);
```

Example 8.2 Second iteration of the user-defined **String** class using the nine steps of the object development process.

```cpp
// File: ex8_2.h
//
// Contains the class definition of String, using the nine
// steps of the object development process.
//

class String
{
private:
  char *d_string_p;  // pointer to string of characters
public:
  // Constructors
  String();
  String(const String& string);
  String(const char *str);

  // Destructor
  ~String();

  // Assignment
  String &operator = (const String& string);
```

```
String &operator = (const char* str);

// Manipulators
String &operator += (const String& string);
String &operator += (const char* str);
// Concatenation (to this string)

// Accessors
int length() const;
String operator + (const String& str) const;
String operator + (const char* string) const;
// Concatenation (to a new string)

// Lexical Comparison Operators
int operator == (const String& string) const;
int operator == (const char* str) const;
int operator != (const String& string) const;
int operator != (const char* str) const;
int operator < (const String& string) const;
int operator < (const char* str) const;
int operator <= (const String& string) const;
int operator <= (const char* str) const;
int operator > (const String& string) const;
int operator > (const char* str) const;
int operator >= (const String& string) const;
int operator >= (const char* str) const;


// overloaded conversion operator converts String to char*
operator char*()  // converts to standard type
{
  return d_string_p;
}

// friend—for overloaded I/O operator of ostream class
friend ostream& operator << (ostream& s, String &str);

};
```

There are many ways to describe the abstract object represented by the **String** class. You should compare the two class descriptions given so far in this section with the equivalent **String** class available with your C++ compiler. You should also consult the C++ standard library when it becomes available, or Plauger's book on the draft ANSI standard for a C++ library that is listed in the References.

Additional steps are appropriate if the goal is to develop classes that encourage the use of reusable software components. The suggestions of Johnson and Foote are typical of methods for development of reusable classes of objects. The goal is to create classes that not only represent relevant data abstractions but also are easily tested. Their suggestions are presented in Table 8.2.

These rules are helpful when designing large systems with complex classes. They are probably too much for the simple examples that are presented in this chapter.

We now present the final description of our **String** class, illustrated in Example 8.3. The new features include a set of nonmember (free) functions to perform other actions. As before, you should compare this class with the **String** class available with your system. (The file is listed under the name **String.h** in the CHAP8 directory on the disk provided with this book.)

The class description is complete and shows the effects of the different iterations of the object development process. The methods (member functions) are small, each performing specific actions on selected types of operands.

There are many instances of overloading operators such as <= and += in order to have simple programs to compare and concatenate strings. You should note the proper use of constant pointers within the member functions implementing these operations for concatenation to new strings and to existing ones.

Note also the presence of free functions to perform compare and concatenation. These free functions are used when the first argument is a null-terminated character array, rather than an object of class **String**. This is an indication of the completeness of our **String** class.

As indicated above, the class is described in Example 8.3. The implementations of the member functions will be given in Example 8.4.

Table 8.2 Some methods for encouraging reusable classes.

1. Introduce recursion into the class to aid in abstraction.
2. Eliminate case analysis in the development of member functions.
3. Reduce the number of arguments.
4. Reduce the size of methods.
5. Class hierarchies should be deep and narrow.
6. The top of the hierarchy should be abstract.
7. Minimize access to variables.
8. Subclasses should be specializations of larger classes.
9. Split large classes into several smaller classes.
10. Factor implementation differences.
11. Separate methods that do not communicate.
12. Send messages to components instead of the object itself.
13. Reduce implicit parameter passing.

Example 8.3 The user-defined include file **String.h**.

```
//////////////////////////////////////////////////////////////
// File: String.h
// Contains the class definition of String, as well as
// non-member overloaded operator functions.
//////////////////////////////////////////////////////////////

class String
{
private:
  char *d_string_p;   // pointer to string of characters

public:
  // Constructors
  String();
  String(const String& string);
  String(const char *str);

  // Destructor
  ~String();

  // Assignment
  String &operator = (const String& string);
  String &operator = (const char* str);

  // Manipulators for concatenation (to this string)
  String &operator += (const String& string);
  String &operator += (const char* str);

  int length() const;

  // Concatenation (to a new string)
  String operator + (const String& str) const;
  String operator + (const char* string) const;

  // Comparison Operators (lexical)
  int operator == (const String& string) const;
  int operator == (const char* str) const;
  int operator != (const String& string) const;
  int operator != (const char* str) const;
  int operator < (const String& string) const;
  int operator < (const char* str) const;
  int operator <= (const String& string) const;
  int operator <= (const char* str) const;
  int operator > (const String& string) const;
  int operator > (const char* str) const;
  int operator >= (const String& string) const;
  int operator >= (const char* str) const;
```

```
  // overloaded conversion operator converts String to char*
  operator char*()  // converts to standard type
  {
    return d_string_p;
  }

  // friend — for overloaded I/O operator of ostream class
  friend ostream& operator << (ostream& s, String &str);
};


// Non-Member (Free) Operators
String operator + (const char* str, const String& string);
int operator == (const char* str, const String& string);
int operator != (const char* str, const String& string);
int operator > (const char* str, const String& string);
int operator >= (const char* str, const String& string);
int operator < (const char* str, const String& string);
int operator <= (const char* str, const String& string);
```

Of course, we need implementations of the member functions for this class. The source code implementations of these functions are presented in Example 8.4. (The file is listed under the name **String.c** in the CHAP8 directory on the disk provided with this book.)

There are many member functions because there are many opportunities for operator overloading. This leads to a large number of potential test cases.

Most of the details of implementation of the methods are straightforward. However, there are several features of the code that you should note. We have made frequent use of the special pointer **this** in several function definitions. You should also note the heavy use of passing arguments by reference, using the ampersand symbol (&) after the name of the argument.

Example 8.4 File **String.cpp**: Implementation of member functions for the **String** class.

```
/////////////////////////////////////////////////////////////
// File Name: string.cpp
// Contains member and nonmember function definitions.
/////////////////////////////////////////////////////////////

#include "string.h"

static char *init (const char *str)
{
  int size;
  char *string = new char[size = strlen(str) + 1];
```

```
    memcpy(string, str, size);
    return string;
}


// constructor
String::String()
{
  d_string_p = init("");
}


// constructor
String::String(const String& string)
{
  d_string_p = init(string.d_string_p);
}


// constructor
String::String(const char* str)
{
  d_string_p = init(str);
}

// constructor
String::~String()
{
  delete d_string_p;
}


String & String::operator = (const String& string)
{
  return *this = string.d_string_p;
}


String & String::operator = (const char* str)
{
  int len = strlen(str);           // get length of str
  char *s = new char[len + 1];     // alloc mem for s

  strcpy(s, str);                  // copy str to s
  delete [] d_string_p;            // dealloc mem of old string
  d_string_p = s;                  // reinitialize pointer
  return *this;                    // return
```

```
}


String &String::operator += (const String& string)
{
  return *this += string.d_string_p;
}


String &String::operator += (const char* str)
{
  int len = length();      // get length of str1
  len += strlen(str);      // add length of str2
  char *s = new char[len + 1];   // alloc memory

  strcpy(s, d_string_p);        // copy str1 to new str
  strcat(s, str);               // concatenate strings
  delete [] d_string_p;         // dealloc mem of str1
  d_string_p = s;               // reinitialize pointer
  return *this;                 // return
}


// returns length of string
int String::length() const
{
  return strlen(d_string_p);
}


String String::operator + (const String& string) const
{
  String str = *this;    // create new object

  str += string;         // concatenate strings
  return str;            // return new object
}


String String::operator + (const char* str) const
{
  String Str = *this;  // create new object
  Str += str;          // concatenate strings
  return Str;          // return new object
}
```

```
// The following functions use the standard string.h
// library function, strcmp(), to overload operators.
// strcmp() returns 0 if the strings are equal, < 0 if
// str1 is lexicographically less than str2, and > 0 if
// str1 is greater than str2.  The actual return values
// are being tested in these functions.

int String::operator == (const String& string) const
{
  return ( strcmp(d_string_p, string.d_string_p) == 0 );
}


int String::operator == (const char* str) const
{
  return ( strcmp(d_string_p, str) == 0 );
}


int String::operator!=(const String& string) const {
     return ( strcmp(d_string_p, string.d_string_p) != 0 );
}


int String::operator != (const char* str) const
{
  return ( strcmp(d_string_p, str) != 0 );
}


int String::operator < (const String& string) const
{
  return ( strcmp(d_string_p, string.d_string_p) < 0 );
}


int String::operator < (const char* str) const
{
  return ( strcmp(d_string_p, str) < 0 );
}


int String::operator <= (const String& string) const
{
  return ( strcmp(d_string_p, string.d_string_p) <= 0 );
}


int String::operator <= (const char* str) const
{
```

```
    return ( strcmp(d_string_p, str) <= 0 );
}


int String::operator > (const String& string) const
{
  return ( strcmp (d_string_p, string.d_string_p) >  0 );
}


int String::operator > (const char* str) const {
  return ( strcmp (d_string_p, str) >  0 );
}


int String::operator >= (const String& string) const
{
  return ( strcmp(d_string_p, string.d_string_p) >= 0 );
}


int String::operator >= (const char* str) const
{
  return ( strcmp(d_string_p, str) >= 0 );
}


// Next functions also use the overloaded operators that
// were defined above to operate on operands of different
// types.

String operator + (const char* str, const String& string)
{
  String newstr = str;      // create new object
  newstr += string;         // concatenate strings
  return newstr;            // return object
}


// pass str as parameter to overloaded operator function
int operator == (const char* str, const String& string)
{
  return ( string.operator == (str) );
}


// pass str as parameter to overloaded operator function
int operator != (const char* str, const String& string)
```

```
{
  return ( string.operator != (str) );
}


// pass str as parameter to overloaded operator function
int operator < (const char* str, const String& string)
{
  return ( string.operator > (str) );
}


// pass str as parameter to overloaded operator function
int operator <= (const char* str, const String& string)
{
  return ( string.operator >= (str) );
}


// pass str as parameter to overloaded operator function
int operator > (const char* str, const String& string)
{
     return ( string.operator < (str) );
}


// pass str as parameter to overloaded operator function
int operator >= (const char* str, const String& string)
{
  return ( string.operator <= (str) );
}


// overloaded I/O operator
ostream &operator << (ostream& s, String &str)
{
  // << is friend of String class
  s << str.d_string_p;  // get output string from str
  return s;             // return output
}
```

It is unlikely that there are any other operations that might be needed for an implementation of a **String** class.

8.6 Concepts Related to Objects

Many disciplines in computer science have concepts that are somewhat related to objects in object-oriented programming. One example is the entity–relationship, or E-R, model that is common in database design. Another is the information model that is frequently used in artificial intelligence and expert systems. We will discuss each of these models briefly in this section.

An E-R diagram represents a set of fundamental quantities, known as entities, and the relationships between them. The labeling of arcs in the E-R diagram indicates the nature of the relationships between the different entities connected by each arc.

An E-R diagram can serve as a starting point for a preliminary set of objects. The diagram's relationships often suggest some possible methods, or transformations, on objects in the system.

This method is only a first step in the development of a complete description of the objects and methods in a system because the E-R diagram generally lacks any self-transformations of an object. Thus constructors, destructors, and initializers are not generally evident from E-R diagrams. Tests for equality are typically not clear. Many other common methods are not easily represented in E-R diagrams.

These observations of the utility of E-R diagrams in objects can be summarized as follows:

- If an E-R diagram already exists, use the entities as initial choices of objects and methods. Pay particular attention to the need for self-transforming methods such as constructors, destructors, and initializers.
- If no E-R diagram exists, then don't bother writing one. Instead, proceed to the description of objects using the process in Table 8.1 directly.

We now turn to the discussion of information models. Information models are often used in artificial intelligence. They represent connections between different aspects of a system. The term *object* is often used in information modeling and has a different meaning from that of this book.

Notations for information models are far from standard. The arcs of the diagram represent relationships between the various "aspects" of the system. The arcs are labeled indicating that the relationships are one-to-one, many-to-one, one-to-many, or many-to-many. Some information modeling systems suggest avoiding the use of many-to-many representations by refining the "aspects" if necessary. These notations can indicate aggregation, in which one object is logically composed of several other objects.

A set of attributes for the "aspects" is also provided as part of an information model diagram.

Another common feature of information models is the is-a relation. This can help to determine if an object is a subobject of another, indicating inheritance.

Note that the information model diagrams as described here do not convey any information about the organization of attributes, or the passing of attribute values from one "aspect" to another. The diagram contains no attribute information. All attribute information is stored in the attribute list. As with E-R diagrams, no explicit information about constructors, destructors, initializers, etc. is directly available.

8.7 Design Representations
for Object-Oriented Systems

In this section we will describe one commonly used notation for representation of object-oriented designs. It should be noted that there are many representations used for object-oriented analysis and design, just as there are many representations used for both procedurally oriented and data flow–oriented analysis and design.

Some of the methodologies used for object-oriented software development are the Booch method and object modeling technique (OMT).

We can have two different views of a system: the object model and the interface model. We will discuss these two views in order.

In the object model representation, we will use an extended entity–relationship (E-R) notation. We will use the convention that the name of a class will be given in uppercase and the instances of a class will be given in lowercase.

Our starting point for this discussion is the object diagram given in Figure 8.5 in Section 8.1.6. Such diagrams provide a good high-level view of an object-oriented system.

The object diagrams can be refined further by incorporating the cardinality of each relationship in the diagram. Figure 8.6 illustrates this. The numbers on the side or top of a relation indicate the number of items on each side having the relationship. The cardinality can be one of the following: a precise value, a range of values, the symbol * denoting 0 or more, or the symbol + denoting 1 or more. We have used the + and a range in Figure 8.6.

An object model should be expanded until it describes the essential abstractions of objects in the system. Unfortunately, the object model, as indicated so far in this section, is inadequate to describe fully the relationship between different objects.

In view of this limitation, we will attempt to incorporate the interfaces between objects in our model. There are several methods of doing this.

Figure 8.6 Addition of cardinality information to an object model notation.

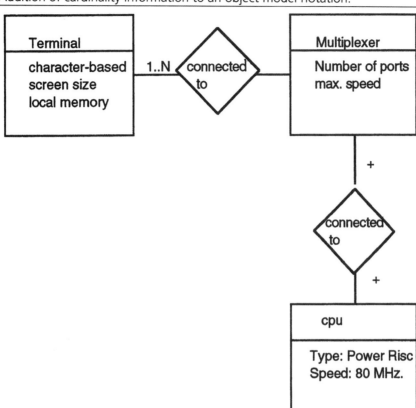

One method is the use of state tables. The terms "state diagram," "state machine," and "finite state machine" are often used instead of "state table." This is one of the oldest methods for describing systems. It certainly predates any of the current efforts in object-oriented design.

A state table for the terminal concentrator system might have six states, which we will call **TIR, CIR, CPUIR, CPUOR, COR,** and **TOR**. The acronyms stand for terminal input ready, concentrator input ready, cpu input ready, cpu output ready, concentrator output ready, and terminal output ready, respectively.

We illustrate the states for the terminal concentrator system in Figure 8.7. The notation is slightly different from the most common one in that we have not specified the initial state where the inputs to the system arive (from the keyboard) and the final state where the outputs leave the system for good (when they are displayed on the terminal screen).

Figure 8.7 A state diagram for the terminal concentrator system.

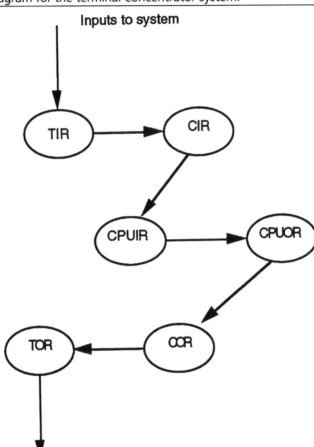

Inputs to system

Outputs from system

It is useful to know how to use existing representations for systems, when attempting to describe them in object-oriented terms. We often have an object model for a system. Our suggestions for the use of existing information models and diagrams in object modeling can be summarized as follows:

- If an information model diagram exists, use it to determine initial relationships, especially those of aggregation.
- Examine attribute lists, for indication of data structures and a preliminary set of transformation to operate on the values of these attributes.
- If no information model is available, then proceed directly to a description of objects in the system.

For additional information on E-R diagrams and information modeling, consult the References.

Summary

Design representations can make a system easier to understand by using a graphical representation to provide a high-level view, hiding relatively unimportant details. Common design representations for procedurally based designs include flowcharts and data flow diagrams. Pseudocode is also frequently used.

The first step in designing an object-oriented system is to determine the relevant objects. Objects have attributes, and for each instance of an object, the attributes can take on a set of possible values. Determination of the attributes of an object and the set of possible values helps in the development of the function prototypes for the class.

Objects should not be defined in a vacuum for realistic descriptions of systems. The interfaces for a particular class may make it difficult to use other classes already present in the class library. Thus the class library must be examined, either by a catalog (listing) of the classes or by using a software tool called a browser.

The interface of the class should be consistent with that of related classes performing similar services.

Preexisting classes in the class library should be examined for the possible availability of usable friend functions.

The development of a set of objects for a system should be an iterative process. Candidates for objects should be able to pass the multiple example and other tests. Attributes of objects can be found by the **has-a** relationship. A derived class must be related to a base class by the **is-a** relationship. Other relationships between classes can be found using the **uses-a** relationship.

Design representations for object-oriented systems can be either graphical or text-based. Graphical ones are often based on information models or entity–relationship (E-R) graphs.

EXERCISES

1. Take any non-object-oriented program that you have written with approximately 50–300 lines of code. Write a flowchart for this program.

2. Repeat Exercise 1, writing a data flow diagram.

3. What are the objects in the system you chose for Exercises 1 and 2? List the attributes and the set of possible attribute values for each.

4. Take any object-oriented program that you have written with approximately 50–300 lines of code. Write a flowchart for this program.

5. Repeat Exercise 4, writing a data flow diagram.

6. Consider the development of an external computer system to evaluate how well a human subject is learning the use of a computer. The user is to interact with the I/O devices of monitor, keyboard, trackball, and mouse. The "user object" has an attribute called "experience level," which has the possible values "novice computer user," "frequent computer user," and "experienced computer user." List other possible attributes that might be appropriate for describing the user. (For simplicity, assume that there is a single software application running and that the user is not familiar with it.)

7. Rewrite the **String** class of Examples 8.3 and 8.4 to avoid the use of free (non-member) functions.

8. Write a description of the **String** class discussed in Section 8.5 using an **Array** class as a base class.

9. Write a description of the **String** class discussed in Section 8.5 using a **List** class as a base class.

10. How does the **String** class given in Examples 8.3 and 8.4 compare with the **String** class available in your class library?

11. Describe how you would test the member functionts in the **String** class given in Examples 8.3 and 8.4. How would you test the free (non-member) functions?

An Example: A Graphical Database

9

In this chapter we will describe the design and implementation of a simplified example of a graphical database system. The objective of this system is to enable a user to manipulate and traverse simple graphical images. We will take the approach that the system is to be designed from scratch, so that there is no need to reuse any existing structures or code. In particular, we will not attempt to incorporate any code that we had developed previously as part of a procedurally based system.

In order to illustrate good software engineering practice, we will now follow the policy of giving our files names that indicate their contents, rather than indicating their position within a chapter of a book. This is appropriate, since we have already learned the fundamentals of C++ and are anxious to apply the techniques of object-oriented software design to more realistic problems. The files are named properly on the disk included with this book.

9.1   Requirements

For simplicity, we will limit our discussion to polyhedral figures, that is, three-dimensional figures made up of a finite collection of "faces," each of which is a two-dimensional polygon. For short, we will refer to these polyhedral figures as polyhedra. The polygons themselves are bonded by a finite collection of line segments called "edges."

Some examples of polyhedral figures are cubes, tetrahedrons, and prisms, which are illustrated in Figures 9.1, 9.2, and 9.3.

We have shown the cube in Figure 9.1 without any direct indication of the hidden edges or faces. The same is true for the prism in Figure 9.3. The representation of the tetrahedron in Figure 9.2 does have a dashed line representing a hidden edge. This hidden edge is part of the boundary of two hidden faces. It is possible for a single polyhedron to obscure more than one hidden surface.

We will show hidden edges and faces in the illustrations when they are not obvious from the viewpoint given for the object and their inclusion in a diagram does not clutter the image too much.

A three-dimensional geometric figure can be considered as a solid object with a boundary, as a solid object without a boundary, or as a region in space described by its boundary surfaces. For simplicity, we will consider only the surfaces of the polyhedra in our database.

The operations that we will perform on these polyhedra will be construction, destruction, determination of their orientation in space, and the determination of which faces of the polyhedra are visible to an observer at a certain position and looking in a particular direction. The display of these polyhedra using a graphics package is highly machine-dependent and will not be described in this book.

We briefly discuss some of the motivation for the information that will be included in our analysis.

In order to determine if a face is visible from a viewpoint in a particular direction, we must be able to determine which points on the surface are hidden by other surfaces. Figure 9.4 illustrates this point. The faces labeled **A**, **B**, and **C** in the figure are visible since, from our perspective viewpoint, there are no points of the surface between our viewpoint and the rear surface. We take our viewpoint to be at infinity along the **z** axis (coming out of the page). The other two faces of the prism are not visible from this viewpoint. Note that different faces will be visible and others will be hidden if either the viewpoint or the viewing direction is changed.

One common computer graphics algorithm used to solve this problem uses the orientation of the face and sorts all points on the surface of the polyhedron by their **z** coordinates. This algorithm is called the **z**-buffer algorithm. The sorting is done for those points with their **x** and **y** coordinations related by an expression based on the type of projection onto a hypothetical plane seen from the viewpoint. For more details, consult any standard reference on computer graphics.

The orientation of a face can be determined by taking the cross-product of two directed vectors that describe two adjacent edges. The orientation of the edges is such that the interior of the face is always to the left.

We will not use any of the mathematical computations or viewing algorithms in the discussion that follows. (This is only a tiny portion of the set of operations that would

Figure 9.1 A cube.

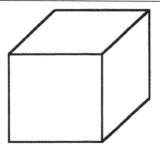

Figure 9.2 A tetrahedron.

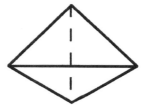

Figure 9.3 A prism.

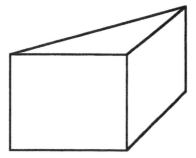

be required of even the simplest graphics package.) We will not combine two polyhedra by taking the union of their boundaries or interiors, as is shown in Figure 9.5; remove a polyhedron from within another one, as is shown in Figure 9.6 or apply any geometric transformations to the polyhedron such as translation, rotation, or shrinking.

One final observation should be made about the requirements. A typical computer graphics system distinguishes the modeling step, in which geometric objects are represented in "world coordinates," from the display step, in which the object is displayed on a monitor in what are called "normalized screen coordinates." Normalized screen coor-

Figure 9.4 Illustration of visible and hidden faces.

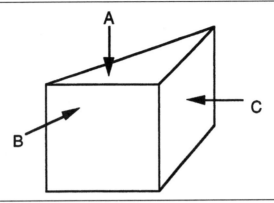

Figure 9.5 Combination of two polyhedra.

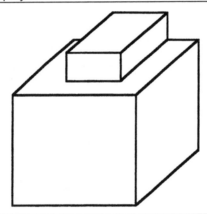

Figure 9.6 Removal of one polyhedron from another.

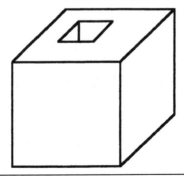

a monitor in what are called "normalized screen coordinates." Normalized screen coordinates usually range from 0.0 to 1.0 in each direction (x, y, z).

Some computer graphics display systems use a range of 0.0 to 1.0 for the normalized horizontal (x) screen coordinate, 0.0 to 0.75 for the normalized vertical (y) screen coordinate, and 0.0 to 1.0 for the normalized z screen coordinate, which appears as an oblique line. This is done to account for the aspect ratio, which is the ratio of the horizontal dimension of the monitor (or terminal) screen to its vertical dimension. We will not treat this alternative arrangement of normalized screen coordinates in this book.

The transformation from world coordinates to normalized screen coordinates is something like

```
//World-to-screen algorithm.
for (x = *MIN; x <= XMAX; x += increment)
   for (y = YMIN; y <= YMAX; y += increment)
      for (z = ZMIN; z <= ZMAX; z += increment)
        {
        x_screen = (x - XMIN)/(XMAX - XMIN);
        y_screen = (y - YMIN)/(YMAX - YMIN);
        z_screen = (z - ZMIN)/(ZMAX - ZMIN);
        };
```

The six constants **XMIN**, **XMAX**, **YMIN**, **YMAX**, **ZMIN**, and **ZMAX** are chosen to represent the portion of real world space that will be displayed. Any clipping of the object is done in world space so that the world-to-screen algorithm can be applied directly. (The term *clipping* refers to the restriction of the amount of an object that can be viewed in a fixed area such as a rectangle of limited size.) For our purposes, we will ignore the world-to-screen transformation and concentrate on the geometric object in world coordinates.

9.2   Determination of Objects for Representation of Polyhedra

In this section we will develop the objects for an object-oriented system that meets our requirements. There are several natural choices here. We can let any allowable geometric object (in this case a polyhedron) be an object in the sense of object-oriented programming.

An alternative approach is to let the fundamental object in our system be a face of a polyhedron. Other possibilities include letting edges or even vertices (which are merely points) be objects.

Let's examine each of these possible organizations from the perspective suggested in Chapter 8. For clarity, we will discuss each of these possible organizations in a separate subsection. After we have considered all these organizations, we will select the best one at the end of this section. Member functions for the organization chosen will be given in Section 9.3.

9.2.1 USE OF POLYHEDRA AS FUNDAMENTAL OBJECTS

If we use polyhedra as our fundamental objects, we certainly meet the "multiple examples" criterion. Possible attributes include the number, size, and shape of the individual faces, orientation of each face relative to a fixed orientation and viewpoint, number of edges, and number and location of vertices. The object's attributes must have some way of indicating the set of faces that make up the object and which edges belong to which face.

We list some of the possibilities for attributes in Table 9.1. We will not worry at this stage about which attributes are primitive and which ones can have their values derived from values of other attributes. These issues will be addressed in the next iteration of object determination.

Table 9.1 Attributes of polyhedra.

Attribute	Types of Values
Number of faces	Integer, >= 4
Shape of faces	Some figure known from plane geometry. Includes "triangle," "square," "rectangle," "rhombus," "pentagon," etc., as well as a catchall name such as "other" for unknown figures.
Size of faces	**float**
Orientation of faces	Angles (3)
Set of edges for each face	Set of edges (pairs of type **Vertex**)
Number of edges	Integer
Length of an edge	**float** (not a primitive attribute)
Number of vertices	Integer
Set of vertices for each face	Set of vertices (triples of type **float**)
Location of vertices	Triples of type **float**

Some of these attributes are clearly redundant. For example, the length of an edge can be computed from the coordinates of the vertices that are its endpoints. Hence the length of an edge is not a primitive attribute.

Note that there are many possibilities for inheritance with such a class description.

There are many possible relationships between the various attributes, and this suggests that the definition of the methods for this class, not to mention the implementation of these methods, might be very complex. Part of this complexity is due to the potential relationships involved with polyhedra such as those shown in Figures 9.5 and 9.6.

We have several options, including the following:

- Representing the "internal" and external attachments illustrated in Figures 9.5 and 9.6 using an explicit attribute.
- Representing the "internal" and external attachments illustrated in Figures 9.5 and 9.6 implicitly.
- Not representing any of the "internal" and external attachments illustrated in Figures 9.5 and 9.6.

It is not immediately clear that we have isolated the most fundamental objects in this system. Thus we will follow the next step in the process of object development that was described in Section 8.2. This means that we should list some potential member functions.

Constructor functions would have to be heavily overloaded, because of the different possibilities for polygons. Destructor functions would have to be carefully written but seem to pose no special difficulties at this time.

Since we are probably thinking of some sort of list or other standard data structure for the set of faces, the member function to compute the number of faces seems to be easy enough to write.

Determining the size and shape of a face is more complex. The value of the attribute "shape" is probably meaningless if the face is not well known to us. It is likely that the most common value of this attribute will be "other."

For the value of the size attribute, we could use some formula known from plane geometry for the areas of well-known figures such as triangles, squares, and rectangles. More complex shapes can have their areas computed by using some sort of decomposition into triangles, whose areas can be computed easily. There are several such triangularization algorithms. Each of them might lead to an (overloaded) member function to compute the area of a face. The important thing to note is that the area of a face is a well-defined concept.

We probably wish to determine precisely which faces are adjacent to each individual face. This in turn leads us to a new relationship, "is adjacent to," and a corresponding member function.

The set of edges and the set of vertices are also well-defined concepts, at least for the types of figures likely to occur in most computer graphics applications.

The remaining attributes appear to have well-defined values, at least at first glance. However, the orientation of individual faces may be difficult to determine. The problem becomes clear when we consider Figures 9.5 and 9.6. We don't have any way of specifying if a face is internal or external to a polyhedron, or if a polyhedron has "holes." To some extent, these issues are more appropriate for a topological description of an object than a geometric description. To simplify matters, we will assume that the individual edges for each face will be given and stored so as to make sure that if we move along each edge, the face will be traversed in a counterclockwise manner. We will ignore topological features of polyhedra for the present.

This revised set of attributes appears to provide a fairly complete description of the geometric properties of any polyhedron, at least for any that we are likely to imagine. The member functions might be the following:

```
Polyhedron()
~Polyhedron()
Number_of_faces()
Shape_of_faces()
Size_of_faces()
Orientation_of_faces()
Set_of_adjacent_faces()
Is_adjacent_to()
Set_of_edges()
Set_of_vertices()
Number_of_edges()
Length()
Number_of_vertices()
Vertex()
```

As was mentioned earlier, some of these member functions might be complicated to implement. Note also that several of the member functions are actually appropriate as member functions of a lower-level class such as **face**, or even **edge**.

9.2.2 USE OF FACES AS FUNDAMENTAL OBJECTS

We now consider another possible organization of the fundamental objects. If we let a face of a polyhedron be the fundamental object in the system, then the complexity of the interrelationships between its attributes is reduced. The attributes of a face object are the size and shape of the face, orientation relative to a fixed viewpoint (only one, since there is one face that serves as the object under consideration), number and orientation of edges, and number and location of vertices. This certainly reduces the amount of complexity of the attribute relationships.

The downside is that we can't represent complete polyhedra as simple objects. We have to combine faces in order to create polyhedra.

Let's list some of the possible attributes of an object of a class called "face" in Table 9.2. Note that many of the attributes were also used in the proposed polyhedron class.

We might want to represent the higher level of object (polyhedra) as collections of faces.

We probably wish to determine precisely which faces are adjacent to each individual face. This in turn leads us to a new relationship, "is adjacent to," and a corresponding member function. We probably won't need the aggregate "set of adjacent faces" that we had when polyhedra were used as our fundamental objects.

The member functions might be the following:

```
Face()
~Face()
Shape_of_face()
Size_of_face()
Orientation_of_face()
Set_of_adjacent_faces()
Is_adjacent_to()
Set_of_edges()
Set_of_vertices()
Number_of_edges()
Length()
Number_of_vertices()
Vertex()
```

Table 9.2 Attributes of faces.

Attribute	Types of Values
Number of edges	Integer, >= 3
Shape of faces	Some figure known from plane geometry. Includes "triangle," "square," "rectangle," "rhombus," "pentagon," etc., as well as a catch-all name such as "other" for unknown figures.
Size of faces	**float**
Orientation of faces	Angles (3)
Set of edges for each face	Set of edges (pairs of type **Vertex**)
Number of edges	Integer
Length of an edge	**float** (not a primitive attribute)
Number of vertices	Integer
Set of vertices for each face	Set of vertices (triples of type **float**)
Location of vertices	Triples of type **float**

Note that many of the member functions for the **face** class were also member functions for the **polyhedron** class described in Section 9.2.2. As we noted there, some of the functions make use of the hierarchical relation between faces, edges, and vertices.

9.2.3 USE OF EDGES AS FUNDAMENTAL OBJECTS

Let's continue the process. We can use an edge as the fundamental object. If we do this, then the endpoints are appropriate attributes. Note that this information includes the length of an edge and its orientation implicitly.

The set of adjacent edges also provides important information about higher-level objects. An edge is a very simple object, since it is essentially a line segment. However, there are several levels of complexity needed to create a polyhedron from knowledge of the line segments or edges that are part of the polyhedron.

Let's list some of the possible attributes of an object of a class called "edge" in Table 9.3. The length of an edge is clearly not a primitive attribute and so we discard it.

The member functions for the **edge** class might be the following:

```
Edge()
~Edge()
Set_of_adjacent_edges()
Is_adjacent_to()
Set_of_vertices()
Length()
Number_of_vertices()
```

As we observed when discussing the **face** class, many of the member functions were also member functions for other potential classes.

Table 9.3 Attributes of edges.

Attribute	Types of Values
Set of vertices for each edge	Set of vertices (triples of type **float**)
Location of vertices	Triples of type **float** (possibly redundant)
Set of adjacent edges	Set of **edges**

9.2.4 USE OF VERTICES AS FUNDAMENTAL OBJECTS

The last option that we consider for possible objects is the individual points that make up the vertices. This appears to be a poor choice because there is only a single attribute (the location, or coordinates of the vertex) and because creation of a polyhedron using just the information conveyed by the location of the vertices appears to be extremely complex. It is clear that this choice should be rejected immediately, without further consideration.

9.2.5 SELECTION OF FUNDAMENTAL OBJECTS FOR DESCRIBING POLYHEDRA

We thus have three options left to consider for our relevant classes: polyhedra, faces, and edges. Each of the options meets the criteria of having a rich set of attributes and a collection of relationship to the other possible classes.

Let's examine some tentative class descriptions for each of these options. For the simplest relevant object, the edge, we have only a few attributes: vertices, the set of adjacent vertices, and orientation. Since an edge is actually just a line segment, the orientation attribute is easily replaced by marking one of the vertices as the first vertex and the other as the second. This specifies a direction for the edge.

Each of these classes will use a more fundamental object: the **Vertex** class. Therefore the class descriptions will reflect the inheritance from this class.

This discussion suggests that we might want to implement **Vertex** as a class rather than as a triple of coordinates. This is consistent with good object design.

9.3 Class Descriptions

In this section we present one possible organization of the relevant classes. For each class, we provide the class description and the member functions. The classes are shown in Examples 9.1 through 9.4, with a main driver program presented in Example 9.5.

There are some departures from the organization suggested in the previous section. For example, none of the classes will have a constructor function. This was done deliberately, because we will use the template-based list classes presented in Examples 5.11 and 5.12.

Each template will require the use of a default constructor, and we will have the compiler construct one for each of the classes **Vertex**, **Edge**, **Face**, and **Polyhedron**.

Since we are unlikely to need them for our relatively simple examples, we will not include any destructors in order to save space.

We have included a **friend** operator << of the **ostream** class in order to be able to print the contents of each vertex.

One possible organization of the **Vertex** class might be something like the one presented in Example 9.1.

Example 9.1 The file **Vertex.cpp**.

```
//
// FILE: vertex.cpp
//

#include <iostream.h>


class Vertex
{
public:
  double x, y, z;   // coordinates

  // Constructor
  Vertex(double x1 = 0, double y1 = 0, double z1 = 0);
  friend ostream & operator << (ostream &s, Vertex &);
};



// Default constructor.
Vertex :: Vertex(double x1, double y1, double z1)
{
  x = x1;
  y = y1;
  z = z1;
}



ostream & operator << (ostream &s, Vertex &V)
{
```

```
        cout << "First coordinate :" << V.x << endl
            << "Second coordinate: " << V.y << endl
            << "Third coordinate: " << V.z << endl
            << endl ;
      return s;
    }
```

The **Vertex** class is used to describe the **Edge** class. One possible description of the **Edge** class is shown in Example 9.2. Note the inheritance of the properties of the **Vertex** class. In addition, for reasons to be given later, we will wish to use linked lists and list iterators with this class. Thus we have included the file **list.h** in this example, in addition to the file **vertex.cpp.** This header file is the class descriptions and member functions for the linked list implementation of Examples 5.10 and 5.11 and will not be presented in the book, although it is listed on the disk included with this book.

Example 9.2 The file **Edge.cpp.**

```
//
// FILE: edge.cpp
//

#include "vertex.cpp"
#include "list.h"
#include <math.h>
#include <iostream.h>

typedef int boolean;


class Edge : public Vertex
{
public:
  Vertex first, second;
  void init( Vertex, Vertex);
  boolean is_adjacent_to(Edge E);
  double length;
  double direction_cosines[3];
  friend ostream & operator << (iostream &s, Edge &);
};
```

```
// Initializer
void Edge :: init(Vertex v, Vertex w)
{
  double temp, temp_x, temp_y, temp_z;

  first =  v;
  second = w;

  temp_x = w.x - v.x;
  temp = temp_x * temp_x;
  temp_y = w.y - v.y;
  temp += temp_y * temp_y;
  temp_z = w.z - v.z;
  temp += temp_z * temp_z;

  if (temp == 0.0) // the default
    {
    length = 1.0;
    direction_cosines[0] = 1;
    direction_cosines[1] = 0;
    direction_cosines[2] = 0;
    }
  else // actually create length, dir_cosines
    {
    length = sqrt(temp);
    direction_cosines[0] = temp_x/length;
    direction_cosines[1] = temp_y/length;
    direction_cosines[2] = temp_z/length;
    }
}



boolean Edge ::is_adjacent_to(Edge E)
{
  // to be determined later
  return 1;
}



ostream & operator << (ostream &s, Edge &E)
{
  cout << "First vertex :" << E.first << endl
     << "Second vertex :" << E.second << endl;
  return s;
}
```

We have chosen to implement the set of adjacent edges as a linked list. Other organizations are possible, and even are to be preferred, if an abstract set class is available in the class library.

These two classes lead to the development of classes for faces and polyhedra. Of course, there is a higher level of inheritance, because the **Edge** class depends on the **Vertex** class, and the **Face** class will inherit from both. Note that this class and the previous two classes presented here contain a method of output using the **ostream** class as a **friend**.

The outline of our definition of the **Face** class is given in Example 9.3.

Example 9.3 The file **Face.cpp**.

```
//
// FILE: face.cpp
//


#include "edge.cpp"


typedef int boolean;

class Face : public Edge
{
public:
  List<Edge> set_of_edges;
  List<Vertex> set_of_vertices;
  double direction_cosines[3];
  char * shape; // Perhaps String?
  void init(List<Edge> &,  List<Vertex> &);
  boolean is_adjacent_to(Face F);
  int number_of_edges;
  double area;
  int number_of_vertices;
  friend ostream & operator << (ostream &s, Face &F);
};


typedef int boolean;


void Face:: init(List<Edge> &temp_edge_set,  List<Vertex>
       &temp_vertex_set)
{
```

```
   set_of_edges = temp_edge_set;
   set_of_vertices = temp_vertex_set;
   shape = "Unknown shape";
   number_of_vertices = 0;
   number_of_edges = 0;
   area = 0;
   direction_cosines[0] = 1;
   direction_cosines[1] = 0;
   direction_cosines[2] = 0;
}



boolean Face :: is_adjacent_to(Face F)
{
   // Details coded later.
   return 1;
}



ostream & operator << (ostream &s, Face &F)
{
   cout << "Shape: " << F.shape << endl
        << "area :" << F.area << endl
        << "Number of vertices : " << F.number_of_vertices
        << endl << "Number of edges: "
        << F.number_of_edges << endl;
   return s;
}
```

The highest-level class in this discussion is **Polyhedron**. This class will inherit from the **Face** class, the **Edge** class, and the **Vertex** class. The corresponding class description for the highest-level class might look something like the class shown in Example 9.4.

Example 9.4 The file **polyhedr.h**.

```
//
// FILE: polyhedr.cpp
//

#include "face.cpp"
```

```
class Polyhedron : public Face
{
private:
  List<Face> set_of_faces;
  List<Edge> set_of_edges;
  List<Vertex> set_of_vertices;
public:
  void init(List<Face> &, List<Edge> &, List<Vertex> &);
  ~Polyhedron();
  double direction_cosines[3];
  int number_of_faces;
  char * shape;   // Perhaps String?
  double surface_area();   // Total area of faces.
  double volume();
// orientation Orientation_of_polyhedron();
  int number_of_edges;
  int number_of_vertices;
  friend ostream & operator << (ostream &s, Polyhedron &P);
};



void Polyhedron :: init(List<Face> & F, List<Edge> & E,
      List<Vertex> &)
{
  direction_cosines[0] = 1;
  direction_cosines[1] = 0;
  direction_cosines[2] = 0;
  number_of_faces = 0;
  shape = "Unknown";
  number_of_edges = 0;
  number_of_vertices = 0;
}



// Destructor
Polyhedron :: ~Polyhedron()
{
}



// Total surface area of all  faces.
double Polyhedron ::  surface_area()
{
  // determine later
  return 0;
}
```

```
double Polyhedron :: volume()
{
  // determine later
  return 0;
}


ostream & operator << (ostream &s, Polyhedron &P)
{
  cout << "Shape: " << P.shape << endl
     << "Number of vertices : " << P.number_of_vertices
     << endl << "Number of edges: "
     << P.number_of_edges << endl
     << "Number of faces: " << P.number_of_faces << endl;
  return s;
}
```

The initial organization of these four classes was not as complex as it seemed at first glance. It seems best to use the **Polyhedron** class in our description of graphical objects, inheriting properties and methods from the lower-level classes.

You should note that we have many unanswered questions about our objects, including how to access them using what we have called **List_of_Vertices**, **List_of_Edges**, and **List_of_Faces**. We will discuss some of these points in the next section when we consider higher-level organization of objects into a database.

9.4　A Graphical Database

The problem addressed in the first three sections of this chapter is a very old one in computer science. There have been computer graphics systems that performed the computations of this chapter as early as the 1960s. (Sutherland, 1965). The relatively stable state of these implementations meant that there are many possible criteria that can be used for the evaluation of our development.

The goal now is to expand our collection of objects in order to develop a graphical database. A graphical database allows the easy entry and retrieval of different graphical entries.

Some of the criteria to be used for evaluation of our system are

- Support for abstraction and information hiding.
- Efficiency of implementation.
- Consistency with modeling practices of most users.

We should expect our object-oriented solution to provide more support for abstraction and information hiding than a procedural one, simply because of the nature of object-oriented programming. Any thing else would indicate some degree of failure.

What is the state of abstraction of our system? There is clearly no problem in the interfaces to the **Edge** object if we define the edges making up the face to belong to a linked list structure or to a circular linked structure. The only changes would occur in the lower-level classes and the implementation of their methods. Similar statements would hold for the **Face** and **Polyhedron** classes. This is the high level of abstraction that we expect.

The measurement that we will apply to the efficiency of implementation is the number of unnecessary transformations of data because of our class organization. If this setup is done efficiently, then we will assume that the C++ compiler will implement the computations efficiently.

The next criterion for evaluating our system is the efficiency of the search of databases. What we have in mind here is a system with such a huge number of polyhedra in a database that the efficient search of the database is essential to the usability of the system.

One common database representation of polyhedra (Giloi) is to have a polyhedron stored as a list of pointers to the faces. Each face is stored as a collection of pointers to edges, which in turn are stored as pointers to pairs of vertices. This organization is consistent with our organization of our classes and thus we expect our class structure to lead to efficient database searches.

The final criterion to be considered is the degree to which our class structure agrees with the way that most users of computer graphics systems interact with their systems.

Let's begin with the basic goals of a database: storing entries and searching for entries according to one or more keys.

We clearly want some level of indirect access to keys associated with pointers to objects. For lower-level connections, such as linking sets of faces to a polyhedron, we need a method similar to the behavior of access to a polyhedron from a set of polyhedra.

Nearly every known algorithm of computational geometry (using computers to describe and represent geometric objects) processes the edges of a face in some kind of sequential order. A similar statement is true for processing the set of faces in a polyhedron or vertices in an edge. Fortunately, we have already developed a class description and set of member functions for a general, template-based linked list object in Chapter 5. We even developed an iterator class for lists using templates.

We can use these previously developed template classes here. They are included in the code given in Examples 9.2, 9.3, and 9.4 by means of the inheritance mechanism.

We need at least one more structure to allow us to display scenes that consist of sets of polyhedra. The most common structure on graphics workstations is a display list, and therefore we will describe graphical scenes using a list of polyhedra, which is the final organization in our hierarchy.

The overall design of the database is suggested by the main driver program, which is given in Example 9.5. There are several things to note about this program.

We have used list structures and list iterators several times within the main driver function. The set of faces for the polyhedron has been constructed as a list. The number of faces is obtained by using the list iterator and simply incrementing a counter when each face is found.

Example 9.5 The file **main.cpp**.

```
//
// FILE main.cpp
// Contains the main driver function for the
// polyhedron class.
//


// The main function will describe a polyhedron
// with 6 vertices, 9 edges, and 5 faces.
//


#include "polyhedr.cpp"
#include <iostream.h>

main()
{
  Vertex a, b(0.0, 1.0, 0.0), c(1.0, 1.0, 0.0),
     d(1.0, 0.0, 0.0), e(1.0, 0.0, 1.0),
     f(1.0, 1.0, 1.0);

  Edge  E1, E2, E3, E4, E5, E6, E7, E8, E9;
  E1.init(a, b);
  E2.init(b, c);
  E3.init(c, d);
  E4.init(d, a);
  E5.init(b, e);
  E6.init(e, a);
  E7.init(c, f);
  E8.init(d, f);
  E9.init(e, f);

  cout  << "VERTICES:" << endl << a << b << c
     << d << e << f;

  cout  << "EDGES" << endl
     << E1 << E2 << E3 << E4 << E5 << E6
     << E7 << E8 << E9 << endl;
```

```
/////////////////////////////////
// Initialize Face 1 (front of prism).
/////////////////////////////////
List<Edge> LE1;
LE1.insert(E1);
LE1.insert(E2);
LE1.insert(E3);
LE1.insert(E4);
List_Iterator<Edge> LE_iterator1(LE1);
LE_iterator1.init();

List<Vertex> LV1;
LV1.insert(a);
LV1.insert(b);
LV1.insert(c);
LV1.insert(d);
List_Iterator<Vertex> LV_iterator1(LV1);
LV_iterator1.init();

Face F1;
F1.shape = "square";
F1.area = E1.length * E2.length;
F1.number_of_vertices = 4;
F1.number_of_edges = 4;


cout << F1;




/////////////////////////////////
// Initialize Face 2 (right of prism).
/////////////////////////////////
List<Edge> LE2;
LE2.insert(E5);
LE2.insert(E9);
LE2.insert(E7);
LE2.insert(E2);
List_Iterator<Edge> LE_iterator2(LE2);
LE_iterator2.init();

List<Vertex> LV2;
LV2.insert(b);
LV2.insert(e);
LV2.insert(f);
LV2.insert(c);
List_Iterator<Vertex> LV_iterator2(LV2);
LV_iterator2.init();
```

```
Face F2;
F2.shape = "square";
F2.area = E5.length * E9.length;
F2.number_of_vertices = 4;
F2.number_of_edges = 4;

cout << F2;


////////////////////////////////////
// Initialize Face 3 (back of prism).
////////////////////////////////////
List<Edge> LE3;
LE3.insert(E6);
LE3.insert(E9);
LE3.insert(E8);
LE3.insert(E4);
List_Iterator<Edge> LE_iterator3(LE3);
LE_iterator3.init();

List<Vertex> LV3;
LV3.insert(a);
LV3.insert(e);
LV3.insert(f);
LV3.insert(d);
List_Iterator<Vertex> LV_iterator3(LV3);
LV_iterator3.init();

Face F3;
F3.shape = "rectangle";
F3.area = E6.length * E9.length;
F3.number_of_vertices = 4;
F3.number_of_edges = 4;

cout << F3;


////////////////////////////////////
// Initialize Face 4 (top of prism).
////////////////////////////////////
List<Edge> LE4;
LE4.insert(E3);
LE4.insert(E7);
LE4.insert(E8);

List_Iterator<Edge> LE_iterator4(LE4);
LE_iterator4.init();
```

```
List<Vertex> LV4;
LV4.insert(b);
LV4.insert(c);
LV4.insert(f);

List_Iterator<Vertex> LV_iterator4(LV4);
LV_iterator4.init();

Face F4;
F4.shape = "triangle";
F4.area = E3.length * E7.length/ 2.0; // right triangle
F4.number_of_vertices = 4;
F4.number_of_edges = 4;

cout << F4;


///////////////////////////////////
// Initialize Face 5 (bottom of prism).
///////////////////////////////////
List<Edge> LE5;
LE5.insert(E1);
LE5.insert(E5);
LE5.insert(E2);

List_Iterator<Edge> LE_iterator5(LE5);
LE_iterator5.init();

List<Vertex> LV5;
LV5.insert(a);
LV5.insert(b);
LV5.insert(e);

List_Iterator<Vertex> LV_iterator5(LV5);
LV_iterator5.init();

Face F5;
F5.shape = "triangle";
F5.area = E1.length * E5.length/2.0; // right triangle
F5.number_of_vertices = 3;
F5.number_of_edges = 3;

cout << F5;


///////////////////////////////////
// Now construct polyhedron.
///////////////////////////////////
Polyhedron P1;
P1.shape = "Prism";
```

```
// Compute the number of faces.
// Other computations are similar.
List<Face> LF;
LF.insert(F1);
List_Iterator<Face> LF_iterator(LF);
LF_iterator.init();
LF.insert(F2);
LF.insert(F3);
LF.insert(F4);
LF.insert(F5);
int i = 0;
for (LF_iterator.init(); LF_iterator.forward != 0; ++LF_iterator)
  i++ ; // All work is done in iterator.
P1.number_of_faces = i;


// Insert polyhedron into list for potential use.
List<Polyhedron> LP1;
LP1.insert(P1);
List_Iterator<Polyhedron> LP_iterator1(LP1);
LP_iterator1.init();

cout << endl << "POLYHEDRONS:" << endl << P1 << endl;
}
```

The output from this program is presented below. Note that some of the values of members of the object P1 are meaningless because they were not initialized. We used a counter within a loop controlled by an iterator to compute the number of faces. Other computations would be similar, but require us to eliminate duplications in the list. These computations are omitted.

Output from the programs of this chapter:

```
VERTICES:
First coordinate :0
Second coordinate: 0
Third coordinate: 0

First coordinate :0
Second coordinate: 1
Third coordinate: 0

First coordinate :1
Second coordinate: 1
Third coordinate: 0
```

```
First coordinate :1
Second coordinate: 0
Third coordinate: 0

First coordinate :1
Second coordinate: 0
Third coordinate: 1

First coordinate :1
Second coordinate: 1
Third coordinate: 1

EDGES
First vertex :First coordinate :0
Second coordinate: 0
Third coordinate: 0


Second vertex :First coordinate :0
Second coordinate: 1
Third coordinate: 0


First vertex :First coordinate :0
Second coordinate: 1
Third coordinate: 0


Second vertex :First coordinate :1
Second coordinate: 1
Third coordinate: 0


First vertex :First coordinate :1
Second coordinate: 1
Third coordinate: 0


Second vertex :First coordinate :1
Second coordinate: 0
Third coordinate: 0


First vertex :First coordinate :1
Second coordinate: 0
Third coordinate: 0
```

```
Second vertex :First coordinate :0
Second coordinate: 0
Third coordinate: 0


First vertex :First coordinate :0
Second coordinate: 1
Third coordinate: 0


Second vertex :First coordinate :1
Second coordinate: 0
Third coordinate: 1


First vertex :First coordinate :1
Second coordinate: 0
Third coordinate: 1


Second vertex :First coordinate :0
Second coordinate: 0
Third coordinate: 0


First vertex :First coordinate :1
Second coordinate: 1
Third coordinate: 0


Second vertex :First coordinate :1
Second coordinate: 1
Third coordinate: 1


First vertex :First coordinate :1
Second coordinate: 0
Third coordinate: 0


Second vertex :First coordinate :1
Second coordinate: 1
Third coordinate: 1


First vertex :First coordinate :1
Second coordinate: 0
Third coordinate: 1


Second vertex :First coordinate :1
Second coordinate: 1
Third coordinate: 1
```

```
Shape: square
area :1
Number of vertices : 4
Number of edges: 4
Shape: square
area :1.732051
Number of vertices : 4
Number of edges: 4
Shape: rectangle
area :1.414214
Number of vertices : 4
Number of edges: 4
Shape: triangle
area :0.5
Number of vertices : 4
Number of edges: 4
Shape: triangle
area :0.866025
Number of vertices : 3
Number of edges: 3
Shape: triangle
area :0.866025
Number of vertices : 3
Number of edges: 3
 Shape: triangle
area :0.5
Number of vertices : 4
Number of edges: 4
 Shape: rectangle
area :1.414214
Number of vertices : 4
Number of edges: 4
 Shape: square
area :1.732051
Number of vertices : 4
Number of edges: 4
 Shape: square
area :1
Number of vertices : 4
Number of edges: 4

POLYHEDRA:
Shape: Prism
Number of vertices : 210
Number of edges: -31752
Number of faces: 5
```

Summary

In this chapter we described several approaches to the development of an object-oriented treatment of a graphical database system for polyhedral objects. We chose one alternative based on the perceived complexity of the system's description.

The system was developed using the guidelines presented in Chapter 8. We made extensive use of the object hierarchy (**polyhedron**, **face**, **edge**, and **vertex**) in the development of our system. Inheritance was a major feature in the design of the classes for this system.

The previously developed template classes **List** and **List_Iterator** were very useful here.

EXERCISES

1. Suppose that we were only interested in a computer graphics system that used two-dimensional polygons. One way to design such a system would be to take the object-oriented system designed in this chapter and remove all three-dimensional features. Do this, writing the two-dimensional classes and member functions using inheritance. Are any other organizations possible?

2. How extensible is the system organization of this chapter? Extend the system to include portions of circles as part of the **Edge** class.

3. Design the system using a different organization for the object hierarchy.

4. Encode the world-to-screen transformation suggested in this chapter.

5. Encode the missing member functions for the **Vertex** class.

6. Encode some of the member functions for the **Edge** class.

7. Encode some of the member functions for the **Face** class.

8. Encode some of the member functions for the **Polyhedron** class. Compute the number of vertices and edges correctly.

9. Examine a graphical database system such as that discussed in Giloi's book or any commercial system for which you have good documentation. The systems should have procedurally driven designs. (See the References for a complete bibliographic listing of Giloi's book.) Compare such systems with the object-oriented one described in this chapter.

Making the Transition to an Object-Oriented System

10

I n this chapter we describe a common problem when making the transition to an object-oriented system—what to do with a "legacy system." We use the term *legacy system* to mean a system that was developed before the current software development methodology of the organization. Frequently such systems have little available documentation and are hard to understand. Hence any change, especially to a new methodology such as object orientation, involves a great deal of effort just to understand the existing system.

10.1 Introduction

In many software engineering projects, the first step is the determination of requirements or specifications. In real-world situations, this includes the choice of programming language, host computer (on which the software will be developed), target computer (on which the software will be run when the system is complete), operating system, and programming support tools, perhaps including some for CASE (computer-assisted software engineering). It also includes a description of the timing and storage space needs of the system. This is a key step in the classical waterfall model of the software life cycle.

Our approach is somewhat different from this classical method in which all the requirements are set in advance. Our approach is much more like that of the software design model called rapid prototyping. In this method, the system is designed to meet a minimal set of requirements. The system is then either changed or discarded and built anew as new specifications or requirements are changed or added. Support for rapid prototyping is considered to be one of the major advantages of C++ as a programming language.

Prototyping is especially important when updating legacy systems. The documentation may be missing or not consistent with the code, which is likely to have had many changes made to it during its lifetime. The fact that the original computer hardware and most of the software with which the system had to be interoperable are very much out of date is much more important.

In this chapter we will describe a software system that was already built in the C programming language. The software provides a simulation of a file system, which is a major component of an operating system. We will also consider the actual disk movement as well as the writing of data to and from computer memory.

This software system will have fairly good high-level documentation, probably better than what is available for many legacy systems. Our intention is to describe the process of transforming an existing, procedurally designed system into an object-oriented one. General issues of software maintenance will not be discussed in this book.

The remainder of this chapter is organized as follows. In the next section (Section 10.2), we will describe procedurally based specifications for a simulation of a file system.

In Section 10.3, we will describe the high-level design of the procedurally based simulation, using a well-documented main program and set of procedures. Input and output in the original C program have been changed to use the C++ I/O operators << and >> to operate on iostreams.

The details of the procedurally based implementations of disk operations, memory–disk transfers. and I/O are discussed in Section 10.4.

In Section 10.5, we will describe additional features of the procedurally based design that allow a more complex structure of the simulated disk, using a hierarchical organization for the simulated file system. Source code is not given in this section because of its length but is available on the disk included with this book. This section may be omitted by a reader desiring only an overview of the transformation of existing procedurally based systems into object-oriented ones.

In Section 10.6, we study the process of transforming the procedurally based simulation into one that is object-oriented in nature. Here we describe changing procedurally based requirements into object-oriented requirements.

In Section 10.7, we will present some of the code for an object-oriented program to perform the file system simulation.

Finally, in Section 10.8 we compare the two sets of requirements and designs. We also discuss general issues that are likely to arise when transforming procedurally described systems into object-oriented ones.

10.2 Specifications for a File System Simulation

The initial requirements are that the system will be able to move blocks of data from memory to the disk and from the disk to memory. We will concentrate on the actions that our program will perform and on how we will communicate our wishes to various portions of the program.

The most important thing that we need at this point is a discussion of a user interface. The program is to be totally interactive and prompt the user to enter data in a predetermined form. There is an initial message explaining the system and then prompting the user for input from a small set of options. A high-quality user interface should also provide checking of the input for errors and have a method for the user to be able to correct any input errors. Since we are designing a simple system, let us assume that the user is perfect and never makes errors. Thus no error checking of input is needed.

The input commands will allow data to be entered into memory directly. Data can be entered into memory directly, sent from memory to disk, or sent from disk to memory in units called blocks. Our system will be able to move data in blocks that are accessed in memory by identifying a starting memory location and to access blocks of data on the disk by the track and sector numbers identifying this block.

A limited set of the specifications of the system is thus as follows:

Functional Requirements

- Provide opening message to user.
- Move data into memory directly, from memory to disk, or from disk to memory in fixed-sized units called blocks. Any movement of data to or from the disk must access the block using the track and sector numbers that uniquely identify the block. A block in memory is specified by identifying the starting position.
- Obtain input commands interactively. The input is read in one line at a time. If the first input character is `'i'`, then the next input line is a variable of type **int**, which is the type that we are using for data. The function **put_in_memory()** is then called with the parameter data that was read in. After the function **put_in_memory()** is called, control returns to the main program.
- If the input is `'d'`, then the next three input lines will contain variables of type **int**. These three lines represent the values of the memory location **mem_loc** and the disk location specified by **track** and **sector**, respectively. The function **mem_to_disk()** is then called with the parameters **mem_loc**, **track**, and **sector** read in. After the function **mem_to_disk()** is called, control returns to the main program.

- If the input is `'m'`, then the next three input lines will contain variables of type `int`. These three lines represent the values of the memory location `mem_loc` and the disk location specified by `track` and `sector`, respectively. The function `disk_to_mem()` is then called with the parameters `mem_loc`, `track`, and `sector` read in. After the function `disk_to_mem()` is called, control returns to the main program.
- Input is read in without error checking.

Some of the functions that we will need are

```
void print_disk();

void print_mem();

void mem_to_disk(int mem_loc, int track, int sector);

void disk_to_mem(int mem_loc, int track, sector);
```

The functions `print_disk()` and `print_mem()` are used to display the contents of the simulated memory and disk on the screen. The functions `mem_to_disk()` and `disk_to_mem()` are used actually to move blocks of data from memory to disk or from disk to memory. The three parameters `mem_loc`, `track`, and `sector` are each of type `int` and indicate the starting locations of the blocks of data in memory or on the simulated disk.

The user will have to be able to tell the software if data is to be moved from memory to disk or from disk to memory. In our system, data needs to be placed in memory before it can be sent to the disk. Thus we need some additional functions:

```
opening_message();

get_data();

put_in_memory();
```

To make life as simple as possible, we will require that the input commands are entered one per line, with `'i'` for input into memory, `'d'` for writing to disk from memory, and `'m'` for writing from disk to memory. A command of `'d'` or `'m'` means that three additional parameters are needed to specify the memory location `mem_loc` and the two parameters `track` and `sector` needed to specify a disk location. The command `'i'` means that data is to be sent to memory from the keyboard and thus is to be followed by the data. We will assume that the data is of type `int` and that only one such data item will follow the command `'i'`.

Functions

`void opening_message(void)`

Presents an opening message explaining the system and its purpose to a user. **`opening_message()`** has no parameters and returns no value.

`void get_data(void)`

This function has no parameters. It reads its input one line at a time. It has no parameters and returns no value.

If the input is '**i**', then the next input line contains a variable of type **int**, which is the type of data that we are using for the disk. The function **`put_in_memory()`** is then called with the parameter data that is read in. After the function **`put_in_memory()`** is called, control returns to the main program.

If the input is '**d**', then the next three input lines will contain variables of type **int**. These three lines represent the values of the memory location called **mem_loc** that is used to mark the start of a block of memory as well as the **track** and **sector** that are used to mark the start of a disk block. The function **`mem_to_disk()`** is then called with the parameters **mem_loc**, **track**, and **sector** that were read in. After the function **`mem_to_disk()`** is called, control returns to the main program.

If the input is '**m**', then the next three input lines will contain variables of type **int**. These three lines represent the values of the memory location called **mem_loc** that is used to mark the start of a block of memory as well as the **track** and **sector** that are used to mark the start of a disk block. The function **`disk_to_mem()`** is then called with the parameters **mem_loc**, **track**, and **sector** that were read in. After the function **`disk_to_mem()`** is called, control returns to the main program.

If the input is '**p**', the contents of the simulated memory will be printed.

If the input is '**P**', the contents of the simulated disk will be printed.

If the input is either '**q**' or '**Q**', the program will terminate.

`void put_in_memory(int data)`

Parameter is of the type of data that we will enter into memory. It returns no value.

`void disk_to_mem(int mem_loc, int track, int sector)`

Parameters are of type **int**. It returns no value.

`void mem_to_disk(int mem_loc, int track, int sector)`

Parameters are of type **int**. It returns no value.

`void print_disk(void)`

Prints the contents of the array simulating the disk. It returns no value.

`void print_mem(void)`

Prints the contents of the array simulating memory. It returns no value.

We need to have some method of conveying the major features of the design. It would be nice to have some formal way of describing this. However, formal design methods are not common and are often hard to use. In the absence of such methods, we will do the next best thing—incorporate the description of the design into the documentation of a prototype that will serve as the basis for the program itself.

We will write the design in two parts. The top-down design will indicate the major modules of the system and their relationship. The data flow design will show some of the flow of data through the system.

These two representations of the design are clearly well suited to graphical methods. However, we will choose a somewhat less attractive representation of the design using text to simulate the boxes and lines that are part of the graphical model. The reason is that such a representation can easily be kept as part of the system documentation and as part of the source file containing the code for the system.

We now consider the design of the system. We will use a top-down approach to our design by choosing appropriate functions and by "stubbing in" their definitions. Stubbing in means that even if we do not know precisely how the function will perform its actions, we include a description of the function in the design. For example, we do not yet know the structure of the disk but we can still indicate the printing of its contents by using a function called **print_disk()**. The process of stubbing in requires that all parameters to a function be described in the function header. It is good practice to include documentation of the name, type, and purpose of each parameter used inside a function.

The function **print_disk()** is then stubbed in to the system in a form something like the code shown below:

```
//
// This function prints the contents of the simulated disk.
// PARAMETERS : none
// VALUE RETURNED: none
//

void print_disk(void )
{
  cout << "In print_disk\n";
}
```

The function **print_disk()** has been set up with no parameters and no values to be returned. We may change this later, but for now it seems sufficient.

We must decide about the passing of variables to the functions in our prototype either by parameters to the functions or by means of global variables. Dunsmore and Gannon (1980) suggest that global variables are better for the original design of very small programs but are a poor idea for larger programs and are especially poor for the design of a program that will need to be modified many times (as this one will). We will therefore avoid the use of global variables as much as possible.

10.3 Procedurally Based System Design

We now show the high-level procedural design of the system. It has three parts: documentation of the top-down design of the system, documentation of the flow of data through the system, and a stubbed-in set of functions.

In order to facilitate the discussion of the transition to an object-oriented system later in this chapter, we will illustrate the code using the C++ I/O features with **cout** and **cin** instead of the C language functions **printf()** and **scanf()**) that were originally used in the C code. We have also used a C++ comment style instead of the comment style typically used in the C language.

In a realistic programming environment, these two steps might be useful if the existing C source code will be reused to a large extent in the development of the object-oriented system in C++.

On the other hand, the effort needed to carry out these two steps might be pointless if most of the code has to be rewritten to emphasize an object-oriented approach. Clearly, the amount of potential reuse is the deciding factor.

Example 10.1

```
//
// DESIGN  OF DISK/MEMORY MANAGEMENT SYSTEM  PROTOTYPE
// DESIGN TEAM: A. B. See
//         C. D. Eff
//         G. H. Eye

// DESIGN LEADER:
//         A. B. See
//
// DESIGN DATE: February 30, 1995
//
// HOST COMPUTER: Sun SPARC 2
//
// OPERATING SYSTEM: SunOS 4.1.3 (Solaris 1.1)
//
// COMPILER: UNIX C++ Compiler v 3.0
//
//


//   FUNCTION BLOCK DESIGN:
```

```
//
//        |-----------|
//        |   main()  |
//        |———————————|
//              |
//              |
//              |
//        |---------------------|
//        |   opening_message() |
//        |—————————————————————|
//              |
//              |
//              |
//        |-----------|
//        | get_data()|
//        |-----------|
//              |
//              |
//              |
// _____  |_____
//        |     |         |        |              |
//        |     |         |        |              |
// ----------   |    -------------  |   ---------------
// put_in_memory()  | disk_to_mem() |   print_mem()
// ----------   |    -------------  |   ———————————
//                                  |
//        |              |
//        |              |
//    -------------    ------------
//    mem_to_disk()    print_disk()
//    -------------    ------------
//
//
```

```
//
//                  DATA FLOW DESIGN


// input choice:

// --- 'i', data  -->      put_in_memory()

// --- 'd', mem_loc, track, sector        -->    mem_to_disk()

// --- 'm', mem_loc, track, sector        --> disk_to_mem()
```

```
//  --- 'p' --> print_mem()

//  --- 'P' -->  print_disk()

//


//
//
//                 MAIN

//
//
//   List of functions in program.

void  opening_message(void ) ;
void get_data(void ) ;
void put_in_memory(int data) ;
void mem_to_disk(int mem_loc, int track, int sector) ;
void disk_to_mem(int mem_loc, int track, int sector) ;
void print_mem(void ) ;
void print_disk(void ) ;

#include <iostream.h>
main(void)
{
  char ch;

  opening_message();
  get_data();
}




//
// FUNCTION opening_message()
// This function prints an opening message.
// CALLED BY: main()
// FUNCTIONS CALLED: none
// PARAMETERS : none
// VALUE RETURNED: none
//

void  opening_message(void )
{
  cout <<"Welcome to the FILE SIMULATION SYSTEM \n\n";
```

```
    cout << "The purpose of the system is to demonstrate";
    cout << "some of the\n";
    cout << "features of a file system.\n\n";
    cout << "This first phase will show some of the";
    cout << "commands\n";
    cout << "to move data to and from simulated memory";
    cout << "and disk.\n\n\n";
}



//
// FUNCTION get_data()
//

// This function gets input data for the system.  It will
// accept data of the form 'i', 'd', 'm', 'p', 'P', 'q', or
// 'Q'.

// If the input is 'i', then the next parameter will be of
// type int and will be used to fill up a memory block by
// calling the function put_data().

// If the input is 'd', then the next three variables will
// be passed to the function mem_to_disk() as the parameters
// mem_loc, track, and sector.

// If the input is 'm', then the next three variables will
// be passed to the function disk_to_mem() as the parameters
// mem_loc, track, and sector.

// If the input is 'p', then the function print_mem() will
// be called without any parameters.

// If the input is 'P', then the function print_disk() will
// be called without any parameters.

// If the input is 'q' or 'Q', then the function will
// terminate and  return control to the main program.

// If the input is not either 'q' or 'Q', then the function
// get_data() will continue execution, calling the
// appropriate functions.

// The function will repeat the evaluation of input until a
// 'q' or 'Q' is entered, at which point the function
// returns control to the main program.
```

```
//
//
// CALLED BY: main()
//
// FUNCTIONS CALLED:
//          put_in_memory()
//          mem_to_disk()
//          disk_to_mem()
//          print_mem()
//          print_disk()
//
// PARAMETERS : none
//
// VALUE RETURNED: none
//
//

void get_data(void )
{
  int ch;          // for input command
  int data, mem_loc, track, sector;

  // loop runs forever until a quit command is given
  for( ; ; )
  {
  cout << "\n\n";
  cout << "Select an option:\n";
  cout << "\n";
  cout << "i        insert directly into memory .\n";
  cout << "d        move data from memory to disk\n";
  cout << "m        move data from disk to mem\n";
  cout << "p        print memory\n";
  cout << "P        print disk\n";
  cout << "q        quit\n";
  cout << "\n\n";
  cin >> ch ;
    switch (ch)
    {
    case 'i':// place data directly into memory block
      cin >> data;
      put_in_memory(data);
      break;
    case 'd': // need three parameters
      cin >> mem_loc;
      cin >> track;
      cin >> sector;
      mem_to_disk(mem_loc, track, sector);
      break;
```

```
         case 'm': // need three parameters
           cin >> mem_loc;
           cin >> track;
           cin >> sector;
           disk_to_mem(mem_loc, track, sector);
           break;
         case 'p':
           print_mem();
           break;
         case 'P':
           print_disk();
           break;
         case 'q':         // exit get_data()
         case 'Q':
           return;
         }      // end switch
      }       // end for
   }          // end get_data


   //////////////////////////////////////////////////////////
   // FUNCTION put_in_memory()
   //////////////////////////////////////////////////////////


   // This function places data into memory initially.
   // It has a parameter that represents the data that is to be
   // placed into each of the memory locations forming the
   // first available block.
   // CALLED BY: get_data()
   //
   // FUNCTIONS CALLED:none
   //
   // PARAMETERS: data (type int)
   //
   // VALUE RETURNED: none
   //
   //////////////////////////////////////////////////////////


   void put_in_memory(int data)
   {
     cout << "In put_in_memory - parameter is";
     cout <<  data << "\n";
   }
```

```
////////////////////////////////////////////////////////
// FUNCTION  mem_to_disk()
////////////////////////////////////////////////////////
// This function controls the movement of blocks of data
// from the simulated memory to the simulated disk.  It has
// three parameters: mem_loc, track, and sector.
//
// CALLED BY: get_data()
//
// FUNCTIONS CALLED: none
//
// PARAMETERS : mem_loc, track, sector
//
// VALUE RETURNED: none
//
////////////////////////////////////////////////////////
void mem_to_disk(int mem_loc, int track, int sector)
// int mem_loc is the  starting point of memory block
{
  cout << "In mem_to_disk - parameters are";
  cout << mem_loc << track << sector <<"\n";
}



////////////////////////////////////////////////////////
// FUNCTION disk_to_mem()
////////////////////////////////////////////////////////
//
// This function controls the movement of blocks of data
// from the simulated disk to the simulated memory.  It has
// three parameters: mem_loc, track, and sector.
//
// CALLED BY: get_data()
//
// FUNCTIONS CALLED: none/
//
// PARAMETERS : mem_loc, track, sector
//
// VALUE RETURNED:  none
/
////////////////////////////////////////////////////////

void disk_to_mem(int mem_loc, int track, int sector)
// int  mem_loc is starting point of memory block.
{
  cout << "In disk_to_mem -");
```

```
  cout << "parameters are %d %d %d \n";
  cout <<  mem_loc, track, sector);
}



//////////////////////////////////////////////////////////
// FUNCTION print_mem()
//////////////////////////////////////////////////////////
// This function prints the contents of simulated memory.

// CALLED BY: get_data()

// FUNCTIONS CALLED: none

// PARAMETERS : none

// VALUE RETURNED: none

//////////////////////////////////////////////////////////
void print_mem(void )
{
  cout << "In print_mem\n";
}



//////////////////////////////////////////////////////////
// FUNCTION print_disk()
//////////////////////////////////////////////////////////

// This function prints the contents of the simulated disk.

// CALLED BY: main()

// FUNCTIONS CALLED: none

// PARAMETERS : none

// VALUE RETURNED: none

//////////////////////////////////////////////////////////
void print_disk(void )
{
  cout << "In print_disk\n";
}
//////////////////////////////////////////////////////////
//            END OF PROGRAM
//////////////////////////////////////////////////////////
```

It is important to note the use of some simple design principles in this first prototype. We have chosen to write a modular design, with each of the functions needed stubbed in.

Note that the design is in the form of a documented program. This is because we want to avoid duplication of effort. It will be easier to test our program by testing the component functions individually and then placing them into the final program.

10.4 Implementation Details for a Procedurally Based Disk Simulation

We can start to flesh out the bodies of the two functions **mem_to_disk()** and **disk_to_mem()** that were stubbed in earlier. We interpret memory as a two-dimensional array of data elements whose type is the same as we considered earlier that is, the data is of type **int**. The contents of memory locations are addressed by simply giving their location. Since we will be moving blocks of data from memory to disk and from disk to memory, we also want to think of memory as being composed of blocks that can be accessed by knowing the starting location of a block and the number of elements in the block. Hence we will also want to be able to view memory as a two-dimensional array of blocks of data.

The disk is a more complex system, since a disk is inherently a two-dimensional object. We access elements on the disk by determining the disk block in which they occur. A disk block has its position determined by two parameters—the track and sector of the block. Think of a disk as being a set of concentric rings. Each ring is assumed to have the same capacity for storing data even though the rings of smaller diameter have the data packed more densely. By analogy to a phonograph record, these concentric rings are called *tracks*. There is another division of the disk into *sectors*. Each of the tracks is considered to be divided into the same number of sectors.

In actual disks, there is a read/write head that moves relative to the disk. The head can move along a particular track through various sectors, or can move to different tracks while remaining along the same sector. For our purposes, it doesn't matter if the read/write head is fixed and the disk spins or if the disk is fixed and the head moves. A fixed-head system allows the disk to move along a sector and the head can move in and out, reading data as necessary. A fixed-disk system has the head move along tracks or read different sectors by moving along rays emanating from the center of the disk. In most large computers, there are many read/write heads and many "platters" making up a disk system for the sake of simplicity we consider only one platter and one read/write head.

The natural way of simulating the disk is by a two-dimensional array of data elements. On most computer disks, movement of the read/write head in and out while staying in the same sector is slower than changing sectors while staying in the same track. Therefore we will access a block of data by reference to the pair (**track**, **sector**) instead of the pair (**sector**, **track**). An element of the disk is then found by knowing the track and sector numbers that tell which block the element is in and the offset of the element from the start of the block.

As with memory, there is another way of treating the disk. We can consider a disk to be a three-dimensional array of data, with the data indexed by three numbers: the track, sector, and offset from the start of the disk block.

We will fix the following constants for use in our setting of the system requirements.

Example 10.2 Constants for the file system simulation.

```
constant int BLOCKSIZE = 10 ;
constant int NUM_TRACKS = 50 ;
constant int NUM_SECTORS = 4 ;
constant int NUM_MEM_BLOCKS = 10 ;
constant int MEMSIZE = 100; //NUM_MEM_BLOCKS*BLOCKSIZE
```

There are additional specifications.

Data Movement

Movement from memory to disk and from disk to memory is determined by specifying the **track** index and **sector** index on the disk and the memory block index in memory for each block. The track index is in the range 0..**NUM_TRACKS** – 1. The sector index is in the range 0.. **NUM_SECTORS** – 1. The memory block index is in the range 0..**NUM_MEM_BLOCKS** – 1.

Note that there is a lot of leeway in the specifications given so far for this project. All of the lower-level decisions, such as how the disk and memory are to be organized, how to error check, or how to implement the parsing of input, are left to be determined during the design of the system. The design involves decisions about the following functions:

disk_to_mem(int mem_loc,int track, int sector)

Parameters are of type **int**. The first parameter represents a memory location in the range 0..**NUM_MEM_BLOCKS** – 1. The second parameter represents a track number in the range 0..**NUM_TRACKS** – 1, and the third parameter represents a sector number in the range 0..**NUM_SECTORS** – 1. This function will move a block of data that is specified by a track and a sector number to a memory location specified by the parameter **mem_loc**.

mem_to_disk(int mem_loc, int track, int sector)

Parameters are of type **int**. The first parameter represents a memory location in the range 0..MEMSIZE – 1. The second parameter represents a track number in the range 0..NUM_TRACKS – 1, and the third parameter represents a sector number in the range 0..NUM_SECTORS – 1. This function will move a block of data that is specified by a memory location to a disk block that is specified by a track number and a sector number.

void print_disk(void)

Prints the contents of the array simulating the disk. Details are given later.

void print_mem(void)

Prints the contents of the array simulating memory. Details are given later.

We have several choices here depending on the organization of the disk and memory. One solution is to have one-dimensional arrays for both the simulated memory and the simulated disk. The corresponding declarations are

```
MEMSIZE = NUM_MEM_BLOCKS * BLOCKSIZE;
DISK_SIZE = NUM_TRACKS * NUM_SECTORS * BLOCKSIZE ;
int data
int track , sector;   // track and sector parameters
int mem[MEMSIZE];     //  a one-dimensional array
int disk[DISK_SIZE];
int mem_loc;
```

If we use this organization, then we will have to impose the disk and memory structures upon the program commands as they execute. This organization does not support the availability of high-level structures in the C language.

If we wish to preserve the block structure, one alternative is to design the disk as a two-dimensional array and to require that the memory organization should be in the form of a one-dimensional array.

```
int data
int track , sector;   // track and sector parameters
int mem[MEMSIZE];     //  a one-dimensional array
int disk[NUM_TRACKS][NUM_SECTORS];
int mem_loc;
```

This causes us one problem—we don't have any way of indicating the contents of a block. For now, we can't use this organization.

If we use a three-dimensional array for the disk, then we will be able to access every disk element directly. Clearly, we should use a similar arrangement for the organization of memory, so we could have memory declared as a two-dimensional array. In this organization, the structure of a block of data is relatively unimportant, since it has been incorporated into the disk itself. This is the organization that we will use for this project.

```
int data
int track, sector; // track and sector parameters
int mem[NUM_MEM_BLOCKS][BLOCKSIZE];
int disk[NUM_TRACKS][NUM_SECTORS][BLOCKSIZE]
int mem_loc;
```

What are the ramifications for the rest of the design? If we consider the disk as a three-dimensional array, then we can use the first two parameters to act as identifiers of blocks and use the third dimension as a counter for indexing the elements in the block. The simulated memory can be handled in a similar manner using the first parameter to identify the block and the second one to act as an index of the block elements. Because of the modular way that the program has been written, no changes need to be made to the main program or to the functions **get_data()** or **opening_message()**.

The functions **print_mem()** and **print_disk()** are the easiest to implement, so we consider them first. They require no parameters, and the disk and memory organizations make them easy to design. In fact, the coding of these two functions is so simple that we can do it right now.

The original functions were stubbed in and looked like

```
print_mem(void)
{
cout << "In print_mem\n";
}


print_disk(void)
{
cout << "In print_disk\n";
}
```

The output statements can be removed, and the simple loops to allow us to print the contents can be inserted easily.

```
void print_mem(void)
{
  int i, j;

  for(i=0; i < NUM_MEM_BLOCKS; i++)
    {
    for (j = 0; j < BLOCKSIZE; j++)
```

```
        cout << mem[i][j];
      cout << "\n";
      }
  }

void print_disk(void)
{
  int i, j, k;

  for(i=0; i < NUM_TRACKS; i++)
    {
    for (j = 0; j < NUM_SECTORS; j++)
      {
      for (k = 0; k < BLOCKSIZE; k++)
        cout << mem[i][j][k];
      cout << "\n";
      }
    cout << "\n";
    }
}
```

This is somewhat minimal in that there is no appropriate heading for the output. This might be marginally acceptable for a system in which the output is written to a file, but it is not at all appropriate for an interactive system. The formatting of output should be done at a later stage, since it is not yet critical to the design. We will not consider it at this time.

It is now time to look more closely at the structure of memory and the disk. We have a situation something like that shown in Figure 10.1, assuming a value of 10 for **BLOCKSIZE** and that the value of **NUM_MEM_BLOCKS** is at least 9.

An element in memory is then found by directly specifying the block number and the offset from the start of the block. For example, if the value of **BLOCKSIZE** is 10 and the value of **NUM_MEM_BLOCKS** is 10, then the last element in memory can be found by specifying a value of 9 for the block number and a value of 9 for the offset. The next-to-last element has a block number of 9 but an offset of 8, and so on.

We can relate the value of the variable **mem_loc** that we have previously used to the values of the block number and offset by the formulas

```
mem_loc = block_number * BLOCKSIZE ;
block_number = mem_loc / BLOCKSIZE;
offset = mem_loc % BLOCKSIZE;
```

Note that the values of **MEMSIZE** or **NUM_MEM_BLOCKS** do not figure into these formulas. Note also that the location of a particular memory element is found by adding the offset of the element from the starting position in the block to the value of **mem_loc**.

Figure 10.1 Structure of memory.

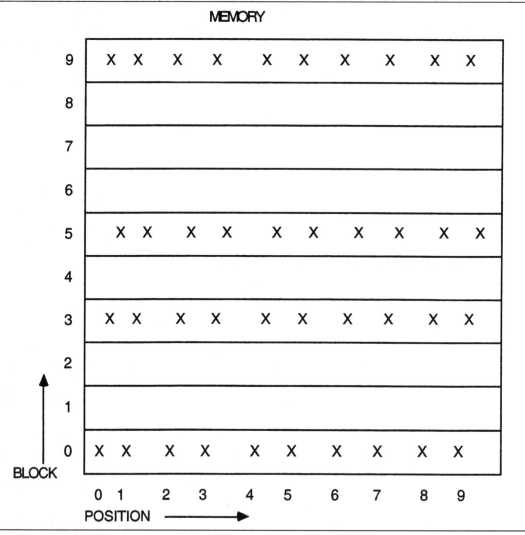

What about the three remaining functions, **put_in_memory()**, **mem_to_disk()**, and **disk_to_mem()**? In each case, we need to make a decision about where the block of data should be placed. There are several ways of doing this.

Consider the problem of placing a block of data into memory. We need to be able to find an available place for the insertion of a new block. There are two situations that we need to consider: one or more blocks available or nothing available.

If one or more memory blocks are available, then we have a situation something like that of Figure 10.1. In Figure 10.1, an uppercase X indicates that the memory location is already in use and a blank space means that the space is available for insertion of data. Recall that we are assuming that data is transferred in blocks and not as individual memory locations.

Our system will use the "first-fit" method of inserting blocks into memory. In the first-fit method, we start at the beginning of memory and ask for the first available block that is large enough for the data to be inserted.

The result of using this method on the insertion of the

Y Y Y Y Y Y Y Y Y Y

into the memory configuration displayed in Figure 10.1 is shown in Figure 10.2.

We still have to consider the disk. We will use the same method of first fit to find available blocks, but with a slight difference. We will choose to fill up the disk by filling up all blocks on the first track, then all blocks on the second track, etc. On each track, we will fill up the sectors in increasing numerical order. This is the first-fit method applied to both the tracks and sectors, in order.

This takes care of the situation when there is room in memory for the storage of the desired data. If there is not room, then we have three choices. We can terminate the program with an appropriate error action. We can continue the program execution by swapping the block of data from memory to the disk and thus free up the memory block. The third option is unacceptable: we continue execution of the program in an error state. Options 1 and 2 are used in many computer systems. We will arbitrarily choose the second option if memory is full; that is, we write a memory block of data onto the disk.

A similar problem occurs when the disk is full. In this case, we have no place to put extra data and so we select the first strategy of terminating execution of our program with an appropriate error action.

Everything looks fine from the point of view of how to access blocks of data on the simulated disk or simulated memory. However, there are some things that we have overlooked. For example, we need to have some mechanism of determining if a block of space in memory or on the disk is available. We have to store such information somewhere and access it somehow. Finally, we have to know the state of the simulated disk and memory initially that is, we have to initialize the system.

Real operating systems store information on what space is available in memory in what is historically called a free list or free vector. We will use an array to store the information for memory this array will contain as many entries as there are blocks in memory, **NUM_MEM_BLOCKS**. Recall that the dimension of the simulated memory is **MEMSIZE**, which is the product of **NUM_MEM_BLOCKS** and **MEMSIZE**. Similarly,

Figure 10.2 Result of insertion using the first-fit method.

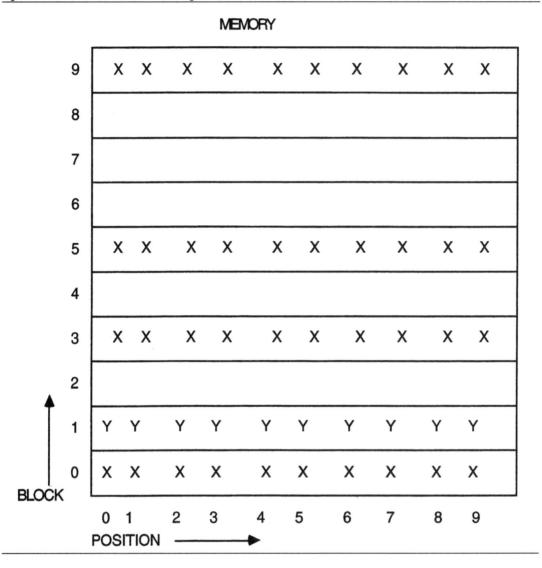

the availability of blocks on the disk is kept in a two-dimensional array. Thus we need the two new data declarations

```
int free_mem_list[NUM_MEM_BLOCKS];
int free_disk_list[NUM_TRACKS][NUM_SECTORS];
```

in order to keep a record of the available blocks. If a block is available, then we should have a 0 in the corresponding "list" if the block is in use, then we should have something else such as a 1 in the appropriate place.

We now know enough to do the design. We will follow the general principle of using a function to encapsulate an action that is repeated. The two functions **put_in_memory()** and **disk_to_mem()** require us to find an available memory block. Therefore we will define a new function, **find_mem_block()**. This function uses the first-fit algorithm for obtaining a free block. We have to check the array called **free_mem_list**. The algorithm seems simple:

```
mem_block_number = 0
do
   {
   test free_mem_list[mem_block_number]
   mem_block_number ++
   }
while free_mem_list[mem_block_number] != 0
```

This works perfectly if there is a free block. If none is available, then we would continue searching until we exceed the amount of memory allotted to our running program. The correct algorithm also test for failure:

```
mem_block_number = 0
do
   {
   test free_mem_list[mem_block_number]
   mem_block_number ++
   }
while (free_mem_list[mem_block_number] != 0) &&
              (mem_block_number < NUM_MEM_BLOCKS);

if (mem_block_number == NUM_MEM_BLOCKS)
   printf("Error - no available memory blocks\n");
```

We will need to perform a similar search for free blocks on the disk. For the disk, the algorithm is

```
track_number = 0;
sector_number = 0;
do
   // search each track, one sector at a time
   do
      {
      // search a complete track
      test free_disk_list[track_number][sector_number];
           sector_number] ++;
      }
   while ( free_disk_list[track_number][sector_number] != 0 )
```

```
                    && (sector_number < NUM_SECTORS);

      track_number ++;
      sector_number = 0;

   while (free_disk_list[track_number][sector_number] != 0 ) &&
                  (track_number < NUM_TRACKS) ;

   if (track_number == NUM_TRACKS)
      cerr << "Error - no available disk blocks\n";
```

It is time to take stock of our progress. We have designed a fairly elaborate system for moving data blocks to and from memory. Let us suppose that we have actually coded the program to carry out the algorithms and data structures in the design. It is important to note that we really cannot do exhaustive testing of any major software project because of the complexity of the system. For example, there are **NUM_MEM_BLOCKS** possible memory blocks. The number of possible combinations of memory block availability includes

1 case of no blocks available,
NUM_MEM_BLOCKS cases of exactly one block available,
NUM_MEM_BLOCKS * (**NUM_MEM_BLOCKS** – 1) / 2 cases of exactly two blocks,

and so on for a total of 2 raised to the power **NUM_MEM_BLOCKS** possible groupings of memory alone. The number of possible disk block combinations is exponential in the number **NUM_TRACKS** + **NUM_SECTORS**, and the total number of combinations to be tested is astronomical. It is quite common to have systems that are so complex that complete testing would require centuries.

As was mentioned earlier in this chapter, the original source code for the system has been changed to C++ from C code by replacing the calls to the functions **printf()**, **scanf()**, and **getchar()** by the C++ I/O operators **<<** and **>>**, using the standard iostreams **cout** and **cin**. For simplicity, the file-based I/O using pure C language constructions has been left unchanged.

10.5 Source Code for Procedural System (Optional)

The code presented in this section is based on a procedural design of the system and will be given in Examples 10.4 through 10.9. The overall organizational structure of the code is indicated by the **Makefile** that is presented in Example 10.3. The source code performs the appropriate disk operations such as moving blocks of data between simulated memory, the simulated disk, and a user. This is the lowest level of the file system simulation.

Robin Morris of AT&T provided some help in the original C language implementation of this program, using the design given in the previous sections of this chapter.

Exampl.e 10.3 `Makefile` for a procedurally oriented file system simulation.

```
## makefile for disk simulation program
## the executable file is named disk_mem

disk_mem: memory.o move_dat.o print.o disk.o main.o
        cc -o disk_mem memory.o move_data.o print.o disk.o\
        main.o

memory.o: memory.c header.h
        cc -O -c memory.c
move_dat.o: move_dat.c header.h
        cc -O -c move_dat.c
print.o: print.c header.h
        cc -O -c print.c
disk.o: disk.c header.h
        cc -O -c disk.c
main.o: main.c header.h
        cc -O -c main.c
```

In Example 10.4, we present the header file that is common to all source code files for this system.

Example 10.4 Header file **`header.h`** for a procedurally oriented file system simulation.

```
/*********************************************************/
/**   HEADER FILE header.h                       **/
/*********************************************************/


#define NUM_MEM_BLOCKS 10
#define NUM_TRACKS 50
#define NUM_SECTORS 10
#define Blocksize 10
#define MEMSIZE 100

int data;
int track,sector;
int mem[10][10];
```

```
int disk[50][10][10];
int mem_loc,location;
int free_mem_list[10];
int free_disk_list[50][10];

struct disk_info
{
  int track_no;
  int sector_no;
};

struct FIFO
{
  int block;
  struct FIFO *next;
} *mem_que;


/* Function prototypes */
void initialization(void);
void opening_message(void);
void get_data(void);
void print_disk(void);
void print_mem(void);
put_in_mem(int data);
disk_to_mem(int track, sector);
mem_to_disk(int_mem_loc);
```

Example 10.5 File **main.c** for a procedurally oriented file system simulation.

```
/**********************************************************/
/****                    MAIN                        ****/
/**********************************************************/

#include "header.h"
#include <iostream.h>
main()
{
  initialization();
  opening_message();
  get_data();
}


/**********************************************************/
```

```
/****          FUNCTION initialization()              ******/
/****                                                ******/
/**** CALLED BY: main()                              ******/
/****                                                ******/
/**** FUNCTIONS CALLED: none                         ******/
/****                                                ******/
/**** PARAMETERS:   none                             ******/
/****                                                ******/
/**** VALUE RETURNED: none                           ******/
/****************************************************************/

void initialization(void)
{
  int i,j,k;

  for (i=0; i<NUM_MEM_BLOCKS; i++)
   {
   free_mem_list[i] = 0;
   for (j=0; j<Blocksize; j++)
     mem[i][j] = -99;
   }

  for (i = 0; i < NUM_TRACKS; i++)
    for (j = 0; j < NUM_SECTORS; j++)
     {
     free_disk_list[i][j];
     for (k=0; k<Blocksize; k++)
     disk[i][j][k] = -99;
     }

  mem_que = (struct FIFO *)NULL;
}



/****************************************************************/
/****           FUNCTION opening_message()            ******/
/****                                                ******/
/**** This function prints an opening message.       ******/
/****                                                ******/
/**** CALLED BY: main()                              ******/
/****                                                ******/
/**** FUNCTIONS CALLED: none                         ******/
/****                                                ******/
/**** PARAMETERS:   none                             ******/
/****                                                ******/
/**** VALUE RETURNED: none                           ******/
/****************************************************************/
void opening_message(void)
```

```
{
  cout << "Welcome to the FILE SIMULATION SYSTEM.\n"
    << "The purpose of the system is to demonstrate some"
    << "of the.\n"
    << "features of a file system.\n\n"
    << "This first phase will show some of the commands"
    << " necessary\n"
    << "to move data to and from simulated memory and"
    << "disk.\n\n\n";
}



/**********************************************************/
/****                                              *******/
/****             FUNCTION get_data()              *******/
/****                                              *******/
/**** CALLED BY: get_data()                        *******/
/****                                              *******/
/**** FUNCTIONS CALLED: many                       *******/
/****                                              *******/
/**** PARAMETERS:   none                           *******/
/****                                              *******/
/**** VALUE RETURNED: none                         *******/
/**********************************************************/

void get_data(void)
{
  int ch;
  int data,mem_loc,track,sector;

  for(;;)
    {
    cout <<"\n\nSelect an option:\n";
    cout << "i......insert data into memory directly.\n";
    cout << "d......move data from memory to disk\n";
    cout << "m......move block from disk to memory\n";
    cout << "p......print memory\n";
    cout << "P......print disk\n";
    cout << "q......quit\n";
    cout << "\n\nEnter Option >> ";
    cin >> ch;
    cout << "\n\n");
    switch(ch)
      {
      case 'i':
        cout << "Enter data:\n";
        cin >> data;
```

```
        if (put_in_memory(data) != -1)
          break;
        else
          return;

      case 'd':
        cout << "Enter mem_loc, track, sector:\n";
        cin >> mem_loc >> track >> sector;
        mem_to_disk(mem_loc,track,sector;
        break;

      case 'm':
        cout << "Enter mem_loc, track, sector:\n";
        cin >> mem_loc >> track >> sector;
        disk_to_mem(mem_loc,track,sector;
        break;

      case 'p':
        print_mem();
        break;

      case 'P':
        print_disk();
        break;

      case 'q':
      case 'Q':
        return;

      default:
        cout << "Invalid Selection, Try Again\n";
        break;
      }   /* end switch */
  } /* end big for loop */
}
```

Example 10.6 File **memory.c** for a procedurally oriented file system simulation.

```
#include "header.h"
#include <iostream.h>

/**********************************************************/
/**** FILE memory.c                                   ***/
/**********************************************************/
int find_mem_block()
```

```
{
  int mem_block_number=0;

  do
    {
    if (free_mem_list[mem_block_number] != 0)
      mem_block_number++;
    }
  while ((free_mem_list[mem_block_number] != 0) &&
          (mem_block_number < NUM_MEM_BLOCKS));


  if (mem_block_number == NUM_MEM_BLOCKS)
    {
    printf("Error - no available memory blocks\n");
    return(-1);
    }
  else
    return(mem_block_number);
}



int free_memory(void)
{
  struct disk_info disk_block;
  int block_num,i;

  disk_block = find_disk_block();
  if (disk_block.track_no == -1)
    {
    cout << "Memory and Disk full \n";
    return(-1);
    }

  block_num = mem_que->block;
  mem_que = mem_que->next;
  for (i=0; i<Blocksize; i++)
    disk[disk_block.track_no][disk_block.sector_no][i] =
                mem[block_num][i];

  free_disk_list[disk_block.track_no][disk_block.sector_no]
                = 1;

  for (i=0; i< Blocksize; i++)
    mem[block_num][i] = 0;
  free_mem_list[block_num] = 0;
```

```
  }


update_mem_info(int location)
{
  struct FIFO *current,*new_node;

  free_mem_list[location] = 1;

     /*  Adds location which is the block just filled
     to the mem_que so that we can keep up with which
     location was filled in first (order).      */

  new_node = (struct FIFO *) malloc (sizeof(struct FIFO));
  new_node->block = location;
  new_node->next = (struct FIFO *)NULL;
  current = mem_que;
  if (current == (struct FIFO *)NULL)
    mem_que = new_node;
  else
    {
    while (current->next != (struct FIFO*)NULL)
      current = current->next;
    current->next =new_node;
    }
}
```

Example 10.7 File **disk.c** for a procedurally oriented file system simulation.

```
/***********************************************************/
/***** FILE: disk.c                                    ****/
/***********************************************************/

#include "header.h"
#include <stdio.h>

struct disk_info find_disk_block()
{
  int track_num = 3;
  int sector_num = 0;
  struct disk_info block;

  do
    {
    do
      {
```

```
        if (free_disk_list[track_num][sector_num] !=0)
            sector_num++;
        }
    while ((free_disk_list[track_num][sector_num] != 0) &&
            (sector_num < NUM_SECTORS));

    if (free_disk_list[track_num][sector_num] != 0)
        {
        track_num++;
        sector_num=0;
        }
    }
while ((free_disk_list[track_num][sector_num] != 0) &&
        (track_num < NUM_TRACKS));


if (track_num == NUM_TRACKS)
    {
    cout <<"Error-no available disk blocks \n";
    block.track_no = -1;
    block.sector_no = -1;
    }
else
    {
    block.track_no = track_num;
    block.sector_no = sector_num;
    }
return(block);
}
```

Example 10.8 File **move_dat.c** for a procedurally oriented file system simulation.

```
#include "header.h"

/*************************************************************/
/***    FILE: put_dat.c                             ****/
/*************************************************************/
int put_in_memory(int data)
{
  int loc_found = -1;
  int i;

  if ((loc_found = find_mem_block()) == -1)
    {
    if (free_memory() == -1)
```

```
        return(-1);
      else
        loc_found = find_mem_block();
      }
  for (i=0;i<Blocksize;i++)
    mem[loc_found][i] = data;
  update_mem_info(loc_found);
  cout << "Infomation stored in memory\n";
}




mem_to_disk(int mem_loc, int track, int sector)
{
  int block_num,i;
  int chances=0;

  do
    {
    if (free_disk_list[track][sector]  != 0)
      {
      cout << "Information is already stored at track"
          << track
          << " and sector" << sector << endl;
      cout << "Enter new track and sector numbers:\n";
      cin >> track >> sector;
      chances++;
      }
    }
  while ((free_disk_list[track][sector] != 0) &&
          (chances < 2));

  if (chances != 2)
    {
    block_num = mem_loc/Blocksize;
    for (i = 0; i < Blocksize; i++)
      disk[track][sector][i] = mem[block_num][i];
    free_disk_list[track][sector] = 1;
    free_mem_list[block_num] = 0;
    for (i = 0; i < Blocksize; i++)
      mem[block_num][i] = 0;
    }
}
disk_to_mem(int mem_loc, int track)
```

```
int sector;
{
  int block_num,offset,i;
  int chances=0;

  do
    {
    block_num = mem_loc/Blocksize;
    offset = mem_loc%Blocksize;
    if (free_mem_list[block_num] != 0)
        {
        cout << "The mem_loc specified is not available\n";
        cout << "Enter mem_loc:\n";
        cin >> mem_loc;
        chances++;
        }
    }
    while ((free_mem_list[block_num] != 0) &&
                  (chances < 2));

  if (chances != 2)
    {
    for (i = 0; i < Blocksize; i++)
      mem[block_num][i] = disk[track][sector][i];
    update_mem_info(block_num);
    }
}
```

Example 10.9 File **print.c** for a procedurally oriented file system simulation.

```
/*************************************************************/
/***        FUNCTION print_mem()                   *******/
/**** This function prints an opening message.      *******/
/****                                               *******/
/**** PARAMETERS:   none                            *******/
/****                                               *******/
/**** VALUE RETURNED: none                          *******/
/*************************************************************/
#include "header.h"

void print_mem(void)
{
  int i,j;
```

```
    cout << "                 LAYOUT OF MEMORY  \n\n\n";
    for (i = 0;i< NUM_MEM_BLOCKS;i++)
     {
     cout << "Block = " << i ;
     for (j = 0;j < Blocksize; j++)
       if (mem[i][j] != -99)
         cout << mem[i][j]);
     cout << "\n";
     }
     cout << "\n\n\n";
}



/**************************************************************/
/****             FUNCTION print_disk()            *******/
/****                                              *******/
/**** PARAMETERS:   none                           *******/
/****                                              *******/
/**** VALUE RETURNED: none                         *******/
/**************************************************************/

void print_disk(void)
{
  int i,j,k;

  cout << "                 LAYOUT OF DISK  \n\n\n";
  for (i = 0; i < NUM_TRACKS; i++)
    for (j = 0; j < NUM_SECTORS; j++)
      {
      if (free_disk_list[i][j] != 0)
      {
      cout << "Track " << i << "Sector "<< j ;
      for (k = 0; k < Blocksize; k++)
        {
        if (disk[i][j][k] != -99)
          cout << disk[i][j][k];
          }
        cout << endl;
            }
        }
    cout << "\n*** All Tracks and Sectors not Printed are"
         << "Empty ***\n\n";
}
```

10.6 Reengineering a Procedurally Based System into an Object-Oriented One

The subject of this section is one of the most difficult problems in the area of object-oriented software. While there have been many articles written on the subject, there is little consensus about appropriate methodologies for performing this transformation in general. It is not completely clear that any of the existing methodologies are general or if they succeeded in particular situations because of the nature of the application domain of the software.

Notice that our problem is actually one of reengineering an existing system. The fundamental issue is whether we should develop an entirely new set of requirements for our system, obtaining the design from the new requirements, or use the existing, procedurally oriented ones in order to develop a new design. In each case, we would use the new design as the basis for the remainder of activities during the software's life cycle.

Note that we are somewhat better off than the traditional reengineering practitioner because we have the existing requirements, design, and source code available to us.

The tutorial book by Arnold listed in the references provides more information on this aspect of reengineering.

This problem is somewhat easier than that of the previous few paragraphs. The object-oriented requirements naturally suggest some objects. These objects will lead to a potential organization for the objects that represent the data that is used in the program. The organization is usually a hierarchy, because of the inheritance structure of many objects.

However, we have to be careful to distinguish the object hierarchy of the data from the hierarchy of the program. Even with an object-oriented approach, the program must begin its execution somewhere and must maintain a flow of control. The control flow of the program is what is commonly referred to as the program hierarchy.

We will transform the procedural requirements of the simulation system to object-oriented requirements by using the following guidelines. The guidelines are based on the domain analysis techniques used by R. Prieto-Diaz in his research on software reuse.

1. List all major actions performed by the system in complete sentences.
2. Group the nouns in the sentences by placing them into one of three categories: object, medium, or system.
3. Determine all parallel relationships between the actions of the sentences and the three classes of nouns determined in the previous step.

4. Use these as the initial set of candidates for objects. (This will be similar, but not identical, to the set of objects determined in step 1).

These guidelines should be taken as a starting point, with more specific steps generally being necessary.

The relevant terms found are listed in Table 10.1.

Table 10.1

Action	Medium	Object	System
Print	Memory	Memory	Memory
Print	Disk	Disk	Disk
Put	Disk	Block	Disk
Insert	Disk	Block	Disk
Insert	Memory	Block	Memory
Delete	Disk	Block	Disk
Write	Memory	Block	Memory
Delete	Memory	Block	Memory
Write	Disk	Block	Disk

The two subsystems of our disk–memory simulation are the disk and memory subsystems. There are two "mediums" in our system: the "disk" and "memory." The rest of the terminology is straightforward.

An examination of this data suggests that there are only a few actions that are applied to objects: printing, reading, and writing. "Deleting" appears to be a misnomer—we are only overwriting the information in a memory block. Note also that we can combine printing of the disk and memory into repeated printing of the individual blocks that make up these simulated "media." Reading and writing can take several forms, often including some sort of initialization.

10.7 An Object-Oriented Disk Simulation Program

The class organization causes several changes to the existing, procedurally developed solution. These changes affect the number and type of operations given as member functions, the placement of functions into files, and documentation. Of course the code itself will change considerably. Nonetheless, its roots in the procedural system remain clear.

The program will have three important types of objects: block, disk, and memory. These objects will be organized so that the classes **Disk** and **Memory** can inherit from the base class **Block**.

The organization of the object-oriented design is different from that of the procedural one. The use of an object of type **Block** as the primary object allows the routines **mem_to_disk()** and **disk_to_mem()** to be simplified considerably. Other routines can be replaced by simple function calls.

For example, the header file can be eliminated, since there is no need for prototypes for member functions, and the **Block** class contains the common structure. All functions in the file **move_dat.c** can be placed into other files as member functions or developed as simple composition of functions relating the disk to memory.

10.8 Source Code for an Object-Oriented Solution

In this section we will present some C++ code that describes the procedurally based simulation of the file system. The code will perform the appropriate disk operations such as moving blocks of data between simulated memory, the simulated disk, and a user.

The documentation has been changed to reflect the information hiding and abstraction available in object-oriented programming.

Our new system will have three files, which are shown in Examples 10.10, 10.11, and 10.12. The algorithms for disk and memory operations are the same as in the procedural version of the system.

Most of the code is straightforward. However, you should note the use of conditional compilation using the **#ifndef** ... **#endif** construction in Example 10.11 to make sure that a header file is included only once.

Example 10.10 File **Block.cpp** for object-oriented file system simulation.

```
//
// FILE block.cpp
//
```

```
#include <iostream.h>
#include <iomanip.h>



//
// Description of base class Block.
//
class Block
{
private:
#define BLOCKSIZE 10
  int contents[BLOCKSIZE];
public:
  Block();
  void init();
  void clear();
  void put(int info); // Put info into each entry.
  int get(); // Returns info in block.
  void print();
};



Block:: Block()
{
  init();
}



void Block:: init()
{
  int i;

  for (i = 0; i < BLOCKSIZE; i++)
    contents[i] = -1;
}



void Block:: clear()
{
  int i;

  for(i = 0; i < BLOCKSIZE; i++)
    contents[i] = 0;
}
```

```
int Block:: get()
{
  return (contents[0]);
}




void Block:: put(int info)
{
  int i;

  for (i = 0; i < BLOCKSIZE; i++)
    contents[i] = info;
}




void Block :: print()
{
  int i;

  for (i = 0; i < BLOCKSIZE; i++)
    cout << setw(4) <<contents[i];
  cout << endl;
}
```

Example 10.11 File **disk_mem.cpp** for object-oriented file system simulation.

```
#ifndef block_cpp
#include "block.cpp"
#endif
#include <iostream.h>


//
// Description of the class Disk.
//

class Disk: public Block
{
private:
  #define NUM_TRACKS 50
  #define NUM_SECTORS 10
  Block contents[NUM_TRACKS][NUM_SECTORS];
  int free_disk_list[NUM_TRACKS][NUM_SECTORS];
```

```
public:
  int track,sector;
  Disk();
  void init();
  struct disk_info find_disk_block();
  Block get(int trck, int sec);
  void put(int trk, int sec, Block b);
  void clear(int trk, int sec);
  void print();
};



struct disk_info
{
  int track_no;
  int sector_no;
};




Disk :: Disk()
{
  init();
}




void Disk:: init()
{
  int i, j;

  for (i = 0; i < NUM_TRACKS; i++)
    for (j = 0; j < NUM_SECTORS; j++)
      {
      free_disk_list[i][j];
      contents[i][j].init();
      }
}




struct disk_info Disk :: find_disk_block()
{
  int track_num = 3; // Reserve first 2 tracks.
  int sector_num = 0;
  struct disk_info d_info;
```

```
    do
      {
      do
        {
        if (free_disk_list[track_num][sector_num] !=0)
              sector_num++;
        }
      while ((free_disk_list[track_num][sector_num] != 0) &&
              (sector_num < NUM_SECTORS));

      if (free_disk_list[track_num][sector_num] != 0)
        {
        track_num++;
        sector_num=0;
        }
      }
    while ((free_disk_list[track_num][sector_num] != 0) &&
            (track_num < NUM_TRACKS));


    if (track_num == NUM_TRACKS)
      {
      cout <<"Error-no available disk blocks \n";
      d_info.track_no = -1;
      d_info.sector_no = -1;
      }
    else
      {
      d_info.track_no = track;
      d_info.sector_no = sector;
      }
    return(d_info);
  }


//////////////////////////////////////////////
Block Disk :: get(int trck, int sec)
{
  Block temp;
  int i, j;

  temp.put(contents[trck][sec].get() );
  return temp;
}
```

```
////////////////////////////////////////
void Disk :: put(int trk, int sec, Block b)
{
  contents[trk][sec].put( b.get());
}


void Disk::print(void)
{
  int i,j,k;

  cout << "             LAYOUT OF DISK \n\n\n";
  for (i = 0; i < NUM_TRACKS; i++)
    for (j = 0; j < NUM_SECTORS; j++)
      {
      if (free_disk_list[i][j] != 0)
      {
      cout << "Track " << i << "Sector "<< j ;
      contents[i][j].print();
      cout << endl;
      }
      }
  cout << "\n*** All Tracks and Sectors not Printed are"
       << "Empty ***\n\n";
}




//
// Description of the class memory.
//

class Memory: public Block
{
public:
  #define NUM_MEM_BLOCKS 10
  Block memory[NUM_MEM_BLOCKS];
  struct FIFO
    {
    int block;
    struct FIFO *next;
    } *mem_que;
public:
```

```
  // Constructor
  Memory();
  void init();
  int free_mem_list[NUM_MEM_BLOCKS];
  int find_mem_block(); // Returns a block number.
  void free_memory();

  // Functions to update memory.
  void update_mem_info(int location);
  void put(int loc, Block b);
  Block get (int loc);
  int mem_loc;
  void print();
};


//////////////////////////////////////////////////
Memory :: Memory()
{
  init();
}


//////////////////////////////////////////////////
void Memory :: init()
{
  int i,j,k;

  for (i = 0; i < NUM_MEM_BLOCKS; i++)
   {
   free_mem_list[i] = 0;
   memory[i].init(); // Uses Block :: init()
   }
  mem_que = (struct FIFO *)NULL;
}


//////////////////////////////////////////////////
void Memory ::put(int loc, Block b)
{
  memory[loc].put( b.get() );
}


//////////////////////////////////////////////////
Block Memory ::get (int loc)
{
  Block temp;
```

```
      temp.put(memory[loc].get() );
      return temp;
    }


//////////////////////////////////////////////////
int Memory :: find_mem_block()
{
  int mem_block_number=0;

  do
    {
    if (free_mem_list[mem_block_number] != 0)
      mem_block_number++;
    }
  while ((free_mem_list[mem_block_number] != 0) &&
         (mem_block_number < NUM_MEM_BLOCKS));

  if (mem_block_number == NUM_MEM_BLOCKS)
    {
    cout << "Error - no available memory blocks\n";
    return(-1);
    }
  else
    return(mem_block_number);
}


//////////////////////////////////////////////////
void Memory :: free_memory(void)
{
  struct disk_info disk_block;
  int block_num, i;
  Block b;

  block_num = mem_que->block;
  mem_que = mem_que->next;
  memory[block_num].init();
  free_mem_list[block_num] = 0;
}


//////////////////////////////////////////////////
void Memory :: update_mem_info(int location)
{
  struct FIFO *current;

  free_mem_list[location] = 1;
```

```
          // Adds location which is the block just filled
          // to the mem_que so that we can keep up with which
          // location was filled in first (order).

  struct FIFO * new_node = new (struct FIFO) ;
  new_node->block = location;
  new_node->next = (struct FIFO *)NULL;
  current = mem_que;
  if (current == (struct FIFO *)NULL)
    mem_que = new_node;
  else
    {
    while (current->next != (struct FIFO*)NULL)
      current = current->next;
    current->next =new_node;
    }
}




///////////////////////////////////////////////////
void Memory:: print(void)
{
  int i,j;

  cout << "              LAYOUT OF MEMORY   \n\n\n";
  for (i = 0;i< NUM_MEM_BLOCKS;i++)
   {
   cout << "Block = " << i ;
   if ( memory[i].get() >= 0 )
     memory[i].print();
   cout << "\n";
   }
   cout << "\n\n\n";
}
```

Example 10.12 File **main.cpp** for object-oriented file system simulation.

```
//
// File main.cpp
//


#include "disk_mem.cpp"
#include <iostream.h>
```

```
  // Global variables.
  Disk disk;
  Memory memory;
  Block temp; // For temporary storage.


  // Function prototypes.
  void opening_message(void);
  void get_data(void)


  main()
  {
    opening_message();
    memory.init();
    disk.init();
    get_data();
  }




  //////////////////////////////////////////////////////////
  // FUNCTION opening_message()
  //

  void opening_message(void)
  {
    cout << "Welcome to the FILE SIMULATION SYSTEM.\n"
      << "The purpose of the system is to demonstrate some"
      << "of the.\n"
      << "features of a file system.\n\n"
      << "This first phase will show some of the commands"
      << " necessary\n"
      << "to move data to and from simulated memory and"
      << "disk.\n\n\n";
  }




  //
  // FUNCTION get_data()
  //

  void get_data(void)
  {
    char ch;
    int data, mem_loc, trk, sect;
```

```
for(;;)
  {
  cout <<"\n\nSelect an option:\n";
  cout << "i......insert data into memory directly.\n";
  cout << "d......move data from memory to disk\n";
  cout << "m......move block from disk to memory\n";
  cout << "p......print memory\n";
  cout << "P......print disk\n";
  cout << "q......quit\n";
  cout << "\n\nEnter Option >> " ;
  cin >> ch;
  cout << "\n\n";
  switch(ch)
    {
    case 'i':
      cout << "Enter data:\n";
      cin >> data;
      temp.put(data);
      memory.put(memory.find_mem_block(), temp);
      break;

    case 'd':
      cout << "Enter mem_loc, track, sector:\n";
      cin >> mem_loc >> trk >> sect;
      temp = memory.get(mem_loc);
      disk.put(trk, sect, temp);
      break;

    case 'm':
      cout << "Enter mem_loc, track, sector:\n";
      cin >> mem_loc >> trk >> sect;
      temp = disk.get(trk, sect);
      memory.put(mem_loc, temp);
      break;

    case 'p':
      memory.print();
      break;

    case 'P':
      disk.print();
      break;

    case 'q':
    case 'Q':
      return;
```

```
        default:
          cout << "Invalid Selection, Try Again\n";
          break;
      }  /* end switch */
  } /* end big for loop */
}
```

10.9 Comparison of Object-Oriented and Procedural Solutions

Let's examine the two proposed organizations for the system. The C language procedurally designed one presented in this chapter uses arrays and structs in order to represent data. It is very easy to manipulate lower-level details that should be hidden from a programmer.

For example, it is easy to write I/O functions that directly act upon the individual members of a disk block, defeating the block orientation of the procedural system.

The C code consists of approximately 317 lines of code. (We have used the measure "NCNB," or noncommented, non-blank lines of code.) Any measurement of lines of code should be taken as a reasonable approximation and not as an absolute number.

On the other hand, the object-oriented C++ program provides a higher level of abstraction and information hiding. Access to private data is allowed only by using member functions.

The C++ code consists of approximately 301 noncommented, nonblank lines of code. These are broken into many small member functions, including several functions that were not present in the original, procedurally developed system coded in C.

At first glance, the systems would appear to have the same level of complexity, since the number of noncommented, nonblank lines of code is essentially the same for each system development. However, the C++ system is less complex, because its functions are simpler.

The C++ code combines some of the member functions to eliminate several of the more complex routines that were in the C source code. The C source code consists of 12 functions, with an average size of 317/12 or 26.25 noncommented, nonblank lines of code per function. On the other hand, the C++ code consists of 25 functions, of which 23 are member functions and can be reused easily. This is an average of approximately 12 noncommented, nonblank lines of code per function.

Clearly, the C++ implementation of this system is easier to understand than the C implementation.

Summary

In this chapter we presented two designs for a simulation of the operation of a simple disk–memory system. The first design was a procedurally oriented one, which we took to be the description of an existing system.

The focus of the chapter was the transformation of this design into an object-oriented design. We reengineered the procedurally oriented design by the simple method of examining the operations of the existing system and changing them into object-oriented actions. This provided us with an example of the reengineering process.

We also provided a description of a more complex problem—adding a file system hierarchy and a method of file access to the procedurally described disk simulation system.

EXERCISES

1. Implement the free list for access to memory blocks in our project as a bit vector. A bit vector is a memory unit that is used to simulate the contents of a boolean array. The bits are either 0 or 1, and this means that the memory location corresponding to the position of the bit is either empty or full.

   The function that manages the free list should use each bit to represent a specific memory block. We can determine the first bit that has a value of 0, using a function to select the bit by shifting the input until the bitwise exclusive OR of the number and the octal number 0000 has the value xxx1, where we don't care about the first three octal digits. The exclusive OR operator will return a value of the form xxx1 if the rightmost bit is a 0, which is the situation that we want.

   The header for the new function **find_free_block()** should be of the form

   ```
   find_free_block(list_vector)
   double list_vector;
   {
   // The body of find_free_block goes here.
   }
   ```

   with the free list passed as a parameter named **list_vector**.

   Are there any differences implementing this in the procedural and object-oriented systems?

2. Change the system to have two possible environments—a user-friendly one, in which the user is prompted for input with an opportunity to correct incorrect or missing data, and an environment in which a user has no interaction because all of the commands come from a file. This second situation is commonly called a batch

system. Specifically, the software should be able to take either of two execution paths. If the system receives the command for interactive input and response, then the software should respond as before. However, if the command is for the software to act as a batch system, then all of the user interface commands and prompts should be removed from the software.

The information about whether the system is to be interactive or batch should be obtained as early as possible in the execution of the program. The command line

    program1

means that the program is interactive the command line

    program1 input

means that the program is batch and reads commands from a file named "**input**" and the command line

    program1 input output

means that the output should be written to a file named "**output**." This means that our program should be able to handle the case of one, two, or three command-line arguments. If the number of arguments is one, then the program is meant to be interactive. If there is more than one argument, then the program is a "batch" program and the second command-line argument is the name of the input file. If a third command-line argument is given, then it represents the name of the file to which output is to be written. If there are any additional command-line arguments, they should be ignored.

Are there any diferences implementing this in the procedural and object-oriented systems?

3. Consider the additional features of the procedurally oriented system to include simulation of higher levels of the file system: grouping disk blocks into files and lacing the files into directory structures.

(a) Determine the fundamental data objects in this system. Are the fundamental objects the disk, the memory, disk or memory blocks, single data elements for either disk or memory, or something else? As part of your analysis, include the possibility of reusing libraries of transformations on these data objects and the possibility of having new classes of objects inherit properties from existing classes of objects.

(b) Determine the allowable operations on each of the classes that you have determined in part a of this problem.

Reserved Words in C++

asm	float	signed
auto	for	sizeof
break	friend	static
case	goto	struct
catch	if	switch
char	inline	template
class	int	this
const	long	throw
continue	new	try
default	operator	typedef
delete	private	union
do	protected	unsigned
double	public	virtual
else	register	void
enum	return	volatile
extern	short	while

Syntax Summary of C++

2

The syntax summary is given in *yacc* format. In this format, the first character string (in this case "program") is where the pattern matching begins. The leftmost character string in each block is a nonterminal, which is to be expanded into one of the options provided after the colon. Different options are separated by single vertical bars and appear on different lines. Matching continues until each nonterminal in the sequence of replacements is replaced by a terminal. Terminals are actual characters or strings in a C program. We have used italics for nonterminals and have separated each block of possible matching by a semicolon on a line by itself, followed by a blank line. Also, a pair of braces in italics means that the terminals and nonterminals inside can occur either zero or an arbitrary number of times. Braces, commas, semicolons, and other punctuation marks in normal fonts are to be treated as required characters. (In some versions of yacc, these punctuation marks must be enclosed in single quotes.)

program :
    external_definition
    | *external_definition program*
    ;

external_definition: :
      function_definition
      | *data_definition*
      ;

function_definition: :
      function_declarator function_body
      | *decl_specifier function_declarator function_body*
      | *function_declarator ctor_initializer function_body*
      | *decl_specifier function_declarator ctor_initializer function_body*
      ;

ctor_initializer :
      mem_initializer_list
      ;

mem_initializer_list :
      mem_initializer
      | *mem_initializer , mem_initializer_list*
      ;

mem_initializer :
      complete_class_name ( )
      | *complete_class_name* (*expression_list*)
      | *identifier* ( )
      | *identifier* (*expression_list*)
      ;

function_declarator :
      declarator { *parameter_list* }
      ;

parameter_list: :
      identifier
      | *identifier , parameter_list*
      ;

function_body :
      type_declaration_list function_statement
      ;

function_statement :
        { *declaration_listopt statement_list* }
        ;

data_definition :
        externopt type_specifieropt init-declarator_list ;
        | *staticopt type_specifieropt init-declarator_list* ;
        ;

compound_statement :
        { *declaration_listopt statement_listopt* }
        ;

declaration_list :
        declaration
        | *declaration declaration_list* ;
        ;

statement_list :
        statement
        | *statement statement_list* ;
        ;

statement: :
        compound_statement
        | *expression* ;
        | **if** (*expression*) *statement*
        | **if** (*expression*) *statement* **else** *statement*
        | **while** (*expression*) *statement*
        | **do** *statement* **while** *expression*
        | **for** (*expression_1* ; *expression_2* ; *expression_3*) *statement*
        | **switch** (*expression*) *statement*
        | **case** *constant_expression* : *statement*
        | **default** : *statement*
        | **break** ;
        | **continue** ;
        | **return** ;
        | **return** *expression* ;
        | **goto** *identifier* ;
        | *identifier* : *statement* ;
        ;

declaration:
> *declaration_specifiers init_declarator_listopt* ;
> ;

declaration_specifiers :
> *type_specifier declaration_specifiersopt*
> | *sc_specifier declaration_specifiersopt*
> ;

sc_specifier :
> **auto**
> | **static**
> | **extern**
> | **register**
> | **typedef**
> ;

type_specifier :
> **char**
> | **short**
> | **int**
> | **long**
> | **unsigned**
> | **float**
> | **double**
> | *struct_or_union_specifier*
> | *typedef_name*
> ;

init_declaration_list :
> *init_declarator*
> | *init_declarator* , *init_declarator_list*
> ;

init_declarator :
> *declarator initializer*
> ;

declarator :
> *identifier*

```
        | { declarator  }
        | * declarator
        | declarator ( )
        | declarator [constant_expressionopt  ]
        ;


struct_or_union_specifier :
        | struct { struct_declarations_list  }
        | struct identifier {struct_declarations_list }
        | struct identifier
        | union { struct_declarations_list  }
        | union identifier { struct_declarations_list}
        | union identifier
        ;


struct_declarations_list :
        struct_declaration
        | struct_declaration struct_declarations_list :
        ;


struct_declaration :
        type_specifier struct_declarator_list
        ;


struct_declarator_list :
        struct_declarator
        | struct_declarator ,  struct_declarator_list
        ;


struct_declarator :
        declarator
        | declarator : constant_expression
        | : constant_expression
        ;


initializer :
        = expression
        | = { initializer_list}
        | = { initializer_list , }
        ;
```

initializer_list. :
> *expression*
> | *initializer_list* , *initializer_list*
> | { *initializer_list* }

type_name   :
> *type_specifier abstract_declarator*
> ;

abstract_declarator :
> | (*abstract_declarator*   )
> | * *abstract_declarator*
> | *abstract_declarator* ( )
> | *abstract_declarator* [*constant_expression*]

typedef_name :
> *identifier*
> ;

enum_name :
> *identifier*
> ;

class_name :
> *identifier*
> ;

expression :
> *primary*
> | * *expression*
> | & *expression*
> | - *expression*
> | ! *expression*
> | -- *expression*
> | ++ *lvalue*
> | --*lvalue*
> | *lvalue* ++
> | *lvalue* --
> | **sizeof** *expression*
> | **sizeof** (*type_name*   )

        | *allocation_expression*
        | *deallocation_expression*
        | (*type_name*) *expression*
        | *expression binaryoperator expression*
        | *expression* ? *expression* : *expression*
        | *lvalue assignoperator expression*
        | *expression* , *expression*
        ;

allocation_expression :
        new *placement new_type_name new_initializer*
        | **new** *placement* (*type_name*) *new_initializer*
        | **new** *placement new_type_name*
        | **new** *placement* (*type_name*)
        | **new** *new_type_name new_initializer*
        | **new** (*type_name*) *new_initializer*
        | **new** *new_type_name*
        | **new** (*type_name*)
        | :: **new** *placement new_type_name new_initializer*
        | :: **new** *placement* (*type_name*) *new_initializer*
        | :: **new** *placement new_type_name*
        | :: **new** *placement* (*type_name*)
        | :: **new** *new_type_name new_initializer*
        | :: **new** (*type_name*) *new_initializer*
        | :: **new** *new_type_name*
        | :: **new** (*type_name*)
        ;

placement :
        (*expression_list*)
        ;

new_type_name :
        type_specifier_list
        | *type_specifier_list new_declarator*
        ;

new_declarator :
        * *cv_qualifier_list new_declarator*
        | * *cv_qualifier_list*

    | * *new_declarator*
    | *complete_class_name* :: * *cv_qualifier_list new_declarator*
    | *complete_class_name* :: * *cv_qualifier_list*
    | *complete_class_name* :: * *new_declarator*
    | *new_declarator* [*expression*]
    | [*expression*]
    ;

new_initializer :
    (*new_initializer_list*)
    | ( )
    ;

deallocation_expression :
    delete *cast_expression*
    | **delete** [ ] *cast_expression*
    | :: **delete** *cast_expression*
    | :: **delete** [ ] *cast_expression*
    ;

primary :
    identifier
    | *constant*
    | *string*
    | (*expression*)
    | *primary* ( )
    | *primary* (*expression_list*)
    | *primary* [*expression*]
    | lvalue . *identifier*
    | *primary* -> *identifier*
    | **this**
    ;

lvalue :
    identifier
    | *primary* [*expression*]
    | *lvalue* . *identifier*
    | *primary* -> *identifier*
    | * *expression*
    | [*lvalue*]
    ;

name :
  identifier
  | *operator_function_name*
  | *conversion_function_name*
  | ~ *class_name*
  | *qualified_name*
  ;

qualified_name :
  qualified_class_name **: :** *name*
  ;

class-specifier.
  class_head { *member_list* }
  | *class_head* { *member_list* }
  ;

class_head :
  class_key
  | *class_key base_spec*
  | *class_key identifier base_spec*
  | *class_key identifier*
  | *class_key class_name*
  | *class_key class_name base_spec*
  ;

member_list :
  member_declaration
  | *member_declaration member_list*
  | *access_specifier* :
  | *access_specifier* : *member_list*
  ;

member_declaration :
  declaration_specifiers
  | *declaration_specifiers member_declarator_list*
  | *member_declarator_list*
  | *member_declarator_list*
  | *function_definition*

      | *function_definition* ;
      | *qualified_name*
      ;

member_declarator_list :
      member_declarator
      | *member_declarator_list* , *member_declarator*
      ;

member_declarator :
      | *declarator*
      | *declarator pure_specifier*
      | *identifier* : *constant_expression*
      | : *constant_expression*
      ;

pure_specifier :
      = 0
      ;

base_spec :
      : *base_list*
      ;

base_list :
      base_specifier
      | *base_list* , *base_specifier*
      ;

base_specifier :
      complete_class_name
      | **virtual** *complete_class_name*
      | **virtual** *access_specifier complete_class_name*
      | *access_specifier complete_class_name*
      | *access_specifier* **virtual** *complete_class_name*
      ;

access_specifier :
      private
      | **protected**
      | **public**
      ;

conversion_function_name :
      operator *conversion_type_name*
      ;

conversion_type_name :
      type_specifier_list
      | *type_specifier_list ptr_operator*
      ;

operator_function_name:
      operator *operator_name*

operator_name :
      new
      | **delete**
      | +
      | -
      | *
      | /
      | %
      | ^
      | &
      | |
      | ~
      | !
      | =
      | <
      | >
      | +=
      | -=
      | *=
      | /=
      | %=
      | ^=

```
        | &=
        | |=
        | <<
        | >>
        | >>=
        | <<=
        | ==
        | !=
        | <=
        | >=
        | &&
        | ||
        | ++
        | --
        | ,
        | ->
        | ->*
        | ()
        | []
        ;
```

template_declaration :
      template *< template_argument_list > declaration*
      ;

template_argument_list :
      template_argument
      | *template_argument_list* , *template_argument*
      ;

template_argument :
      type_argument
      | *declaration*
      ;

type_argument :
      class *identifier*
      ;

template_class_name :
    template_name < template_arg_list >
    ;

type_argument :
    template_arg
    | *template_arg_list , template_arg*
    ;

template_arg :
    expression
    | *type_name*
    ;

try_block :
    try *compound_statement handler_list*
    ;

handler_list : *handler handler_list*
    ;

handler. :
    catch { *exception_declaration* } *compound_statement*
    ;

exception_declaration :
    type_specifier_list declarator
    | *type_specifier_list abstract_declarator*
    | *type_specifier_list*
    | ...
    ;

throw_expression :
    throw *assignment_expression*
    | **throw**
    ;

exception_expression :
    throw { *type_list* }
    | **throw** {}
    ;

type_list :
>
> *type_name*
> | *type_list* , *type_name*
> ;

Identifiers

An identifier in C++ is a sequence of letters, digits, and underscores. The first character of an identifier must be either a letter or an underscore.

Operators are given below. Their precedence and associativity are given by the precedence table.

The binary operators are

```
*  /  %  +  -  >>  <<  <  >  <=  >=  ==  !=
&  ^  |  &&  ||  ?:
```

The assignment operators are

```
=  +=  -=  *=  /=  %=  >>=  <<=  &=  ^=  |=
```

Review of the C Language

A C program consists of one or more functions together with any necessary data declarations. A C program may consist of several source code files.

Each variable in C must have a type. The elementary data types in C are **int**, **float**, **double**, and **char**. There is no boolean data type in C.

C is a case-sensitive language. This means that symbols named i and I represent different variables. The custom in C is to have nearly all of the program written in lower-case letters.

C is a weakly typed language. While each variable in C must have a definite type, type checking is usually not done by the C compiler. Type changes and conversions are common and often lead to unexpected results.

Variables in C can be initialized using an assignment statement. Uninitialized variables can have garbage values. The value of a variable can be kept fixed throughout a C program if we declare it to be a constant at the time of its initial definition.

Output in C can be done using the **printf()** function. Each value to be printed must have a control specification. Possible specifications include **int (%d)**, **char (%c)**, **float (%f)**, **double (%f** or **%e)**, **octal (%o)**, **hexadecimal (%x)**, and **string (%s)**. Field size can be controlled by including a field specification such as

```
printf("%5.2f",x)
```

with **printf()**. Characters can also be printed using the **putchar()** function so as to run faster. The function **putchar()** can be used for character output only,

Figure A3.1 The C compilation process.

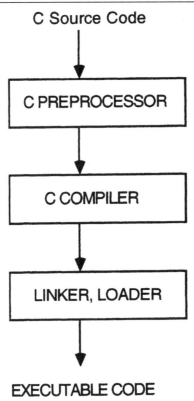

while **printf()** is much more versatile in the sense that it can be used to print any type of expression. A useful function for printing a string of characters is **puts()**.

Input in C is similar to output. We can use **scanf()** for formatted input using control specifications. Character data can be read either using **scanf()** with the **%c** control specification or by using the function **getchar()**. The function **scanf()** uses the address of variables by means of the **&** symbol.

Comments in C programs can be enclosed within the delimiters **/*** and ***/**. They may be placed anywhere in a program.

A variable of type **int** may be given as an enumerated type if its set of allowable values is a fixed set of values, each of which is a constant value of type **int**.

C has several facilities for iteration and for branching of programs. All of these statements are controlled by evaluation of one or more expressions.

Iteration can be done using the **for-loop**, the **while-loop**, or the **do-while-loop**. Each of these is convenient for certain applications. Any type of expression can be used to control the number of iterations of a loop. A **for-loop** is most commonly used when the number of iterations of the loop is essentially controlled by a numeric variable. The primary difference between a **while-loop** and a **do-while-loop** is that the testing of the controlling expression is done at the start of a **while-loop** (before execution of the statements in the body of the loop) and at the end of a **do-while-loop** (after execution of the statements in the body of the loop). The syntax of the loop is quite simple:

```
for (expression1 ; expression2 ; expression3)
    zero_or_more_statements_to_be_repeated
```

In the simplest case, the loop is controlled by a single variable. **Expression1** represents an initial value of this variable while **expression2** represents a condition for termination of the loop based on the final value of the variable. **Expression3** represents the method of having the loop control variable move from initial condition to final condition by incrementing or decrementing. These expressions often use the operators

```
<=
<
>=
>
```

with the obvious meanings. Other operators used are the

```
==
```

operator, which is used to test for equality of two expressions, and the similar operator

```
!=
```

which is used to test for inequality of two expressions. The logical negation operator ! is used according to the syntax

```
!expression
```

and tests if the value of the expression is zero.

The **while-loop** in C has the following syntax:

```
while (expression1)
    zero_or_more_statements_to_be_repeated
```

The last loop structure in C is the **do-while-loop**. This mechanism is like the **while-loop** in that it is appropriate when the number of iterations is not known in advance. The syntax is

```
do
    one_or_more_statements_to_be_repeated
while (expression1);
```

The expressions controlling any kind of loop can be arithmetic expressions such as $3 * x + 1$ or logical ones such as $x < 7$. Logical operators that can be used are <, <=, >, >= , ==, !=, and !. Expressions can be combined using the logical operators **&&** (logical AND), || (logical OR), or ! (logical NEGATION).

Iterations can be nested. We can have **for-loops** that are inside of **for-loops** that are inside of **while-loops**, and so on.

All loops should have the body of their code indented. A **do-while-loop** should be further marked by using blank lines to set off the loop from the surrounding code.

An important use of loops is to process a stream of information. The **while-loop** is especially useful for reading from an input stream. The function **scanf()** can be used to read formatted data and **getchar()** can be used to read in data without requiring any assumption about the format. The file **stdio.h** should be included in order to access the system constant EOF, which is used to indicate the end of the input stream.

Here are the steps:

1. Use the function **getchar()** to read in the input one symbol at a time.
2. The value returned by **getchar()** is to be of type **int** to agree with the range of values used for storage of the character set.
3. The test for EOF is made before we print anything so that there will be no output if there is no input.
4. Parentheses are used to force the assignment of the value returned by **getchar()** to the variable **c** before comparing the value to EOF. They were necessary because of the precedence rules of C, which in the absence of parentheses determine which of the operations **=** or **!=** is performed first.

C uses the == symbol to denote comparison; it is important to distinguish its use from that of the = symbol, which is used to indicate an assignment.

Branching can be done using the **if**, **if-else**, or **switch** statements. The **if** and **if-else** statements are used for determining which of two branches can be followed in the control of a program. The simple **if** statement has the form

```
if (expression1)
    zero_or_more_statements
```

C also has the **if-else** statement. The syntax is

```
if (expression1)
  zero_or_more_statements
else
  zero_or_more_statements
```

An example of an **if-else** statement is

```
if (i == 5)
  printf("The value of i is 5");
```

```
else
    printf("The value of i is not equal to 5");
```

The **switch** statement is used when there are many possible branches in a program's control flow. It can use numerical constants as the choices; the constants can also be given using an enumerated type. The only requirement for the choices in a **switch** statement is that they must be integer constants. The most common syntax of the **switch** statement is

```
switch (expression1)
    {
    case constant_integer_1: zero_or_more_statements_1
    case constant_integer_2: zero_or_more_statements_2
        .
        .

    case constant_integer_n: zero_or_more_statements_n
    default: zero_or_more_statements_default
    }
more_statements;
```

Many combinations of conditional and branching statements can be made within a program. **Switch** statements can be combined with **if** and **if-else** statements in any order. They can be combined with any reasonable number of loop control statements.

There are many facilities for the processing of character data such as **isspace()**, **isalpha()**, and **isalphanum()**. These can all be found in the file **ctype.h**, which can be included in C programs using the C preprocessor.

A fundamental concept is that of an expression. All of the usual arithmetic operators that can be applied to expressions in other programming languages are available in C.

Some of the special operators available in the C language but not generally available in other languages are the incrementation operator **++** and the decrementation operator **--**. C also allows several compound operators such as **+=**, **-=**, ***=**, **/=**, and **%=**. All of these operators can be applied to expressions of type **int**, and the results will be of type **int**. Addition, subtraction, multiplication, and division can be applied to **float** or **double** types and the results will be of type **double**. Mixed-mode arithmetic is possible in C, and the results will always be of type **double**.

C allows a large number of operations to be performed on expressions. Precedence and associativity of operations are critical to a good understanding of how these operations are performed in C. An extensive precedence table is used to determine the order in which operations are performed. Default precedence can be overridden by the use of parentheses.

Expressions in C can have lvalues, which may have values assigned to them, and rvalues, which may not have values assigned to them. Expressions declared as constants cannot have their values changed and therefore are rvalues only. In general, expressions can be used in placed of variables with the same value in any situation in which the expression is used as an rvalue.

Functions are a major tool in building modular programs. C functions can access global variables and cannot be nested.

Unlike several other languages, C does not distinguish between program units that return a value and those that do not. The only difference in C between these cases is the return value. Functions can return values of specified types. Functions that do not return a value can be given the void default type.

Functions in C can have arguments, and they treat these arguments as passing information by value that is, the value of a parameter cannot be changed by the called function. The terms "argument" and "parameter" are used interchangeably.

There are five qualifiers that can be attached to C variables to describe their storage classes: automatic, static, external, register, and **void**.

Automatic variables have their scope within functions and their values disappear after exiting the function. They are not automatically initialized and may contain garbage values unless the programmer takes specific action.

Static variables retain their values on successive entries into a function. They are automatically initialized to 0.

External variables are used to connect variables to functions without being restricted to the scope of the function.

Register variables are used when speed is of the utmost importance this qualifier may be ignored by a C compiler when it generates code.

The **void** storage class means that no memory is set aside for storage of the expression.

Several rules describe the visibility or scope of a variable that is used in a C program that consists of a single source code file:

1. If the variable is defined inside a function, then its scope is that function.
2. If the variable is defined outside every function, then it will be available to any function defined from that point to the end of the file.
3. If the variable is defined outside every function, then it can be made available to any function in the file by declaring the variable to be extern in the function that wishes to use it.
4. The C language does not permit a function to be defined inside another function.

Functions in C may be recursive—they may call themselves.

Library functions must be linked to C programs in two steps: include all appropriate header files to tell the compiler about the number and type of arguments and the type of the return value; and link the appropriate library.

Function prototypes in ANSI standard C provide the compiler with additional information about the return type of the function and the type of each of the parameters. This can help to avoid type errors at run time and will produce more portable code.

The C language has very strong support for the array data structure, which allows elements of the same type to be combined into a larger structure. Arrays in C may comprise elements of any data type.

Array elements may be accessed by using the name of the array (and thus its starting location in memory) and the index of the element. In C, array indices start from 0. Arrays in C may be initialized as an aggregate or by using assignment statements for the entries of the array. All arrays, whether static, external, or automatic, may be initialized.

Character arrays in C may be treated in two ways. One method is to consider only arrays of the same size and to pad any shorter representation by padding with blanks. Another method is to terminate the character string by a special null byte that contains the escape sequence **\0**. Using this special byte terminates the array.

C has no facilities for directly implementing twodimensional arrays, and thus they must be implemented using indirect methods. The typical technique is to use definitions of the form

```
float arr[NUM_ROWS][NUM_COLUMNS];
```

for two-dimensional arrays with a fixed number of elements and

```
float arr[][NUM_COLUMNS];
```

for two-dimensional arrays with a variable number of elements. The number of elements in the second index range must always be specified.

Elements of a two-dimensional array must be accessed by the [row][column] notation rather than by the [row,column] notation. The [row,column] notation uses the "comma operator," which returns a single number and not a pair of indices. The comma operator is to be avoided in C programs because of its unreadability.

Higher-dimensional arrays may also be simulated in C. All of the array dimensions, with the exception of the first, must be specified when the array is declared.

C allows, and in fact encourages, the separation of programs into multiple source code files. The files may be compiled separately and linked later. This is a major feature of the C language and is one of the advanced ways in which C supports good software engineering practice by encouraging modularity at a higher level than just functions.

There are several software development tools available for management of separately compiled files. Among the more popular are the UNIX **make** utility and Turbo C's project facility. The syntax and semantics of these tools vary from system to system.

The scope rules for multiple files are an extension of the scope rules for single files, with the additional feature that external static expressions have their scope limited to the file in which they are defined and cannot be accessed, even if there is an extern declaration in another file.

Pointers are addresses of data in computer memory. They can be used to access objects and to allow the operating system to allocate memory dynamically.

There are two basic operations that can be performed on pointers: the contents operator ***** and the address operator **&**.

Pointers are used extensively with arrays. There are two notations that can be used interchangeably to access the elements of an array:

```
arr[i]
```

and

```
* (arr + i)
```

Pointers can be used with space allocation functions such as **malloc()** and **calloc()**. In order to allocate space using **malloc()** or **calloc()**, we must know the size of the object and its type so that we know how large the object is and how much space must be reserved.

We need to use a cast operator such as in

```
float_ptr = (float *) malloc(sizeof(float) );
```

Pointers are appropriate for the treatment of character strings. A character string is passed as a command-line argument using the construction

```
main(int argc,char *argv[] )
```

in which the interface to the command interpreter of the operating system automatically places a termination byte **\0** at the end of each string in a command-line argument. In order to use functions such as **atoi()**, **strlen()**, **strcmp()**, and others, we must be sure to pass the arguments as character pointers and to have the string terminated by a termination byte **\0**.

Pointers are the only way to simulate passing parameters by reference in C.

The fundamental C language construction for combining data that can be of the same or different types is the struct. Combining data into a struct means that memory can be allocated for its storage and for access to the component parts. Structs can be used to store any combination of data.

Like all other variables in C, any variable that is a struct must be declared as having a type. The syntax of the declaration of a struct type is

```
struct struct_type {
    part1_type part1;
    part2_type part2;
    part3_type part3;
    };
```

A variable of this type can be declared as

```
struct struct_type s;
```

or in conjunction with the type declaration as in

```
struct struct_type {
      part1_type part1;
      part2_type part2;
      part3_type part3;
      } s;
```

The most common use of structs is in combination with pointers that are used for access to a struct variable. The common form is that a pointer to a struct is used as an indirect access to the parts of the struct. If **ptr** is a pointer to a struct with three parts named **part1**, **part2**, and **part3**, then the parts can be accessed by constructions such as

```
(*ptr).part1 = x;
```

or

```
y = (*ptr).part2 + (*ptr).part3;
```

An alternative notation for access to the parts of the struct is

```
ptr->part1 = x;
```

and

```
y = ptr->part2 + ptr->part2;
```

The most important C library function to be used with structs is **malloc()**, which allocates memory of the correct size for the storage of a struct. Since the storage allocator function **malloc()** returns only "pointers to **void**," the cast operation is used to coerce the return type to the desired form.

The call to **malloc()** reserves space in memory for the variable and indicates the appropriate use by the cast operation. Initialization of the space is the responsibility of the programmer. A related function, **calloc()**, can be used to allocate memory for an array of structs; this function will perform initialization of the space to 0.

The portions of a struct; can be of any fixed form, including pointer types. The use of pointers to variables of the same type allows the incorporation of recursive data structures such as trees.

A **typedef** statement can be used together with structured data types to provide the C language version of abstract data types.

Variable-sized portions of data can be incorporated into a common structure by using the C construction called a union. A union permits different portions to have different types at run time depending on the nature of their usage.

An important notion in C is that of a file pointer. In order to use file pointers to access a file, a program has to have a pointer declared as pointing to a variable of the predefined type **FILE**. Files are opened with the function **fopen()** and closed with the function **fclose()**. Files can be opened with permissions to read, write (at the beginning), or to append (to the end of the file). Once a file pointer points to a file and the file is opened, we can read the contents as characters by using the function **getc()**.

The function **getchar()** is a special case of **getc()** and is used when the input data comes from standard input (**stdin**). In a similar manner, **scanf()** is a special case of **fscanf()** in that **scanf()** reads its input from **stdin** and **fscanf()** reads its input from the given file.

The UNIX operating system allows an additional type of file access, based on the notion of a file descriptor. A file descriptor is a number used to denote which entry in the file table of a UNIX process is intended. File descriptors 0, 1, and 2 are reserved for **stdin**, **stdout** (the user's terminal), and **stderr** (usually errors are also displayed on the user's terminal), respectively. A file is created by using the **creat()** UNIX system call. Files can be opened using the UNIX system calls **open()** and **close()**.

UNIX file access also allows a lower-level means of reading bytes of data using the **read()** and **write()** system calls. The UNIX file access commands are more powerful than the general C file access commands, since they allow the programmer to have some control over the access permissions on the files being accessed. UNIX systems allow both the general file access commands and the special UNIX system calls.

C permits operations on individual bits. Bit operations can be used to control the behavior of several different aspects of the contents of memory locations. Typical applications of bit operations include setting or releasing a bit that represents a pixel in a graphics display, reading the contents of a memory location that represents the status of some system function and interpreting the values of particular bits in this memory location, and speeding up access to lists that can be represented as bits in a computer memory location.

Some of the operations that can be performed on bits and the notations used for these operations are

OR	|
AND	&
EXCLUSIVE OR	^
NOT	~
LEFT SHIFT	<<
RIGHT SHIFT	>>

These can generally be used on **int** and **char** expressions.

The bitwise AND and OR operations | and & are different from the logical AND and OR operations || and &&; this can cause serious problems if the two operations are confused.

The ANSI Standard C Library

4

The term ANSI C refers to the definitions given by the ANSI (American National Standards Institute) in their 1989 standard X3.159-D1989. This is essentially the same as ISO (International Standards Organization) standard 9899:1990. For more information, refer to the standard directly or to the book by Plauger listed in the references.

A4.1 Organization

There are many different header files that are necessary in order to access functions provided in the standard C library. These header files are:

errno.h	Error reporting
stddef.h	Common definitions
assert.h	Debugging diagnostics
ctype.h	Character handling
locale.h	Non-US standards (not discussed in this book)
math.h	For mathematics
setjmp.h	Nonlocal goto's in programs (not discussed here)

`signal.h`	Signal detection and handling
`stdarg.h`	Variable number of arguments
`stdio.h`	I/O
`stdlib.h`	Standard library utilities
`string.h`	String handling
`time.h`	Date and time
`limits.h`	Implementation-dependent minimum limits
`float.h`	Implementation-dependent minimum limits

A4.2   Commonly Used Functions

- `void abort(void)`   `stdlib.h`
  Usage: `abort()`

- `int abs(int)`   `stdlib.h`
     `abs()` is the absolute value function for integers.
  Usage: `int_result = abs(int_argument)`

- `double acos(double)`   `math.h`
     `acos()` is the inverse cosine function
  Usage: `double_result = acos(double_argument)`

- `double asin(double)`   `math.h`
     `asin()` is the inverse sine function
  Usage: `double_result = asin(double_argument)`

- `void assert(int expression)`   `assert.h`
     `assert()` macro—places "assertions" about expressions into programs. If the
  value of expression is FALSE (0) when the assert statement is reached, then the
  assert macro will print an error message about the line and the file where the asser-
  tion was FALSE, after which the program will terminate. Checking for assertions
  can be turned off in each source code file where the statement

     `#include <assert.h>`

  occurs, by placing the preprocessor directive

     `#define NDEBUG`

  at the start of the file. It can also be turned off by selecting certain compiler
  options in many cases.
  Usage: `assert(divisor);`

- **double atan(double)**   **math.h**

  atan() is the inverse tangent function

  Usage: **double_result = atan(double_argument)**

- **double atan2(double)**   **math.h**

  atan2() is also an inverse tangent function

  Usage: **double_result = atan2(double_argument)**

- **int atexit(void (*func)(void));**   **std library**

  atexit() function—calls a function when program terminates normally.

  Usage: See your manual.

- **float atof(char *)**   **std library**

  atof() function—changes ASCII string to float

  Usage: **float_result = atof(char_string)**

- **int atoi(char *)**   **std library**

  atoi() function—changes ASCII string to int

  Usage: **int_result = atof(char_string)**

- **long int atol(char *)**   **std library**

  atol() function—changes ASCII string to long int.

  Usage: **long_int_result = atof(char_string)**

- **void *bsearch(const void *key, const void *base, size_t num_elts, size_t elt_size, int (*compare(const void *, const void *)); <stdlib.h>**

  bsearch() function—searches an array of elements pointed to by the second argument, for the key, which is the first argument. It uses a user-defined function to compare two elements in the array. The result returned is a pointer to the first match in the array, or a null pointer if no match is found.

  Usage: **ptr = bsearch(key, arr, nul_elts, elt_size, compare);**

- **void * calloc(int, int)**   **std library**

  Note. Many UNIX implementations have two versions of this function. One is in the standard library and the other is in the **malloc** library. To use the **malloc** library, include the file **malloc.h** and compile with the **-lmalloc** option.

  calloc() returns a pointer to a region containing precisely enough memory to hold an array. The first argument to **calloc()** represents the number of elements in the array and the second argument represents the size of an element in the array. The pointer is to **char** in Kernighan and Ritchie C and the pointer is to **void** in ANSI C. The two **int** parameters should always be positive.

  Usage: **pointer = (pointer_type *)**
                                calloc(number_of_elements, element_size)

- **double ceil(double)**   **math.h**

    ceil() is the ceiling function—returns a double-precision number that is on the next integer boundary greater than or equal to the argument.

    Usage: **double_result = ceil(double_argument)**

- **double cos(double)**   **math.h**

    cos() is the cosine function.

    Usage: **double_result = cos(double_argument)**

- **double cosh(double)**   **math.h**

    cosh() is the hyperbolic cosine function.

    Usage: **double_result = cosh(double_argument)**

- **int exit(int)**   **std library**

    exit() is the exit function—terminates execution of the program and provides the status of the program, which is stored in the argument, to the environment. An argument of 0 indicates successful execution; any other argument is used to indicate an error.

    Usage: **exit(int_status)**

- **double exp(double)**   **math.h**

    exp() is the exponential function.

    Usage: **double_result = exp(double_argument)**

- **double fabs(double)**   **math.h**

    fabs() is the floating point absolute value function.

    Usage: **double_result = fabs(double_argument)**

- **int fclose(FILE *)**   **stdio.h**

    fclose() file function—closes the input file given in the argument, returns value of –1 for error

    Usage: **fclose(file_stream)**

- **int feof(FILE *)**   **stdio.h**

    feof() function—returns 0 unless the END_OF_FILE character has been read from the input stream pointed to by the file pointer; in this case it returns a nonzero value. This is used to detect reading after the END_OF_FILE.

    Usage: **if (file_error = feof(file_stream))**
             exit(file_error);

- **char * fflush(int)**   **stdio.h**

    fflush() is the flush buffer function—empties output buffers if we wish to force their output. Useful in C++ programs when using **printf** and **cout** in the same program.

    Usage: **fflush(file_stream);**

- **int fgetc(int)**   **stdio.h**

  fgetc() function—gets character from an input stream. Identical to **getc()** in use. Somewhat slower than **getc()** because **getc()** is usually implemented as a macro.
  Usage: **ch = fgetc(file_ptr);**

- **int fgetpos(FILE *stream, fpos_t *pos)**   **stdio.h**

  fgetpos() function—returns current position of file pointer into the second argument.
  Usage: **fgetpos(fp, pos);**

- **(char *) fgets(char *, int,FILE *)**   **stdio.h**

  fgets() function—gets the number of characters specified in the second argument from the input stream specified in the third argument and places them in order in the array of consecutive memory locations starting from position 0 in the array specified by the address of the first argument. The number of bytes read will be less than the second argument if EOF is encountered or an error occurs. A new line in the input is read into the array; this is different from the treatment of **gets()**.
  Usage: **str_ptr = fgets(start_addr, num_char, fp)**

- **double floor(double)**   **math.h**

  floor() is the floor function—returns a double-precision number that is on the next integer boundary smaller than the argument.
  Usage: **double_result = floor(double_argument)**

- **double fmod(double)**   **math.h**

  Floating point mod function—returns the remainder after division of the first argument by the second, or returns 0 if division by 0
  Usage: **double_result = fmod(double_arg1, double_arg2)**

- **FILE *fopen(char *, char *)**   **stdio.h**

  fopen() is the open file function—opens the file stream given in the first argument. The second argument is one of the following: **"r"**, **"w"**, **"a"**, **"r+"**, **"w+"**, or **a+**.
  Usage: **file_ptr = fopen(file_name, mode)**

- **int fprintf(int, char *, var_args)**   **stdio.h**

  fprintf() function—prints to the file stream specified in the first argument as output. The output is formatted according to the control specifications in the second argument. The variables that get their values printed are in the remaining arguments. The usage

  fprintf(stdout, control_char_string, other_args)

is equivalent to the usage

```
printf(control_char_string, other_args)
```

See also the functions **printf()** and **scanf()**.

Note: The order of control specifications and arguments to be printed can be changed and any number can be mixed in any order.

Usage: **fprintf(file_ptr, control_char_string, other args);**

- **int fputc(char, FILE *)** stdio.h

  fputc() function—writes its first argument to the output stream specified by the second argument, which is a pointer to a FILE. The return value is the **int** equivalent of the first argument. See also the function **putc()**, which has the equivalent action.

  Usage: **int_val = fputc(ch, file_ptr);**

- **int fputs(char *, FILE *)** stdio.h

  fputs() function—takes the first argument, which is a character string, and places it on the output stream specified in the second argument. The first argument must be terminated by a null byte; this null byte is not written to the output stream. See also **puts()**.

  Usage: **int_val = fputs(char_ptr, file_ptr);**

- **size_t fread(void *ptr, size_t size, size_t num_elts, FILE *stream);** stdio.h

  fread() function—reads up to **num_elts** of the size given in the second argument from the file stream pointed by the last argument. The data is read into the array pointed to by the first argument. Note that the first argument need not be an array of characters. The number of elements read will be less than the third argument if an error occurs or if end of file is encountered.

  Usage: **data_read = fread(ptr, size, num_elts, fp);**

- **void free(void *)** std library

  free() function—releases a memory region previously allocated by a call to **malloc()** or **calloc()**.

  Usage: **free(void_ptr);**

- **double frexp(double, int *)** math.h

  frexp() is an exponential function—breaks the first argument into a double-precision number (used as the return value) and a power of 2 stored in the address of the second argument. The return value is either 0, or else is in the interval [1/2, 1].

  Usage: **double_result = exp(double_argument, int_ptr)**

- **int fscanf(FILE *, char*, var_args)** **stdio.h**

  fscanf() function—reads from the input stream specified in the first argument according to the control specifications in the second argument. The variables that get assigned values are in the remaining arguments.

  Usage: **fscanf(file_ptr, control_string, other args);**

- **int fseek(FILE*, long int. int)** **stdio.h**

  fseek() function—allows random access to a file pointed to by the first argument. The second argument is used as the file offset from the current position, which is specified in the third argument.

  Usage: **fseek(file_ptr, file_offset, current_position);**

- **int fsetpos(FILE *stream, fpos_t *pos)** **stdio.h**

  fsetpos() function—sets current position of file pointer by the second argument.

- **long int ftell(FILE *stream)** **stdio.h**

  ftell() function—returns current position of file pointer. Generally followed by a call to **fseek().**

- **size_t fwrite(void *ptr, size_t size, size_t num_elts, FILE *stream);** **stdio.h**

  fwrite() function—writes up to **num_elts** of the size given in the second argument to the file stream pointed by the last argument. The data is read from the array pointed to by the first argument. Note that the first argument need not be an array of characters. The number of elements read will be less than the third argument if an error occurs or if end of file is encountered.

  Usage: **data_written = fwrite(ptr, size, num_elts, fp);**

- **int getc(char*)** **stdio.h**

  getc() function—gets character from an input stream. This is usually implemented as a macro.

  Usage: **ch = getc(file_ptr);**

- **int getchar(void)** **stdio.h**

  getchar()—gets a character from standard input. This is the equivalent of **getc(stdin);** This is usually implemented as a macro.

  Usage: **ch = getchar();**

- **char * getenv(char * name)** **stdlib.h**

  getenv() function—returns a pointer to a list of environment variables and their values, specified by the argument (assuming that a match occurs). Differs from the UNIX **getenv()** function slightly.

  Usage: **getenv(name);**

- `int gets(char *)`   `stdio.h`

  `gets()` function—reads an input string from standard input and places it in consecutive locations beginning in the one pointed to by the argument. Input is read until EOF or a newline character is read. The newline character is *not* placed into the array pointed to by the second argument. This treatment of the newline character is different from that of `fgets()`.
  Usage: `gets(char_ptr);`

- `int isalnum(char)`   `ctype.h`

  `isalnum` function—returns a nonzero value if the character is in one of the ranges A–Z , a–z, or 0–9; returns 0 otherwise—needs the include file `ctype.h`.
  Usage: `if (isalnum(char_arg) ) ...`

- `int isalpha(char)`   `ctype.h`

  `isalpha` function—returns a nonzero value if the character is in the range A–Z or a–z; returns 0 otherwise—needs the include file `ctype.h`.
  Usage: `if (isalpha(char_arg) )...`

- `int iscntrl(char)`   `ctype.h`

  `iscntrl` function—returns a nonzero value if the character is a control character; returns 0 otherwise—needs the include file `ctype.h`.
  Usage: `if (iscntrl(char_arg) )...`

- `int isdigit(char)`   `ctype.h`

  `isdigit` function—returns a nonzero value if the character is in the range 0–9; returns 0 otherwise—needs the include file `ctype.h`.
  Usage: `if (isdigit(char_arg) )...`

- `int isgraph(char)`   `ctype.h`

  `isgraph()` function—returns a nonzero value if the character is is any printing character except ' '; returns 0 otherwise—needs the include file `ctype.h`.
  Usage: `if (isgraph(char_arg) )...`

- `int islower(char)`   `ctype.h`

  `islower()` function—returns a nonzero value if the character is in the range a–z; returns 0 otherwise—needs the include file `ctype.h`.
  Usage: `if (islower(char_arg) )...`

- `int isprint(char)`   `ctype.h`

  `isprint()` function—returns a nonzero value if the character is a printing character (including ' '); returns 0 otherwise—needs the include file `ctype.h`.
  Usage: `if (isprint(char_arg) )...`

- **int ispunct(char)**   **ctype.h**

  ispunct() function—returns a nonzero value if the character is in the range A–Z or a–z; returns 0 otherwise—needs the include file **ctype.h**.
  Usage: **if (ispunct(char_arg))...**

- **int isspace(char)**   **ctype.h**

  isspace() function:—returns a nonzero value if the argument is one of the following: blank, space, carriage return, form feed, vertical tab, newline; returns 0 otherwise—needs the include file **ctype.h**.
  Usage: **if (isspace(char_arg))...**

- **int isupper(char)**   **ctype.h**

  isupper() function—returns a nonzero value if the character is in the range A–Z; returns 0 otherwise—needs the include file **ctype.h**.
  Usage: **if (isupper(char_arg))...**

- **int isxdigit(char)**   **ctype.h**

  isxdigit() function—returns a nonzero value if the character is a legal hexadecimal character; returns 0 otherwise—needs the include file **ctype.h**.
  Usage: **if (isxdigit(char_arg))...**

- **char* itoa(int)**   **nonstandard**

  itoa() function—changes **int** to ASCII string—not always found in C libraries—see **sprintf()**.
  Usage: **string_val = itoa(int);**

- **double ldexp(double, int)**   **math.h**

  ldexp() is a multiplication function, exponential form—multiplies the first argument by the power of 2 given in the second argument and returns the result.
  Usage: **double_result = exp(double_argument, int)**

- **long int labs(long int)**   **stdlib.h**

  abs() is the absolute value function for integers.
  Usage: **long_int_result = labs(long_int_argument)**

- **double log(double)**   **math.h**

  log() is the natural logarithm function.
  Usage: **double_result = log(double_argument)**

- **double log10(double)**   **math.h**

  log10() is the logarithm to base 10 function
  Usage: **double_result = log10(double_argument)**

• **void * malloc(unsigned int)**   **std library**

   Note: Many UNIX implementations have two versions of this function. One is in the standard library and the other is in the **malloc** library. To use the **malloc** library, include the file **malloc.h** and compile with the **-lmalloc** option.

   malloc() returns a pointer to a region of size number of bytes; pointer is to **char** in Kernighan and Ritchie C and pointer is to **void** in ANSI C. The **int** parameter should always be positive.

   Usage: **pointer = (type *) malloc(size)**

• **int mblen(const char *, size_t)**   **stdlib.h**

   mblen() is used to determine the number of bytes used with a wide (multibyte) character that is pointed to by the first argument. The second argument places a limit on the number of bytes checked. There are several related functions for treating wide characters: **mbtowc()**, **wctomb()**, **mbstowc()**, and **wcstombs()**.

   Usage: **len = mblen(wide_ptr, 2); /* for 2-byte characters */**

• **void *memchr(const void*str, int c, size_t n)**   **string.h**

   Function **memchr()**—examines the first *n* characters of the object given in the first argument for the presence of the second argument (promoted to **unsigned char** for the comparison). Returns a pointer to the character if the character is present, null if the character is not found. See also **strchr()**.

   Usage: **loc = memchr(str1, c, n);**

• **int memcmp(const void*, const void *, size_t n)**   **string.h**

   Function **memcmp()**—compares the first *n* characters of the two objects given in the first and second arguments. (The objects need not be "strings.") Returns a positive integer if first is "greater" than second, negative if "less," 0 if equal.

   Usage: **val = memcmp(str1, str1);**

• **void *memcpy(void *, const void*, unsigned int)**   **string.h**

   function **memcpy()**—behaves much like the function **strcpy()**—copies from the memory location pointed to by the second argument to the location pointed to by the first argument; the number of characters copied is given by the third argument. The value returned is a pointer equal to the first argument.

   Usage: **source_ptr = memcpy(dest_ptr, source_ptr, num_bytes);**

- **void *memmove(void *, const void*, unsigned int)**   **string.h**

  Function **memmove()**—behaves much like the functions **memcpy()** and **strcpy()**—copies from the memory location pointed to by the second argument to the location pointed to by the first argument; the number of characters copied is given by the third argument. This function is somewhat slower than **memcpy()**. The value returned is a pointer equal to the first argument.
  Usage: **source_ptr = memmove(dest_ptr,source_ptr, num_bytes);**

- **void * memset(void *s, int c, size_t n);**   **string.h**

  memset() function—copies the value of the second argument (promoted to an **unsigned char**) to the first n characters of the object pointed to by the first argument.
  Usage: **memset(s,c,n);**

- **double modf(double, double *)**   **math.h**

  Function **modf()**—breaks the first argument into a fractional part used as a return value and an integer part stored in the address pointed to by the second argument.
  Usage: **val = modf(arg1, *int_ptr);**

- **double pow(double,double)**   **math.h**

  pow()—raises the first argument to the second argument. An error occurs if the value of **x** is negative and **y** is not an integer.
  Usage: **double_result = pow(double_arg1, double_arg2)**

- **int printf(char *, var_args)**   **stdio.h**

  printf() function—prints to standard output according to the control specifications in the first argument. The variables that get their values printed are in the remaining arguments. See also the function **scanf()**.
  Usage: **printf(control_char_string, other args);**

- **int putc(char, FILE *)**   **stdio.h**

  putc() function—places the character argument on the output file pointed to by the file pointer specified in the second argument, which is a pointer to a FILE. The return value is the int equivalent of the first argument. See also **fputc()**, which has equivalent action.
  Usage: **int_val = putc(ch, file_ptr);**

- **int putchar(char)**   **stdio.h**

  putchar() function—writes its argument to the output stream **stdout**. The return value is the **int** equivalent of the argument.
  Usage: **int_val = putchar(ch);**

- **int puts(char *)**   **stdio.h**

    puts() function—takes its argument, which is a character string, and places it on the output stream **stdout**. The first argument must be terminated by a null byte; this null byte is not written to the output stream.

    There is one difference between **puts()** and **fputs()**. The function **puts()** always places a newline character at the end of the character stream, while **fputs()** does not. See also **fputs()**.

    Usage: **int_val = puts(char_ptr);**

- **void qsort(const void *base, size_t num_elts, size_t elt_size, int (*compare(const void *, const void *));**   **stdlib.h**

    qsort() function—sorts an array of elements pointed to by the first argument. It uses a user-defined function to compare two elements in the array. The result returned is a pointer to the first match in the array, or a null pointer if no match is found.

    Usage: **ptr = qsort(arr, nul_elts, elt_size, compare);**

- **int raise(int)**   **signal.h**

    raise() function—sends a signal to the program.

    Usage: **raise (signal);**

- **int rand(void);**   **stdlib.h**

    rand() function—returns a "pseudorandom" integer in the range **0..RAND_MAX**. See also **srand()**.

    Usage: **r_int = rand(void);**

- **void *realloc(void *p, unsigned int size)**   **stdlib.h**

    realloc() function—changes the size of the region pointed to be the first argument into one whose size is specified in the second argument.

    Usage: **p = realloc(p, size)**

- **void rewind(FILE *)**   **stdio.h**

    rewind() function—resets the file pointer to the beginning of the file.

    Usage: **rewind(fp);**

- **int scanf(char *, var_args)**   **stdio .h**

    scanf() function—reads from standard input according to the control specifications in the first argument. The variables that get assigned values are in the remaining arguments.

    Usage: **scanf(control_char_string, other args);**

- **void setbuf(FILE *stream,char *buf);**   **stdio.h**

    setbuf() is equivalent to **setvbuf()** with the values **_IOFBF** and **BUF-SIZ** for full buffering and with the values **_IONBF** if **buf** is a NULL pointer.

- **int setvbuf(FILE *stream,char *buf, int mode, size_t size);** `<stdio.h>`

  setvbuf() function—sets I/O buffering, depending on the value of mode. _IOFBF means buffering, _IOLBF means buffering of each line, and _IONBF means no buffering.

  Usage: **setvbuf(fp, buffer, _IOLBF, 80); /* 80 char line */**

- **void (*signal(int, void(*func)(int))) (int);** signal.h

  signal() function—see text for more information. The action can be to ignore the signal, take a default action, or call a signal handling function. See also any advanced UNIX book.

  Usage: **signal(signal_number, action);**

- **double sin(double)** math.h

  sin() is the sine function.

  Usage: **double_result = sin(double_argument)**

- **double sinh(double)** math.h

  sinh() is the hyperbolic sine function.

  Usage: **double_result = sinh(double_argument)**

- **int sprintf(char *, char *, var_args)** stdio.h

  sprintf() function—prints its output to the string specified in the first argument according to the control specifications in the second argument. The variables that get their values printed are in the remaining arguments. See also the functions **printf()** and **scanf()**.

  Usage: **sprintf(result_str, control_str, other_args);**

- **double sqrt(double)** math.h

  sqrt() is the double precision square root function—error if argument is negative

  Usage: **double_result = sqrt(double_argument).**

- **int srand(unsigned int seed);** stdlib.h

  srand() function—returns a "pseudorandom" integer in the range **0 .. RAND_MAX**. See also **rand()**.

  Usage: **r_int = srand(seed);**

- **int sscanf(char *, char *, var_args)** stdio.h

  sscanf() function—reads from character string specified in the first argument according to the control specifications in the second argument. The variables that get assigned values are in the remaining arguments.

  Usage: **fscanf(file_ptr, control_string, other args);**

- **char * strcat(const char *, const char *)   string.h**
  strcat() function appends the contents of the string pointed to by the second argument onto the string pointed to by the first argument at the beginning of that string. The value of the first argument is returned. The end of string character from the string pointed to by the second argument is used to terminate the string. (The null byte character from the first string is overwritten.) See also **strncat()**.
  Usage: **big_string = strcat(string1, string2);**

- **char *strchr(const void*str, int c, size_t n)   string.h**
  function **strchr()**—examines the first *n* characters of the character string given in the first argument for the presence of the second argument. Returns a pointer to the character if the character is present, null if the character is not found. See also **memchr()**.
  Usage: **loc = strchr(str1, c, n);**

- **int strcoll(const char *, const char *)   string.h**
  strcoll() is similar to **strcmp()** except that it uses a local "collating sequence" instead of strict ASCII values for comparison.
  Usage: **int_value = strcoll(string_ptr1, string_ptr2);**

- **int strcmp(char *, char *)   string.h**
  strcmp() function compares the contents of the string pointed to by the second argument with the string pointed to by the first argument. The function returns a negative value if the first string is lexicographically less than the second, a positive value if the first is greater than the second, and 0 if the strings are identical. Since lexicographical order is what is used in dictionaries, this function is useful for sorting alphabetic data.
  Usage: **int_value = strcmp(string_ptr1, string_ptr2);**

- **char *strcpy(char *, char *)   string.h**
  strcpy() function copies the contents of the string pointed to by the second argument into the string pointed to by the first argument at the beginning of that string. The value of the first argument is returned. (The end of string character from the string pointed to by the second argument is used to terminate the string.) See also **strncpy()**.
  Usage: **string_ptr = strcpy(string_ptr1, string_ptr2);**

- **size_t strcspn(const char *, const char *)   string.h**
  strcspn()—returns length of the longest substring of the first argument that consists entirely of characters not in the second argument. See also **strspn()**.
  Usage: **len = strcspn(str1, str2);**

- **`char * strerror(int errno);`**   **`string.h`**

  `strerror()` function—used for mapping error numbers to error message strings.

  Usage: **`strerror(errno);`**

- **`size_t strlen(char *)`**   **`string.h`**

  `strlen()` function—gives the length of the string pointed to by the argument as an **int**; all characters up to, but not including, the end of string marker are counted. The value of the return value is non-negative since the length of an empty string is 0.

  Usage: **`string_length = strlen(string_ptr);`**

- **`char * strncat(const char *, const char *,`**
  `size_t)`   **`string.h`**

  `strncat()` function appends the contents of the string pointed to by the second argument onto the string pointed to by the first argument at the beginning of that string. The value of the first argument is returned. The end of string character from the string pointed to by the second argument is used to terminate the string. (The null byte character from the first string is overwritten.) The third argument limits the number of characters appended; null characters and additional characters after a null character in the second string are ignored. See also **strcat()**.

  Usage: **`big_string = strncat(string1, string2, n);`**

- **`int strncmp(char *, char *, size_t)`**   **`string.h`**

  `strcmp()` function—compares the contents of the string pointed to by the second argument with the string pointed to by the first argument. Only the number of characters specified in the third argument are used and characters after a null character are ignored. The function returns a negative value if the first string is lexicographically less than the second, a positive value if the first is greater than the second, and 0 if the strings are identical. Since lexicographical order is what is used in dictionaries, this function is useful for sorting alphabetic data.

  Usage: **`int_value = strncmp(string_ptr1, string_ptr2, n);`**

- **`char * strncpy(char *, char *, size_t)`**   **`string.h`**

  `strncpy()` function—copies the contents of the string pointed to by the second argument into the string pointed to by the first argument at the beginning of that string. The value of the first argument is returned. (The end of string character from the string pointed to by the second argument is used to terminate the string.) The third argument places an upper limit on the number of characters to be copied. Any characters in the string pointed to by the second argument after a null character are ignored. If the length of the string pointed to by the first argument is less than the third argument, this string is padded by null characters. See also **strcpy()**.

  Usage: **`string_ptr = strncpy(strptr1, strptr2,n);`**

- **char *strpbrk(const char* s1, const char* s2)**   **string.h**

    strpbrk()—returns a pointer to the first character of **s1** of any character in the string **s2**, or null if there is no such character.
    Usage: **loc = strpbrk(str1, str2);**

- **char *strrchr(const char* s1, int c)**   **string.h**

    strrchr()—returns a pointer to the last character of **s1** of the second argument (which is promoted to **char**), or null if there is no such character.
    Usage: **loc = strrchr(str1, str2);**

- **size_t strspn(const char *, const char *)**   **string.h**

    strspn()—returns length of the longest substring of the first argument that consists entirely of characters included in the second argument. See also **strcspn()**.
    Usage: **len = strspn(str1, str2);**

- **char * strstr(const char* s1, const char *s2)**   **string.h**

    strstr() function—returns the location of the first occurrence of the sequence of characters in the second argument in the string represented by the first argument. Null characters are ignored and the function returns a null pointer if the second argument is a null pointer.
    Usage: **loc = strstr(first_str, second_str);**

- **double strtod(char *p, char **temp);**   **stdio.h**

    strtod() function—attempts to convert string pointer to by first argument into a double result. Initial white space is omitted. If an error occurs, then the attempted temporary string being converted is stored in the second argument.
    Usage: **d = strtod(s, temp);**

- **char * strtok(char * s1, char *s2)**   **string.h**

    strtok() function—parses the string in the first argument into a sequence of tokens determined by the characters in the second argument string. The first call to **strtok()** searches the string pointed to by **s1** for the first character *not* contained in the current delimiter string pointed to by **s2**. If no such character is found, then **strtok()** returns a null pointer. Otherwise, it returns the location of the first token in **s1**. Subsequent calls to **strtok()** always use the starting location of any token already found to begin their search. The starting location found at each invocation of **strtok()** uses the previously returned value of the token pointer, which is saved internally as well as being a returned value.
    Note: The second string can be changed in subsequent calls to **strtok().**
    Usage: **token_loc = strtok(char * s1, char *s2);**

- **long int strtol(char *p, char **temp, int base)**   **stdio.h**

  strtol() function—attempts to convert string pointer to by first argument into a long int result in the base specified by the third argument. Initial white space is omitted. If an error occurs, then the attempted temporary string being converted is stored in the second argument.

  Usage: **i = strtol(s, temp,base);**

- **unsigned long int strtoul(char *p, char **temp, int base)**   **stdio.h**

  strtoul() function—attempts to convert string pointer to by first argument into an unsigned long int result in the base specified by the third argument. Initial white space is omitted. If an error occurs, then the attempted temporary string being converted is stored in the second argument.

  Usage: **i = strtol(s, temp,base);**

- **size_t strxfrm(char *, const char *, size_t)**   **string.h**

  strxfrm() function—changes the string given in the second argument (up to the limit of the number of characters specified in the third argument). The transformation preserves order of strings in the sense that any comparisons of the second argument and another string, say **s0**, given by **strcoll()** will also hold between the first argument and the transformed **s0**, if we use **strcmp()** or **strncmp()** for comparison.

  Usage: **strxfrm(str1, str2, n);**

- **int system(char *string)**   **stdlib.h**

  system() function—allows a string argument to be executed by a command processor such as the user's login shell in UNIX. Processing is implementation dependent.

  Usage: **system(string);**

- **double tan(double)**   **math.h**

  tan() is the double-precision tangent function.

  Usage: **double_result = tan(double_argument)**

- **double tan(double)**   **math.h**

  tanh() is the double precision tangent hyperbolic tangent function.

  Usage: **double_result = tanh(double_argument)**

- **int tolower(int)**   **stdlib.h**

  tolower() changes uppercase characters to lower.

  Usage: **low = tolower(ch)**

- **int toupper(int)** `stdlib.h`

  toupper() changes lower case characters to upper.

  Usage: **upper = toupper(ch)**

- **int ungetc(char, char *)** `stdio.h`

  ungetc() function—places the character back on the specified input stream to be read by the next call to a "get" function such as **getc(), getchar(), fgetc(), fgetchar()**, etc.

  Usage: **int_val = ungetc(ch, file_name);**

- **void va_start(va_list, argN);** `stdarg.h`

  va_start() function—begins a list of a variable number of arguments pointed to by the first argument. The second argument is the argument before the ... indicating the variable list.

  Usage: **va_start(va_list ap, argN);**

- **arg_type va_arg(va_list);** `stdarg.h`

  va_arg() function—accesses a list of a variable number of arguments pointed to by the first argument.

  Usage: **va_arg(va_list ap, arg_type);**

- **void va_end(va_list);** `stdarg.h`

  va_end() function—ends a list of a variable number of arguments pointed to by the first argument.

  Usage: **va_end(va_list ap);**

A4.3 Some UNIX I/O C Functions

All of these functions can be found in the standard UNIX library and do not require any include files. They are considered to be system calls in UNIX since they involve access to lower-level operating system routines. Technically speaking, they are not generally part of the standard C library. Some are available on other, non-UNIX, systems.

- **int close(int)**

  close() function—the argument is a file descriptor. It is an error if the file is already closed.

  Usage: **close(fd);**

- **`int creat(char *, int)`**

  creat() function—The first argument is a character string of the file and the second argument is the permissions in octal. The value returned is a file descriptor. If the user is not the super-user and the file already exists, then **creat** returns −1.

  Usage: **`if ((fd = creat(filename, octal_permissions))`**
  `== -1)          error();`

- **`int open(char *, int)`**

  open function—the first argument is a character string of the file and the second argument is the mode. For more information on the mode, consult any book on UNIX system calls. The value returned is a file descriptor. The value of −1 is returned if there is an error such as the permissions being wrong, the file already existing, etc.

  Usage: **`if ((fd = open(filename, mode)) < 0)`**
                          `. . .`

- **`int read(int, char *, int)`**

  read() function—the first argument indicates a file descriptor to read from; the second is a buffer location for buffered reads; and the third argument is the number of bytes that the reader requests. The return value is 0 if we read end of file, −1 if an error, and a non-negative number if the read is successful. The number of bytes that are read may be less than the number requested if there are few bytes remaining; this is not an error.

  Usage: **`#define BUFFER_SIZE some_int`**
          `char buffer[BUFFER_SIZE];`
          `num_read = read(file_descriptor, buffer, bytes);`

- **`int unlink(char *)`**

  unlink() function—removes a link to a file whose name is the second argument.

  Usage: **`unlink(filename);`**

- **`int write(int, char *, int)`**

  write() function—the first argument indicates a file descriptor to write to; the second is a buffer location for buffered reads; and the third argument is the number of bytes that the writer requests. The return value is 0 if we read end of file, −1 if an error, and a non-negative number if the write is successful. The number of bytes that are written must be the number requested; if not, an error occurs.

  Usage: **`#define BUFFER_SIZE some_int`**
          `char buffer[BUFFER_SIZE];`
          `num_written = write(file_descriptor, buffer,`
          `bytes);`

A4.4   Rarely Used Functions

The functions described in this section are rarely used. We will be content with indicating their syntax and giving an example of typical usage (if the usage is not complex). The functions in this section are grouped alphabetically by header file and the header files are also grouped alphabetically.

These functions should be used only when absolutely necessary and then only in conjunction with your user manual and a complete description of the ANSI standard.

HEADER FILE <locale.h>

- `struct lconv * localconv(void);`

- `char * setlocale(int category, const char *locale)`
  `setlocale()` is used for non-ASCII-based locations, especially outside the United States.
  Usage: `setlocale(LC_MONETARY, "");` /* sets the locale for money to the default */

HEADER FILE <setjmp.h>

- `void longjmp(jmpbuf begin, int val)`
  `longjmp()` and `setjmp()` are used for exception handling in C.
  Usage: `if (error_condition)`
          `longjmp(begin, val);`
          `/* val acts as a return value for longjmp() */`

- `int setjmp(jmp_buf begin)`
  Usage: `jmpbuf begin;`
          `...`
          `setjmp(begin);`

HEADER FILE <stdio.h>

- `FILE *freopen(char *filename, char *mode, FILE *stream)`
  `freopen()` is a more complex alternative to `fopen()`.

- `int remove(char * filename);`

- `int rename(char * filename);`

- `FILE *tmpfile(void);`
    tmpfile() creates temporary files.

- `char * tmpnam(char *s);`
    tmpnam() creates temporary names for temporary files.

- `vfprintf(FILE *stream, char *format, va_list args);`
    The function **vfprintf()** is similar to **fprintf()**.

- `vprintf(char *format, va_list args);`
    The function **vprintf()** is similar to **printf()**.

- `vsprintf(char *s, char *format, va_list args);`
    The function **vsprintf()** is similar to **sprintf()**.

HEADER FILE `<time.h>`

- `clock_t clock(void);`

- `double difftime(time_t, time_t);`

- `time_t mktime(struct tm *t_ptr);`

- `time_t time(time_t *t_ptr);`

- `char *asctime(struct tm *t_ptr);`

- `char *ctime(const time_t *t_ptr);`

- `struct tm *gmtime(const time_t *t_ptr);`

- `struct tm * localtime(const time_t *t_ptr);`

- `size_t strftime(char *, size_t, const chr * const struct tm *);`

A4.5   Constants, Variables, and Types

In the header file **<errno.h>**:

```
int errno;
NDEBUG
```

In the header file **<float.h>**:

```
FLT_ROUNDS
FLT_RADIX
FLT_MANT_DIG
DBL_MANT_DIG
LDBL_MANT_DIG
FLT_MIN_EXP
DBL_MIN_EXP
LDBL_MIN_EXP
FLT_MIN_10_EXP
DBL_MIN_10_EXP
LDBL_MIN_10_EXP
FLT_MAX_EXP
DBL_MAX_EXP
LDBL_MAX_EXP
FLT_MAX_10_EXP
DBL_MAX_10_EXP
LDBL_MAX_10_EXP
FLT_MIN
DBL_MIN
LDBL_MIN
FLT_MAX
DBL_MAX
LDBL_MAX
FLT_EPSILON
DBL_EPSILON
LBDL_EPSILON
```

In the header file **<limits.h>**:

The constants in this file for any conforming ANSI implementation are greater than or equal to (in absolute value) the constants given in this list.

```
CHAR_BIT      8
SCHAR_MIN    -127
SCHAR_MAX     127
```

```
USHAR_MAX        255
CHAR_MIN         0 or SCHAR_MIN
CHAR_MAX         UCHAR_MAX or SCHAR_MAX
MB_LEN_MAX       1
SHRT_MIN         -32767
SHRT_MAX         32767
USHRT_MAX        65535
INT_MIN          -32767
INT_MAX          32767
UNIT_MAX         65535
LONG_MIN         -2147483647
LONG_MAX         2147483647
ULONG_MAX        4294967295
```

In the header file `<locale.h>`:

```
LC_ALL
LC_COLLATE
LC_CTYPE
LC_MONETARY
LC_NUMERIC
LC_TIME
CHAR_MAX

struct lconv
{
  char * decimal_point;
  char * thousands_sep;
  char * grouping;
  char * int_curr_symbol;
  char * currency_symbol;
  char * mon_decimal_point;
  char * mon_thousands_sep;
  char * mon_grouping;
  char * positive_sign;
  char * negative_sign;
  char * int_frac_digits;
  char * frac_digits;
  char p_cs_precedes;
  char p_sep_by_space;
  char n_cs_precedes;
  char n_sep_by_space;
  char p_sign_posn;
  char n_sign_posn;
};
```

In the header file **<math.h>**:

    HUGE_VAL

In the header file **<signal.h>**:

    sig_atomic_t
    SIG_DFL
    SIG_ERR
    SIG_IGN
    SIGABRT
    SIGFPE
    SIGILL
    SIGSEGV
    SIGTERM

(See also any advanced UNIX book.)

In the header file **<stddef.h>**:

    NULL
    offsetof()
    ptrdiff_t
    size_t
    wchar_t

In the header file **<stdlib.h>**:

    EXIT_FAILURE
    EXIT_SUCCESS
    MB_CURR_MAX
    NULL
    RAND_MAX
    div_t
    ldiv_t
    size_t   /* unsigned int for sizeof() operator result */
    wchar_t   /* wide character */

In the header file **<stdio.h>**:

    _IOFBF
    _IOLBF
    _IONBF
    BUFSIZ
    EOF
    FILE
    FILENAME_MAX
    FOPEN_MAX

```
fpos_t
L_tmpnam
NULL
SEEK_CUR
SEEK_END
SEEK_SET
size_t
stderr
stdin
stdout
TMP_MAX
```

In the header file <**string.h**>:

```
NULL
size_t
```

In the header file <**time.h**>:

```
CLOCK_PER_SEC
NULL
time_t
size_t
struct tm
{
    int tm_sec
    int tm_min;
    int tm_hour;
    int tm_day;
    int tm_mon;
    int tm_year;
    inttm_wday:
    int tm yday;
    int tm_isdst;
}
```

These constants and the **tm** structure are used by the functions **clock()**, **difftime()**, **mktime()**, **time()**, **asctime()**, **ctime()**, **gmtime()**, **localtime()**, and **strftime()**.

The Draft ANSI Standard C++ Library

The draft ANSI standard for the C++ language is still under discussion as this book is being written. Therefore no definitive description of the library can be given at this time. However, there has been widespread agreement on many of the features that would be required for a standardized language. A description of the contents of a standard C++ class library will probably be available by the time that this book appears.

It should be noted that it is slightly difficult to get information about a proposed language standard before it is formally released to the public for comments. This formal release usually occurs after many months, and often years, of deliberation by a small group of expert representatives from industry, government, and academia.

We will content ourselves with a summary of the principles used in defining the draft ANSI C++ standard library and a list of new header files for this library.

A5.1   Guiding Principles Relating C and C++ Libraries

C++ was intended to be downwardly compatible with ANSI C. It was considered desirable for existing ANSI C programs to be compilable using C++ compilers and to produce the same output. Thus, to a large extent, the C++ standard library will include the C standard library.

The principles used to relate the draft ANSI C++ and existing ANSI C standard libraries are listed below.

- Allow the use of C library functions in C++ programs without change, unless their use conflicts with standards for type checking and protection in C++.
- Many of the changes in the semantics of standard library functions between C and C++ involve the distinction between constant and non-constant pointers. Thus an argument of type

```
char * p;
```

in ANSI C should be replaced by the argument type

```
const char * p ;
```

in several C++ implementations of C library functions.

- C library functions cannot be used in programs without the appropriate C include files.
- A statement such as

```
extern "C";
```

is often present in header files of libraries. In order to use these functions, C++ uses techniques such as conditional compilation, for example:

```
#ifndef __STD_C
...
#endif
```

- When a C construct conflicts with a C++ construct, the C++ construct takes precedence. For example, the construct **wchar_t** that is used for wide characters in the C header files **stddef.h** and **stdlib.h** is a reserved word in C++ and thus may not be defined in any header file.
- There are sequencing problems when C and C++ I/O functions are used in the same program.
- Other constructions in C, such as **malloc()** and **free()**, may not work well when used with the C++ operators **new** and **delete**.
- Conditional compilation, such as

```
#ifdef __cplusplus
// C++ code here
#else
/* C code here */
#endif
```

may help in spots. However, it can make code very hard to read.

A5.2   New Header Files in the Draft C++ Library

Note that the proposed new header files that access portions of the standard C++ library do not end in the **.h** extension. The proposed new header files are as follows:

bits	for bit operations such as masking
bitstring	for compact storage of bit strings
complex	for complex numbers
defines	for common definitions (also called **stddef**)
dynarray	for common template-based storage of arrays
exception	for exceptions
fstream	for I/O streams using files
iomanip	for manipulation of I/O streams
ios	the base class for I/O streams
iostream	for I/O streams
istream	for input streams
new	for the operator **new** with scope resolution
ostream	for output streams
ptrdynarray	for pointers to template-based storage of arrays
stddef	for common definitions (also called **defines**)
sstream	for I/O streams in memory using strings effectively
streambuf	for I/O stream operations
string	for common definitions and operations on strings
strstream	for I/O streams in memory
typeinfo	for common definitions (also called **defines**)
wstring	for strings of wide characters

A5.3   C Header Files in the Draft C++ Library

assert.h	for debugging diagnostics
ctype.h	for character handling
errno.h	for error numbers
float.h	implementation-dependent minimum limits
iso646.h	new relational operator names

`limits.h`	implementation-dependent minimum limits
`locale.h`	for non-US standards (not discussed in this book)
`math.h`	for mathematics
`setjmp.h`	for non-local goto's in programs (not discussed here)
`signal.h`	for signal detection and handling
`stdarg.h`	for variable number of arguments
`stddef.h`	standard definitions
`stdio.h`	I/O
`stdlib.h`	standard library utilities
`string.h`	string handling
`time.h`	date and time
`wchar.h`	wide (non-ASCII) character types
`wctype.h`	wide (non-ASCII) character types

Solutions and Hints to Selected Exercises

Chapter 1

1. Every arithmetic operator can be overloaded, including +, -, *, /, +=, etc. The assignment operator + and the comparison operator == can also be overloaded. The address operator & and the contents operator * can be overloaded. In fact, most operators in C++ can be overloaded. For more detailed information, see the syntax summary in Appendix 2 or the annotated reference manual by Ellis and Stroupstrup listed in the references.

2. Structs cannot be assigned or compared. In addition it is not possible to restrict access to a field of a struct.

3. A **typedef** is a synonym for a name, not a new type. There is no easy way to formalize prevention of type coercion.

Chapter 2

1, 2. You should check for the presence of function prototypes, format of function headers and prototypes, differences in header files, and the syntax of function pointers.

4. One way to do this is to incorporate the precision within the class. For example, we can always allot a **long double** for storage, as in the class description

```
class number
{
  enum precision = {FLOAT, DOUBLE, LONG_DOUBLE};
  long double value;
};
```

Note that we used uppercase constants for the enumeration types, since the enumerated values must be integer constants. The addition operator should be an overloaded member function of the form **operator + (number &);**.

5. Technically, all possible combinations of types are possible and should thus be tested. Since any arithmetic operations for this class will make use of the predefined operations, it is probably sufficient to test each operation for the case of arguments of the same type.

Chapter 3

1. The experiment should consist of timing two dintinct programs. The first will use the qualifier **inline** and the second will not. The examples should be run at least three times, and the average times should be declared.

   On a multi-user system such as UNIX, only the actual time (called **user** time) used by the program should be counted, not the elapsed time. The elapsed time is greatly affected by the other processes running at the time of the program's execution.

3. A simple way to create destructors for classes without pointers is to reset each value of the member data. Thus, we could have

```
~Rectangle()
{
  length = 0.0;
  width = 0.0;
}
```

6. There are only a few test cases for the member functions of the **Rectangle** class, including testing the **area()** and **perimeter()** functions by giving the **int** or **float** arguments instead of **double**.

8. All the functions must now be tested, with special emphasis on the creation of the objects using constructors. If you have confidence in the implementation of inher-

itance by your compiler (as you should for nearly all the products of the major compiler vendors), then you need not test that this works correctly. However, default setting of values of member data should be checked.

9. Member functions belong to a class and can have their access permissions determined by the protection that is set up in the class description.

Friend functions have access to the data of any class that declares them as being friends.

Free functions do not have access to private or protected data of any classes.

Each type of function can be polymorphic, as long as the overloading can be resolved by the compiler.

10. The categories of functions can be determined by the syntax used and their placement within classes. Note that we must also consider operators as functions. The header file is the primary source of information. For the two examples in this section, we have the following.

Member functions

```
String();
String(const String& string);
String(const char *str);
~String();
String &operator = (const String& string);
String &operator = (const char* str);
String &operator += (const String& string);
String &operator += (const char* str);
int length() const;
String operator + (const String& str) const;
String operator + (const char* str) const;
int operator == (const String& string) const;
int operator == (const char* str) const;
int operator != (const String& string) const;
int operator != (const char* str) const;
int operator < (const String& string) const;
int operator < (const char* str) const;
int operator <= (const String& string) const;
int operator <= (const Char* str) const;
int operator > (const String& string) const;
int operator > (const char* str) const;
int operator >= (const String& string) const;
int operator >= (const char* str) const;
operator char*();
```

Friend functions

```
friend ostream& operator << (ostream& s, String &str);
```

Free functions

```
String operator + (const char* str, const String& string);
int operator == (const char* str, const String& string);
int operator != (const char* str, const String& string);
int operator > (const char* str, const String& string);
int operator >= (const char* str, const String& string)
int operator < (const char* str, const String& string);
int operator <+ (const char* str, const String& string);
```

Chapter 4

5. The function **bin_to_dec()** might look like the following:

```
// Function bin_to_dec().
// Assumes input in null-terminated,
// starts with leading 0's stripped off.

int bin_to_dec(char *in)
{
  int temp, val = 1;
  int i = 1; // val starts at 1, ignore first character.

  while (in[i] != '\0')
    {
    temp = in[i] - '0';
    val = val * 2 + temp;
    i++;
    }
  return val;
}
```

Note that the related function **dec_to_bin()** must return a character string or something similar.

6. One version of the program might look something like the code presented below. The code can be improved by overloading the relevant operators.

```
// C++ program to compute the sum of two binary integers.
// Integers are entered as character strings, with the
// characters being either 0 or 1.
// No error checking of the input is performed.
```

```cpp
#include <iostream.h>
#include <string.h>  // prototype of the function strlen()

#define MAXLINE 80

class Binary
{
  char num[MAXLINE] ;
  int len;
public:
  int length()  { return (strlen(num)); };
  int max_len;
  void print();
  void read();
  void convert(Binary x, Binary y);
  sum(Binary x, Binary y, int max_len);
};

void Binary :: print()
{
  int i;

  for (i = 0; i < max_len; i++)
    cout << num [i] ;
};

void Binary :: read()
{
  cin >> num;
  len = strlen(num);
};

//////////CONVERT////////////////////////////////
void Binary :: convert(Binary x, Binary y)
{
  int i;

  extern int max_len;
  exter int larger, first, second ;
  extern int len1, len2;

  if (larger == first)
    {
    for (i = len2 - 1; i >= 0 ; i--)
      y.num[i + max_len -len2] = y.num[i];
    for (i = 0; i < max_len - len2; i++)
      y.num[i] = '0';
```

```
        }
    else
    {
    for (i = len1 - 1;i >= 0 ;i--)
        x.num[i + max_len -len1] = x.num[i];
    for (i = 0; i < max_len - len1; i++)
        x.num[i] = '0';
    }
}


///////////SUM////////////////////////
Binary :: sum(Binary x, Binary y, int max_len)
{
    static int temp[MAXLINE +1];        // initialized to 0
    Binary  xtemp, ytemp;
    int i ;
    int carry = 0;

    count <<"\n";
    // Starts at index 1 to allow carry into leftmost place.
    // Arrays x and y have data in positions 0 ..max_len - 1

    for (i = 0; i < MAXLINE; i++)
        {
        // Convert from int to char.
        xtemp.num[i] = x.num[i] - '0';
        ytemp.num[i] = y.num[i] - '0';
        }

    i = max_len;

    do
        {
        {temp[i+1] = xtemp.num[i] + ytemp.num[i] + carry ;
        if  ( temp[i+1] > 1)
            {
            carry = 1;
            temp [i+1] = (temp[i+1] % 2) ;
            }
        else
            carry = 0 ;
        }
    while (i--);

    temp[0] = carry;
    if (carry == 0)
        for (i = 1; i <= max_len; i++)     // ignore lead zero
```

```
          cout << temp[i];
    else
      for (i = 0; i <= max_len; i++)
        cout << temp[i];
    cout << "\n" ;
}


////////////////////////////////////////////////
int len1, len2;                   // lengths of strings
int first = 1, second = 2, larger;
int max_len = MAXLINE - 1;

////////////////MAIN/////////////////////////////////
main(void)
{
  extern int first, second, larger;
  Binary num1, num2;

  count << "Please enter the first binary number.\n";
  num1.read();
  count << "Please enter the second binary number.\n";
  num2.read();
  len1 = num1.length();
  len2 = num2.length();
  if (len1 > len2)
     {
     max_len = len1;
     larger = first;
     }
  else
     {
     max_len = len2;
     larger = second;
     }
  num1.convert(num1, num2);
  num1.sum(num1, num2, max_len);
}
```

16. There are several ways to write this program. The solution given here uses a cast of a pointer to **void** into a pointer to **int**. The initialized array is passed to the function **print_matrix()**. As was mentioned in Chapter 4, this was suggested by my colleague Will Craven at Howard University. Note the inclusion of **stdio.h** in order to have a function prototype available for **print()**.

```
/* ANSI C program */
#include <stdio.h>

#define SIZE 10
```

```
void print_matrix(void *, int);
int arr[SIZE][SIZE];

main()
{
  int i, j;
  void *temp = arr;

  for (i = 0; i < 3 ; i++)
    for (j = 0; j < SIZE; j++)
      arr [i][j] = i + j;
  print_matrix (temp, 3);
}



void print_matrix(void * p, int count)
{
  int i, j;
  int *arg_array;

  arg_array = (int *) p;
  for ( i = 0; i < count ; i++)
    {
    for(j = 0; j < SIZE ; j++)
      printf("%4d ", *(arg_array + SIZE * i + j) );
      }
}
```

20. The easiest way to do this is to have an object of type **Matrix**, using the **Matrix** class given in Chapter 4. This completely avoids the need for casting pointers to **void** as was given in the previous solution.

Chapter 5

3. The important thing to remember in your class description is that the abstract array class can have the maximum size of the array included as part of the member data for this class. This limit can serve as the maximum size of the stack, thereby making the explicit listing within the member data of the stack class inappropriate.

7. The **assert()** function should be used to provide information in at least two places, regardless of the type of data structure used. It should be used with pointers

to ensure that the **new** operation is successful. It should also be used to ensure that any array access is within the appropriate bounds. In the case of the data structures described in this chapter, it should also be used to avoid attempting to delete data from empty structures (list, stack, queues, etc.) or inserting data into structures that are full.

8. Merging and splitting queues is very common, especially in operating systems. These operations are important when priority queues are used. These are common operations on trees, when trees are used for graphical representation of data.

13. The easiest way to do this is to have the class **Complex** included as a **friend** class so that its overloaded arithmetic operators can be used without change. it is likely that your compiler's built-in class library will already have this class provided, so that developing such a class from scratch will not be necessary.

14. There are several ways to do this. One of the most elegant is to define an abstract data type called **General_Matrix**. This class will have only virtual functions, using the key word **virtual**, and will allow the compiler's run-time system to determine the proper function to use in this polymorphic situation. An alternative is to simply include each of the options in a larger class named **General_Matrix**.

Chapter 6

1. Inconsistent options include

   - **nocreate** and **noreplace**
   - **ios::in** and permission **of S_IWRITE**
   - **ios::out** and permission of **S_IREAD**
   - **ios::in** and **ios::trunc**

7. Unexpected input is a serious problem for interactive programs. You should try to handle input as robustly as possible. One way to do this is to overload the **<<** operator for the class **Complex** with character strings, using the function **strtok()** available in the standard C library. The separate tokens can then be changed to integer or floating point format using other standard library functions.

10. The basic outline of the code is something like the example given below. The name of the file used for the experiment is given as a command-line argument. We have hard-coded the number of iterations as 10,000; you should replace this number with a command-line argument and run the experiment many times.

```
// Program to illustrate the efficiency of the seekg()
// operation.
#include <fstream.h>

main(int. argc, char * argv[])
{
  int i, j;
  fstream s;

  if (argc != 2)
    cout << "Error in number of arguments" << end1;
  else
    {
    s.open(argv[1], ios::in | ios ::out);
    for (i = 0; i < 10000; 1++)
    s.seekg(i, ios::beg);
  s.close();
    }
}
```

Chapter 7

3. The error message is certainly helpful, letting us know that we have attempted to take the square root of a negative number. The problem is that the function has a return value, and the error branch of the code has no return value. This branch is where an exception should be raised.

4. Underflow occurs when a positive number is smaller than the smallest representable positive number on the computer. Negative numbers can underflow if their absolute values underflow.

   Overflow occurs when a positive number is greater than the largest representable positive number on the computer. Negative numbers can overflow if their absolute values overflow.

   Imprecision occurs when either of the operands in a binary operation has either underflow or overflow. It can also occur if the result of a binary operation will either overflow or underflow.

5. Errors in pointer arithmetic are not likely to cause exceptions unless they attempt access to forbidden locations, such as space reserved for the operating system or another process. Errors such as overwriting important data for the process can occur, but are not handled directly by the exception mechanism at this time.

   Each of the other errors can generate an exception.

6. The current state of C++ exceptions does not allow exceptions to be propagated. However, the underlying communications software such as **TCP/IP** will detect errors in lack of response on sockets on which the client is listening.

Chapter 8

6. A user could either an experienced or a novice computer user. He or she could also be experienced in the use of the I/O devices required, or in the software itself.

7. The easiest way to do this is to have each of the free (non-member) functions be a member of the class. Note that in our example, each of the free functions was a binary operator. This means that the name of the object must be provided as an argument and that the class to which the object belongs must be provided as the type of the argument. The rest of the conversion should be straightforward.

   You should be aware of one simplifying factor in this situation that will not always occur. The free functions had the class **String** argument in second position. If we have to change from member functions to free functions, then we must be careful about the relative positions of the arguments within the argument list.

11. Free (non-member) functions can be used with many different classes. They should be tested with each possible combination of different types of arguments. The relative positions of the arguments within the argument list should be considered when designing test cases.

Chapter 9

2. Including arcs of circles in the **Edge** class is straightforward. We should include the center and radius of the defining circle of the arc, in addition to the endpoints.

   One way to do this is to have a new **Arc** class to describe a member of the **Edge** class. Since the center and endpoints are simply triples of floating point numbers, we could have objects in the new **Arc** class inherit their structures from the **Vertex** class.

   We might also describe a new **Circle** class and let the **Arc** class inherit structure from the **Circle** class.

   Other arrangements are certainly possible. None of these should effect the structure of the higher-level **Face** or **Polyhedron** classes.

4. The world-to-screen transformation uses the algorithm that is given in Section 9.1. It is used after the objects in the database have been selected for display. The constants representing the maximum and minimum values of the three real-world coordinates are generally determined by setting what is frequently known as a **window** or **viewport**. Objects entirely outside the window and portions of objects outside the window are ignored when displayed. (This operation is called *clipping*.)

Chapter 10

3. The most appropriate choices for fundamental objects are blocks and files. Since the simulation of disk operations already involves the use of block class, the system can be extended to incorporate files. The new class **File** can inherit locations of data in both the simulated disk and memory using the structure included in a **Block**. Use the technique of Chapter 8 to determine the appropriate member functions.

References

Ada, *Reference Manual for the Ada Programming Language*, ANSI-MIL-STD-1815A, 1983.

Arnold, R. S., *Software Reengineering*, IEEE Computer Society Press, Los Alamitos, CA, 1992.

Barbey, S., and A. Strohmeier, "The Problematics of Testing Object-Oriented Software," *Proceedings of the Second Conference on Software Quality Management (SQM'94)*, Edinburgh, Scotland, July 26–28, 1994, vol 2, 411–426.

Beizer, B., *Software Testing*, Van Nostrand Reinhold, New York, 1983.

Beizer, B., *Software Testing*, second edition, Van Nostrand Reinhold, New York, 1990.

Boehm, B., *Software Engineering Economics*, Prentice Hall, Englewood Cliffs, NJ, 1981.

Booch, G., *Object-Oriented Analysis and Design with Applications*, Addison-Wesley, Reading, MA, 1994.

Budd, T., *Classic Data Structures in C++*, Addison-Wesley, Reading, MA, 1994.

Buhr, R., *Practical Visual Techniques in System Design with Applications in Ada*, Prentice-Hall, Englewood Cliffs, NJ, 1990.

Coad, P., and E. Yourdon, *Object-Oriented Analysis*, second edition, Prentice-Hall, Englewood Cliffs, NJ, 1991.

Date, C. J., *An Introduction to Database Systems*, sixth edition, Addison-Wesley, Reading, MA, 1995.

Deitel, H. M., and P. J. Deitel, *C++ How to Program*, Prentice-Hall, Englewood Cliffs, NJ, 1994.

DeMarco, T., *Structured Analysis and System Specification*. Prentice Hall, Englewood Cliffs, NJ, 1979.

Ellis, M., and B. Stroustrup, *The Annotated C++ Reference Manual*, Addison-Wesley, Reading, MA, 1990.

Giloi, W., *Interactive Computer Graphics: Data Structures, Algorithms, Languages.* Prentice Hall, Englewood Cliffs, NJ, 1978.

Harrold, M. J., J. D. McGregor, and K. J. Fitzpatrick, "Incremental Testing of Object-Oriented Class Structures," *Proceedings of the 14th International Conference on Software Engineering,* Melbourne, Australia, May 11–15, 1992, 68–79.

Hashemi, R., and Leach, R. J., "Issues in Porting Software from C to C++," *Software—Practice & Experience,* **22**, 7, 1992, pp. 599–602.

Humphrey, W., *A Discipline for Software Engineering,* Addison-Wesley, Reading, MA, 1990.

Johnson, R. E. and B. Foote, "Designing Portable Classes," *Journal of Object-Oriented Programming,* vol. 1, no. 2, June/July 1988, pp. 22–35.

Kernighan, B. and D. Ritchie. *The C Programming Language,* second edition, Prentice Hall, Englewood Cliffs, NJ, 1988.

Leach, R. J., *Using C in Software Design,* AP Professional, Boston, 1993.

Leach, R. J., *Advanced Topics in UNIX,* John Wiley & Sons, New York, 1994.

Lorenz, *Object-Oriented Software Development: A Practical Guide,* Prentice Hall, Englewood Cliffs, NJ, 1993.

Murphy, G. C., P. Townsend, and P. S. Wong, "Experiences with Cluster and Class Testing," *Commun. ACM,* vol. 37, no. 9, pp. 39–47, September 1994.

Myers, J. G. , *The Art of Software Testing,* John Wiley & Sons, New York, 1979.

Pfleeger, S. L., *Software Engineering,* Macmillan, New York, 1987.

Plauger, P. J., *The Standard C Library,* Prentice Hall, Englewood Cliffs, NJ, 1992.

Plauger, P. J., *The Draft Standard C++ Library,* Prentice Hall, Englewood Cliffs, NJ, 1994.

Pohl, I., *C++ for C Programmers,* Benjamin/Cummings, Redwood City, CA, 1989.

Pressman, R., *Software Engineering: A Practitioner's Approach,* McGraw Hill, New York, 1992.

Prieto-Diaz, R., and G. Arango, *Domain Analysis and Software Systems Modeling,* IEEE Computer Society Press, Los Alamitos, CA, 1991.

Smith, M., and Robson, D. J., "A Framework for Testing Object-Oriented Programs," *J. Object-Oriented Programs.,* vol. 3, no. 5, June 1992, pp. 45–53.

Stevens, W. R., *Advanced Programming in the UNIX Environment,* Addison-Wesley, Reading, MA, 1992.

Strang, G., *Linear Algebra and Its Applications,* second edition, Harcourt Brace Jovanovich, San Diego, CA, 1980.

Stroustrup, B. "Classes: An Abstract Data Type Faculty for the C Language," *ACM SIGPLAN Notices,* vol. 17, no. 1, January 1982.

Stroustrup, B. "Data Abstraction in C," *AT&T Bell Laboratories Technical Journal,* vol. 63, no. 8, October 1984.

Stroustrup, B. *The C++ Programing Language,* second edition, Addison-Wesley, Reading, MA: 1991.

Stroustrup, B. *The Design and Evolution of C++,* Addison-Wesley, Reading, MA, 1994.

Sutherland, I. E., *Sketchpad: A Man–Machine Graphic Communication System,* TR-296, MIT Lincoln Laboratory, Lexington, MA, January 1963.

Wirfs-Brock, R., B. Wilderson, and L. Wiener. *Designing Object-Oriented Software,* Prentice Hall, Englewood Cliffs, NJ, 1990.

Wirth, N., *Algorithms + Data Structures = Programs,* Prentice Hall, Englewood Cliffs, NJ, 1976.

Yourdon, E., *Modern Structured Analysis,* Prentice-Hall, Englewood Cliffs, NJ, 1989.

Index

LIMITED WARRANTY AND DISCLAIMER OF LIABILITY

About the Disk

The disk contains all the source code examples used in this book. Each example has been tested on at least two different compilers, including Borland C++ version 4.0.

The disk is in IBM PC format and can be read by any software that can read a 3.5 inch, 1.44 MB disk in PC format. It can be read easily on Macintosh computers using the Apple File Exchange program and on Sun workstations using the dos2unix file transfer utility. For more information on these formats, see your system manual.

The files on the disk are arranged to follow the organization of the book. Each chapter of the book corresponds to a directory on the disk. Many directories contain a README file in ASCII format so that the organization of the directory is clear.

In general, the examples in the book are included on the disk with abbreviated names in order to conform to the limited number of characters in an allowable file name on an MS/DOS-based computer. Thus, the third example of Chapter 2 would be found in the directory named **CHAP2** in a file named **ex2_3.c**, and so on.

Some of the examples (especially in the later chapters) are more complicated and require the use of makefiles in order to form systems. In these situations, subdirectories may be used in order to make the program structure clear. Any subdirectory contains README files with the necessary makefiles and instructions on appropriate use.